Confessions of an Accidental Mouseketeer

Confessions of an Accidental Mouseketeer

Lonnie Burr

BearManor Media
2009

Confessions of An Accidental Mouseketeer
© 2009 Lonnie Burr

Image from *Children's Playmate*, © 1957 by children's Better Health Institute, Benjamin Franklin Literary & Medical Society, Inc., Indianapolis, Indiana. Used by Permission.

All rights reserved.

For information, address:

BearManor Media
P. O. Box 71426
Albany, GA   31708

bearmanormedia.com

Cover design by John Teehan

Typesetting and layout by John Teehan

Published in the USA by BearManor Media

ISBN—1-59393-326-6

Table of Contents

1. Under The Dining Room Table 1
2. Baby Lon in Babylon 17
3. The Charles Dickens School of Dance 29
4. Judy Garland, Natalie Wood, Melanie Griffith and Me 41
5. The Teeniest Existentialist 59
6. Spoiled Bling-Bling Rotten 91
7. Mickey Mouse Offer I Could Not Refuse 115
8. No Matrix for Matriculation 165
9. The Rest Was Almost Silence 191
10. Showbizaphobia 203
11. Chilling Draft & Snake Eyes in Vegas 243
12. On The Road (or Not a Kerouac In Sight) 273
13. Sour Apples are Worse Than Sour Grapes 285
14. Some Tough Guys Can Dance a Little 325
15. Renaissance Mouseketeers (or The Middle Ages?) 343
16. Such Women Do Not Exist 377
17. The Desperate Silence of Testosterone 389
18. Back Home, Candide Weeds His Garden 405
    Appendix 431
    Index 443

For Diane who means more to me and has done more for me than any other person in my life.

For Floomerfelt, Leibniz, Asta and my late daughter Syny whose unconditional, feline love is far beyond the Greek concept of sophrosyne, the Navajo goal of *hozro* and the fragile feelings humans are capable of expressing on rare occasions.

"The unexamined life is not worth living."
– Plato, *Timaeus* ca. 360 B.C.

Chapter 1
Under the Dining Room Table

Before I acted in films with Elvis, Dustin Hoffman and Jean-Claude Van Damme; before I danced and sang with Ginger Rogers, Sammy Davis and Carol Channing; before I directed and took over the lead in my first produced play, was awarded for my poetry, reviewed theatre and film or signed my first published book; before I performed on Broadway with Robert Preston and Bernadette Peters; before I was directed by Spielberg and Fosse and Gower Champion; before I became a permanent part of the Smithsonian Museum of American History; before I received my high school diploma six days after turning fifteen and finished my M.A. at nineteen; before I dated Barbara Parkins and had sex with a hooker in Paris on a Disney expense account at eighteen; before I attempted to take my life at twenty—I accidentally became a permanent part of pop culture.

I am certainly not a legend, nor a David Copperfield hero of my life, but I have been lumbered with brobdingnagian, iconic ears since the age of eleven when I became one of the four boy Mouseketeers to last the entire filming of the original *Mickey Mouse Club* (1955-59).

Thus, I foreshadowed Warhol's cynical, hackneyed quote about everyone having his or her fifteen minutes of fame, except my allegedly fleeting celebrity has lasted over six decades and will inevitably dominate my obituary, ending not with a whimper but with a squeak.

The very first time I wore a claustrophobic, smelly, wool bear suit with chafing muslin padding, peering out from the bear head's nostrils as best I could as I sweated profusely and danced to "The Humphrey Hop" in take after take as my persona Mouseketeer Lonnie on Stage 1 of the Disney Studios in Burbank, California, we were filming the first season of the popular kids' series in 1955. I had just turned twelve.

Our show premiered later that year on October 3, 1955 the same day as Capt. Kangaroo, and we promptly booted Howdy Doody off the air. The approximately 360 black and white episodes have somehow been resurrected in the '60s, '70s, '80s, and 1995-2002 bringing forth two new versions and making it to CDs and DVDs. There is even showbiz rumor in 2009 of a fourth remake of the MMC. Disney has *Spin and Marty, The Hardy Boys,* and *The Annette Series* on DVD, perhaps they will reissue the entire original MMC one year at a time.

My career in entertainment, however, had started at a much younger age and included performing on *The Colgate Comedy Hour* for an ailing Eddie Cantor on the stage of the El Capitan Theatre just north of Hollywood and Vine and which, ironically, is now owned by Disney.

In over ten episodes of this kinescoped TV variety show, I exchanged punch lines with Bob Hope, Martin and Lewis, Ed Wynn, who reminded me I had guested in 1952 on his earlier television show (see autographs in Appendix), and danced with Donald O'Connor. The majority of my shows were with Eddie.

My professional showbiz debut was actually earlier at age five in 1948 with a live performance of my song/dance/imitations act as well as playing multiple roles on a local Altadena, California radio show for kids and dancing with my adagio partner on local television in Pasadena.

The Enchanted Lady, who was the producer, writer, director and played the lady—and she really thought she was enchanted—cast me to play various roles such as Buster the Beetle, Prince Charming and the evil, laughing frog; even a kid knows these are very different guys. This began my long career as a "character man" only as a boy. On the same medium I was later the "Oh boy, Chef Boy-ar-dee!" commercial spokes-kid for two years, became Tiny Tim on the radio version of Dickens' *A Christmas Carol* nationally on *Stars Over Hollywood* and maintained the child lead, Chris Martin, for about a hundred broadcasts on the NBC radio soap opera *Dr. Paul*, which aired live at NBC's West Coast Radio City at Sunset and Vine, now long gone.

I moved on to national TV, film and theatre as an actor and occasional song-and-dance guy in 1949. I rode a horse with the Lone Ranger, Clayton Moore, whom I never saw as a child, nor later as an adult, without his face covered, to sell Cheerios. I played the title character of the segment, "The Minister's Son," on an episode of *The Roy Rogers Show* with Dale, Roy and Trigger (pre-taxidermy) and I did my own riding in

Under the Dining Room Table 3

On location with Roy Rogers. I played the title role of "The Minister's Son" on The Roy Rogers Show, *1951.*

my first guest star TV lead as the eponymous character "The Holy Terror" in 1951 at eight on *The Range Rider*. We were on location in Lone Pine, California and for close-ups I was shot on the bed of a speeding pickup truck riding the back of the series star, Jock Mahoney, a former stunt man and Sally Field's stepdad, who was on his hands and knees as I gripped the reins and appeared to gallop feverishly to escape kidnappers.

In the last scene of the episode I am a reformed holy terror and very polite to my dad, played by veteran character actor Lyle Talbot, and everyone else. As a result I wear a gift from the Range Rider: a buckskin outfit, with fringe shirt and pants just like his—very cool at eight. My only problem on the shoot was covering a fire with a blanket to signal where I was after being kidnapped, which the Rider had taught me earlier. The smoke kept getting in my eyes, which watered, and my nose, which sneezed and the smoke made my face all black after every take, so the makeup had to be taken off and put on from scratch. We finally redid the makeup one more time and I got it on the fourth take. I have never taken up smoke signaling again.

My only *Space Patrol* gig was another cereal commercial and my only recurring role before the Mickey Mouse Club was on one of the first TV sitcoms, *The Ruggles*, starring character actor Charlie Ruggles. I played Oliver Quimby the snooty, snotty next-door neighbor as a foil for the "real" boy/girl twins in the Ruggles' home. This show was filmed on the West Coast and led the way for television to move from the East Coast to the West Coast.

Cecil B. DeMille directed me in the Oscar-winning film *The Greatest Show on Earth* which starred Jimmy Stewart, Betty Hutton, Charlton Heston and a cast of thousands—or thereabouts. Burgeoning auteur Joseph Losey used me in the U.S. remake of *M*, the German film that made Peter Lorre a star. (The frequently incorrect internet has it that I was a victim, which is patently false since they were all girls.) I did a scene early in the film that is viewed from the interior of a barber shop with kids playing as they crossed the street and were overheard by the denizens of the haircut hangout.

I played war-hero-turned-actor Lon McAllister's son in my first film *Yank in Korea*, shot in 1950 and released in 1951, and I was the only person in *Hans Christian Andersen* who was directly related to the Danish storyteller, which occasioned publicity shots in period costume with the star, Danny Kaye. My second film, three melodramatic, fictional

I grew a feather on my head for The Strawberry Circle, *my third play and first stage lead at the Pasadena Playhouse, 1952.*

episodes of the popular daytime television show *Queen for a Day*. Leonard Nimoy told me at a party that this film was his first adult screen role.

My first theatre role was at the Pasadena Playhouse when I was six and my third play there, at eight, was my first stage lead in *The Strawberry Circle*. I never ran into Gene Hackman, Charles Bronson, nor Dustin Hoffman who all did early work at the Playhouse. There were many other radio, film, theatre and TV roles as well as commercials, modeling and live performances before I signed a seven-year contract with Disney in 1955.

But my very first dramatic act was in the year I turned three, 1946, and I recall it much more vividly than all of the preceding.

On a visit to my grandparent's furniture store I became mesmerized by a miniature cactus plant and so I latched onto its myriad, tantalizing stickers. As abundant shafts of pain were tweezed from my tiny hand amidst cacophonous wailing and a plethora of tears, I learned a lesson: all that glisters is not gold. I add to Chaucer's moral that it is usually not even fool's gold and that is even truer in showbiz than it is in actual life.

Howard A. Babin and Dorothy Doloris Burr met in a small Kentucky town and turned their young love and fabulous dancing ability into a relationship and a career. They toured from 1936 to 1941, finally marrying in 1939, from Detroit to Bridgeport, New Jersey to Ohio, from Niagara's Cataract House to the Hi-De-Ho Club as the dance team Dot and Dash. They made a living, barely, were very, very good but did not prove a viable threat to Fred and Adele Astaire, even though they headlined over a youthful Doris Von Kappelhoff, who hailed from nearby Cincinnati, Ohio and later became a star under the name of Doris Day.

My mom Dot was tossed around a lot which is silently assumed by the female in such endeavors, although it is never mentioned in the job description: ADAGIO PARTNER SOUGHT (masochist preferred). She sustained sundry injuries culminating in Dash dad impaling Dot mom's cranium on a pointed chandelier hanging precariously over the dance floor. Dorothy, from whence Dot, thence Dot and Dash, finished the number smiling bravely while drops of blood trickled down her pate. She was rewarded by the audience with a slightly more than average hand.

Mom insisted that she and Howard retire to less dangerous pursuits. Mom's wounds healed and the former pros danced only for their own pleasure. Dot had two years of business college, the most education in the family, and performed related duties as a secretary.

I think it was during this period that my dad Dash decided to be a jockey. Mom was not thrilled but at least she was not in danger. Dad trained with the later famous champion Eddie Arcaro and during Dad's riding a fellow trainee fell from his horse and a following equine stepped

The very elegant team of Dot and Dash in a 1934 publicity photo.

on his head, squashing it as Dad passed. Then he stopped wanting to be a jockey. He had not quite finished high school but had training from his dad in lathe work and as a machinist, so he machined.

During the years they were no longer pros, the former Dot and Dash inseminated with gusto, or so I assume, and within two years they became producers of a slash (The literate actually call this a virgule.) - Leonard Burr Babin. The equation reads . + - = / and occurred on May 31, 1943 in Dayton, Kentucky, smaller and some distance from Dayton, Ohio.

Muhammad Ali, Abe Lincoln and I are all sons of 'ol Kaintuck but I absconded with more alacrity than Abe & Ali, at age three, due to my mother's resolve to vicariously seek fame and fortune in the glittering streets of Californ-

Slash (me), Dot and Dash, who is already keeping his distance in early 1945.

I-A. Of course, she would never have stated it like this for it was all done for the benefit of her brilliant, multi-talented three-year-old son.

As they sought to kidnap me on the morning of our departure from all the blue lawns of Kentucky that I recall as green or covered with snow, I threw myself in highest dudgeon under my grandparents' dining room table. I refused to be abducted and the normally "perfect" Lonnie child vented a startling tantrum. It seemed to me at three to be the most effective hiding place since it made it very sticky for adults to access and shoes scurrying about never glower, shout nor slap. John Updike confessed to the same ploy as a child in one of his memoirs but neither the august author nor I were correct.

I believe that my fear, flight and concealment were motivated by the terror of leaving what I had accepted as my entire three-year-old world. I was having order destroyed by chaos. I most certainly would miss my gramma who was always preoccupied with my well being and was the source of the most and best presents and treats.

"Oh, pleeeeeaaaasssssseee, Dorth, don't hit him!" She was my knightly defender. My deracination brings up an extremely youthful trauma of betrayal. I have had a fear of betrayal for much of my life and it has less to do with paranoia than it does with reality. This dining room havoc in my third year may have also begun my personal theory of chaos—all life is chaos and I must do everything I can to prevent the inevitable disaster, failure, tragedy or snafu.

My grandparents, Glade and John, were integral to Mom and me; Howard would have preferred they stay away permanently. John and Glade were the only financial success and security in my mom's family from prior to my birth to my grandmother's seventies. My dad's family, I

Riding Lemuel Gulliver's horse and acting unafraid, 1946.

later assumed because he had married a non-Catholic, was absent all of my life except for one of his brothers and his wife in two visits to California when I was quite young. To my knowledge, none of them were even close to being as well off as the Burrs.

The Grands had a bigger-than-mom-and-pop furniture store at this time on the Cincinnati, Ohio side of the Ohio River, directly across from Covington, Kentucky. It was inside amidst these homey groupings that the cruelly didactic cactus lurked.

My actual recollections of these first years are few and vague—no rosebuds in May: forcing a smile and hiding fear in a photo of me jauntily posed astride a pony that seemed to me a Clydesdale out of Lemuel Gulliver's meanderings; laughing and peeing on my grandfather's lap for which, as best I was able to judge, he never forgave me; the roiling, threatening Ohio River outside the store; being bundled up like an arachnid's prey for winter with only my eyes and nose exposed as I was pulled on a red sled not named rosebud through the numbing white winter landscape which was curiously outlined in blue.

Whether in front of a house, drinking and dining in a night club or restaurant or posing as Dot and Dash, my mom and dad, like most young couples, appear to be an attractive, snappy young duo having a ball, the future clearly theirs, even though this did not prove to be the case. I recognize them instantly from ancient, yellowed, grainy photos before I was born, even though I never do remember seeing them look quite that way. Without these visual props I cannot conjure up an image of them other than in their thirties after we began living in California and I trudged toward my fourth year.

Dorothy was very attractive and frequently exposed excellent teeth that complemented her hazel eyes and auburn hair that later magically turned blonde on occasion. She was only 4'11," yet joyfully lied declaring it "eleven and three quarters, just shy of five feet." Her very shapely figure, more Monroe than either Hepburn, was accented by stylish clothes, high French heels, the higher the better, and hair worn up for dressy do's and decorated by tasteful gewgaws which was a penchant of the era. She died of a pulmonary embolism at 89 in 2003.

Howard, who only divulged his hated middle name, Ambrose, to me when I was almost twenty, was a sharp dresser and maintained an extremely trim, well defined, 5'6" frame until withering from pancreatic cancer before his death at 64 in 1980. His dark hair was always neatly

Here I am in costume with Danny Kaye for Hans Christian Andersen, *1952.*

slicked straight back and his look of dapper unpredictability never left him. He brought me my French and, to a lesser degree, German genes.

Gladys Olga Nethersole Andersen Burr, Gram, was about 5'4" and pleasantly portly. She had an olive complexion, dark hair and a quite broad nose that led me later to hidden speculations about miscegenation, since her grandparents had owned slaves. Her grandfather was Danish sea captain Karl Eimer Andersen, third cousin to Hans Christian Andersen, and it was he who emigrated to America and brought me my Danish blood. I was the first blond in the family since these roots. There was also some Scots/Irish from this side of the family, perhaps the DNA of Gram's fiery temper and strong opinions which never ceased to explode at anyone disagreeing with her about anything. She was 105 when she died but if I had ever mentioned my speculation about sexual interaction with a slave before her birth she probably would not have seen 55.

"Leonard" Burr Babin was arbitrarily designated as my name by Mom and Gram and came from my grandfather John Leonard Burr. I did not find out that he had adopted Dorothy, making him my step-grandfather, until I was in my late 50s and he had been dead almost twenty-five years. My family's secrets never aspired to Sophocles, Ibsen, nor O'Neill but they were sealed just as tightly. The family history was solidly behind the myth that this English Burr fellow led me directly to Aaron Burr and Benjamin and William Henry Harrison as progenitors. I believed it and all the family acted as if they did but I felt no loss when the triad was disappeared as kin on later revelation.

Gram was divorced and Mom was about seven when she somehow hooked the young John Burr scofflaw and renegade. She transformed him into the strictness of her lifestyle from his youth as a gambler and womanizer around "sporting houses." He could hold three dice and throw only two and became known as a teenager as "The Deacon with the Wicked Wrist." He did manage to hold onto smoking, betting on the ponies and holiday imbibing after he was reformed by marriage. He quit smoking in his sixties.

Coming from a different gene pool, John was the only tall member of the family at six-feet plus. He limped as the result of losing two toes while hopping freights as a wild young vagabond and almost broke his back when he turned his Indian motorcycle upside down on railroad tracks in his early teens. He only completed sixth grade, the same as Glade, as Gladys was called. She never appeared to notice that he took his loss of freedom out on everyone else, smirking and needling us at every chance offered, although he was cautious not to disparage Glade. She would say he meant nothing by it—it was just his "dry, English wit."

Lacking a full formal education, this couple, particularly Gram, was very business savvy and more than diligent, working sixteen, sometimes eighteen-hour days seven days a week before and during the Depression even though they had no boss to blame.

They did lose everything in the early 'thirties due to listening to their friend the banker, but they set back industriously working and became more successful and stable in America long before meaningless pixels made billionaires of some and millionaires of fortunate hangers-on and investors with either insight or luck. Few if any of Glade and John Burr's achievements had to do with luck.

My meager reflections and recollections of my three years of evolving before growing up in Southern California are impressionistic: the chilling snow, the hot piss, the cactus clenching pain, and my panic under the table. Otherwise, this part of my life is a tabula rasa from gurgling and crawling to babbling and toddling.

Between the facts and the fables of memory there exists this paradox: wherein lies the truth?

There will always be some discrepancies even when using the most disciplined objectivity and total honesty. This is true for the historian, the journalist, the biographer, the witness and all other professionals and nonprofessionals. The court reporter makes mistakes just recording with no interpretation whatsoever.

Our lives are frustratingly obscure to us because of our emotions and doubts, fallibilities and beliefs, perceptions and dreams, insights and recalled images. Almost no one desires to be regarded as evil. Even most sociopaths make an attempt to establish the rightness, logic and veracity of their actions, words, emotions and/or their dialectic.

The human view of reality is, at best, an amalgam of recalled incidents, sometimes dubious notes or photos or newsprint and mental pictures rather than quiddity, the thing in itself. It is more like a series of episodes and contradictory, sometimes confusing paradigms that capture—if we are perceptive, persistent and fortunate—the essence of what was, as opposed to the exactness of who we are and were, what we say and said, how we act and acted, what we do and did, and, more abstrusely, why we do or did things the way we do and did.

Like a murky Expressionist stage set or film scene, events in our lives are more supra-real than real, more extended and rounded than precise and angular, more hidden in shadows than illuminated by bare, bright actuality.

I write this more or less chronological series of events, insights and experiences, sometimes fast forwarding, sometimes regressing, of eclectic personal interactions and feelings in my life as genuinely as I can.

Have I ever acted badly? Of course, but these moments occur even more rarely. Have I ever done something for which I feel or felt shame? Of course, but these moments occur even more rarely. Am I a cruel, misanthropic person? No, absolutely not. I confess to being difficult and capable of anger mitigated by the words "on some occasions." I do have problems with depression which started sometime before I became a teenager and was not clinically discovered until I was in my twenties.

Do I ask for understanding or forgiveness? No. A little indulgence, though, would be appreciated.

Although I believe myself to be what Richard III pretends to be, "a marvelous, proper man," neither a Machiavellian devil, nor a saint, I struggle and quite often succeed in being ethical and moral and principled. I appear to do this more than most I have encountered without the crutch of a deity while far too many belie their sanctimonious hypocrisy by merely mouthing words and acting as they please. I read or hear about my superiors in this arena, not knowing what knowledge is accurate rather than fictional. Mother Teresa and her ilk seem to me like a foreign species, however laudable and beatified, of which I am not a member nor could I ever be a member.

The kindest, most understanding, most selfless person, including Aquinas, Donne and former President Carter who apparently was guilty of more than one instance of mental sexual hijinks, has struggled with evil thoughts and desires and urges. It is only in the denial of inherent evil potential that all humans confront and carve out whatever identity, happiness and peace that they are capable of achieving in their unique lives.

Since I first discovered and devoured Kant in my late teens, I have been convinced of his posit that humans have no choice in prejudging things, for that is how the human mind functions. Bigotry, as opposed to prejudice, is learned, not inherent, and can be corrected or at least held in abeyance. For that matter, one can succeed and change prejudging—at least to some degree.

I have been astute most of my life at what psychologists now term "thin slicing", our unconscious mind's ability to instantly recognize patterns of behavior and situations, according to Malcolm Gladwell in his 2005 book *Blink*.

Still, I am sometimes confused. I am sometimes confounded. I sometimes fail. I do maintain, however, a sense of right and wrong despite battles as a puerile idealist lost quite early on to decades of intellectual and emotional cynicism.

"Do the others speak of me mockingly, maliciously?" is the title of a Delmore Schwartz poem in which he finds, as have I, that they do. Delmore and I have also found that we do the same to them. I only add that we must try to be successful in suppressing what we feel like doing and it is an ongoing struggle. This is an unpleasant part of the human psyche. As opposed to a glib aphorism about caring, there is something wrong with this human condition and other innate human foibles and there is something we can do about it. I have worked on doing this for many years and I have been fairly efficacious much of the time, but certainly not always.

More importantly, all of the above does not escape absurdity and humor, two of the essentials of life, my saints being Ionesco, Groucho Marx (but not his brothers, nor Karl), Mort Sahl, Peter Sellers and, of course, Mel Brooks.

So, here is Lonnie Burr, although my name is neither Lonnie nor Burr.

Chapter 2
Baby Lon in Babylon

In an aging two-door Austin, the now forgotten American automobile and not the British sports car, the three pilgrims Babin, Dorothy, Howard and Leonard (a name unknown to me until I was six and never used by anyone, for I was always and will always be Lonnie), set off to seek fame and fortune. We were mashed in with necessities, odds and ends, clothes, one small piece of furniture Mom could not part with, and sundry food products. We must have resembled an upscale version of *Grapes of Wrath* migrants. I actually played Steinbeck's Granpa Joad, more than twenty years my senior, in 2003 in the stage version of the film at Ford's Theatre in Washington, D.C. Henry Fonda played the grandson in the movie.

We did lack Hank Fonda, whose reputation for moody ill will I found absent when we had a casual, one on one, ten-minute-or-so exchange about single malts and other scotches right after his opening that evening in the Broadway-bound play *The First Monday in October* at the Kennedy Center in Washington, D.C. It was his last stage performance.

Fonda was still wearing his costume of a judge's black, floor-length robe. I dislike crowds and went to the farthest bar set-up and he joined me. No one else but the bartender was around and we did not introduce ourselves. I wisely said nothing about his long career, his very good work that night, my childhood celebrity, nor show business. We exchanged as two veteran scotch drinkers with no knowledge of each other at an anonymous bar. Both of us were not in favor of a heavy peat taste and found that we both liked a rarely-stocked-by-bars single malt called Dalwhinney—smooooooooth.

The Babins' arduous six-or-seven-day crossing of the States by auto is shadowy to me vis-à-vis my only partially successful avoidance of the car's jump seat, which opened via a pull-up chrome handle from the auto's rear and which I feared would swallow me whole as if I were a petite Jonah. This might have been the inception of my claustrophobia. I renounce vagina dentata since I was born via caesarian section, the most awful and painful experience in my mother's life and of which I was reminded unceasingly for the entirety of her years. The often visited tortuous event was categorically and imperatively my fault, satanic embryo, at least in this instance, that I proved to be.

If we saw the Grand Canyon or any other noteworthy Americana, I do not recollect it. I only recall extreme boredom, dingy little rooms in motels and greasy meals on greasy tables in greasy cafes.

Dorothy and her mom thought my affinity for dancing and singing to any music from the radio, player piano—or even whistling—was "swell." Mom swore until her death that a few months after uttering my first sentences I asked for dance classes. She noted gleefully that I was really drawn to getting attention and laughs.

Voila—she had a new dream. Rarely sharing her thoughts with anyone unless airing a grievance against them, Dot decided that if she could not make it in *the* showbiz then her son *would*. Her goal in the gaudy, gold-paved nirvana "La-La-land" was to make Lon a star.

Ham, the nickname everyone called my dad but never made any sense to me, had given up his dancing for a nine-to-five job and family life. It became clear to me as an adult that he furtively held this against his wife *and me*. Things could only deteriorate further when I eclipsed him in earning power in my twelfth year. The year I turned sixty a distant Babin family member made contact with me and it was explained, finally, that Ham was a contraction of Howard and Ambrose. This seems ridiculously simple but it had never been broached to me by any family members before.

Throughout Ham's life he excelled at dancing with a partner but his unvoiced dreams obviously disappeared. He was not going to be like George Raft, a dancer turned actor whom many said he resembled. I like to think he reconciled himself to being forever successful socially, on a dance floor, with any lady he chose. At that he was only excelled by Mr. Astaire who stated he practiced perpetually while Dad practiced as little as possible.

Eventually we seemed to somehow miss Hollywood and arrived in California disembarking in Highland Park, a small town in the San Gabriel Valley of Southern California just east of the San Fernando Valley and adjacent to Pasadena, which is heralded for its Rose Parade, Rose Bowl and little old ladies. Highland Park is not heralded for anything of which I have ever heard. My parents rented a room in the small home of a couple and we shared their one bathroom and kitchen, a practice not uncommon at the time. World War II had ended the year before and the subsequent prosperity and glow was yet to come.

This bungalow was about fifty feet from the Arroyo Seco, the very first freeway in California and, to my knowledge, the world. This budding smog factory was begun in 1925, halting construction during the Depression, then continuing and being completed after World War II. In 1946 it snaked from Pasadena to downtown Los Angeles, where hardly anyone ventured unless, like Ham, they worked there.

I loved sitting on the small front porch and eye-balling the automobiles as they whizzed by at up to 45 miles an hour! It seemed like multi-hued lightning to me. The transition from eastern provincialism to the auto-as-male-identity state was a snap for me.

The gruff and strict married renters became my bugbears. Having been warned copiously about not breaking their rules, I was sure a violation would garner me a tossing onto the freeway in front of a huge, speeding Packard. If I survived, I would face my mom's formidable temper (inherited from Gram) and my dad's comparable wrath.

Thus, one morning I emerged early to play on the front porch when "somehow" a milk bottle got knocked over. They still delivered things to your door in 1947, although I was more partial to the smells emanating from the Helm's Bakery truck and the treasures of the Good Humor Man.

The crash of breaking glass and the *glug-glug-glug* of the flooding milk terrorized me thoroughly. In hindsight I may have felt some connection to my later discovery that I was allergic to milk, hence, this accident was some kind of Jungian foreshadowing, therefore unavoidable and *not my fault*.

I fled up the street. Realizing relatively soon that I was not being chased by a mob with torches and pitchforks, I slowed to a walk and began speculating about a grilled cheese sandwich on white bread dipped in catsup, accompanied by a tart dill pickle, fries with more catsup and a cherry phosphate, all favorites. I planned to stop at the first soda fountain I encountered. How I was to pay for these delicacies in my penniless abandon never occurred to me, nor slaked my mounting desire.

The street stopped, making a "T" at a cross street, so I turned right, as opposed to left towards the dangerous Arroyo Seco, and began climbing a hill that I recalled from a car ride that led to downtown Highland Park and food. I did not notice a two-toned car pull ahead of me and park. A strangely clad man got out and slowly ambled over to greet me. His pants, shirt, socks, shoes, tie, the entire ensemble, was a monochrome black highlighted by a shiny metal badge and a thick, black leather belt which held a weapon much larger than the cowboy cap pistol I had recently discovered and coveted.

I had been warned to avoid nefarious strangers but this guy was unthreatening and smiled broadly. He squatted down to my level and instantly became my buddy. Since this singular early experience I have found it highly unlikely for anyone dressed in this monistic fashion to show any endearing equanimity, except in very unusual instances.

His concern for my safety and my grieving parents allowed him access to my precocity and I gave him my address. I jumped at the opportunity to ride in his shiny, black and white vehicle with the two neat chrome searchlights by the cozy wings.

The visible ire of Dot and Dash on our arrival prompted my bud to calm them to prevent a virgule thrashing. Perhaps his parents had the temper of tragedians, too. He complimented my excellent memory and polite behavior which seemed to pacify them and extracted exculpatory smiles but the instant he left Ham gave a fierce growl about whomping my bare bottom as veins ebbed and flowed freely throughout his body.

I was made airborne and whisked off to the privacy of our bedroom. Dad unbuckled his belt to set about strapping me as I cried and cowered; Dickens would have loved it. My mom decried this version when I mentioned it as a mature adult. She insisted he did nothing with the belt using only his hand to whack my nude behind. I capitulated to her memory but thought to myself, "Why then, pray tell, did he take the belt off? A compulsive surge of gas, perchance?" Family legend has it that he merely thwacked my bum with his calloused palm for a short period of time, which seemed rather long to me, when Mom grabbed me up and shouted that if he ever laid one digit on me again she would abandon him.

In hindsight, this classical father-son battle is a categorical victory and I won the lady. I wailed louder in what I would like to think was a bravado-taunting fashion. To my dismay, I could not hold, nor did I yet own, a football to spike. Ham bellowed profanely at us and screeched off in the Auburn.

However much this schism may have appealed to Ham, he reconsidered. In this separation scenario he would lose access to my mom's body, his main squeeze and best dancing partner ever, as well as the moola my grandparents gave us. He had no family, nor friends, in California and no encouraging prospects back in Kentucky.

He had already begun his job, which he quickly settled into, as a short haul, home-nightly trucker for an L.A. metallurgy company. After rejecting being a machinist because of the "cooped up," inside nature of the chores, he enjoyed being outside, on the road, daily and he continued doing it for over thirty-five years despite earning less than a machinist and almost everyone else who was not a day laborer.

He returned a few hours later redolent of what I would learn to identify as bourbon. He never rampaged my rear end again but he abandoned both of us regularly, anywhere from one to three weeks from one to three times a year, after any substantive argument, versus daily hostile exchanges, with Dot.

He did engage in frequent recriminations of me. For instance, he would snarl at me for mixing my vegetables with the potatoes or meat, which he believed normal people did not do, and making noises while chewing, which I did not do but he did. His absences lasted until my parents divorced in celebration of my fifteenth birthday and my almost simultaneous high school graduation.

From this moment forward I began suspecting that Howard Ambrose Babin had decided that Dorothy's threats, nagging and absorption with me, herself and my career, along with John and Glade's undisguised contempt and meddling and controlling through their money were enough grounds for divorce. So with no official documents, no swelling orchestra, no pompous declaration, Ham got a divorce, in effect—long before I was fifteen—from me, his son Lonnie. There were to be no visitation rights.

We escaped further coughing à la Arroyo Seco and acrimony from the rentees by renting, as always with Gram's help, a larger, separate "apartment" in a much bigger, two-story house a few miles north but still in Highland Park. We had a larger bedroom, a living/dining area and a tiny kitchenette of our own; in addition we could use the downstairs common area which included a large living room, dining room and the biggest kitchen in any of my dwellings. The large, upstairs bathroom was shared with other tenants on the second floor; there was a second full bath downstairs. This arrangement was in a nicer section of Highland Park, a negligible distinction at best.

The front door was reached by a set of concrete steps from the sidewalk to the wooden steps of the wide porch that ran along the entire front of the house. There was a large fireplace in the living room which is useless in California except for one or two moody days a year, but it appealed to my vague recollections of home and hearth warmth from Kentucky.

The large backyard had an unusual series of six connected single-car garages that were used more for storage than General Motors products. A wonderful, densely foliated area in the center of the yard afforded a great place to hide and chase wild or imagined beasties. There was a big incinerator, for everyone burned most of their trash until much later when incinerators were banned since they fouled the air, which was done much more efficiently by automobiles and large money-making plants.

One Sunday afternoon this was the setting of a neighborhood brouhaha when an ill-advised opossum, looking to me like King Kong's pet rat, sought sanctuary in the thicket and when spotted and chased somehow escaped and squeezed into the basement through the two exterior wood doors. The renters and nearby others stopped pasting Green Stamps into their books to save money on things and soon became an audience that acted as if a lion was holed up in there.

The tension and drama went on for about an hour until, much to the dismay of the women, kids and most particularly the opossum, it was resolved in a typically human fit of violence. I learned that fear of marsupials is a greatly overrated pastime and seemingly friendly humans are very dangerous.

Outside the kitchen overlooking the backyard we had a screened porch from which I watched for birds or occasional critters. Back in our main room I lounged on the floor in front of the large, freestanding radio and listened to *Burns and Allen, Amos 'n Andy, Gangbusters* and *Inner Sanctum*, which scared the hell out of me even though I did a good imitation of the eerily creaking door in the show's opening. Mom knitted and dad drank beer, ate peanuts and passed wind. In the comfort of our not yet global era we all still believed that there was something to this imagination business. We still made our own pictures in our minds and were not hypnotized by image manipulators on larger than life film screens and the lesser than life TVs.

One unpleasant activity that troubled me as a kid was napping. The first time this came to a crisis level was at this location. I was forced to do it and it was nearly impossible after about four. I do not believe I can blame it on nightmares despite having some that were dillies; some came from my imagination and others were suggested by outside sources. Mom did a number of unusual things as a loving parent. I distinctly remember scary images from one movie. I tracked down the title much later as an adult: *The Beast with Five Fingers*. In this 1946 horror flick a disembodied hand walks upstairs to strangle someone and it scared the beejeesus out of me. What parents would take a little tyke of four or five to such a

Tapping in front of the chorus in the twice nightly, six nights a week Las Vegas production of George M, *1980.*

movie? It is bad enough that Bambi's mom got killed but lethal hands without a body are quite a bit more graphic and terrifying.

In all candor, this was a rare instance and I also discovered Fred Astaire when I saw the film *Three Little Words*. The movie had little substance but I did not notice. I was fascinated by Fred and he was, as always, absolutely spectacular. I was sold on his dancing, suave style and excellent haberdashery choices. Plus, it proved that you did not have to look like Cary Grant to get the girl.

Finally, in my thirties I forced myself to catch a few winks due to an exhausting schedule. I was playing my second version of the musical *George M* in Vegas, which means a "tab" version—no intermission, some songs and much of the dialogue excised, running time about ninety minutes. We performed two shows a night, six nights a week and finished at about 2:30 a.m. Since it has always been difficult for me to relax right after stage work, I did not get to sleep until early in the morning in this 1980 run.

A further complication was added when I had to fly on the earliest flight out of Vegas to the Disney Studios in Burbank. Our original filming of the MMC 25th Anniversary TV special on NBC was stopped after rehearsal but before we started on camera by the 1980 SAG strike. As soon as the issues with management were resolved, Disney wanted to shoot, so I had to be there. My casting in the musical was subsequent to the strike beginning and our special halting production.

This double workfest ran for about ten days and I was managing only three to four hours of sleep a night working two jobs that involved physicality, dancing and singing, as well as acting. Catching up on shut eye was mandatory so I found a way of adapting Pavlov to my sleep habits without all of the salivating.

I managed to sleep with my cheek on my hand so I could keep from screwing up my fine, pain-in-the-cerebellum blond hair which after rehearsing, doing a show, playing tennis, riding in a convertible, almost anything, would then require washing, drying, combing and spraying. The alternative to this whole process was that my hair was a total mess and I do not enjoy looking disheveled.

My hair was an asset but too much work all of my life until my 60s when I began shaving my head. Like most blond males, my hair was thinning on the top and I was not about to do a comb-over and look like Zero Mostel, nor wear a piece. I save a bundle on hair stylists and sundry products and shave every 7 to 10 days in about 10 minutes. I no longer have stiff, blond hair that had a slightly sweet smell, despite my finding the most effective "no scent" hair spray. It was also a mite sticky to the touch.

My worst wrangles about napping as a kid were with my grandmother, which was atypical since she pretty much let me get away with a lot. Within a year of our departure from Kentucky my grandparents moved to California. They sold their house, furniture store and other properties for my grandmother could not take the separation. John was less thrilled but where Glade went, he went. They would see their darling grandson and their beautiful, misused daughter weekly, if not daily. They did their best to ignore Dot's husband—or "Buzz."

My grandfather had nicknames of his own for everyone—except Glade. Our cousin Billy was "Doc" because he read a lot and imperiously let all know that he knew the answer to almost everything. I did not get Buzz for Dad until I was told that it was short for buzzard.

Talk about your fun in-laws!

They lived with us for a desperate few months, which brought forth the napping scrapping, until they bought a house in Altadena, just north of Pasadena. They then acquired a store on Colorado Boulevard and began stocking their new furniture emporium. Dorothy and Glade vied for ascendance over the three-male roost. As they bickered, we three generations of males tried to remain safe and not take sides. It was a haven for anyone seeking high blood pressure.

Exterior of Slapsy Maxie's supper club, 1947.

Between Dad, Mom on one side and Gram and Gramp at Slapsy Maxie's. Slapsy Maxie Rosenbloom was a fighter-turned-actor and restaurateur, 1947.

The two combatants for the throne acquired a surly, petulant, well-clawed, adult Siamese cat with whom I had instantaneous and urgent issues. Being of an inquiring young mind and disliking the snarling, hissing, scratching feline, I sought to verify the laws of physics that dictate that the puss always lands on its paws and right side up. Avoiding the treacherous rapiers, I threw the snarling nasty as high as I could into the air and, lo and behold, she landed on all fours. Her weapons neutralized by disorientation, I tried twice more to insure the verity of the experiment. The noise adversely alerted the ladies of the fiefdom away from their preoccupation with over-cooking and over-salting food in the southern tradition.

Running in from the kitchen like crazed Assyrians, they were horrified by my torture of the poor, yowling grey beast with black shadings. I was excoriated as a minion of Beelzebub. I felt as if my nascent science research should have been lauded as the working of a mind that might emulate Einstein or at least Edison. With dignity, I gathered my four-year-old fury and declared I would not suffer ignominious treatment further—I was moving out!

I tromped upstairs, followed by the ladies, packed a small bag and journeyed back down to the foyer. They appeared to be holding back tears or something at my bold venture. I found nothing unusual in a four-year-old running away from home; after all, I had tried at three after the spilt milk.

I gave a final glower and with a little effort opened the oversized front door and slammed it behind me. Like Candide and Balso Snell, I was off on a great adventure to make my way in the world.

The world greeted me unkindly in the form of a huge, ferocious dog barking feverishly, his tail as erect as the hairs on his back as I descended the wooden steps to the concrete landing while he claimed the sidewalk. I was afraid he would attack even though he may have been angry at someone else or possibly just rolled in some starch.

I quickly returned to the porch and edged slowly to a rocker and sat, dropping my valise at my feet. The canine added saliva slinging to his savage repertoire. I flashed on scary accounts of mad dogs and the excruciatingly painful *series* of shots *in the stomach* if you were ravaged by such a beast as it ripped and gashed away at your flesh. I was not distracted by the cries of hysterical concern for my well-being from Mom and Gram, now observing at the window next to the front door.

I reasoned that this feral, surely diseased Cerberus—having left two of his heads at the ferry—was not going away, nor would he be distracted by a squirrel, a cat, nor even a siren blaring the way for a fire engine. So, I edged toward the front door dragging my bag and re-entered. I was met by the glassy, red eyes of the women as they worked to hide their overwhelming sorrow at my horrid misadventure. They were damn near incoherent.

They averred they would accept me back with the proviso that I never toss kittums ceiling-ward again. I agreed if they accepted my proviso to not acquire other felines, and certainly not a dog, without my consultation.

Upstairs I unpacked my things and carefully put them away. I may have been mean to a cat but I was neat, goldarn it. Besides, if I had succeeded in leaving and married a beautiful heiress before being elected President, I would have missed my first dancing lessons.

Chapter 3
The Charles Dickens School of Dance

In 1947 streetcars still clanged and *clickety-clacked* in the streets of Southern California, the metal tracks making car tires slide careening hither and yon when changing lanes, so my mom drove carefully in downtown Highland Park to Mrs. Burke's School of Dance.

Despite the fact that Dot and Dash, James Cagney and most vaudevillians learned by watching and doing rather than taking dance classes, Mom resolved that it was time for my formal dance training. We parked for free—no greedy meters cluttering all the sidewalks yet—and entered the rear of a building to climb steep wooden steps straight up to the second floor. We then walked down a long hallway.

Like my dad, I did not like to rehearse and my mother was always at me to keep at it. I argued that if I knew the exercises, steps or dances, then why did I have to keep repeating them? A year after beginning classes she had me doing a *tour jeté* over and over when I slipped and bloodied my small proboscis. I reasoned that if I had not been forced to rehearse the accident would not have occurred. She became less strict about my practice since I retained things quickly and well and she did not want to pay for a nose job. Later, as an adult, I naturally rehearsed but I am still not a stickler about it.

The hall ended at an open door and we found a large room devoid of furniture except for a few wooden chairs. The floor was shiny and I assumed the wood had been polished since the word vinyl was not yet part of the language. A door back up the hallway opened to a smaller room used for tap dance and was also polished but scuffed with black marks, taps being harder on floors than ballet slippers. Both rooms had tall mirrors covering one wall and wooden hand rails on the opposite wall. I learned the rails were called *barres* used by shaky, grasping, little (or large) hands to help support weak ankles and often stubbed toes.

Each room had an area to hold a record player for 78-rpm records and other paraphernalia for music. The tap room had no windows and was lit only by overhead lighting. The ballet room had very large windows with glass transoms that were opened or closed by a long stick with a hook on the end. I sometimes worried about "getting the hook."

It is impossible to make a living by teaching dance to adults unless you focus only on the rod-up-your-tookus, pixilated world of ballroom dance. So, one must mostly teach children in order to make the endeavor economically viable. This requires the patience of a saint, the focus of a lapidary and the zeal of a myopic Pointillist. Dance teachers, like musicians, are usually a little "off center."

The proprietress, Mrs. Elsie Burke, who was never *ever* addressed as anything other than Mrs. Burke, was a Dickensian type. She was a squat, densely packed martinet who brooked no humor, nor individuality. Her white-grey hair was wrapped very tightly in a chignon on all occasions and was set off by her pinkish, almost translucent skin. She struck me as a petite, pale version of George Washington with the addition of large, matronly breasts that might make Stuart Gilbert peeved.

Our agon began.

This solemn, elderly, five-foot tyrant was inevitably clad in a leotard, fishnet stockings, ballet shoes, a pastel tutu and a finely woven, unbuttoned sweater with a chain and clasps below her throat to keep the top in place. I figured she had no other attire until our first recital because she never changed, except for a scarf about once a month.

Her minatory wood cane came to above her waist and only left her grasp for necessities like changing a record or blowing her nose in a ladylike fashion. This made her always at port arms to *smartly* strike a child's limbs or rear when he or she talked, erred or in some other way garnered her disfavor. She did not, of course, beat the crap out of kids as in *Oliver Twist* but she did not spare the rod and the era allowed for errant children to be disciplined rather than buying them ammo for their Uzis. When Mrs. Burke shouted, "Diaphragm *in*, behind *under*, back *straight*!" everyone scurried to obey.

Mr. Burke, who got no billing anywhere, was named Fred and affected a hair style and outfits that emulated the other Fred—Astaire—sometimes even wearing a handkerchief loosely tied about his neck. He was older than the Mrs. and taught tap but was actually better at "eccentric dance," the peculiar, humorous, limber movements used to best effect by Ray Bolger and Buddy Ebsen.

The rail-thin Fred was a standup comedian compared to his wife but he was easily bemused. He persisted in calling me *Lennie* even after both my mom and I corrected him for weeks then gave way to his capabilities. If he had encountered me later, *if* he recognized me, he would still call me Lennie Burr—if he knew I had a last name.

Back in ballet class we learned to stand properly, point our toes arching the ankle, move our arms precisely, keep our diaphragm in and butt under and the five positions for feet, arms, legs and all the body. These were innovatively titled: first, second, third, fourth and fifth position. We learned exercises at the *barre* and those done in the center of the room, which precariously left nothing to hold onto, nor fall against, save ourselves, other little people or the floor. This became problematic and fearfully embarrassing—not to mention a tad painful—to many tykes.

After we warmed up our extremities and got the blood flowing, we then would work on steps, thence to combinations of steps: *pas de bourrée, changement, changement, glissade, assemblé* and so on. This falderal confused everyone including me, although I am of 35 or 40+% French extraction. A smidgen of pidgin *Français* is mandatory in figuring out what in the hell was going on in this dance form and, significantly, to translate prior to any cane "touches."

Ballet is formal and precise; it does not allow for much innovation, or any improvisation. If I forgot a step in a solo tap routine when we made live appearances as Mouseketeers, I would just make something up and no one, except other Mice who remembered my routine, would have an inkling that things were different. Ballet, however, is an extremely disciplined discipline and, ironically, unbending.

Ever the innate individualist—one of the tenets of being American—I insisted as child, teen and adult on thinking for myself and finding my own way. I found ballet a bit like dancing in a cell. The minute anyone coerces me to do things one way only, I resist; I then find another way to do it. Ballet was not my style.

Contrarily, American tap came from the street in the late 19th century, although it may have precedents in immigrants from European clogging, and moved onstage in minstrel shows, then vaudeville and thence to burlesque. It is much more informal and a boon for individual thinkers and creators. It is the height of existentialism; ergo, I really took to it.

Tap does not demand the same precise control of the body and most "hoofers," the term for tappers although it is used to mean all dancers by many, do very little with their arms and torso. They concentrate solely on their feet and the percussive beats they punch out to and with the music or as they accent or syncopate against the music. The separate beats of tap rely heavily on the absence of sound too, silence becoming a substantive change from so many double, triple and occasionally quadruple clicks we clack out. It is quite like drumming with your feet.

Astaire changed all of that with his graceful style. Then Gene Kelly took tap more into the world of athletics. These two innovators were the best, the most distinctive, tappers and dancers and they epitomized the use of the entire body instead of just the heels and toes and sometimes the side of the foot. They are the *sine qua non* of tapping. This does not mean Greg Hines was not a great hoofer, nor that Baryshnikov, surprisingly, was okay tapping in *White Nights*.

The freedom and unique sounds of tap are akin to the insouciance of jazz versus the classical symphony's unerring precision or the exacting stiffness of ballet. Both are aesthetically fulfilling and we all have our own world of preferences. I could not watch an entire ballet performance if I was paid to do it in spite of taking classes for six years and understanding it more than most people. I managed to see Nureyev on a backstage TV while doing my second run in *West Side Story* just south of San Francisco and he, like Baryshnikov, was great.

My early facility and ease with tap dancing might explain why I was "into" jazz before and during my teen years in the 'fifties while everyone else was consumed by rock 'n roll. I thought Little Richard, Elvis and Chuck Berry were great for dancing fast with girls and Mathis and Sinatra for pressing important matters with young ladies, but that was all. I preferred Miles Davis, Dave Brubeck and Stan Kenton, Oddly, I was also drawn to Debussy, Beethoven and Ravel.

I took ballet classes but was one on one with Fred Burke in private classes for my flaps, shuffles, and heel digs before moving on to cramp rolls, riffs, time steps, trenches, tap turns and sundry combinations of all the moves associated with a craft which, like acting, can ascend to art. My best and last teacher—for after a time you really do not learn much but invent by yourself—was Dee Blacker, who started her classes with a short routine to loosen up the ankles, feet and legs.

Mr. Burke and I moved quickly into creating rhapsodic, intricate combos of sounds and moves. The steps are linked musically by "breaks," the fourth variant of a step that leads to the next step combination and ends a musical phrase. I used my ballet arm moves even though my teacher let his arms hang at his sides most of the time. I soon had my first tap routine while I was learning mostly more exercises in sequence in ballet. I did start doing adagio, combinations of dance steps and lifts with little girls, and that was more interesting but I was not a patient child and tap was much more fulfilling. I was also later not a patient young man and it has taken me some adult decades to be a much more even-tempered, although I am sure I could find someone who would disagree with this statement.

The formidable Burke woman, with my mom as her ally, wanted me to wear what the other two boys in the mostly girl class wore: *tights*!

Using the blackest of black materials and a Lone Ranger mask, this little fellow was never going to be seen in such an outfit anywhere, ever. The onus of males dancing, even social dancing with girl partners, even square dancing, let alone the unspeakable ballet, was still occupation non grata for the testosterone-driven guys of the 'forties and 'fifties.

Tights would have exacerbated the problem beyond comprehension. I had enough trouble with my blond, wavy hair and "peaches and cream" complexion and the women who consistently commented on them much too loudly in public. The unmanly adjectives "beautiful" and "pretty" came up far too often in relationship to my burgeoning male ego.

My firm convictions sufficed and I sidestepped the girlie appearance that seemed not to bother the two other guys by managing a compromise. I wore a T-shirt, boxer bathing trunks with no pattern, black socks and ballet shoes. It might have appeared bizarre to most, but this tiny individualist did not care.

The late comedy performer and writer Dick Clair (*Carol Burnett Show* and co-creator of *Mama's Family*) evoked guffaws at my 40th surprise birthday roast referring to my "relentless heterosexuality." The intimations of this exaggerated rubric grew apace from my early ballet epiphanies. It also most likely led to a short lived trait as a youngster that made my mother apoplectic. I gave it up after a year or so—honest.

Along with the two other guys there were almost a dozen little girls and I found this off-putting at first but I do not link it to my early, recurring nightmares about being kidnapped to a jungle and ravaged sexually by scantily clad, very large-breasted Amazon women. I readily perceived the upside and all of the lubricious opportunities for surreptitious glances, horny speculations and careful-to-not-show fantasies. The erotic was an early priority for me.

When in a store or a room but never on a street or sidewalk, I would "accidentally" fall down or drop something and sneak a peek up a woman's dress. I was choosey and gravitated toward the most alluring. Achieving two or more women on one drop was the ultimate goal. This mini-obsession is frozen in an image of old time five-and-dime stores redolent of lunch counters, wooden floors, popcorn and candy scents and the perfume or cologne or powders that every woman then wore.

Katharine Hepburn had not convinced many women, nor did the "war to end all wars," to wear pants so they were costumed in dresses or skirts covering a panoply of slips, chemises, panties, nylons, garter belts and who knew what else? I was driven by my inquiring eyes and imagination. These inaccessible forests of silk and other soft, fascinating materials was also fed by my quest for certainty about what in the heck was up there that they kept so private and mysterious and that men seemed to be so consumed by.

My mother's horrified reactions wrought forcible jerking of my arms, wrists and ears that were demeaning and unpleasant to me. Her exhortations were stressful, too. I knew it was inappropriate, which is why I tried to make it look accidental. But even in success, all I saw were panties and such. I hoped, I surmise, to someday catch a bad lady who wore no panties enabling me to discover what women saucily concealed. Thus, I would discover what the world was all about.

As an adult I have absolutely never had the urge to splay out and peer up a female's dress.

Well…at least I have never practiced such a disgusting and antisocial procedure since turning five.

Six?

Honest!!!

Long before finishing my years of ballet I knew that it was not a fit. In tap almost everything was easy and exciting, as if I had some rhythmic, archetypal recognition. I had talent and some of it was at least to some degree genetic via Dot and Dash. My parents, until they divorced, never lost the ability to stun other dancers on the floor who flared out in a circle, ceasing their dancing, to watch and enjoy and applaud the former dance team's grace and facility at the Palladium, the Aragon Ballroom and the other venues we frequented when I was growing up.

Ballet, however, being more exacting and precise, prepared me and my body much better than my eight years of tap and more of jazz dance for sports, working onstage, acting and just about anything that was physical in my life. Training for ballet is helpful to every child, girl or boy, and particularly those that are awkward or retiring and shy. The only negative to avoid is toe work for girls. Dancing *en pointe* is damaging and dangerous when muscles and sinews are still growing into their fruition.

Doing "wings" as part of my tap routine at age eight, 1951.

To me tap was exotic and the Frog ballet business was foreign. But it did facilitate eventually doing pint-sized lifts and routines with girls along with tap solos and group numbers in Mrs. Burke's recitals. This got me on TV as an amateur for the first time, dancing with first Judy Bogart, then Gwendolyn Stevens, Judy Kaye and Bee Jee Kunkle. Bee Jee and I became local Pasadena television hits in 1948 as I simultaneously premiered on radio as an actor.

My mom adapted and changed Mr. Burke's steps and routines into an act with songs and imitations for me to do solo. I workshopped them at "community sings" locally and won talent contests. My impressions included Cagney, Eddie Cantor, Jimmy Stewart and the now-forgotten Ted Lewis.

Mom's little Lon star trek was en route so she shelled out for pro photos. At the time they were idealized, shadow fraught, touched up prettifications that made everyone look like a screen idol with glittering teeth and perfect hair. My prettiness did not require as much correction as some, although the term would seem problematic for people who have known me since my twenties. As an adult I have primarily played heavies, the bad, tough guys who got their nickname from the heavy makeup and beards worn as a convention in silent films. As a teen I longed for facial scars to make me tougher looking, a reaction to all the ego-fondling ladies as a child and the complications of being in addition to pretty, not very tall, three years ahead in school, and an "egghead" (intellectual) which are traits for a boy that beckon to bullies and other guys. Before I turned twenty I received a large scar cutting through another childhood scar on my left jaw line and under it. The first one was a mass on my lower left jaw that was burned off with radium. This sounds life threatening now, but nothing has ever come of it and it was hardly noticeable on the jaw line.

The second was the result of a car accident at seventeen on Coldwater Canyon right in front of the fire station above Sunset Boulevard. The incompetent and/or novice doctor at the tiny Beverly Hills Emergency Hospital near Wilshire and little Santa Monica to which I was rushed by ambulance had apparently read too much Mary Shelley for he reattached the flap hanging from my jaw and a smaller one above my left eye in an ugly, crude manner.

I kept the scar after recovery and it afforded me some visual credentials as a heavy rather than a pretty boy juvenile. The scars were not eye magnets but they balanced the blond hair and solid features. By this time my complexion had become peaches, cream and some zits. Decades later I was advised that the scar kept me from commercial work and I had it cleaned up as well as possible in my early forties by a plastic surgeon but it still is visible unless I have a beard, which I have had since 1995.

The Charles Dickens School of Dance 37

Another problem that attached itself to performing forced me into outfits as hideously egregious as tights, for example a white, double-breasted, short-pants suit accoutered with a colorful bow tie, bright suspenders and white shoes. My mother foisted these upon me at about five or six and I was so damn cute that I am sure many males and male kids

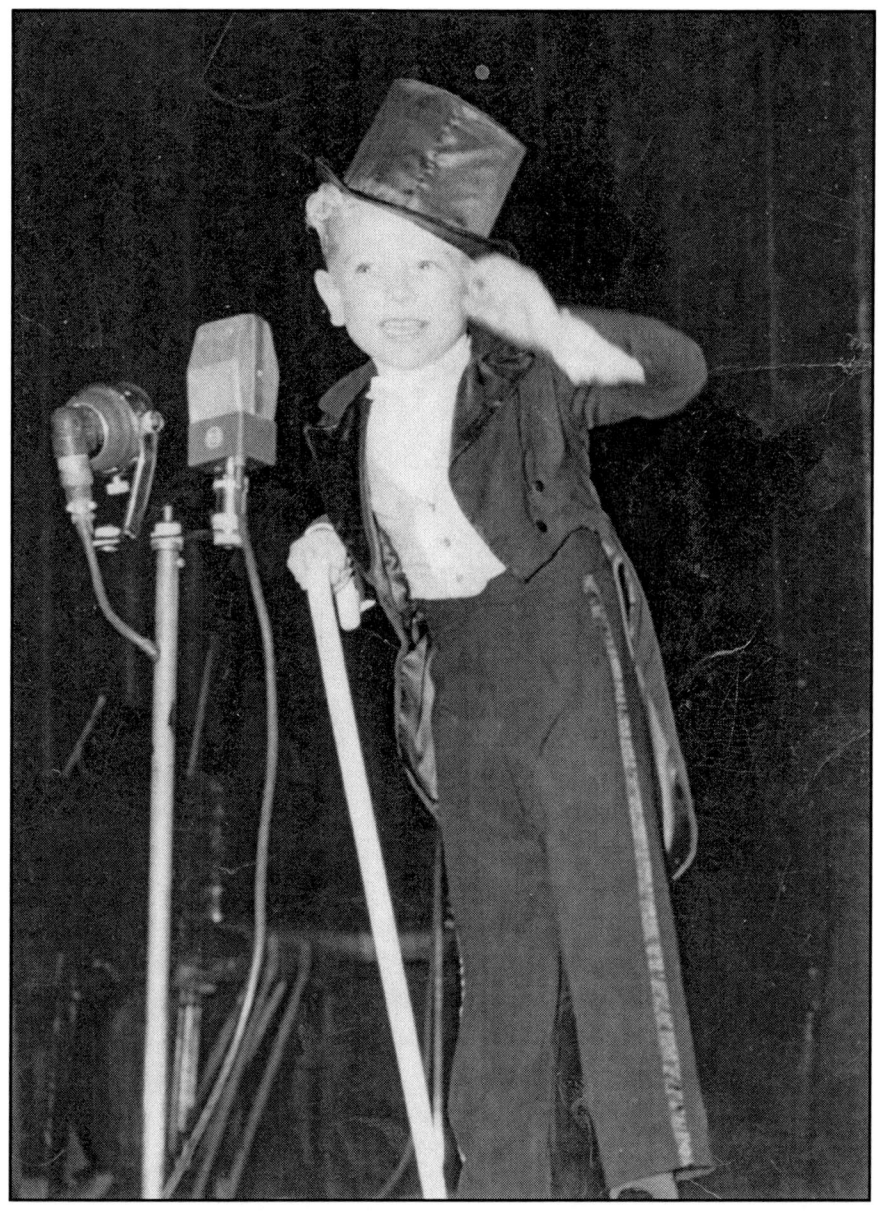

Singing, dancing and imitations, top hat and cane included, first paying job, 1948.

> **The Home of**
> **Saturday Night Vaudeville**
>
> **CIVIC AUDITORIUM**
>
> **PASADENA, CALIFORNIA**

Pasadena Civic Auditorium where I debuted as a professional, 1948.

wanted to beat me up on sight. Some discerning females of varying ages most likely felt the same urges.

I claimed my haberdashery choices from my mom, with much ado, at seven or eight and to this day I constantly scorn bow ties and suspenders even for formal events. There are other appropriate options.

My amateur days led me to win not just decrees and newspaper subscriptions but actual shekels—a whopping *three dollars* from a *Herald Examiner* competition. Mom, naturally, pocketed it all. Someone had to contribute to my grandmother's constant gifts for classes, photos, and so on. I finally landed my first paying gig after turning five in 1948 and received $25, quite respectable for the era, by performing my dancing/singing/imitations act at a Policeman's Benefit at the Pasadena Civic Auditorium, a large still-extant structure built in 1932 in the "Italian Renaissance Style." However, no one has ever declared an actual renaissance in Pasadena.

It was in the last days of vaudeville shows and was titled "The Home of Saturday Night Vaudeville" and luckily I did not slip and slide following the seals or other animal acts that made dancing iffy and stinky on vaudeville stages. I was a hit, did an encore and made more in a few minutes than my dad did in a few days. This went over badly with Ham who did not attend my performances.

Costumed in white tie, top hat and tails, I tapped and sang my rendition of Ted Lewis' hit "When My Baby Smiles At Me" and my encore, which Dot would have pushed me on to do even if the audience had thrown many mushy watermelons, was "If You Knew Susie" à la Cantor with some imitations thrown into short vamp sections.

I later reprised this number, mouthing to a playback of Eddie, on *The Colgate Comedy Hour* when Cantor was ill due to his heart problems and could not take the rigors of his frenetic style of dancing as he sang. The director, Cantor, producers and choreographer asked to see my turn as Eddie and opted for my standing in for him when we kinescoped it live for TV.

He was a small man and the number was done solo, "in one," which is right in front of the foremost downstage curtain, but separated from the live audience by the orchestra pit at the El Capitan theatre. The fuzzy,

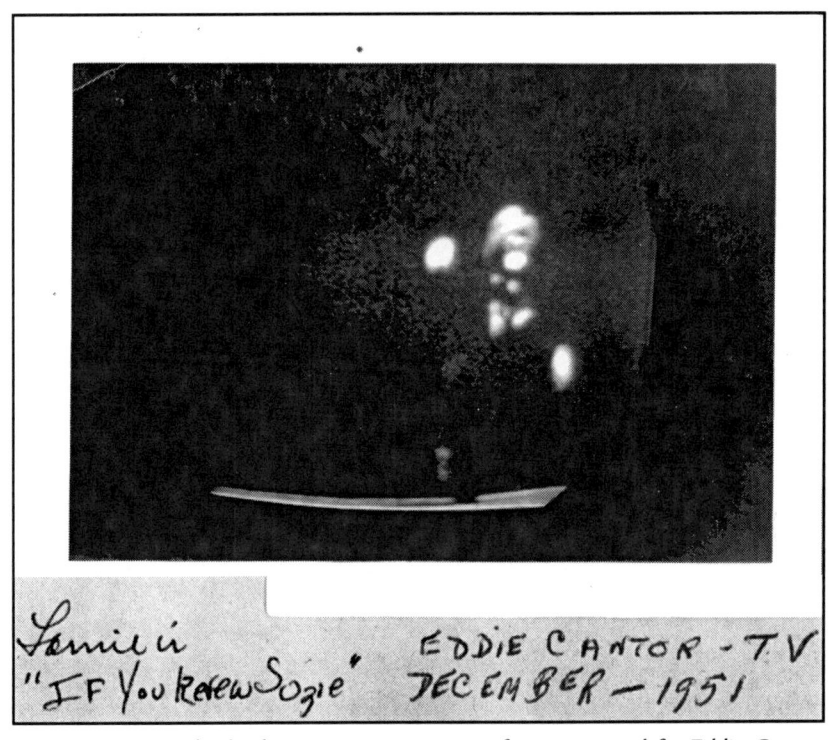

From Mom's scrapbook, that's me at age seven performing as and for Eddie Cantor, photographed off the TV screen.

technologically volatile kinescope images, most of which have decomposed, that appeared on TV screens were helped by the use of only long shots and the black and white result left no one doubting that it was Cantor rather than me. I have a snapshot proving it actually happened this way.

Performing in "black-face" started in the late 19th century in minstrel shows and it was blacks who wore the stylized makeup. It was then moved to vaudeville and burlesque and even movies often with whites as well as blacks wearing the makeup. Many stars, including Jolson, would not have been as well known without their "black-face" routines; it was a staple for Cantor, too. Dark black makeup—originally burnt cork was used—was applied to the face leaving the eyes and mouth highlighted by no further covering or heavy white makeup outlines. The hands were covered with white gloves. Such an act became thoroughly unacceptable in the 'sixties, but was still requested and considered no problem through most of the 'fifties.

My appearing for Cantor with no billing is one example of the never-ending duplicity of showbiz, especially film, with matte shots—parts of background and/or foreground masked so something different can be substituted in editing—and *trompe l'oeil* and presently decades of digitalization. By the mid-1950s on the Mouse Club, to give the impression of someone or something disappearing or appearing from nowhere, we "froze," the performer walked into or out of camera frame or the prop was added or subtracted and on "Action" we all began moving again. Hence, he, she or it appeared or disappeared.

By 1949, my pro status established, I turned six and was making money in network TV, radio, theatre, film, commercials in more than one medium, modeling and live performance. Mom was thrilled but not sated while Dad was mum and appalled. Gram was proud and boastful and Gramp thought I should act more like a real little boy.

Unquestionably, I liked the attention, compliments and the reification that I was a worthwhile kid deserving of the Big Time.

The downside was that instead of a reward I was rudely thrust into what was spuriously called a place of learning. In spite of many of my teachers, I somehow eventually became educated. This misguided concept requires a disregard for being an individual and becoming a cog in the group mentality, with most of the group rather slow and tedious—unless one became a rebel with a cause, say like common sense or actual ratiocination.

Chapter 4
Judy Garland, Natalie Wood, Melanie Griffith and Me

A short list of the child and later adult stars who attended the same unique school that I did includes Judy Garland, Mickey Rooney, Betty Grable, Donald O'Connor, Debra Paget, Natalie Wood, Bobby Driscoll, Lauren Chapin, Connie Stevens, Ryan and Tatum O'Neal (although not simultaneously), Patty McCormack, the Cowsills, four of *The Brady Bunch*, Brenda Lee, six of the Mouseketeers (but not Annette which she verbally confirmed in the 'nineties), Sammy Ogg, Sue Lyon, Tony Butala (The Lettermen), Peggy Lipton (*The Mod Squad*), Brian and Carl Wilson of The Beach Boys, Annette O'Toole, dancer/choreographer Tommy Rall, Barry Gordon, Yvette Mimieux, Tuesday Weld, Jill St. John, Valerie Bertinelli and MacKenzie Phillips (*One Day at a Time*), Val Kilmer and Melanie Griffith.

Except for my first week of my senior year in high school, I spent all of my pre-college years at Hollywood Professional School, known as HPS. I started before all the Mouseketeers, was joined by Ronnie Steiner and his two brothers who had a song, dance and comedy act; Ron was only on the MMC the first season and we were joined at HPS by four more Mouseketeers after the MMC folded.

Of course, hundreds of other kids in show business and sports—some stars, some not—also attended like ice skater Peggy Fleming and Olympic gymnast Muriel Davis (whom I dated and who later had a short showbiz career). Stars like Bob Mitchum, Alan Ladd, Spike Jones, Mickey Rooney and Peggy Lee had their children enrolled as well. I briefly dated Cynnie Troup who is the daughter of pianist/vocalist Bobby Troup and his first wife Cynthia. After their divorce, Bobbie married Julie London, making her Cynnie's stepmother, and Bobbie changed Julie from an actress into a popular jazz singer.

Located on the corner of Hollywood Boulevard and Serrano, a few miles east of the hubbub of Hollywood and Vine, and below Griffith Park and the well known Observatory, HPS was opened and created to solve the complications of education for children who worked in films; this later became even handier for television. There are various stories of it being founded in the mid-'thirties, but it is impossible to be precise; it closed in 1985. Prior to Mickey and Judy, schooling for performing children was not dealt with as a priority.

Unlike public schools, HPS was geared specifically to show business schedules and was college accredited so the curriculum covered all of the mandatory classes; it excluded sports and almost all extracurricular courses like home economics and shop. The school day ran from 8:30 am to 12:30 pm five days a week, with afternoon school and summer school for those who wanted or required it. Given the hours, there were no breaks for food. The school started with kindergarten and ran through twelfth grade, although I found that far too many years to waste, so I managed it with more alacrity.

There were five class periods with four short intervals to hit your locker or the sometimes overcrowded bathrooms and move to another classroom. To my knowledge, not one of my former schoolmates has turned into Quasimodo as the result of wearing weighty back packs hung much too low. We also had no adding machines and computers, therefore, these crutches were not integral to our minds, nor our homework, and most of us can still function if there is no electricity. We were not distracted by texting or listening to our favorite music incessantly. The short school day allowed auditions, classes, agent visits, and workouts for skaters or gymnasts who needed more time for training efficiency.

By the 1930s a teacher or tutor was provided on movie sets and this individual would accommodate all grades in a private area away from the sound stage furor. The children read, did assignments, homework, wrote essays and took tests so that they could pass to the next grade. At HPS the faculty and material was sensitive to these absences for a day or for weeks or—less often—months.

Kids worked only eight hours a day but still six days a week in the 'fifties, as we did on the MMC, with five days of school. The workday was four hours of performing, rehearsing, recording, costumes and makeup and three hours, usually in small increments, of school with one hour for lunch.

The Disney lot made much of our "little red schoolhouse" which was a trailer painted red and set up with a larger teacher's desk as you entered and school desks in two rows with a middle aisle for access. It was parked just off Dopey Drive outside Stage One and was directly across from the costume/makeup/sound departments making quick access for the Mice and only around the corner from the studio film theatre where the parents were rounded up and required to stay.

The time increments were never less than fifteen minutes in the 'fifties, and teachers always sought at least an uninterrupted half hour or more. It is taxing enough to remember your lines, lyrics and dance steps while sweating under Klieg lights, or worse, keeping down the stress of "Action!" but those duties are heavily distracting when you have to jump immediately into geometry or an essay. The time loophole existed and Disney management took advantage of it as often as possible.

Children in show business also had to get a mandatory physical exam every six months to be eligible to work. Mom drove me down to some department or other in L.A. They thwacked my back, chest and knees, splayed my tongue with a wooden stick, listened to me breathe with ice-cold instruments and had me read an eye chart.

My mom's vanity about her glasses extended to me so she taught me how to cheat on the eye test. I would finagle to use my best eye first and memorize the chart characters to get by with the "weaker" eye. She never took me to an optometrist nor an eye doctor that I recall and although I played a number of "glasses types," always intellectuals, superior types who were usually wealthy, I used prop glasses with clear lenses or no glass at all which helped the Director of Photography for there was no light reflection to worry about which costs time, thus, money.

I was shocked at sixteen when I was forced to get goggles for my long-desired driver's license. I was myopic and astigmatic so things were both fuzzy and distorted to some degree. The fact is that you cannot realize this until you are shown a clear image via a machine or spectacles for what you see is only what you see and you assume everyone else sees the same things in a similar way. It is possible to doubt the accuracy of your vision when someone else is better but you figure they are just that, better at seeing, just as they might be better at basketball.

I have asked numerous ophthalmologists and optometrists why they always use the same charts. Anyone can know them by heart or cheat as I did. They have no answer and the only one I have found is that you want to see as accurately as you can so you are on your own honor system. It is still a bad system for depth perception and color blindness because they are very personal and abstruse forms of perception.

I had begun living with my grandparents before I turned sixteen and I was forced to get prescription glasses to pass my driving visual exam, but I proceeded to drive day and night with shades on. The sins of the mother followed hard upon. This made my night driving vision less than what we all hope for in the other vehicle operators, although it never caused an actual problem. I converted after about a year to having clear glasses as well as sunglasses.

The old HPS building may very well have been new when it opened but it was repainted many times and showed some cracking and age when I started. It was small in relationship to public schools, was plainly painted in a two-tone cream and black and it resembled a slightly extended, two-story box with a small playground adjoining it for the youngest grades. Being a private school, tuition was charged but it was not a huge burden (especially for my grandmother) and it made for a much better student-to-teacher ratio than in public forums.

Sometime in the 'forties Mr. & Mrs. Mann bought HPS and eventually became President and Principal, respectively. We all assumed that Mr. handled the business end of things for he was seen less frequently, did not teach and did not remonstrate at everyone much of the time.

Mrs. Mann was a formidable presence who also did not teach but was seen daily unless you were wise and fortunate enough to avoid her. She was large in height and wide in girth and was definitely not formed after Giacometti's figures. She had short, dark hair and fierce black eyes and she dressed in plain business dresses—neither frivolously colored nor patterned. You did not want to ever mess with Mrs. Mann—her name "She The Man"—said it all.

Mr. Mann was also large and rotund but he seemed more equable on the rare encounter. Perhaps his lack of exposure to the little savages assuaged his composure.

Almost all members of the teaching staff—some of whom were very kind and lovable—were odd in some way. The lovely, aged Mrs. Doss, who had some kind of palsy, seemed to assume that I had a urinary tract challenge in tenth grade for she issued me a pass to the bathroom every day which I used to break the tedium and furtively sneak a smoke outside.

Miss Anderssen, who would have grandly eschewed the label Ms. if it had become fashionable then, would lounge on her large desk and dramatically drop English grammar rules to leap off on a riff about sailing down the Nile. Or she might begin chomping on a few petals from the frequent roses in a vase on her large desk and say, "Umm, scrumptious." She always meandered back to her English demesne of gerunds et. al. and most of us learned basic English rather well.

Anderssen stopped me once from running in the halls, being late for class, and challenged me by saying, "Lonnie, I have always regarded you as a little Greek God and Greek Gods do not run from class to class." Honest. I was taken aback and lacking Eilert Lovborg's vine leaves for my hair, I apologized, and walked briskly away.

The irascible Mr. Scherick (chemistry) was alleged to have thrown a smart aleck male student down the stairs and followed up with a chair but even when physical punishment was not frowned on that seems a bit much and was most likely school myth. If apocryphal, it is true that when he growled and charged a surly female student she kneed him; but the matter never came up again. Allegedly, this student was a girl with whom I was later involved. Still, his lab always smelled like the worst bloozer imaginable and I have since disliked sulphur more than any other chemical.

Mr. Hawkins had balance challenges that made his social dance classes hilarious. Due to showbiz kids being the majority of HPS students, dance and acting were offered as electives, exceptions to the policy that the school offered only the classes mandatory for college admission. We all concluded that Hawkins' occasional vertigo had less to do with the Hitchcock film and more to do with Smirnoff.

There are more idiosyncrasies, like the constant sneer of Mrs. Snell, but it is best to leave deceased instructors and their foibles lie. The perceptions of hormone-stressed, parent-driven, showbiz-obsessed teens are not necessarily the most accurate, nor altruistic of observations.

A very tiny minority element was included in the student body: those who had been expelled, usually from more than one institution whether public or private. There was a Hispanic hipster—very rare amidst all the white faces but not unique like a black student, teacher or staff member, not one of whom did I encounter in ten years. This guy was somehow connected to drugs and wore very brightly colored suede shoes that impressed me. The barely teenaged actress Beverly Aadland, who had just had or was having an underage affair with swashbuckler film star Errol Flynn, was also a schoolmate.

The 1950s was a period of closet bigotry in California and most other states that were not in the South where prejudice was in the open and shouted from the rooftops. In California it was evident by being constantly unnoticed and unmentioned but a fact of life everyone avoided. There were no black families in my neighborhood, no black kids at my school; they were confined to certain areas in downtown Los Angeles. The "N" word was used easily by men and women just as "wetbacks" was for Mexican people and other denigrating terms for nonwhite groups or religions. The only black friend I had as a kid was when I was about seven or eight and took up roller skating by going to the roller derby school in downtown L.A.

My grandmother was a big fan of wrestling on TV, but when roller derby was started in the early 'fifties in L.A., San Francisco and later Chicago, she went nuts. It was very clear who the good guys and bad guys were and she hated the bad guys and the bad girls even more. This was a rough sport and more dangerous than the showboating wrestlers. Skaters could literally break their necks and a fist fight between the opposing team males or females was common. It was like two cycle gangs having it out and the bad guys always fought dirty.

My mom was a fan too, just not as rabid as my grandmother, who subscribed to the *Roller Derby News*, the only paper I ever saw her read. Mom drove and we braved the dangerous area of downtown Los Angeles at night to see the games in person after becoming fans. Their ignoring the hazards of Los Angeles particularly at night showed their devotion and I became a fan, too, which is what led me to the training school. This is one of two places that I met, talked with and saw my black friend George: at the school and the pro games.

At the school we skated on a banked track, just like the one used in the sport. It was in a building that only allowed a few feet from brick walls on three of the four sides of the oval and the fourth was a long drop to a concrete floor. If you were put over the rail, which means being knocked over the padded railing around the upper, outside of the track, you could get really hurt and we did not wear helmets the way the pros did. A large, teenage bully disliked me and started trying to run me over the rail and into the wall. Primarily we sped around the track to improve our agility and balance but we did informally check—bump each other with shoulders, elbows or hips—and jam—go out from the pack of skaters and try to pass them and unofficially score. There were no actual teams, nor games, but being kids and teens we wanted to emulate the real Derby.

This guy almost had me once; I was still growing and only about 5' 3" and he was close to six feet. George blocked him hard and knocked him down. George was six feet and a very lanky teenager about fourteen or fifteen, which was comparable to the bully's size and age. George told him to leave me alone or he would deal with him. The bully left me alone after that and I greatly appreciated this, so George and I became friends. I had told my mom how he protected me and she was very friendly toward George. Having been in show business, Mom had less prejudice than the others in the family.

I did not appreciate the green track dust infiltrating my hair, giving it a greenish cast that was hard to get out. Some guys at HPS accused me, actually my mom, of bleaching my hair blond. After the green mist I got from the dust of the skating track even more rumors started.

George and I began calling each other "cousin," which startled some folks when we did it at the pro games and at the school. My grandmother, who like everyone in the family had a limited education, was from the South and bigoted but she somehow did not mind. Maybe Mom told her how George helped me with the white bully. Gram laughed and found it amusing when 'cuz and I greeted each other. George's mom came with him to the pro games and she was a very nice, refined woman and the five of us would exchange pleasantries when we encountered each other before taking our seats. I only lasted at the school for a couple of years but we attended the games until I started doing the MMC just before turning twelve.

Associating with people of color, except on occasion in showbiz, was very unusual for my family and the era. It took me until my teens to demand that my family stop using negative terms when talking about different foreign or minority groups. It had been their way of life since they were kids growing up in Kentucky. They ceased doing it in my presence but what they did on their own I had no control over. I have always assumed they continued saying what they wanted to when I was not present.

This was in the late 'fifties and very ahead of the times. I attribute it to my own sense of right and wrong and my religious teachings regarding the equality of people in the eyes of God, which most of the family adhered to only when they were under surveillance on Sunday, not socially, nor at home even on the day of rest. This seems to be the case much too often with many people who insist they believe in a God and his edicts.

Back at HPS, however ornery our few banditos were, I never heard of, nor read about youthful serial killers anywhere in the 1950s. Lillian Hellman shocked everyone by writing about one bad seed but we never saw headlines reading "SCHOOL CHUMS WHACK OVER A DOZEN."

Nor was the phrase, nor the concept of the "gifted child" in use at this time. The word "genius" was used, perhaps a bit too readily, for extremely intelligent, perceptive, facile, different kids but we were always expected to go to school and do our stuff like everyone else—skipping grades was frowned upon. Without being able to skip classes or in some way move into classes that were less boring, intelligent students tended more toward misconduct and worse. I was three years ahead and still bored in most classrooms.

It was readily discerned beyond my mom's and gram's opinions that my abilities were in the gifted class. I have never considered myself a genius but I have always realized from a very young age that there was a distinct difference between me and most if not all of my peers. My stringent definition for genius, and a few others like artist, came into play. There was definitely a divergence between me and other kids my age, even many three years older than me, and that was a stigma that kept other kids on the defensive if not completely antagonistic.

I was unyielding in my pursuit of circumventing these social negatives in order to be accepted as "one of the guys." I did not always succeed but I managed quite a good fit despite my mental acuity, my effortlessly solid memory, smart-ass perception and my appalling prettiness for a fellow.

In the eleventh grade at age thirteen, my SAT score was just under 1600. My memory was misidentified as photographic; my deductive and inferential capabilities were sharp. I was fourteen my senior year and achieved my A.B. and M.A. by twenty. It would have been nineteen if I had withdrawn from a conflict with one Samuel Selden, the officious, pedantic, ineffectual Chair of the UCLA Theatre Department.

Having a textbook on playwriting published and used in your own classes does not a playwright (nor a playwriting teacher) make. Selden held only his views and would allow no others. We disagreed about more than one thing but our defining agon was his strict labeling of what a play was and was not and how one created a drama or comedy. I was never sarcastic, but I could not accede to his pedestrian, generalized percepts. He found this unacceptable with a capital "H" for hubris and he required that I take an extra unit, requiring a third semester, when he rejected a full production of my first full-length play as my final project in order to achieve my master's degree.

My play, *Icons Are Not in Vogue*, was a modern American comedy after Oscar Wilde. The head of playwriting at UCLA, Dr. Savage, who had just published the definitive translation of *Wozzeck,* one of Büchner's plays, thought my effort was fine after being present at an unstaged reading, as the one-unit project required. He recommended it but, lacking the tenure of the Chair, he was overruled by Selden.

The real star of the department, Dean Melnitz, who co-authored the text for most theatre departments in the U.S. at the time, *The Living Stage*, suggested I write a paper for the meaningless unit after we agreed on a subject. I compared the Euripides *Antigone* and the later Roman Seneca's play on the same myth, received an A+ from Melnitz and a grand letter of recommendation from him for my Ph.D. work. Cambridge was receptive and complimentary about a paper I had written on Theatricalist productions in England and that was my early plan after a semester or two away from slogging through three college degrees.

Long before my Pyrrhic victory over the long forgotten Selden, my troubles at HPS started in the first grade. The other students and the teacher were disconcerted by my answering nearly all the questions that came up so I was promoted into the second half of grade one. This was the only class I skipped.

From 1948-58 I managed to complete the twelfth grade right before turning fifteen. I took afternoon classes at times and summer school once to affect all my necessary classes to advance three years prior to the ninth grade. My marks were straight A's for some time and always good with only the occasional "B" and very rare "C" inevitably in a high school course I did not like and that was taught boringly by a boob. I was also motivated by learning after a couple of years that having straight A's was not the smartest choice for social assimilation.

I have always been prouder of the acceptance I achieved with my older peers than my grades and awards. This success was not among the accomplishments my mother and grandmother constantly, to my embarrassment, touted. The one or two other eggheads were not treated well. I was not the BMOC, but later in life I have been referred to as one

The happy student at age 10, 1953.

by former HPS students who considered me just that.

    I was liked and accepted enough to get invited to all but the most in-group parties, was elected eleventh grade President both semesters and the next year Student Body President twice. I hung out easily with guys and dated chicks three or more years older than me. My scholastic awards were secondary to dating Gretchen, Rosie and other young ladies with whom I was relentlessly occupied.

    There were other difficulties in my ascendancy beginning in the first grade but they were all superable and school was easy for me, like tap and jazz, except for the occasional clash with a curmudgeon or a thought-challenged fanatic.

The female principal prior to Mrs. Mann's tenure, was an austere, out-of-Hawthorne, vituperative, 19th century harridan who insisted my mother come to her office at HPS because she claimed I could not read.

Dot was not pleased. I had started walking and talking, making sentences and sense, and reading much earlier than most kids and I was now four months into my fifth year. Mom joined me in this virago's office and I read well. It was deduced that I was so scared of this forbidding monster that I was too nervous to read for her without backup.

One for LB, zero for Ms. Vader.

Other problems were germane to the baffling process of growing up rather than being attributable to my precocity. PRECOCIOUS, adj. 1. Unusually advanced or mature in development, esp. mental development.

It has always greatly frustrated me that when this word precedes child there is an ineluctable pejorative connotation. Some precocious kidlets are an ache in the scrotum to be sure but not *all*. Profiling, like typecasting, although rife, is frequently fallacious. Pugilistic pursuits were not in the forefront of my life but they came up from time to time. If I had gone to public school instead of HPS I would probably have been put upon much more in the 'fifties, whereas today I would most likely have been snuffed.

When I was challenged by Ronnie Grubb, the toughest guy in school who managed to survive as a poor white kid in the black ghetto around USC and the Los Angeles Coliseum, I fought this older, bigger, badder enemy. I managed to survive through his magnanimity.

We were on the landing by the wide steps to the second floor and the chem lab and across from the huge Diego Rivera-like mural of workers when we circled and sparred. He chose to use open hands to my fists. He called the fight off when it was clear that I had had enough and my face was not very bloody but completely bright red. I just kept wading in although it was clear I was losing badly. We became friends of sorts because I was tougher than he figured, assuming, I supposed, that I would run away in tears as most intellectual kids. I doubt if his benign actions would be emulated today.

My real bravery was and is in speaking up for what I believe to be right, and for myself. I have done some things that might be called brave, certainly not heroic, like on a snow vacation in Mammoth, northeast of

L.A. with Barbara. She and I and another couple had climbed up a high hill and I do have some fear of heights. She was higher than I was, lost her hand grip and started to slide down. I jumped from where I was, digging my toes into the snow, and stopped her descent and mine, which would have definitely injured both of us if not killed us, if I had not acted instinctively. It was a long way down. Some park wardens and snow experts climbed up and brought us and the other couple down.

I tried to play the tough guy at HPS but that was to supplant the pretty boy, egghead, child star image that people got hung up in—otherwise, why would I have gotten into the scrape with the Mexican gang guys with just big, tough, nutty Earl Plantico at a party. At the same party I challenged a guy to cut his wrist with my pocket knife and, when he refused, I cut my own wrist to prove I was not afraid (and that bright boys can be extremely stupid). This is an interesting precursor to my means of attempting suicide at twenty.

An earlier occasion was a sparring match with a girl in the second or third grade. Ms. Tammy was extremely aggressive verbally and physically, a female bully. She was not given to Ronnie's sense of right and wrong, nor deep thought. I won all of our verbal exchanges. This prompted her on one occasion to bop me on the nose. I bopped her back and we were in a melee when the horrified teacher intervened and pulled us apart for a trip to the Principal's office.

Years later in our very late teens I ran into Ms. T and I found her as aggressive as when we were tykes. This was not helped by our both drinking booze at an HPS grad's party in an apartment whose front window looked out upon the Sunset Strip. Her insults led to my better ones and she reached over a three-seat, portable bar and grabbed my long, 'sixties hair and began yanking. I grabbed her pony tail to show I was a sport.

This standoff continued until she grabbed a heavy, glass ashtray and aimed for my left eye, the better of the two. She missed my eye and my glasses, which were actual glass, not plastic, and could have caused shard cuts of dastardly result, and succeeded in clunking me on the forehead.

Stunned for a millisecond, both of us let go of mutual hair holds and I perceived some bleeding above my glasses. Before it was fashionable, I started to pursue female equality on a physical basis by taking a poke at her with my right when I was grabbed roughly and hauled away. The hauler was a fat, older, larger, alcoholic bully named Les, a former upper classman who with cheating or money or some way had managed to graduate. He was on her side and would not listen to any first blood arguments from me.

I have been very pleased not to see Ms. T ever again. I have no knowledge about her sexual orientation but it seems lucid to me that she maintained a super high testosterone level, even for a male, over a very long time. I came away from this with the insight that if you are not physically imposing, nor an abusive, combative type, it is best to guard your forehead and your ass around pugilistic women and their bulbous, drunken, bully amigos.

At seven I married school days with riding. I had asked for and my grandmother bought me my first horse, Baby Doll, a difficult palomino that we boarded at the Hollywood Stables near HPS and I would ride after school and once in a while on the weekend I took longer rides. I won four ribbons in my first gymkhana at eight but not with this palomino, who would grab the bit in her teeth and try to knock me off. She almost got me once but I used a cutting saddle, rather than a sloping necked roping saddle, and, being a dancer, I laid out flat and grabbed the horn when she ran

On Blue Boy, getting ready to head for the hills, Hollywood Stables, 1953.

through the low branches. I disdained using the horn unless necessary.

Winning ribbons was on my second horse; I dropped Baby Doll after six months—pretty but a pain. Blue Boy was a bluish-gray, half Arabian Blue Roan, quarter horse gelding mix with black points and a black roached mane. He looked like a tiny, tough horse that Roman warriors might ride. All he lacked was a tiny warrior to ride him.

He also loved to roll and had done so in some barbed wire when very young so he had black marks on him. He was only fourteen and a half hands, compact and very fast. He also stopped so short he would slide his rear end underneath him. He was known as an outlaw when he was a rental. He would take people out and stop short, throwing them off and return for grub. He must have liked me and my weight because he never tried it with me.

I once counted him in the dress ring rolling back and forth sixteen times without stopping. He tried it once with me on him while crossing the L.A. River, usually only a slender stream, riding over the Hollywood Hills to Burbank. This meandering trickle can become a dangerous torrent in not too many minutes when it rains. I jumped from the stirrup, saving my left leg, and I knew he was not trying to hurt me. Blue just had this passion for rolling.

I managed him with no problems when we encountered a rattler on the trail once. Another time he listened to me and did not panic when we found ourselves in some quicksand. I backed him slowly out and we went on our way. I had to give Blue up when I started the MMC at eleven and I have never been interested in riding again. I am not sure why that is and Diane loves to ride, for she used to ride on a posting saddle and jump and all that Brit rigmarole growing up back in Bethesda, Maryland. It did not occur to me at the time but perhaps this being a cowboy as a kid was another way to seem like a tougher pretty boy. Being a little bit of a bad boy helped, too.

Mrs. Mann caught me cutting class in the eleventh grade. I was down at the Hut, a small hot dog stand very close by that everyone hung out at for good, greasy eats, the jukebox and just "hanging." The dirt behind it served as a parking lot for students with cars and anyone else who could not find a parking place on the even-then crowded Hollywood Boulevard and connected side streets like Serrano.

Mann decided that a hooky playing thirteen-year-old child star and eleventh grade president needed to be made an example of so, after chas-

Feeling sophisticated in my gold lamé tuxedo jacket at a grad night event in 1958, a few days after my 15th birthday.

ing and visually identifying me as I sprinted away in the large dirt lot, she suspended me from school for a week. Since absenting myself from class was my original intent, I chose to think of this as a profound victory. It did nothing negative to my grades either.

My mom's fantasies about my photographic memory were a direct result of my ease at memorizing lines, lyrics, dance steps, school work, and most things. Since early learning is more a matter of memorizing by rote as opposed to reasoning or deduction or induction, it was a simple mistake to make. I later concluded that I actually had an eidetic memory, which has more to do with calling up images than photographing words and pages. When I entered college, I was always sought out for study groups prior to a test.

Students from public schools that competed with HPS made slurs about the validity of a diploma from our school. There was typical competition between young people of different schools and all envied our talented actors, singers, dancers, musicians, skaters and stars. Our occasional "Aud Calls," short for shows we put on in our tiny auditorium, were inevitably cool entertainments. Other schools made do with much less although some later stars came from Hollywood High and other public institutions.

Given our pixilated, mostly geriatric instructors, I worried about the efficacy of my learning as well. After the oppression and nastiness I received from Mrs. Seamen, the last teacher we had on the Disney series, her intimations regarding my lack of capability frustrated me greatly. So, I enrolled in North Hollywood High, a public school close to my home in the San Fernando Valley, the area disparaged by snobs in Beverly Hills, Holmby Hills and Malibu.

The only guy I knew at NoHo High was beaten up the first week because he knew me; the student body did not take kindly to celebrities. I did not talk about my situation but Mouseketeer Lonnie was recognizable everywhere via our fourth year reruns daily on the tube. Nothing in my books, classes, requirements or assignments was more difficult than HPS.

One teacher made me his assistant and I learned quickly that my grade was contingent more on calling the role and other clerical work to make his job easier than on my scholastic prowess. The much larger teacher-to-student ratio made learning or asking a question more difficult than at HPS so I left NoHo and graduated from Hollywood Pro and soon after made the leap to college with nary a problem.

Scooter or *All for Love*, a satirical male role reversal on Terry Southern's satirical novel *Candy* was my first novel after a first novella, used my pre-college academic experiences as satirically heightened situations and prototypes. Miss Anderssen becoming Miss Meanderson, Mr. Sherick became Mr. Shrike and so on. But my success in college and graduate school can only be to a large degree attributed to what I had learned, my intelligence not being the sole ingredient.

Not all who graduated from HPS were intellectual whizzes, not all went on to college, not all did well, not all got their graduate degrees. Some did do these things and became, among other things, teachers. Whatever the efficacy of the instructors, the shorter hours and the somewhat restricted curriculum, it was possible to learn and be intellectually

Behind the wheel of our new two-tone Mercury Turnpike Cruiser for the HPS annual in 1958. Although I was not old enough for a license, being included in the annual's "car pages" was a California right of passage, so there I am, looking cool!

viable beyond high school.

I consider my college experiences of learning more suspect than those at the Hollywood Boulevard school. Much of all education in my experience involves merely memorizing things and regurgitating the teacher's POV (film term: point of view) accurately. I have always preferred the heuristic approach which I only experienced with a very few of the teachers to whom I have been exposed.

In a heuristic format the student is led to a place wherein he or she may learn subjectively, in an individual fashion, without the tyranny and obduracy of one teacher's concept of the subject, and move on from there. The very unusual exceptions to the vast majority of "educators" I have been stuck with are a very few individuals, like Dr. Morgan at CSUN, who inspire their students to comprehend and speculate beyond the teacher's own parochial box.

My years at three institutions of higher learning garnering an A.A., B.A. and M.A. in theatre arts and two semesters toward a Ph.D. in English literature and later non-degree oriented studies in philosophy and art, as well as my infrequent experiences as an educator myself, lead me to conclude that I have never had reason to doubt my misgivings about the teacher to student relationship and the possibilities of learning, rather than memorizing, in any class.

But returning to my five-year-old entry into the mishmash of academe and the for-money-only performing career, one thing became shockingly clear long before I read Nietzsche's dictum—on the cover of either *Newsweek* or *Time—God is Dead*. I had become desperately concerned about this entity's absence, not to mention *its, his, her* or *their* dismal, cruel, violent and unfair record in all ages and venues.

Chapter 5
The Teeniest Existentialist

Alone in the darkness and isolation of a child's bed, confronted by trillions of quadrillions of dots or pixels of nothingness, what is the most important question we ask? Am I safe? Am I loved? Am I cool? Will I soon get laid?

NOOOOOO.

IS GOD?

NOT, "Is there a God?"

IS GOD?

It is simpler yet more prolix than this recurring query in Tom Stoppard's play *Jumpers* and I am convinced that every single child tussles with this humongous humdinger in one way or another from very early on in life. Not one of us knew that Camus would think that anyone who held hope for the human condition was a fool. Oh, well.

To put it in a more quaint context, Mel Brooks in the persona of the 2,000 Year Old Man, observed that the leader of the first Cave People, Phil, was the biggest, nastiest bully and all feared him. When the tribe witnessed him being disintegrated by lightning the 2,000 Year Old Man, then a mere youngster of 103, said, "There's Something Bigger Than Phiiiiilllllll!!!!"

Children and their protectors are BOTH vulnerable. Surely, a young child's mind reasons, there must be some shield, some solace from the constant dangers of daily life, the need for food and comfort, the lack of pain, not to mention ennui along much of the way, and eventually, incontrovertibly—DEATH.

Excluding incompetent or uncaring Bozos and pathologically evil and abusive parents, who are still in the minority despite making huge headways in the last half of the 20th century and into the 21st, we all live in terror of our good and honorable progenitors' inane, sophomoric and frequently futile efforts to protect us and nurture us.

What did they tell us to do when the fish died?

FLUSH IT DOWN THE TOILET!

And how large do they build commodes?

Note: never mention any of this to a Freudian, or worse, a "therapist," for you are setting yourself up for fifty minutes of murky platitudes and rude hemming and hawing, the end result of which will be that you have to solve this problem by yourself. They do not, nor will they, make a chemical for it that will allow you to obviate the question.

Kids realize earlier than anyone acknowledges that those trusted the most, loved the most, whether kind and benevolent or irascible and frightening, those needed the most all screw up much of the time.

Even the best-intentioned and knowledgeable and caring parents make mistakes. They forget to feed us. They don't feed us when we want. They don't feed us WHAT we want. They argue. They fib and even lie. They falter. They become self-consumed or other-consumed or work-consumed. They show anger a lot. They use violence in varying formats, if not against us, which is edgy in a "politically correct" society, against someone else or themselves or an animal or a wall. As an angry, depressed young man I went through more than one door or wall with my fist and it would not have been salutary for me to raise a child. Fortunately, I chose not to be a father.

Children only have to hear about violence, rather than experience it, to know the depth and fear of it. There is violence in life, in newspaper photos and radio accounts, on television and for far too long in cartoons and games and song lyrics and our madly proliferating technologies. Violence is everywhere. We all live in the same house, the same world. The argument that viewing violence will decrease the occurrence of it has some merit but the great, overbearing amount that surrounds us every day can only be deleterious. Most kids can sense violence before it happens or is imminent. They infer violence that has happened in the past no matter how craftily hidden.

There are other issues, naturally, since some adults and other kids smell funny. Parents and adults and bullying kids make demands and give orders. Tall people are too often in your tiny face, like Aunt Agatha with the obscene mustache pushed down but not hidden by makeup. She does not seem to gather that her face looks uglier than a Picasso and is more threatening than a huge clown face or one of the execrably vivacious big-

My protectors, Mom and Dad, abandon their child for a night of fun; Gram and Gramp take over and I get under the dining room table again, 1946.

headed characters at Six Flags, Disneyland and other torture venues. Ever see the child who runs from Mickey Mouse's huge head and face?

Uncle Iggy has foul breath and sees to his needs but not yours and weird Uncle Feelie—well, let us not go to that family retreat.

At some point all youngsters look for something bigger than Phil: our parents or one of them, other family members, friends, pets, teachers, cops, priests, the President and so on. We feel extremely insecure once we comprehend that there are many guys bigger and tougher than moms, dads, Phil, and all protectors and mentors. Somewhere out there surely lurks a Promethean Nicholson Schwarzenegger Darth Vader that has gone not just over but way past the Dark Side and wants to grab YOU.

A shocking cactus grasp, boogey men under the bed or disgusting masses of heaped spinach bother most kids, but my earliest recalled, unmentioned, palpable fear was this bedtime contemplation. I lay there with my eyes closed and beheld a universe in which I was less than a speck on a speck on a speck of one grain of sand in an impossible-to-ever-traverse endless desert on a planet that was a miniscule mote in a galaxy light years away in one of billions of other universes that are way beyond the third power to the ninth watchamacallit and so on and so on *ad infinitum*.

It scared the living shit out of me.

Hyperbole, I am happy to relate, but actually that would have been more easily reconciled than this too often visited *cauchemar* (French for nightmare; I learned it from a T.S. Eliot poem.).

All of this, I deduced, had to do somehow or other ultimately with dying. By the age of five or so I had a definite grip on the idea of death. Not for me personally surely, but for anyone else. Happily no one I knew closely died until much later in my life—in my thirties.

Maybe it was a pet dying, like old Nobby our nipping, limping, temperamental Boston Terrier, although frankly I was glad he was no longer around, that made the death syndrome scan for me. It could have been the flushed fish or the State Fair chameleon or my pet white rat who froze to death, hard as an ice cube, because my grandmother insisted he and his cage remain on the enclosed porch because it gave her the willies; she could not sleep with a caged, tiny white rat in the house. Anyway, death, like defecation, happens.

Being analytical by nature, which is a deficit I have to guard carefully for others get easily intimidated by this ability, I tried to make sense out of the death to drifting-in-endless-space-time-continuum conundrum.

But I found that no premise is acceptable to a normal human being who is honest and cannot be easily deceived by sophistry. I was convinced I had to make some sense of this gargantuan paradox.

Why am I here if I am going to die someday, or much worse, tomorrow? Who will protect me when everyone appears to be not just fallible but subject to monstrous errors, chance, accidents, disease and death sooner or later? What is the point of it all? Is there anything at all I can do about this horrendous situation? Who dealt me these rotten cards?!

Most of us are led to believe that our cards come from Some Big Dealer in the Sky. *He* somehow reconciles it all and thinks everything is hunky-dory.

These overwhelming questions attacked me perhaps earlier than some others and long before we were drilled in school in the 'fifties about preparing for a nuclear holocaust, to which I wondered to myself, "What is the point of diving under a desk if you understand the words nuclear and holocaust"?

I formulated a syllogism:
I am Scared.
I am useless, as are they.
Ergo,
GOD!

I wondered, naturally, if I was different from other kids, some kind of aberrant alien, as all kids do, as I puzzled these Sisyphean ciphers. But, all kids are afraid of the dark, of being alone, of being adrift in anarchy. Surely I could not be the only tiny whelp seeking some kind of reassurance.

The world view begins in your mother's moist, warm, dark womb. All is good because there is no light. Let there be light, whether you prefer a God or Claudius shouting it, and you are superciliously flushed into a squintingly BRIGHT different existence. Then I was slapped soundly on my butt. Although rear-thumping is no longer *de rigueur* it was still in vogue for my coming out party.

A shocking, eye-bewildering, ass-thwacking, world-shattering birth is assuaged by being nestled in your mom's or some woman's boobs. Much, much better and there is sustenance afoot, so to speak. This does not last all that long and there is a constant flood of new, loud, sun or Fresnel lens-augmented experiences to endure until you are moved to a tiny bed or crib. And now, you are alone for the first time, except for other wailing strangers who deafen you, and to whom you vociferously wail back.

This jammed together aloneness startles you and you become overwrought. You cry in some indecipherable language, "What is going on here? I was all warm and protected and, yeah, I'm not too cold, but this is all wrong."

No one cares. Separation, abandonment, betrayal—these feelings are first, foremost and never to be denied as accurate.

Soon you go home and have reconciled this on-again (tits, warmth, mom, humans) and off-again threat over some months, but then you are moved farther away into your own room! Worse, falling hard upon, you are left with someone who is not your mom, not even that distant, shifty entity: your dad (or dads), maybe grandparents or other relations. Finally, you are dumped with "sitters" and… *Knock it off, Dude.*

Moving along, you sort all this out and learn to tie your shoes and dump INTO the bowl and say, "I skate peas and okra and mime mad as peck and mime not gonna trake it anyfour!" Or something like that. Paddy Chayefsky said it more clearly in *Network*, his great satire.

A few years later you believe mom or someone actually gets your messages and things are not chaotic but under control. Then you are abandoned and forsaken in another foreign place when you are four or five—now, earlier with pre- and pre-pre-school—with a mob of others about your size who are aggressive, unpleasant, smelly, loud, and threatening. Some are much bigger than you and are too often called Phil.

You are lorded over by control freak teachers demanding you do this, this way only, and NOW. QUIET! DO IT! NOW! This is bad, this is unfair, this sucks.

You secretly widen your search for some bodyguards, and mindguards if there is such a thing. If mom or dad or Phil is not so hot, then who is? Dogs, cats, birds, and rats die; fish get flushed. Family members, however distant, go kaput. Queens and presidents get assassinated. Young, famous people keel over. Even the Pope goes up in a puff of smoke.

Everyone dies. I die. *Help*! It is the most frightening feeling you can experience.

This may be why I need it to be slightly chilly to sleep for I do not contend well with heat and worse with humidity at any time and this is exacerbated by trying to go to sleep. This has been a constant all my life. I sweated in my childhood bed and these negative projections heightened my secretions. They were not, more is the pity, your typical nocturnal secretions. That came later. I did have a terse bout with enuresis (bedwetting), but it was over swiftly. The sweating is with me today unless the sheets and room are cold enough.

Fortunately, my mom made an effort to explain things. Unfortunately, not all she explained was accurate but if I had relied on my dad for knowledge I would know nothing and barely be able to speak. I was told about the birds and the bees and did not share my fears that either the bird or the bee had to be not just uncomfortable but surely wounded. Some large-breasted women gave me a turn, but I instinctively puckered and all was well.

My mom's ultimate contribution, from her point of view, and much more important than white lies (those done for the good of someone else), was getting me personal and up close with "God" early on. I had huge hopes this would calm my fears.

So here is this great God guy, whom you better always capitalize or HE will smite thee, and he protects you and comforts you and when you go to your dirt bed HE sends you to this wonderful heaven where you can pet and cavort with friendly tigers and rhinos and there are absolutely no serial killers, lawyers, politicians or used car salesman and, best, no agents. Absolutely no one will ever smear Vick's VapoRub on your chest and jam it up your nose past your eyeballs so you cannot breathe nor fall asleep and maybe not survive because you are ill. Terrific.

The Teeniest Existentialist 65

Mom and I are pleased God is not a German philosopher, 1947.

 Most avoid considering all this Sartre drivel until nine or twelve or forty-six, but finally there is a problem solver and HE is immutable, omniscient, omnipresent and frequently benign.
 !!! F-R-E-Q-U-E-N-T-L-Y ? ? ?
 Prior to going bonkers in the late 19th century and giving Cosima and Ricky Wagner some discomforting nights, Freddy Nietzsche decided that God was dead. A weekly national magazine, catching up about a century later, shrewdly thought it would make a nifty mag cover—after all, they have to come up with fifty-two a year. My mommy, however, had found God alive for herself, me, Howard and much of her side of the family. Are you going to believe some Eastern magazine billboarding a nutty, Kraut philosopher's edict—or your mom?
 When the cover was published in the 'sixties, I was definitely in the expatriate German's camp but I was incessantly inculcated as a child into God's camp. Fortunately, I was young enough to have missed the Hitler Youth movement. My dad became a turncoat and the Papacy would have excommunicated him if they had only heard about it.
 The Babins were devout Catholics, the many of them, explaining how Howard was lumbered with the middle name Ambrose, which he

loathed thoroughly, from St. Ambrose, meaning immortal in Greek, which is many eggs short of a dozen in terms of accuracy. Unlike Ham, Dorothy was an only child and so am I.

Many of the Babins became nuns and priests so they went to mass and so on more or less as a condition of employment. Ham, apparently, was not as convinced about HIM and after Mom spirited him (Dad) away from the fold to the dregs of humanity in Los Angeles, she had her liturgical way with him. Woe is Ham.

Dot's family were dyed in-the-rayon Christians who believed unequivocally in some Christian God or other but none of them held allegiance to any particular dogma, except maybe the Masons. They knew for damn sure that they were not the unscrupulous and untrustworthy Catholics, like that suspicious Kennedy family. The very concept of anyone being a Muslim or any other thing they considered un-American would have discombobulated all of my family members.

My mother was formally led to the church not by a miracle, nor a TV messenger from above but by those who sought her out via Matthew 24:14: "And this gospel of the kingdom shall be preached in all the world for a WITNESS [my caps] unto all nations; and then shall THE END COME [my caps]."

This quote from the New Testament is why Jehovah's Witnesses have been harassing people religiously at their front doors since the religion was founded in the late 19th century when it was known as the International Bible Students Association. I always took great exception to that last bit, "…and then shall THE END COME." I have pretty nearly always been categorically adverse to the idea that the end will come anytime soon, and certainly not in my lifetime.

Less mystical than William Blake, my mom's conversion was more of a door job. There has been abundant humor at the expense of the JWs, their accepted acronym, but most people do not have a clue as to what the followers of this religion actually believe. They are merely a pain in the pulpit and a joke.

A fundamentalist Xian religion, these folks do not utilize, nor fixate on, reptiles. This is a positive point. They do, however, believe that the Bible, to be precise THEIR translation of the Bible [*The New World Translation*], is the literal and infallible truth and words of God, one Jehovah. They are resolved that even the paradoxes and equivocal symbolism of the books of Daniel, Revelation and the rest in the Old and New Testament are explainable, are fact and are accessible.

In the film Queen For A Day *I am the city slicker left looking down my nose at the "real" kid from the farm, 1951.*

My mom was swept away with their beliefs and like all kids that was good enough for me. Howard was swept away, too. In addition to attending the Kingdom Hall, the JWs' equivalent of a church, mosque or synagogue without the expensive architectural demands and theatrical frou-frou, home Bible studies were scheduled a minimum of once a week.

My mother told me as an adult that we began our studies by the time I was six and that I was baptized soon after, along with my dad the fallen Papist, in one of the JWs' huge annual conventions, this particular one in San Francisco or as the JWs might refer to it, Gomorrah on the Bay. They must have gotten a really good deal on hotels and the site rental to justify going to this place.

I have photos of this trip and recall the tedium of traveling by auto from L.A. to S.F. over many long, boring hours, but I have no memory of early Bible studies or my immersion in water. In light of my claustrophobia it seems that I should recall the latter but Mom insisted it happened.

Gram's sister Mamie and one of her sons, "Doc" Billy, followed Mom's lead. Billy's brother Vernie put more faith in cigarettes and beer and his sister Pudd was more lukewarm to it but her daughter Bev became adamant and fervent, much more so after her first husband—having impregnated her prematurely—vanished. Bev's stepfather, Bob, sidestepped it and simply hung out and carped about things. He was an uncivil engineer.

The first scene of Bible studies I can conjure was when I was about eight in the dining room of our most terrific home in the Bluebell Estates in North Hollywood. I found it comforting to have it at a dining room table which enabled me, if the need should arise, to dart underneath. I made a promise to myself I would not look up any dresses if I had to assume this position.

Our meetings began with prayer and then a section of the Good Book would be read in a slow, solemn manner with each person at the table picking up where the last had left off. The Grand Inquisitor, the more seasoned, learned Witness who came to conduct the study and who was not a family member, would discuss the text with us and sum it up. Then he asked questions and we talked about the passages and finally there came a final prayer.

These were not humor-filled hours. I especially had to be very careful what I said and how I phrased it. This was earnest, serious GOD business. All of us knew, though it was never referred to in this way, that for our quotidian Safe Passes from GOD, enabling us to get through another day still breathing, we all had to be constantly aware of HIS requirements, HIS orders, HIS demands, even HIS whims.

The Almighty trusted hardly anyone, or so it appeared, so HE constantly queried and tested people like me and Job and insisted vehemently on uninterrupted attention and recognition. HE got super-wrath-ful if any icon or thing came before HIM, like a flag or Mammon or the Golden Arches which had not yet begun their domination of humans.

This might represent the JWs in a somewhat stilted, dictatorial way, as are many other beliefs founded in fiction, but they were not so strict as to ban dancing in all forms. Lipstick was allowed, but only for women. They are very rigid about other things, like smoking, although a number of Witnesses furtively smoked at least while I was a medium-grey sheep in the fold.

Being immersed and mind-bent into these beliefs at a very persuadable age, I grew up in essence studying for the ministry, for all Witnesses are preachers by definition, at least door-to-door if not behind a pulpit. I read the Bible regularly, quoted it, went to meetings at the Hall on Sunday and walked house to house on Saturday morning in the hope of saving all those poor, tormented suckers out there who believed in a, dare I say it, DIFFERENT, hence nugatory GOD or God or god, or—the horror of all horrors—those pitiful, deluded yahoos who believed in NO god AT ALL! Death to the Infidels, I say! They have no heavenly insurance policy! No beatific security! No heaven, No forty virgins—they got NADA, dude!

Given the Old Testament's heavy-handed smitings, battles, warmongering and other related festivities, it is good that the Witnesses are not a violently oriented religion. They did and do have beliefs that trouble me greatly, but they are not nearly as dangerous as the Scientologists and the one major religion that I found after 9/11 that has a single word, Jihad, for what any other religion, whether fomenting them currently or not, has for the phrase HOLY WAR.

As I accrued life experiences and read philosophers as well as my Bible as a teen in college, my doubts vis-à-vis religion and the illogical, unexplainable paradoxes of the Jehovah's Witnesses and all of Christian belief bothered me a lot. I read about Judaism and Buddhism and other religions as well.

I followed a long road to find a livable balance within the indifference of daily life, what the Greeks might refer to as sophrosyne or the Navajo as *hozro*, differing but similar paths to balance and harmony in life that are sought after via religion and OTHER means. I found I could not take this or that one god, this or that one path of worship, as law, as my belief, as my *raison d'être*. If I come to find this a mistake in some other world that I do not believe exists, so be it, as Edward Albee and Catholics frequently say.

All beliefs of a common, ritualistic, god-driven makeup require a brobdingnagian *jeté* of faith, to wit certain premises cannot be deductively, nor inductively, arrived at. You are told, "You just have to believe." If you cannot join Kierkegaard in leap-frogging across the abyss you have to find some other way to "move on," the hackneyed, zeitgeist phrase being actually appropriate, with your life and find what beliefs you can truthfully live with and manage to construct a life with and manage to sleep well with every night.

In my seventeenth year, a junior in college, I ceased my private, ongoing Bible studies and further extended my ongoing search. I eventually settled on concepts, however harrowing at times, that I, Lonnie, could accept.

This offered me blessings in freeing me from Witness beliefs that I found unconscionable. For example their interpretation of Leviticus and his eating constraints: (Leviticus 7:37) "Whatsoever soul it be that eateth any manner of blood, even that soul shall be cut off from his people." This is translated to mean that an ill or dying person cannot, by God's mandate, get a blood transfusion. The previous verse makes it lucid that Leviticus is talking literally and solely about eating, "…of fowl or of beast, in any of your dwellings." It is the same with cloven hoofs for the Jews; certain animals carried disease and this edict was written to SAVE lives AT THAT TIME by forbidding you from eating things that could literally kill you.

Using "eateth" to mean transferring blood from one human to another that may save a life is convoluted philosophically and ethically and morally. Additionally, it is an obtuse approach to linguistics that patently begs the question. Even with the complications of HIV and other viruses and bacteria, life-saving transfusions are still a positive, humane action to cautiously pursue, in my world view.

It is interesting that the Witnesses are not vegetarians given all the anti-blood thought. My grandmother was a vegetarian all her life and died at 105 but she was never a JW, nor did she consider founding a religion. The Witnesses also do not believe Christ was born on December 25th but that Nimrod, the first man in the Bible who hunted for fun rather than subsistence, was buried on that date, and a fir tree was brought in to signify his death.

I disagree with their anti-abortion dictums for even an early procedure for an entity that has NO CHANCE of a life as defined by "existing as a human." A humanoid individual in a lifelong coma who is unable to

This man said he was a producer, but I didn't believe him, 1946.

eat, think, speak, evacuate—or do anything but breathe unless another human does it for them is to be allowed to live. To me this is as wrong as the Crusades, the Inquisition and 9/11. I know a Witness who had such a child that is now maturing to middle age. I can only find this very wrong, truly sad and I avoid being present.

The truth for me is that my main conflict in my mid-teens, leading to my religious downfall, was sex. The JWs have a common belief that coitus must be abhorred and shunned until you are married. Once this is accomplished, you are welcome to join well over 50% of married people by divorcing and screwing like crazed woodchucks. They also shun an unmarried woman who gives birth. It is a male-oriented religion so they are not as hard on men and, after all, it is not so obvious, for guys do not fatten really quickly until they turn forty.

The other nine commandments I could handle pretty easily. I gambled a little bit as a youth but never got caught up in it and for most of my life considered it a stupidity that I had little interest in indulging. I have never murdered anyone, although some thoughts of that nature have crossed my mind. I have coveted my neighbor's and other guy's wives but I have never acted upon this urge. I do drink, so I am weak on that one. I smoke and I swear, too.

To get down to it, not coveting women was beyond me. I noticed that many of the commandments, for that matter, seemed beyond adherence by more than one or two of the Witnesses I encountered—the flesh be horny.

It became vividly clear to me at sixteen that I could not abstain from these surges and prompts that propelled me sexually until I was wed. I hoped to never wed at that time in my life but if caught in the black widow's web it was not going to ruin me until maybe around the andropause, the term for male menopause.

I had begun dating at nine which was early for the 'fifties and these girls were inevitably older. If not in mortal fear of screwing up my continuing-to-live pass from god, I would have coited by at least thirteen if not younger instead of merely having a wallet with a raised circle the size of a silver dollar, like those unexplained corn fields only much smaller, that I maintained to let others know that I was both cool and ready, however unprepared I might have been.

The results of my forbearance resulted in some bamboozled and hotly frustrated young ladies. From fumblings at breasts, or their beginnings, maddeningly covered and sometimes augmented, I moved on to "Roman hands and Russian fingers" and ostensibly most else but the deed itself. Like all great philosophers and prophets, I had concluded that all was fair game as long as my penis did not penetrate a vagina. This is an unequivocally positive thesis precluding both pregnancy and most possibilities of disease, disease in the 1950s being very tame in comparison to the 21st century.

Beyond being denounced on more than one occasion as a clit tease, other ramifications accrued anent my Witness beliefs.

There was a loud hullabaloo at HPS regarding my refusal to iterate the Pledge of Allegiance to the flag. You recall it was that Jehovah guy who made Othello seem pretty wishy-washy on the jealousy issue? Allegiance to anyone or anything, conflicting with the "render unto Caesar" palaver, includes not just bronze doo-dads but craven flags and most likely now dot coms. Nobody does it better, nor above, Jehovah.

I showed respect by standing at attention for the Pledge, but I would not say the words, nor put my hand on my heart. This was an inviolate teaching of the Witnesses and the law backed it up by the Supreme Court in a ruling in the year I was born, 1943, making it acceptable for a child to not salute the flag if it was against the kid's religion.

It was still a very controversial social issue at the time. Even before the evil McCarthy and his nasty office boy Nixon, the beliefs I was taught were labeled as very close to a queer, pinko Commie bastard anarchist's theses. The warrior queen Dot fought the good battle for Jehovah with me at her side against the towering, scowling figure of Mrs. Mann. We fought tooth and scripture and ultimately prevailed without the need of an orthodontist.

I was allowed to stand silently and there was no violence, nor shouted epithets either in class, nor outside the classroom, not even whispered innuendos. This was not an innocuous choice to fight for in the 'fifties and it would have caused monstrous problems for me and my mother if I had attended a public school. I later assumed that my fellow students just chalked it up to my general weird geniusness and over-sized ears schtick and went about their business.

So, for the formative years of my life I believed in, studied and followed the precepts of a Christian God. Having God on my side did not preclude my diving under my desk in practice for a Hollywood Hiroshima. I knew it was useless but the teachers insisted, so I went through the motions. Although my beliefs waned and then left, the specter of the draft, for which I had thought I would escape as a Witness conscientious objector, began wagging its destructive finger my way. Uncle Sam seemed to have lost his dressed-to-the-teeth striped pants and was wearing a black shroud and carrying a big scythe.

I knew I would be lost and not survive the service, just as I knew I would not endure if I somehow wound up in prison. What was I going to do when I was called up? Young people today have not a clue as to how overwhelming and frightening this was to young men before the draft was abolished in 1973. This clouded my life on many occasions before I was confronted by the situation in the mid-sixties after I had abandoned my conscientious objector religious excuse.

The end of my search for god left me alone facing an unfair, cruel world at seventeen, but I was no longer as scared as I was when I was deluded by faith into believing the unbelievable. I made peace with myself and what I believe we are all offered in life, some much better; some far worse, than others.

Take into account that Thomas Jefferson thought everyone should question the existence of any god and even went so far as to cut out the miracles and inconsistencies of the Bible arriving at what became known as the Jefferson Bible, which contained only forty-six pages. Our third president felt that if there were a god he, she or it (which is not the way he would have phrased it) would prefer being believed in through reason rather than from fear. My reason overcame my dread but not my misgivings regarding zealots.

Since I finalized my youthful teleological struggles I have come to suspect anyone who is zealous about anything. Beliefs that are not imposed on others, that do not lead to jihads and attacks, are acceptable. Beliefs that make hate and violence and individual or mass murder acceptable, worse, encouraged, are to be rebuked, denied and shunned.

To get on in the world it is best to politely keep these views private, which is appropriate and safer, but to declare that all the world must believe as your group does is fascism and fanaticism and I will not abide it.

A final note on eschatology as well as scatology—i.e. obscenity, excrement, etcetera. I eschewed eschatology (eschatology, n. Theol. Any system of doctrines concerning final matters: death, the Judgment, future state, etc.) in my late teenage years. I had begun writing before that and I thought it hypocritical that almost everyone used the "F" word but it was never heard on radio, seen in print, nor in plays, films, TV—at least not in the 'fifties and 'sixties. This bothered me. There were the Joyces, Henry Millers and D. H. Lawrences, but it still was stifling and unreal for authors, especially in dialogue. In 2009 it is hard to avoid the word, hence, I have also eschewed scatology as much as possible in this volume except for a few usages that are "hidden" by dots or dashes—sorry about that.

Most of us know the quote, "…the law is a ass—a idiot," said by Mr. Bumble in Charles Dickens' *Oliver Twist*. I think it is much worse. I think the law is a religion.

The Law God issues strict edicts which are guarded by Popes (judges) that are argued by Prelates (lawyers) from whom the Popes ascend, whose

I played Italian fascisti murderer Capitano Aldo Finzi in the play Tamara *1989-90. Finzi's Law God, Mussolini, is in the photo behind me and my Luger.*

only goal is to win, with nary a thought to right versus wrong, good versus bad, fair versus unfair, moral versus immoral. The High Priests are the legislators motivated primarily by money and power who compose, write and, when they feel like it, change the Law God's edicts. The underpaid Priests who risk their lives every day, some heroes, more than a few villains, are the police whom we need but even the valiant, good ones are greatly outnumbered and outgunned by the bad guys in 2009. This religion exists in every nation and, ergo, is even larger than the three or four largest religions in the world.

Rhadamanthys and his evil minions who first perpetrated the oppressive Law Lord upon us have led me to a Kafkaesque foreboding in my few encounters with any of the representatives of this nugatory institution. Too much of the religion of law is the antithesis of the order, protection and security it is touted to be. I learned to fear and loathe and assiduously avoid anything to do with courtrooms and the law before I read Kafka's illuminating book propitiously titled *The Trial.*

As mentioned, my introduction to the law at three by the cop who took me home was benevolent. The rest were not the same. My second one, on Colorado Boulevard in front of my grandparent's furniture store in Pasadena, was more fascistic. Tommy Crook and I were using our bean shooters to hit the hubcaps of passing vehicles. We had no idea that what we were doing was a major felony punishable by death.

This second guy in a monochrome black outfit with a badge, night stick and a huge weapon and, being California, always eyeless shades, gruffly accosted us and threatened us with jail time. Learning from whence we had hailed, he pulled us inside the Burr's Furniture Store and scared my tough, former hooligan as a youth, Gramp.

John had a fear of the gendarmes after having been beaten thoroughly by some of the graft-driven, violent cops in Louisville, Kentucky when he was in his teens. Like many things in my family and most families, his uncharacteristic fear and from whence it emanated was never discussed, but cryptic allusions and my inferences made it clear the potential uber-thugs made him come unglued in the presence of their uniforms. The tyrant left us in John's custody with a threat of instant incarceration with raving maniacal murderers and possible torture if we repeated our un-American crime against nature of shooting peas at hubcaps.

During the run of the MMC I had my first introduction to the gravity and abuse of law courts. A neighbor sued us for $50,000, a great deal in the 'fifties. I later deduced that they were so deluded that they thought a Disney child star made lots of money, which shows a complete lack of comprehension of how Disney has always done business. The Disney Studio was legendary as being the cheapest major in Hollywood and things have gotten worse, not better, since Walt's demise in 1966. Translating $50,000 to 2009 would mean we were being sued for about half a million.

We were not friends with our next door neighbors and they kept loud, fierce hunting dogs. Both of our back yards were fenced and that was the canines' usual domain, but our front yards were open. One afternoon their eldest son, around seventeen or so, had three of the hunters chasing around without leashes on their front lawn.

The only full-sized pet I had managed to be allowed was a Boxer that I got when I was about ten. Most likely this could be attributed to the fact that no matter how much I contributed to taking care of the animal it would be more work and expense for Dot and Dash and they were not pet people, a group I have always been unable to understand. Animals really help humans to have a positive perspective on life and they are a great calming influence in most cases.

So the Boxer, named Donnie by my mom—how cute: Lonnie & Donnie (*YUCK*)—joined our family. He was full grown when he came to us and fine with humans but we soon learned he would attack any dog, any size, however huge or ferocious and even if he or she came with a buddy or two or three.

I had Donnie on a leash, but he broke from me and plowed into the middle of the neighbor's three hunting dogs. He was getting the best of them when the obtuse teen tried to break them up by using his hands, apparently not bright enough to grab a hose and spray them, use a broom or rake or jump into a passing Sherman tank.

He sustained a minor cut on his thumb that required two or three stitches and this prompted the suit. If they won, the 50K would be more than I made on the original run of the series and all of my minimalist residuals.

I know not why, but I was quite intimidated by going to court and testifying as a witness. Unlike Gramp, I had not been beaten badly by a bunch of cops, nor had I yet read the author of *The Metamorphosis*, but I did feel like a lowly cockroach and I had done nothing wrong, nor illegal, so why did I feel guilty? I managed to get through it without having a nervous breakdown and the cheap shyster my mom hired (who kept hitting on her in my presence as though she were not married and I was the invisible son) actually bumbled into a legal victory.

Two or three stitches is not life threatening, the three hunting dogs were unleashed, no one made him use his hands to separate them, there was no way to prove whether he received his cut from one of his own dogs or mine and we were exonerated but did get stuck with the shyster's fees.

I was not a paragon of virtue, the perfect boy that Mom and Gram touted, but my risk-taking was minor. I did ditch school, knowing it would not affect my grades and I was only caught once. Then the Beverly Hills cops tried to bust me for GTA, grand theft auto, in my fourteenth year. Nothing was ever filed against me, not even actually breaking curfew, so I still never had a record as a juvie.

I liked sneaking out at night for adventures. It started during the MMC mid-'fifties with my buddy Ivan. When staying at his house in Toluca Lake, or he at mine on Bluebell, we would quietly embark, sometimes with bologna sandwiches on white bread with mayo and Cokes and prowl the neighborhood. We were discreet, furtively jumping into bushes or behind a parked car when auto lights approached; we were never caught having our relatively innocent adventures. I pilfered one of my grandfather's cheap, large, greenish- hued cigars on one occasion, which managed to turn me a similar tinge of green. I was edified and found my future was not in cigar smoking.

The GTA episode involved our new 1957 Mercury Turnpike Cruiser, a two-toned vehicle with the first, flat rear window that by pushing a button would go up and down, and the first, and I hoped last, push button, dash mounted automatic transmission. It was bought for my senior year at HPS and my buddy Dave got a picture of me in the driver's seat in the annual car page despite my being fourteen and lacking a driver's license. My grandmother's money and some of my Disney earnings paid for the vehicle and I appeared, after my mom, on the registration and title.

I snuck the cruiser out of the garage, the farthest point from my parent's bedroom, and my first stop was at a licensed driver's house because I did not want to break the law. We picked up some other kids and three more cars full of teenagers and obeying the driving laws, we snaked down to the PCH (Pacific Coast Highway) to Leo Carrillo ("Hey, Cisco, Hey Pancho!") Beach near to Malibu. We listened to radio rock 'n' roll, had somewhat innocent sex, at least for me, drank some warm beer and smoked cigarettes—no grass, no cigars.

Returning home on Sunset in Beverly Hills, Rocky, soon to emerge as an incarcerated juvenile delinquent, was in the lead car and began changing lanes and switching first his left and then his right turn signal on and off. You do not have to do much of anything late at night in Beverly Hills to get the attention of the boutique cops who protect the wealthy. We all got pulled over and transported en masse to the BHPD.

The hostile officers threatened me with a felony grand theft auto charge in the hope of scaring the crap out of me, which they figuratively succeeded in accomplishing. When my enraged mom arrived it became clear that my name was on the title and they hemmed and hawed but released me into her custody with no charges being filed.

Dot was not so magnanimous. You would have thought I had broken a milk bottle, run away and maybe raped a nun. She punished me severely, not physically but in her mental, pre-Gitmo psychological fashion—I was totally grounded for three months.

At fifteen-and-a-half before getting my driver's license I got my first speeding ticket in my Corvette on Pass Avenue in Burbank near two of the film studios. The car was given to me by my grandparents when I turned fifteen for I was to get a special license to drive to and from UCLA when I started college in September of 1958. My grandmother accompanied me, the minor, to court for the ticket and I got a scolding and six-month probation.

After I was sixteen I had my second courtroom experience. I had received two speeding tickets in the same month and I was threatened with jail time. I did not get a benevolent judge but the inexplicable vagaries of court room logic saved me. My lawyer had gone to USC and he knew the judge had his degrees from UCLA. My guy made a humorous aside vis-à-vis their schools that got me off with probation and a small fine. I garnered that right and wrong have very little to do with courtroom procedure.

My next courtroom appearance was in my early thirties when I filed a suit in small claims court to get the full, promised fee for an article I wrote in 1975 on Bernie (Bernadette Peters) with whom I had appeared on Broadway and even taken out on a date on another occasion. The magazine *In The Know*, which had done a piece on Mouseketeer Lonnie and Diane when we were still in New York, had promised me $500, with a $250 advance for this piece and then did not pay the second half.

The letter of agreement I wrote, which I always do if there is no formal contract, was clear and they refused to acknowledge my numerous attempts to contact them. I filed for proceedings, went through the time and expense of the legal bureaucracy and arrived in court. The magazine sent a youthful representative with whom I had had no interaction.

I was asked for my documentation and the head guy in a black robe who sat above us and functioned as a judge but was called something else, not arbitrator, and got really bent out of shape if you addressed him as

Diane and Lonnie in Riverside Park near our west side apartment in Manhattan, taken for In The Know, *1974.*

your honor or judge, ruled in my favor, after asking the other guy a few questions or for any supporting material. He did not have any. The robed presence ordered the magazine to pay the remaining $250.

I made the near-fatal error of politely asking permission to speak and, when given this opportunity, I brought up the fee for filing which I had incorporated into my petition to the court. He had not referred to it. With no explanation the black-robed individual said, "The judgment is reduced to $200." I was not quite brain-challenged enough to inquire what I had done wrong to lose fifty bucks.

Further legal complications were encountered when the $200 was not paid after the correct time allowed for it. I went to the Van Nuys court and inquired about my missing funds and a uniformed clerk explained that the only way to implement acquiring the reduced $200 was to pay $100 to employ a U.S. Marshal to collect it.

In a stretch of unlikely humanity and off the record, the clerk explained this magazine had previous judgments against it and Marshals going to the office found no money nor anything else of attachable value; in other words there was old furniture, one or two old typewriters but nothing that would bring in enough money to pay what was owed me according to the court. Like Orenthal James and others with enough money, they knew how to misuse the system and get away with it. I could use $100 of the reduced-to-$200 half of my payment to go for it, but that left me with only $150 for the already-printed piece. I left the halls of "justice" wiser and convinced definitively that my concept—that everything that can go wrong in a court of law and inevitably would get worse than expected—was accurate.

In 1979 my dad was dying of cancer and had not as yet gone into remission from the chemo. I was having some drinks at a bar with Diane and left when the bar closed. When you are drinking you make unwise decisions, particularly when you are younger, and when the car in front of you is going 25 in a 35 mph zone—you also are much more easily angered by booze. I angrily raced around the slowpoke and was pulled over by two Chippies in a squad car. They gave me the walking tests etcetera and arrested me for DUI, placing me in handcuffs this one and only time in my life. My destination was the hoosegow but the cops drove me to a house and arrested a burglar who they cuffed and threw in with me. We did not chat.

I was asked to take a breath test and I inquired if that was mandatory under existing law; the cop would not answer my question. The "implied consent" law was in effect, if you drove you had to agree to take a test to get your license, but could choose from breath, urine or blood. I took the worst of the three, the breath test.

The only good thing to come out of this dreadful experience is that I made some moola for a *Los Angeles Magazine* article on "what to do" when pulled over for DUI. I did advise the hardest test for them vs. the driver, the blood work, but I did not, nor do I advocate driving and drinking.

Diane was with me when I was busted, had called her father's friend, a lawyer in L.A., put up my bail and I spent only about two or three hours in a cell. Fortunately, I was not put in with any gangbangers, killers or hardened types, but I was still exceedingly uncomfortable. You cannot really comprehend what it is to be handcuffed and then put into a cell until it happens—and I hope to never experience that feeling ever again.

Alvin Greenwald, the lawyer and a friend—we have enjoyed many good times with him and his wife Audrée—did not handle this type of law and suggested his son, who recommended another young lawyer, who happened to be a friend of his. The ninny kid lawyer, despite the arresting officer writing on the citation that I was a female, was not doing well in my estimation. Realizing he was failing me and still getting paid, I asked him for my options and pled *nolo contendere*.

The judge sentenced me to one-year probation and a fine. The DMV, as a separate system, took my license away for six months and in L.A. that is a lot like being in jail anyway. Diane (when she could) and my dad (in remission from his cancer) helped me get around for the next six months. One year after the parole was over, I had the record expunged, which is accepted legal protocol and, therefore, there is no record of my only scrape with the law. I have never had another incident involving alcohol and driving, nor any other misdemeanor or felony.

The Popes, prelates and priests of the law work on the private front, too. I have had problems with the over-zealous Disneyland security on two occasions. The first was when I took Diane to my old stomping grounds in Anaheim in the late 'seventies and paid full entry to the "happiest place on earth." While in line for a ride in Fantasyland, I was accosted by a rude female security guard. It was hot and we were stuck in the sun, perspiring. My shirt was unbuttoned to allow some relief but my belly button was not showing. I was curtly ordered to button up my shirt; the rule, she said, was that only three buttons were allowed to be unbuttoned. I had unbuttoned four. I had to comply immediately or I would be thrown out of the park.

I did not say "Heil!" to that but I noted that right in front of me in line was a young girl, around twelve or thirteen, who was barely covered by tight short shorts and a halter over her burgeoning breasts to good effect displaying herself, the questionable participation of her parents and a sexist dichotomy. When I politely inquired why I was singled out I was threatened with being restrained and taken to the security cop jail facility.

I toyed with the idea of going through with it and then hitting the 5 p.m. news with "Mouseketeer Attacked by Security at Disneyland."

Where do you want to go? "The Hoosegow!"

I opted for complying. I do understand, though, how first year Mouseketeer Billie Jean Beanblossom and two of her grandchildren later might have been mistreated by Disneyland Security after being accosted by thieves in the parking lot, leading to her suit which she, of course, lost. Disney and City Hall are about the same thing most of the time.

In 1980 the entrance security guard at the Ball Street gate, which is inaccessible to the public, stopped Cubby and me, with our wives, from entering. We had been told to enter at this gate in order to have our cars inside the Park during rehearsals. We both assumed later that his animus toward us was that we both had long hair and beards, thus making us disgusting Hippies, who had not been in vogue since the 'sixties and 'seventies.

We identified ourselves as Mouseketeers Cubby and Lonnie, at which he was nonplussed. He talked to different people on his phone and after fifteen minutes of standing around we were allowed to enter. No apology was issued by this private flatfoot; the management apologized but their heart did not seem in it. I think they were not too pleased about the hair and beards, either.

So, prior to moving out on my own at twenty, I knew the law for its overwhelming intimidation, unfairness and unjustness. In the iniquitous, chummy, absurd, morally suspect land of litigation an individual is capable of receiving a death sentence despite the judge, the jury and everyone else knowing he or she is innocent. Or, like Orenthal James Simpson, you can do whatever the hell you want and get away with it. All you need is lots of greenbacks, a nefarious, devious attorney and you will be free (unless you screwup big time again).

You would be told that it was a shame you were sentenced to life without possibility of parole or death, "but that's the law." It is the Law God's will so you march off to the long dirt bath or some dangerous, unpleasant decades because HE decrees it. The subject is closed.

How many people have been wrongly convicted by lies perpetrated by either the prosecutors and/or their witnesses? It does happen but it is certainly not the majority and now, with DNA, it is harder to make these horrid mistakes but the system and the Law God have no concerns about the truth. They give you some money and they apologize about the last ten or twenty years you have lived a horrible life in prison but now you are out and can do just as you want to, no more taking it up the rear, no more being beaten daily, no more tiny jail room.

"Oh, yeah…and sorry about that."

Being an independent thinker, sometimes liberal, sometimes conservative, I am for the death penalty but every avenue must be thoroughly reviewed but not twenty times taking a decade. No case that disallows the truth to be presented to a jury, for example previous instances of malfeasance, should ever occur. There should be no way that a defense attorney can hide the truth because of a mistake in the way the truth is obtained. But the Lord God of the Law declares that there is no truth but the LAW and the way in which it is used (or misused) is the ONLY thing of significance.

This is a part of American culture that I loathe because it is purely the result of human wrongdoing. Acts of God, or if you prefer, acts of nature are not avoidable. There are dictators and mass murders and worse systems of law than ours but I live here and no one complains about this iniquitous legal system which the Law Godhead maintains.

People must be held accountable for their actions but there should be FAIR adjudications instead of "the letter of the law" written not by a god nor gods but fallible, corruptible, sometimes evil lawmakers and their ilk and implemented by sometimes mean, sometimes discombobulated, sometimes clearly crazy underlings and the rest through judges, some of whom are mean, discombobulated or crazy, too.

My most recent run-in with the law began in 1998 and lasted for about six years after Screen Actors Guild brought an arbitration against the Disney Studio over non-payment for reusing films from the 360 or so segments of the original MMC. Arbitration is a word I have come to learn means in the favor of the wealthy, management, the corporations and the politically powerful. SAG spent millions of dollars of actors' dues money and lost the case. Disney spent millions they could write off.

A friend of Diane's knew someone who worked at SAG and reported that Mouseketeer Darlene Gillespie, who had already won a suit against Disney, and her fiancé Jerry Fraschilla, were there daily over many weeks agitating for this suit. The arbitration was reported by the ineffably obtuse media as being about disgruntled Mouseketeers grousing when, in actuality, it covered all the segments of the show and the many more other actors in *Spin & Marty*, *The Hardy Boys*, Annette's series, Darlene's series and so on. Other actors, including Buddy Ebsen, showed up at the Mouseketeers' meeting with SAG's outside counsel to have the suit described to us.

According to the *New York Times*, after Mouseketeer Darlene and her fiancé, Jerry Fraschilla, were convicted of shoplifting, but served no jail time, they were accused in a felony stock swindle. Fraschilla pleaded guilty to multiple counts of fraud and was sentenced to eighteen months. Darlene pled not guilty, went to trial and was convicted on twelve counts of conspiracy, securities fraud, mail fraud, obstruction of justice and perjury. She was ultimately sentenced to two years in prison. Before she was convicted and Fraschilla was jailed, they married. After the marriage neither could testify against the other. After Darlene was prosecuted, she could no longer be used as the main witness against Disney in the arbitration.

The outside law firm hired by SAG asked me to lunch. They wanted me to become their main witness to garner fair residuals for all the actors and the Mouseketeers for constant reuse for over forty years. I listened to them, and declined.

I am the only adult Mouseketeer—except for Annie before and after raising her three children—who continued performing in the entertainment industry consistently as an actor/dancer/singer and, in my case, writer, choreographer and director. I knew that no matter the outcome of the suit, my earning capacity would be negatively affected for the rest of my life. The result would be as bad, perhaps worse, as the situation my mom and I were put into by Disney in regard to signing my seven-year contract (which is detailed in the chapter on my MMC years).

I thought the outside counsel was approaching the case incorrectly in many ways. They did not seek out people I suggested who, like the respected man of music Buddy Baker and others who worked on our series, were adults at the time the show was shot. They could have been extremely useful in giving witness to what they knew and recalled; it is easier to discredit childhood memories than adult recollections.

The legal firm SAG hired had also agreed to link our case to another one from Universal about FILM residuals on a Universal movie that I believe was made before the formalization by SAG of residuals for films in 1960, and which was not retroactive. Our TV contract in 1955 had residuals written into it; by record, the first rerun money began for TV in 1952 after agreements signed in 1948 by SAG and the studios. It did not seem wise to me to conflate these two separate entities, one about a television series and the other about a movie. The contracts were from different time frames and for two very distinct and disparate media. It could only work negatively against the MMC case.

In addition, the sixth-run-only residuals stated in our contract were paid beyond that on later runs of our show in the 'seventies and 'eighties, which seemed to me to set a legal precedent. My calls to SAG also got us small residuals for reuse on these reruns as well as a number of TV retrospective specials that recut and reused clips of our show. I believe there is also a legal possibility that by cutting and changing an existing filmed or taped show already aired that it may constitute a new show, as it had for *The Carol Burnett Show* previously, hence, subject to new payments.

I can prove nothing, but it is my thought that SAG, being goaded by Mouseketeer Darlene and Fraschilla into a suit involving hundreds of actors, knew they had to proceed or they would have problems with all the actors in the union who had acted in almost any TV series from the 'fifties forward. Whatever the outcome, it would be difficult for SAG to survive such a massive litigation scenario.

However, if SAG followed a path that ostensibly showed they were doing what they must do to protect film and TV actors, and then *lost*, the problem would go away. Disney, like every major studio, has all of the best entertainment law firms, and this is a very specific niche in the law, on retainer. Thus, it is nearly impossible to get skilled entertainment counsel to pursue them. In addition, they are a billion+ dollar company and what lawyer, not being paid hourly, working on a one-third contingency, wants to go up against a behemoth like that with the best specialists in the field? And what individual or small group, like the Mouseketeers or the more disparate actors on *Spin & Marty*, has the money to pay for full courtroom research and aggressive litigation?

If SAG had won the arbitration it also would have affected all the major studios in the same way and they are all owned by even bigger corporations than Disney. They would not allow that to happen.

Finally, SAG has to deal with Disney and every other corporate film company or independent every day, week, year, decade or century and will have to until TV, films and commercials are no longer made. This now includes the ongoing computer, cell phone, iPod and all other emerging alternative outlets which are proliferating and the unknowns about these markets and the money that can be made. These issues led to one of my other union's strike, the WGA in 2008, and the ongoing problems with SAG in 2009. Without closure, SAG would have left itself open to litigation by one or all of the 125,000+ members and former members of the guild for not properly pursuing all actors' best interests.

Darlene and Fraschilla invited the Mice and any other actors present at the SAG meeting to their law firm's offices to learn further information. Most of us attended. Fraschilla referred to a "confidential, anonymous" letter to the SAG lawyer of record, not the outside firm that was hired for the arbitration, to which he and Darlene had been privy. This SAG law representative broke all the rules of the legal profession by showing them this letter. I was the anonymous letter writer to whom Fraschilla referred and I had made an accurate and innocuous statement in it in which I wrote, that unlike Mouseketeer Darlene, I had no monstrous animus against Disney, but I did agree that the studio owed us all money and I would gladly participate in the arbitration process.

Darlene never ceased fervently ranting about how badly she had been treated by Disney. I read that she had settled a previous lawsuit—that Disney had reduced to Municipal Court so that the most the award could be was $25,000—for the usual undisclosed amount. I assume the Disney counsel viewed it as an inexpensive nuisance suit and settling would keep it out of media focus.

During his reading of my letter, Fraschilla threatened to "punch him in the nose," referring to me, the anonymous letter writer. Although he declared himself to be a former Marine and a Congressional Medal of Honor winner, which I did not believe for a second, I was not worried by the threat. It is illegal to threaten someone with violence and he made the statement in front of many witnesses in his lawyer's office. Although not the case at that time, it is now illegal under the Stolen Valor Act of 2005 to say you were awarded the Congressional Medal of Honor if you were not. I happen to think it is insulting to some real American heroes. In the opinion of the blog popcultureaddict.com he is "…a con man convicted multiple times named Jerry Fraschilla." In 2005, Mr. & Mrs. Fraschilla were back in court accused of another felony, scamming by filing fake documents to collect from a class-action lawsuit, making fraudulent claims of over $300,000. In 2009 this case is unresolved.

I did call SAG regarding their staff lawyer's malfeasance in disclosing my letter directly to Darlene and Fraschilla and I received an apology from them. The then SAG President Richard Masur also called me and left a personal message of apology on my answering machine at home. The guilty, female legal beagle left SAG soon after this occurrence.

I testified by phone for the arbitration, as did the others who did not live in Southern California. I was hardly "prepped" at all. I imagine the same was true of the other Mouseketeers. Any legally informed person will tell you that no witness can be effective if not properly "prepped"—prepared for adversarial questions by opposing counsel. The situation for the novice in testifying in the quagmire of illogical and slanted verbiage with which you will be attacked leaves you not knowing what to do, or how to say or present things, even though you are being truthful and honest. Without a prep you will be ineffective and screwed by the other side.

As to the 2.5% of GROSS for merchandising the Mouseketeers received in our first season seven-year contract as opposed to the second and third season contracts, which I can only assume have the same clause, the arbitration process as it was explained by a lawyer at the SAG meeting could not address the merchandising segment of the contract—the arbitration rules forbade it. Remember that arbitrations are always in the favor of big money.

After the negative SAG arbitration decision, I sought out more than one legal firm and no one was interested in taking on Disney for the merchandising rights even though, if they won, the firm would make millions.

Our 2.5% of GROSS versus the ADJUSTED net on merchandising was paid out in a few, tiny increments during the 'fifties (see Appendix) but nothing has been paid since then. The Disney lawyers limited it to "…the Artist's endorsement, name, photograph, likeness, silhouette, caricature or voice is or are used…", but these come into play many times. The MMC and Mouseketeer products, as well as new ones that were introduced since the 'fifties and will continue into perpetuity if they make money, are sold with no monies going to the Mouseketeers.

The Law God is unmoved, but there seems to be something questionable about the millions and millions of merchandising products Disney has put out for fifty-three plus years that never fulfills the contract-stated percentage due to the Mouseketeers.

On a more optimistic note, during the 1980 Mouseketeer renascence, I had noticed that character actors who had done one or two roles in Volkswagen movies for Disney had passes to Disneyland and the other Parks. Mouseketeer Tommy and I lobbied for all the Mouseketeers to have these cards. The original Mouseketeers, particularly the nine of us who lasted throughout the filming and Cheryl, are, thus identified with the show by the majority of fans, were and are the mainstays as the human connection between at least two, if not three, generations of kids to Disney as well as their kids and grandkids and great grandkids from our seminal children's television show.

Tom and I were successful for all ten of us and most likely Sherry, only on season two, and we now have these cards arrive every year. We and three guests can get into any of the Parks for free and have been able to since the 'eighties.

I hate lines and crowds and I am not much for rides of any kind, unlike Bobby, who is about three years older than I am, pushing seventy, and really enjoys that sort of thing. Nor can I, as Bob always has, push to the front of a line, explain he is Mouseketeer Bobby and late for a rehearsal or a performance, whether true or not, so he can cut in. Bob has been doing it for decades, his huge smile beaming. He must hate waiting in line more than I do. Thus, I have only used my pass once for visiting relatives from another state. As usual, none of the other Mouseketeers thanked Tommy and me for our successful efforts.

If you cannot fight city hall, and when you do you usually lose, how can you fight a corporation, or worst of all, the evil GOD of LAW? In my mind you cannot. You must decide your position alone, as we all do. The LAW GOD is at minimum as unfair as other gods and there is never a promise of even one virgin for doing the bidding of the god involved

My internal and external colloquies with the inequities of ecclesiastical matters and the law were accompanied during these years of dialogue and exploring and learning by less minatory interests: showbiz and my fame at twelve, dating and arriving at sexual fruition, longing for a license and being given a cool car, expanding my urbane sophistication and the good life via having more and cooler toys. I was not, as many thought, born in the lap of luxury, but I was certainly on the crest of prosperity.

I was both fortunate and unfortunate to be spoiled par excellence for my first twenty years. To varying degrees, my grandmother's indulgences sometimes recurred after I turned twenty, but I rejected her monetary generosity if it required me to adhere to her inflexible orders after our split.

Thereby hangs a golden tale.

Chapter 6
Spoiled Bling-Bling Rotten

A few years before my mother's death in December, 2003 I came upon a book tucked away in her house amidst the remnants and detritus of a lifetime. It was titled *Your Child Year By Year*. Beginning with congratulatory cards on my birth, it set out a template to record my evolution. I was seven months on my first Christmas and I was presented with lots of greeting cards, three rattles, two sterling silver picture frames, a sterling cup, napkin, ring, spoon, and twenty-two stuffed animals— enough to bewilder a zoologist.

Being the only child of an only child is much more than problematic; the concept of sharing does not exist, except verbally. My mom had been spoiled all of her life and those benefits continued through her adulthood—Dad reaping a fair amount by location, location, location. Mom and I were graced by small gifts of clothes and other things and larger gifts of jewelry, money, tuition, trips, cars and houses. Eventually, Mom was given a small resort.

In my situation it was at times beyond the affluence of the few millionaires' kids with whom I came into contact; for instance, I met Peggy Lee at her home in Beverly Hills at a party for her daughter who attended HPS. I was not shown her checkbook, but she certainly had the trimmings to make me think she was a millionaire. Ms. Lee looked nothing like the woman I had seen onstage and her sexy approach to songs was clearly a separate persona. The same was evident at the home of Cyd Charisse and Tony Martin. Kids and parents alike at HPS and later the MMC believed that I came from even more money than my grandparents had, especially after we moved to the Bluebell Estates home when I was nine, having modest dwellings previously, and prior to the Disney series.

I am not writing about abundant old money wealth or robber baron's progeny, but the 'fifties was an era when being a millionaire had a significance as opposed to everyone owning million+ dollar houses and boomer dotcoms buying forty to eighty thousand dollar autos for their sixteen-year-olds and those below billionaire becoming the nouveau hoi polloi. Comparatively, my grandparents were never millionaires but dropped down about $100,000 a year which was doing okay in the 'fifties. I did not get a gull wing 300 SL Mercedes, which I wanted and would have taken used, but I did receive a new convertible Corvette with two four-barrel carbs when I was fifteen. Three months later I was to drive my 'Vette to college.

Glade and John started with only six years of "school 'larnin'" and hardly any capital. They built a substantive, sustaining business through hard work, saving money weekly, giving fair value for cash and being religiously honest, even though they adhered to no formal religion.

Glade had an almost "Rain Man" ability with numbers; she could add, subtract, multiply or divide five digit figures, up to five of them, in her head, as she would say, "with no pencil or paper," and with more speed than a good math student with a calculator. This talent only slackened in her eighties cutting it down to four then three digits and four to three sets of them. She also was more dogged and stubborn than two geminis in the same harness and she never accepted failure or deviation from what she declared as right.

How or why they got into the food industry in the 1920s was never divulged to me or, if so, I have forgotten. They certainly did not take any courses on the subject. I have assumed Gram learned to cook from her mother since there was no TV with 100+ cooking shows. If there was a radio show that gave out recipes, my grandmother had no time to listen to it. They rented and eventually owned a diner near a factory in Kentucky and catered to the employees. It became a hangout for breakfasts, furious lunches and a pretty solid dinner crowd.

Gram was a "bleeder" and one of the times she cut herself very badly but refused to leave rush hour lunch to go to a hospital or a doctor. She also had a fear of physicians all of her life for some unexplained reason, so she stuck her spurting hand in a sack of flour allowing her to finish all the required cooking. After lunch they cleaned her wound and wrapped it up. Another time a robber flashed a knife and demanded money. Gram picked up a bigger knife and chased the galoot out the front door.

They were trusted implicitly by their banker, in a time when you would actually know your banker and he was more like Jimmy Stewart than Lionel Barrymore or Enron execs. Gram proudly averred that they could walk into the bank and be handed twenty grand cash. They actually did this once. My grandmother also left her handbag in a department store with $5,000 cash in large bills inside and when she came back two hours later it had been held for her with all the bills intact. America was quite different then.

I saw my grandmother correct a grocery clerk, before bar codes, when he shortchanged the store in adding up the amount for the goods bought. After all, she could do it in her head faster than the hands at the cash register; actually, she would know the total, including the tax fraction, before it was rung up.

Their banker/friend convinced them to invest in buying rental properties that they could fix up, taking on large mortgages, then rent and eventually sell for a profit. Not owning things outright, after paying off their café, was totally new to them. Gram hated paying interest. They lost the café and their livelihood and these properties soon after the 1929 stock market crash. They had always paid their bills on time and continued to do so until they died but my grandmother never forgot what happened when she listened to the banker who got them in "over their heads," causing them ruination. She vowed to always own property outright. She bought everything including cars, houses, land, apartments, investment properties and stores for "cash on the barrel head."

This practice caused enormous problems when America changed to a borrowing culture from an owning culture after they retired in the 'sixties. This was exacerbated by their elderly trust in two different friends, one a renter with whom they became friends and another—a bowling buddy. The renter was Jim Valint, to whom they sold their last apartment building in which he lived and the bowler was an "aw, shucks" con man in my perception; he was so bland and forgettable, I do not recall his name. He sucked them (and multi-partners) into a Fremont, California land deal that went kaput. They lost their full investment.

Right after the Crash and their losses they began again, refusing to take factory jobs or working for anyone but themselves. However much they were tormented, they did not become sullen about their situation, although knowing my grandmother they surely gave voice to feelings of unfairness and the character of their banker and all bankers.

They made deals on produce and Gramp sold not quite fresh fruit and vegetables door-to-door. Gram scrounged for and cleaned up the veggies and looked for damaged, thrown out, or very under-priced older furniture. Gramp fixed, cleaned and polished the chairs, tables and what-all and began selling these door-to-door as well. He quickly acquired a wagon and a mule and paraded around Cincinnati and outlying areas; they dropped the spoilable produce as soon as possible and stuck to furniture.

In a few years they saved enough to begin their first small second-hand furniture store. By my entrance in 1943, they had a fair-sized store selling only new maple furniture and mattresses. They always loved the maple style and used it in their homes for all of their lives, but why they liked it or how they garnered a knowledge of maple furnishings, and the carpets, lamps and whatnots used in that style has always been a mystery to me. It has never appealed to me at all. I am convinced that "braided rug" should only be a reference to a man's hair piece.

When they followed us to California in the late 1940s they bought an even larger store in Pasadena on the main drag, Colorado Boulevard. Thus, we got to watch the Rose Parade every year and never fought traffic or considered camping out overnight. We sat on comfy furniture, elevated about three feet above the oglers outside on the sidewalk, and watched the festivities from their fifteen-foot-high display windows. We ate and drank goodies, had access to private bathrooms, had no heating or cooling problems and could even go to the second story where they kept the bedroom furniture and take a nap.

Known for their fairness, pleasant nature and honest business acumen, department store chains, like the nearby Biggers, recommended Burr's to customers seeking maple, for it was too confining a specialty to be well represented in mass-oriented businesses. They sold their first home in Altadena and built two houses and six apartment units on a large lot in Monrovia, which is a few miles east of Pasadena.

These were the first properties they owned that they built from scratch on empty land. Gram designed the floor plans and other elements and only employed an architect to finalize and change things that would ensure they were legal. She was quite a creative, bootstrap-pulling gal. She also haggled contractors' prices down and watched them—plumbers, carpenters, painters and other subcontractors—"like a hawk."

When Gram's sister Mamie, two of her sons, Billy and Vernie, and her daughter Pudd, along with her husband Bob and their daughter

Spoiled Bling-Bling Rotten 95

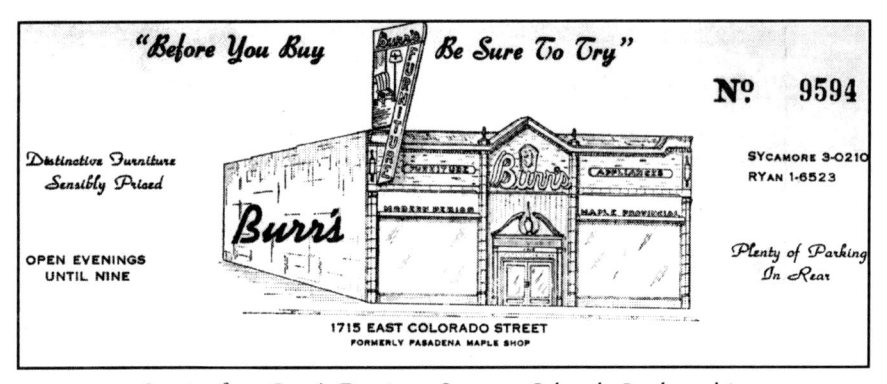

Invoice from Burr's Furniture Store on Colorado Boulevard in Pasadena, California, 1950.

Beverly, followed Gram and Gramp out to California from Kentucky they moved into two of Gram's apartments in her rental properties and were given reduced rents. They continued to do so for decades until Pudd and Bob bought a house, when my grandfather's health and respiratory problems after retirement forced Gram and Gramp to sell and move to Boulder City, Nevada, which is near Hoover Dam about fifteen miles out of Las Vegas in the early 'seventies.

This became their destination because of the desert air for John's breathing problems. There was no gaming in Boulder City, which pleased my gramma, and, most important, was my mom's proximity in nearby Vegas (although they owned two lots in West Palm Springs and had planned to retire there). Mamie, Billy and Vernie remained in their three-bedroom apartment next to the pool until the death of Mame, then Vernie many decades later.

Their apartment buildings were always neat and tidy and well watched after by Gram; John did the repairs unless they were extremely complicated. This was also before rental laws clamped down on whom you could or could not rent to and she was selective, to put it euphemistically. Their units were always full and profitable even with the relatives in tow.

Having labored hard and long through all of her years, my grandmother decided that her daughter and grandson were not going to suffer deprivation in the same way that she and her husband had. We were going to have everything. Hence, after Mom retired from her small profit theatrical agency, she and her second husband were given a small diner, gas station and rental bungalows at the corner of the two lane road that was the last leg to Yosemite and the turn-off to Bass Lake in northern California.

Glade's well meaning largesse to Mom and me was a blessing and a literal curse. In the blessing category are the bling-blings we were both graced with, even though I object to this pejorative neologism that reflects a language further into decline. By my late teens I perceived, as did my mom before me, that these fantastic things were more expensive to us personally than any loss to Glade and John's pocketbook.

My mom, however, was a disciplinarian and rarely spoiled me unless it contributed to the Lonnie path to fame. This is why I got my hair cut by Saul in the Universal Studio barbershop starting at about seven and I noticed that most guys got their shoes shined and a manicure. I was not that interested yet in shiny shoes but when I asked my mom if I could get a manicure she answered in the affirmative, so I got my first manicure, buff no polish if you please, at eight. This was a good place to be seen by casting people, producers and so on for the studio execs got their hair and nails and shoes done here, too. Thus, it was not spoiling me; it was just business as usual.

When my parents divorced and I began living with Gram and Gramp at fifteen, it was not a hard transition in the least.

My (step)grandfather was a prototypical gruff guy at a time when sensitive men were not just suspect but reviled. My dad, in the only simulation of grandfather he ever acquiesced to, followed suit along with John Wayne and other closet-fearing, hard-boiled guys. The word "love" did not come forth from John; Howard said that he loved me once in my life that I remember distinctly; it was very difficult for him. Much later in life, beginning in the late 'seventies, he would use the love word once in a while.

My grandmother, tough but a woman, did speak the love word often but truly the only way either of my grandparents could show love was by giving things or money. These gifts always had multiple strings attached in order to control and shame.

This was not only a sad, depressing, paranoia inducing situation, it created an atmosphere that was insurmountable, like smog in Los Angeles. It could be mitigated and improved at times, but it remained a constant.

Glade was opinionated and unmoving however much she emoted. She affected, controlled and was owed by the entire family including her sister's family. Hers was a life made of maple, not willow. Humans will break free, however, and on rare occasions the monarch was challenged, but it was almost unheard of for her to give in and she only overestimated her power a very few times with anyone.

As Cocky, between my oppressor Sir and The Kid in "Roar of the Greasepaint,...", 1968.

She made that mistake with me and I do not think she ever quite got over it.

After completing my Master's degree at twenty, I was leading the life of a young, affluent wastrel. I drank, party hopped, womanized and carped the diem. I had no debts, no chores, no work. I did not even have to make my bed; my grandmother seemed to love doing these things, like pressing my shirts, and bragging about it. I had no problem with this arrangement. I got an allowance, owned a new Alfa Romeo outright and only had to fork over cash for entertainment, gas and car repairs after the warranty ran out. I eventually would also be getting small but regular residuals from the first syndicated reruns of *The Mickey Mouse Club* (1962-65) after those for the last year of reruns from the original airing of the show.

I tried to find work acting or dancing and singing, but I was typecast as Mouseketeer Lonnie, the cute little blond boy who tapped and jazz danced so furiously. The fact that I was a young man who had done a lot of work on his acting and played many stage roles from *Othello* to Albee to leads in musicals like Cocky in *The Roar of the Greasepaint, The*

Smell of the Crowd in 1968 made no dent in the frequently dim bulbs of casting people and the folks for whom they worked.

The confrontation with my grandmother was likely a subconscious way of breaking away from her control and the effortless and meaningless existence I led. I made a bad, obtuse choice. I brought a somewhat older woman in her thirties back home with me and she stayed overnight in my *pension* on the second floor of my grandparent's house. My grandparents were sound sleepers and had no idea about their guest.

When I accompanied the lady from my second story suite to the door the next morning, introducing her to my grandmother, Gramp being out—I fortunately had double checked her name for I have a block about remembering names—Glade showed her disdain but did not verbally explode until she left.

She ordered me never to invite a female to spend the night again. Other broken rules—like staying out all night, boozing too much, some speeding tickets and other tendencies toward objectionable acts—were brought up.

In spite of the typical vanity and excesses of a burgeoning, self-destructive young male, I explained to my grandmother (in terms less polite as when I did it and ran away in Highland Park at four) that I would move out if she insisted on running my life. She was certainly within her rights demanding that I keep women from staying over night but if I had to give up sex, which was not an option, or only get lucky with women who lived alone, if I could not stay out all night, nor have sex in my room, I was ready to do whatever was necessary.

My grandmother confidently smiled and boasted, "You won't move out. You need the money too much."

This was the worst thing she could have said, assuming, and I have never doubted it, that she wanted me to stay. I was livid and hurt that my character seemed to amount to so little in the eyes of my second mom. It seemed like an abandonment—as it did five years earlier when my mother had blithely gone off to get a divorce and then live the rest of her life in Vegas.

By age twenty my 'Vette had been replaced by a new Thunderbird and two years later the only sports car that Volvo made, a new P-1800 which I had seen on my first European tour, and presently an Alfa, which I promptly got into and drove away. She had underestimated me and overestimated my need for money and objects. She also completely forgot (or chose to forget) my suicide attempt which had come not that many months previously.

I bought a newspaper and looked for the first work in my life that did not involve acting, dancing or singing. I was still writing and getting published, but had not sold anything yet. I looked at apartments. Within two days I had a job selling men's clothes, having a solid knowledge of style and haberdashery, at the May Company and I placed a first and last month deposit on an apartment not too far away. I had grown up in North Hollywood and considered the Valley home so I thought it wise to be near people, places and things that I was familiar with and not that far from work. Coming from beneath the dining room table of your own volition was not the same as leaving the neighborhood. I moved out the weekend after the conflict.

I got some help from my grandfather and two of my cousins, all of whom understood how to properly move furniture since they had at different times worked for my grandfather at their furniture store for extra money. My large Playboy bed would not make it via the stairs and front door. They had to lift it with ropes from outside my balcony and through the sliding glass doors without scratching the wood.

Prudently, I had a savings account, being attentive to my grandmother's business sense, and, with my minimum salary as a salesman, small residuals from the MMC and owning a car outright, I did fairly well. I had taken my more than complete wardrobe and the Danish Modern furniture that was in my large, second story "rooms." All I had to buy was a large bookcase and some dishes and pots and pans, brooms and tools and the usual.

After six months things became more difficult and I had to start making financial issues less pressing. I also had to learn to do all the things that I had not done before as a spoiled kid and teen: washing clothes and dishes, drying, folding, sewing, ironing, cleaning the apartment, repairing things, making the bed, grocery shopping, cooking and all of the seemingly endless "malady of the quotidian" that poet Wallace Stevens referred to in a line of verse. Laura, a lover in my college years, had given me a gourmet cook book and I even tried exotic dishes like vichyssoise. It was pretty good, except I did not cut down the recipe and had the cold potato and leek soup sitting in the refrigerator and staring at me until it went bad after a week or so. My ratatouille was excellent.

I never returned and in many ways still had a pretty large stuffed zoo beginning at my birth in 1943 through my birthday in 1963. The only things I had missed out on by twenty were things my mom blocked, like the BB rifle I lobbied for.

The list of blings is long. One of my first pieces of jewelry was a ring at six that was my birthstone, emerald, with two diamonds on the side. In my forties I discovered that the diamonds were real but I had a good, pretty, green gem, not an emerald. I have inferred that Gram was concerned that I might lose it. As it happens, I have never lost a piece of jewelry and it is the only "costume" item that I have ever owned or given. I still wear it at times and it has a meaning of continuity to me and it looks swell. I have also never bought any jewelry for myself except for some cufflink sets when I collected them in my teens and twenties.

I did lose my grandfather's one carat diamond, which had gone into my first handsome diamond ring as a teen. I had picked out the unique setting for the stone and it was later matched by specially crafted cuff links and studs. I was playing a principal role in a summer stock production of the musical *Irma la Douce* as one of the *mecs* (pimps), Roberto les Diams, in upstate Troy, New York in my first stock after moving to Manhattan.

Since the ring flashed and was right for the role, I wore it in the show as opposed to having it locked up at half hour by the stage manager as AEA requires them to do if the actor so desires—nothing like this is provided for in TV or films. After the matinee I noticed that the stone had come out. I rushed back onstage, the audience gone by now, and searched everywhere on my hands and knees. Pernicious as Gramp had been to me it was part of my family history and I felt a huge loss.

Coming up with nothing, I informed the stage manager and he said that even if found it would most likely not be turned in because diamonds are valuable and impossible to identify as belonging to any particular person. I knew he was correct.

Returning from the dinner break, I inquired again and, getting a negative, I went out to look one last time after the pre-performance stage sweeping had been done. I found nothing. It was an outside, tented venue and the sun was setting. I started for my dressing room when someone opened a tent flap and I caught a glint under a seat in the theatre-in-the round front row. I scrambled to my knees and claimed the family sparkler. I had it reset and it is still my favorite ring, having always preferred it to more glitzy, valuable rings I have received (like my grandfather's ring shaped like a belt buckle with twelve diamonds of varying sizes).

By thirteen I had had a few watches but managed to see, request and get the very first electric watch, a Hamilton, and for many years now a collectible. It was a very unusual triangular shape, similar to my ring, and had a black face which was also not yet common. It was a knockout but in a few years I did not like its thickness, the workings not yet in a thin, elegant carapace. I have never liked the statement, nor the expense of a Rolex and similar heavy, oversized watches. I also have never worn a sign that says please hit me or kill me for my watch. It is not worth the risk just to show off for others. On an appropriate night out I wear the good stuff, as I did every day until about thirty, even in Manhattan, but that is all. The watch was complemented by my black star sapphire ring, cuff links and studs which I eventually gave to my former godson.

All the men in my family were pool players, so besides jewelry and other expensive gifts, I was given my first custom cue and full sized, slate pool table at seven. I actually earned my first bowling ball, another male family favorite, by rolling a league high 213 at twelve. Neither of these pursuits survived past my early twenties.

I might have been prompted to want and receive my first horse at seven because of Dad's and Gramp's interest in the race track. Horse racing did not appeal to me but racing my own horse did. I rode regularly from seven until I started the MMC and I had two horses but after I sold Blue Boy I lost interest in the sport.

There were numerous other gifts, such as a specially tailored, purple and white Vikings football outfit for me at eight, including cleats and a helmet with a new, clear plastic face guard. After my fandom for Crazy Legs Hirsch on the Rams I had moved on to the first scrambling quarterback Fran Tarkenton, who was with the Vikings. I wore this outfit once, luckily not in the wrong neighborhood, and the guys gave me such a bad time that I never wore it again.

My first car, the Corvette when I turned fifteen, was not used by me because the underage license to drive to school and back was not given to me. I was also told that I would be excluded, due to my age, from the mandatory ROTC, which was diametrically opposed to my JW teachings. Neither of these alleged facts became reality and the reasons, which I no longer recall, never were explained to my satisfaction.

I started at the huge campus, my grandfather extremely irked and fearful since he dreaded freeway traffic, but found another problem. I was inured to small, private school classes. In one of my UCLA courses I was in a literal theatre with no stage that would seat, and did in my class, hundreds. I knew I would ostensibly be reading a book, taking notes and

Mouseketeer Karen and I shared a ride in a convertible but not a Corvette in the 1983 Burbank Parade. My young buddy is the car owner's son.

tests but having no interaction with the instructor. This was unacceptable to me also. UCLA was out, at least for the immediate future.

So I attended the closest college to my home, Valley College, a two-year school that yielded an Associate of Arts degree. For once my grandfather approved of something I did because he only had to drive me a few blocks and could shun his fear of freeway traffic.

But I still had the 1958 Corvette bought for my fifteenth birthday—four-speed box, two quad-carbs and fast, fast, fast! Very Cool.

My gram's business sense and frugality offset her magnanimity and the spiffy looking, green and white vehicle we found at a used car lot had over two thousand miles on it. That did little to deter my enthusiasm.

I had literally begun dreaming about how to customize my first car, constantly going over car mags, at about seven or so and in time I changed my 'Vette having it shaved and decked (all decals, metal etcetera taken off the hood and trunk deck), putting in a new grille, moving the dual pipes underneath augmented by headers, inserting backup lights in the bumper openings where the exhausts had come out constantly discoloring the chrome bumper, adding an air scoop to the removable top, beefing up the radio and speakers and painting it purple. People stared approvingly.

This fifteen-year-old college student was disappointed at not being able to drive his cool car, but I was way ahead of everyone else. It would have been a cash loss for Gram to sell it so I was to keep it until I got my license. I talked buddies into driving it, usually taking me and a date places just so they could drive the cool car.

I eventually bought two cars on my own, a beat up older round-backed Volvo, when things got tight after I moved out and I had to sell my Alfa Romeo for money, and finally a new, silver Chevy Impala with wire wheel hubcaps, which is the only car I ever bought on time; I dutifully paid off my GMAC loan.

Two trips to Europe were given to me at eighteen and twenty. The first was a theatre tour of NY and six European countries during which I fell more in love with JoAnne, but was luckily persuaded to move onward and forward.

I did get to see Richard Burton in *Camelot* and in rotten balcony seats was awed by his magnificent voice and acting talent despite the great Julie Andrews and Bob Goulet as Lancelot. Former child star Roddy McDowell played the evil Mordred.

The rest of the theatre events in NYC and the Continent were not memorable. I sagely avoided seeing *Going Madly Dutch* in Amsterdam, but I did see a tedious opera by Mozart in his native Salzburg, Austria and managed to avoid snoring during *Aida*, my interest only focused on the large elephants actually on stage at the *Termi di Caracalla* (the Roman Baths) in Rome. I have always felt that *Porgy and Bess* by Gershwin is the best opera ever written because of its musicality, beauty and tragedy. Besides, you do not require a translator to understand what the hell is going on.

I had the good fortune to work with Broadway hoofers Shirley MacLaine and Sammy Davis, Jr. in "The Rhythm of Life" number in the film of *Sweet Charity*. I had been a fan of Sammy, his brother and dad as The Will Mastin Trio on *The Tonight Show*, but I first saw *Porgy and Bess* as a film at the excellent Carthay Circle Theatre, now built over for an office building. The opening musical sequence is a marvel, as is the opera, but Sammy stood out as Sportin' Life and he acted, danced and sang superbly. I next saw his club act live soon after that at the Moulin Rouge and remember most his version of "Trouble" from *The Music Man*. Robert Preston imprinted the number on Broadway and in the film, but Sammy did it at a faster clip and it was amazingly his own.

He had no star aura on the set and quietly sipped his bucket glass (large cocktail tumbler) of bourbon and coke and was even tempered. But it was Bob Fosse's first film and he did not yet know how to manage things. So he would have all of us standing under the hot lights in our hippie wigs and heavy clothes for long periods while he tried to figure out how he was going to shoot the number. Sammy had leather pants that were also boots, so it was a very hot outfit. Finally, he shouted out to Fosse, "Hey, I'm a superstar and I'm burnin' up. This is not fair." The cast laughed and broke into applause. Fosse gave us a short break.

Fosse's second film was not, as all previous film musicals like his first one, a filming of a musical play. In *Cabaret* Bob changed all intelligent director and choreographer takes on filmed musicals, except for the brain dead, by not shooting numbers straight on but from odd, dramatic POVs, like between a woman's legs here, from behind a bassoon there. Before this lesson in filmmaking the best thing done was overhead shots from Busby Berkeley's musicals over forty years earlier.

I watched and very much enjoyed James Earl Jones in *The Great White Hope* when I was playing *George M* in Cleveland in 1969; I later did one of two episodes of *Lois and Clark* with Jones and when he did not show up for the very unusual, for TV episodics, read-through of the script the producer had me take his lines too. I did *Mack & Mabel* on Broadway with "Pres," the late, great Robert Preston in 1975, and I kibitzed on occasion at a local watering hole just north of Universal with Roscoe Lee Browne in the early 'nineties.

All of these gentlemen had excellent, full, deep voices but the only two even close to Burton is Jones and was Pres. Diane used to come to see *Mack & Mabel* to hear Preston's resonance one more time rather than to see me during the abbreviated Broadway run of the musical.

My second European trip was in 1963, after getting my M.A. in theatre arts at 20 and before the argument and exit from my grandparent's house later in my 20th year. My main purpose, after some fooling around, was checking out Cambridge, for they had shown interest in my attending due to my work on Theatricalist director/producer Terence James Stannus Grey. The Theatricalist approach might stage *Timon of Athens* with actors wearing 20th century Nazi uniforms with appropriate period set design, costumes and props. Those exact costumes were used in the very recent film of *Richard III* starring the wonderful Ian McKellan. They always tried finding new, original ways to approach a play that had been done exactly the same since opening night.

Grey had come from and done some of his subsequent work at Cambridge after becoming a professional director/producer. He was relatively obscure compared to the German Max Reinhardt who was the first Theatricalist and everyone seems to forget that much later the English director Peter Hall merely carried on the tradition, although perhaps with better taste.

This second trip allowed me to see the great Alec Guinness play the tragic lead in *Dylan*, a play about the poet Dylan Thomas, not the singer Bob. I ran into former Disney child star Hayley Mills at the interval. I later guested on one of her TV series, choreographing a dance for the two of us, and worked with her at the Hollywood Bowl in 1990 when she hosted a Disney opening of the summer season and I performed. She was friendly on both of these occasions.

But this planned sortie to St. Moritz, Switzerland, then Paris and finally London turned bad and desperately existential for me and foreshadowed my "nervous breakdown," which translates into that era's euphemistic phrase for attempted suicide.

Aside from European trips, horses, cars, all schooling, dance/voice/acting classes, jewelry, houses and the rest, clothes were a compelling interest in my life. Subsequent to wrenching my sartorial choices from my mom at seven or so, I became known as a cool dresser and a distinctive individualist who took risks no other kids, or teenagers, or older men would dare to attempt.

I wore pink shirts in the 'fifties, a very hazardous and suspect act. A young lady asked me to her graduation from Van Nuys High the same year as mine at HPS and the nights did not conflict. I wore a gold lamé (which now sounds very lame) dinner jacket with black lapels and pocket flaps. This perplexed and astounded many people.

Guys at school emulated me as did many of the male Mice. I designed my first tailored tux at sixteen. I picked a blue/black English mohair material and required a shawl collar versus the common notched collar for the jacket and the unusual matching vest. I required no buttons showing except on the coat sleeves, which is called a fly front, and had the tailor use black silk trim on the coat, vest and slacks. I refused patent leather shoes and found black suede dress loafers in a formal style and added a white, flat not fluffy, lace shirt, a spread collar and an Abe Lincoln tie, avoiding my distaste for bow ties. I was always complimented when I wore it and it lasted me over two decades.

My frequent buying sorties as a child and teen with my grandmother were spectacular, exciting events that could top five hundred bucks, a large amount in the 'fifties. Both my mother and my grandmother felt that a child star, even before he was one, should look like and live like a child star. I agreed heartily. Our outings were a paradigm of an unusually spoiled childhood.

John would drive Glade and me to Highland and Hollywood by Max Factor's and Grauman's Chinese and, almost directly across the street, the Hollywood Masonic Temple where I used to rehearse the *Colgate Comedy Hour*. Gramp then did something for an indeterminate amount of time. Gram and grandson would shop the north or south side of Hollywood Boulevard proceeding east. It was fashionable then and had not achieved the Bowery look, danger and feel of the decades since the 'seventies.

We turned south at Vine near the Pantages and the now-absent-and-soon-to-become-condos Deco Broadway store at Hollywood and Vine across from the original Brown Derby. We never ventured into the Broadway for the styles were not to my liking, preferring a sleeker, less common look. We marched past the first cross street which placed us across from the now long absent NBC Studios where I recorded the radio soap *Dr. Paul* at nights. But we stopped short of Sunset just west of the Palladium and the defunct Moulin Rouge and north of the huge "Music City" record store.

This last stop was Sy Devore's men's shop—"Where the Stars Shop." It was true that Sinatra, Jerry Lewis and other biz hotshots went there and Jerry's suits were always lined with red silk as was the tux I designed and had tailored after high school. I was drawn there because the clothes were excellent, if pricey. As in most men's stores, it was difficult to find something in a size I could wear. Fortunately, a lot of stars are shorter than anyone realizes due to shifty camera work. Sophia Loren actually had to stand in a trench the filmmakers dug so she would not tower over diminutive Alan Ladd in *A Boy on a Dolphin*. Other methods are now used for Dustin, Tom Cruise and other guys even shorter than me.

My gram and I returned by hitting Hollywood on the opposite side and/or returned to a previous store so my grandmother could use her estimable haggling skills on something we did not buy at a shop we hit on the way to Sy's. If there had been a Rodeo Drive then we would have gone there instead but the exorbitant Rodeo-mall and Giorgio's were not yet in existence. I also doubt that my grandmother would have made an appointment to be admitted and pay well over a grand for one shirt which started sometime in the 'eighties, and is surely more outlandish now.

I had an expansive wardrobe for a kid, more dress clothes than Levis and sports wear, which even included hats, gloves, scarves and a top coat—rarely wearable in Southern California. When I joined the first national touring company of the musical *George M* with Joel Grey, one of the chorus guys told me later that when I deplaned by stairs wearing my topcoat, black, stingy brim Sinatra hat and carrying gloves in preparation for winter in eastern cities, he thought I was one of the producers. He was not joking, although given him and the time—1969—he could have been mildly stoned.

It appeared that John was part of my financial excesses but we all knew that it emanated from Glade and if he begrudged my good fortune it would not be voiced. Glade embarrassed me no end with her furious, hard-nosed bargaining but she almost always got a reduction in price or we walked, no matter how much I wanted the item. As adept as she was at this kind of business, I have never had the chops for it but I did watch and, while cringing, learned.

I was taught not to accept the first price and to look at details, not the name of the latest Bozo on a label. In my sixties I still have a few classic clothes that I bought decades ago. I do have Brioni, Valentino, Yves St. Laurent, Countess Mara, Christian Dior and things from Giorgio's. What I am interested in, however, is what my grandmother taught me to look for—good fabric, stitching, tailoring and bargains. I got my Giorgio three-piece suit after searching every shop I could for what I had in mind for over a year and it was reduced to 50% off. If it had not been reduced, I would not have bought it.

When I started college I made these trips by myself. Most of my clothes were still paid for but I never made out as well as I had when Gram was riding shotgun. The only time she accompanied me from that point forward was buying my first car.

The nicest home I lived in as a kid was the one Gram bought for us on Bluebell. She and my mom felt that I could entertain and help my career. I did throw some parties and Carol Lynley and her mom joined Mom and me for lunch while Carol and I were both working for Disney. Much earlier I met Mary Pickford and her daughter at my mom's agency office to arrange a PR "date" for us that never panned out.

The house was a Spanish ranch style architecturally, known back east as a "rambler," with white masonry and a red-tile roof. It sat on a half acre which is relatively large for the even then overcrowded and suburbanized San Fernando Valley of the 1950s.

It had a nice, large front yard and lawn with a winding brick walkway accented by a wishing well that led to the large, aged-wood front door. The back lawn looked over two brick terraces and steps that led to the 18' x 36' pool and separate guest house. The latter could have served as a studio apartment with a small kitchen and bath. We had the space for and were going to put in a tennis court behind the pool when my parents split up officially and Gram, thoroughly disgusted for she did not hold with divorce, sold it for it was in the name of the buyers: Gladys and John Burr.

This Spanish villa had very large rooms and mine, the second and smaller bedroom, had lots of closets, built in drawers and a full private bath. I chose the rug, colors and furniture which began my designing for every environment—room, even when on the road, apartment, condo, house—in which I have lived since. I was nine.

I would be perfectly comfortable in the Bluebell house today, except for its location in the Valley. I do not like entertaining and I do not like strangers coming into my house to clean and break or take. I like things comfortably big enough without feeling like I am lost in a humongous palace and the 2500 square foot home would be just right for Diane, me and our cat Asta.

About a year after I started living with them in the largest apartment in my grandparent's building it was becoming much too crowded in the two-bedroom, one bath with a tiny den unit. They had plans to build another apartment building and a house on a next door lot so they bought two lots and Gram worked out a design for a place a few miles farther west in the Valley.

I had nothing to do with the apartments and pool, but at seventeen I had a great deal to do with exterior and interior design of our house with a pool including the roof line, which extended straight up past the second floor and the half circle driveway in the front yard. The entire second floor with two skylights would be my rooms. I decided on white stucco exterior with a medium light blue trim. Inside I collaborated on rugs, floors and colors. I contributed an architectural element in an exterior atrium space cut out of the family room and open to the outside. The foliage was open to the exterior of the house and viewable inside from a large window in the family room. I chose the plants and discovered my first epiphyte, a staghorn fern, which I had growing off one of the exterior house walls in the atrium.

John and Glade had a master suite off the living room and dining area and I managed to get a spiral, iron staircase in the family room that led to my bedroom/atelier on the second floor. The staircase was painted white, as I had the fireplace stone work painted, and was carpeted in the same color as my bedroom.

Reaching the top of the stairs there were floor to ceiling height, twelve feet across, smoky, variegated mirrors which met an architectural outcrop that contained indirect, blue lighting. To the left was a small study with a small skylight, window, built-in desk and glass enclosed bookcases, both in walnut.

Past that door was an intimate seating area that had sliding glass doors that overlooked the pool, the vista was wider with tall windows on each side. This was cantilevered out from the house and the sliding glass doors opened for air. Unless it is freezing or wretchedly hot I want air blowing through my living space. It was possible to walk behind my chaise lounge, open the glass door and jump from my room into the deep end of the pool. I never tried the jump but a guest once succeeded in doing it without injuring himself—except for my grandmother's fiery reaction.

Farther along on the wall, opposite from the study, were more tall, glass enclosed, walnut book cases—I have always kept a large number of books. In the space here I had a game table with one of my chess sets on top and two chairs which, like all the furniture, were after Eames wood and leather to coordinate with the Danish Modern bed. Past this area were two sliding, louvered-door closets that ran about fifteen feet to the wall against which the bed abutted and which had a built in walnut chest with drawers.

Across from the closets I put my wood hutch that held my records, tapes and other sundries; I set *objets d'art* on top and hung my first choices in original art. The second door on that wall opened to my bathroom and a walk-in closet. I chose black marble with white striations for the walls and vanity top and continued the rug leading to a sunken tub and shower. Now common but then not done, I had the wide mirror outlined with a line of bulbs that emulates the lighting in a makeup room on a studio lot.

Under the larger skylight, back in the main room, was the original Playboy Bed, which I had wanted since first seeing it in *Playboy Magazine*. I did not like the idea of moving on to a round bed as Hefner had. Mine was the original rectangular but had all of the same benefits.

It was custom built for me in Danish Modern, had a large headboard with cubicles for any purpose I chose and on each end stereo speakers were built into the upper headboard and covered with dark material. Sitting on the bed, a lower left cubicle had a small refrigerator and at the foot on the left side a large walnut bar to hold bottles, glasses and cocktail items.

The opposite side was a larger, higher walnut extension from the headboard that housed the tape deck, tuner and turntable. In the center of the headboard was a faux wood drawer that turned over to reveal a large cushion in a color matching the deep blue of the leather on the chairs and chaise lounge.

The skylight, quite unusual for the time, prevented the TV from being suspended from the ceiling as I had wanted, so it was on a matching wooden side table with rollers at the foot of the bed.

The skylight was much more dangerous than the sliding glass doors; neither would be allowed by building codes today and may not have been then. Even though it was safety glass with small, hard to discern wires in it, my female guests and I—allowed when they did not stay overnight—were very lucky not to be sliced and diced.

The rooms had white walls and ceiling, the royal blue materials, the walnut and Danish Modern brown of wood, some brass legs and a very muted, light orange carpet. The orange and blue, both primary colors, sounds gaudy now but were unique, Fauvist and great for a seventeen-year-old intent on getting laid.

Designing the exterior and interior elements of this house and my rooms pleased me in a creative way that was totally different than the disciplines in which I had made my living. Later in life I considered becoming an interior designer but I knew that the constraints and tastes of the client had to be at the forefront and I would not be happy maintaining that necessity.

As a child I was oblivious, except for the arguments and bad sentiments, to the traumatic financial difficulties my parents faced weekly because the shortages always seemed to be assuaged and backed up by my grandparents. I had a very comfortable childhood in the sense of getting what I wanted and being close to overwhelmed by nice, expensive things. But I came to know that there is quite a bit more to life than having a lot of toys.

If I had wanted children I would have made bloody sure that they had duties and chores. Of course, I had duties and chores but they were not boring and endlessly repetitive, like washing dishes or taking out the trash. I did take lessons, went on auditions and worked in various media, acting, dancing and/or singing but that had nothing to do with school, nor growing up, nor working toward becoming a socially adjusted, often happy, productive adult.

My bad fortune led to the kind of chores that thrust a kid into being an instant faux adult with all of the anxieties of failure, ignominy and being lacking in worth. The worst aspect was unconsciously translating success into acceptance and love. If *I* had children, they would have received an allowance but it would arise because of chores around the home. If they did not think it was enough, then they would have to get part time jobs to make more and achieve what they wanted. This is one way to teach that you have to strive for just about everything in life. The Kennedys and other old money families teach their children to give a forceful effort to achieve what they want, that it will not just be handed to them. I would have made it clear that manna from above is a quaint old parable, not a ham on rye whenever your stomach makes a tiny rumble. This truth is more evident in 2009 despite recent economic reversals, at least in American culture, as millionaires have become rife.

Most spoiled children, more now than ever, have a desperate, whining struggle when thrust upon their own devices, however late in life. I set out at twenty to ensure that I would not fall prey to my grandmother's overabundant upbringing and opulent experiences much too early in life. I have survived with no negative involvement with the legal system and no headlines in the tabloids. Considering the problematic on-again off-again nature of my life pursuits—acting, writing, dancing and choreography, directing—I have managed to live in reasonable comfort, if not splendor, and I have never actually faced living on the streets. I have come close a couple of times, but I always found a legal way out.

Never having normal, tedious, quotidian chores and usually having close to everything given to me, I somehow made myself into a person of integrity and predictable, consistent dependability. I do not ever leave a mess and I am inevitably orderly in my living environment and with my bills. I am on time or usually early arriving at work and for all professional appointments and social events. I used to be too early, but I have managed to adjust closer to the actual time as I have matured. It would be very nice if everyone else did the same thing.

I always meet expected deadlines and duties from newspaper, magazine or book assignments to play or radio play rewrites or publisher's manuscript deadlines.

Despite our films, sitcoms and cartoons depicting every single man as a self-consumed, untrustworthy slob and every single woman as an ineluctably tidy, caring person who is always there for anyone who needs her, my experience has proven this to be not quite the case. My attention to quotidian nuisances, being on time, cleaning up, etcetera was and is one of my ways of creating some order out of the chaos of not just show business but my childhood and all of life that we all live and perceive as adults. Since I decided that god does not exist for me, ma and pa did not care and were absent in my mid-teens and no one else was capable nor interested in helping me, I have taken on as much responsibility as I can. This can lead to failure and reversion to depression but I try my best to fend that off and journey on.

In a 2008 *Los Angeles Times Sunday Magazine* article written by Jodie Foster—a former child star who has made it work as an adult. She felt that her mother's rules, many of which she now looks at askance "...set me up to find real stability in an otherwise unstable business. I needed the discipline of a code to feel safe." For me, feeling safe is doing whatever I can to negate the bad possibilities of everything in which I can have an effect. I cannot stop a tornado but I can make sure I do not pay interest by sending bills in late and I can replace things from whence I have gotten them so they will be easily found. Losing my keys or glasses or not finding the research file I want is a very rare exception for me.

In 1854 Peter Mark Roget published the Thesaurus, which has been used incessantly ever since by anyone who is thoughtful. He began collecting words as a child due to a horrendous childhood; his dad died when he was four, his mother was psychotic and other family members suffered from depression (one even committed suicide). Roget needed some stability and order to offset the chaos of his life. The young Peter found his safety in words and the English language. He got this from his fascination with words.

My attention to quotidian nuisances, being on time, and similar traits were and are my way of creating some order out of the disorder of not just show business but my childhood and all of life as most humans perceive and experience it.

I have found that most often if I do not take care of something, remember it and do it, it does not get done or is, at minimum, tardy and sometimes, therefore, costly or causes other problems. I hear the distant clearing of throats as a legion of therapists smile like Hemingway as he spotted another prey he could kill and brag about. It is a good thing that shrinks do not hang the heads of patients on their walls.

Well…at least I've never seen one—yet.

I have managed to let up the desperation of this mandate in the last thirty years, but I can easily fall into it when I let go of the control and assume that Diane, or anyone, will take care of what they have said they will in a timely fashion. It is not an aberration that this type of situation, if left alone by me, will once again remind me that my trust begins with me and is delegated to others very judiciously and cautiously.

I am not parsimonious, although I remain sensible and avoid compulsive spending. I have observed that wealthy people, as opposed to the nouveau riche, are almost always oppressively stingy. They seem incapable of comprehending the difference between being cautious and smart and being cheap.

My grandparents, while dropping down 100K a year, got more than one paper to cut coupons and would spend hours and gas, not yet an actual financial problem, every week going from market to market to save dimes and quarters, long after the Crash of '29. They actually did this sort of thing for their entire lives. The cost of gas today would be much more than all the coupon savings and, even then, they were only saving a dollar or two. My grandmother would say, "A penny [dollar] saved is a penny [dollar] earned."

Gram boasted of my instinct as a child and teen to spy out the most expensive item in a store. She found this endlessly amusing. It was more a case of having an unexplainable aesthetic taste for beautifully crafted, good things, many of which cost more than the mediocre. Another facility that has been in place since my teens is managing to choose things that are less expensive or inexpensive but appear to be the best.

I tried to convince my gramma of my seasoned reasoning and thrift as an adult on my own but she went to her grave after over one hundred years not believing for a second that I was a sensible, thoughtful, independent man immune to buying fits and getting conned out of money for meaningless trivia.

Although I was taught that the world owes me a living, I never believed that the world, nor anyone, owed me anything except love, politeness and, perhaps, true, viable care from a few individuals. That does not mean that I received any of these often, nor that I did not have problems accepting things, expecting them to be rescinded; it seemed that love, the bling-blings and success were taken back or had negative effects soon after they were given. I still am slightly uncomfortable when I am complimented, but no one but Diane knows that this is the truth.

My mom's book *Your Child Year By Year* was never finalized. She stopped making entries when I was about five. Did my family's actions and malfunctions contribute directly to my suicide attempt at twenty?

The catalyst for my drunken actions was betrayal, this by a dark, as Shakespeare would have it, lady who allegedly longed for love forever with me, then after achieving complete surrender from me, casually and speedily she moved on to someone else. Dear Karen. But I was on the road to self-perdition long before I met the mutually depressed and neurotic first Karen.

It was clear to me eventually that I had arrived at twenty being quickly successful in almost all things, achieving the *sine qua non* stardom at twelve, having friends and family, admirers and emulators, and smothering in a surfeit of things, yet I found love and life and bling-blings and success all hollow and useless. I also had a very bad habit of rejecting the very few things I was not good at immediately because I did not want to work at anything. I began changing that fault as soon as I became aware of it.

I am also resolved that the full half of my glittering bling-bling snifter from *Venezia* which I purchased there at eighteen is that I came to know at an early age that materialism is not only thoroughly overrated but it does not give you peace, nor health, nor happiness.

But my resurrection from this abyss of aloneness climaxing in a violent suicide attempt at twenty was preceded by a unique phenomenon that has followed me all of my life and will surely never let go even after my death. It contributed to my problems and depression and my dangerous, fortunately bungled, solution.

The onerous, uncaring businessmen who threatened me into the positive and negative legacy of stardom were particularly unpleasant on the Fiftieth Anniversary of the TV series' premiere in 2005. I felt attacked, hurt and mortified, which is one reason I have never revealed any of the following before now.

Chapter 7
Mickey Mouse Offer I Could Not Refuse

I was cast in *The Mickey Mouse Club* purely by chance—and then something that a person might refer to as hard ball, while the less politically correct might have the phrase force majeure at the tip of their thoughts.

By eleven I was in the ninth grade, having completed all of my three years ahead of the other kids' advancement prior to high school and was a veteran of show business in radio, film, TV, theatre, commercials and modeling. I had just filmed a role on *Father Knows Best*.

My dancing was very good for a boy going through the physical transitions of that age, adjusting to my body's constantly fluctuating spurts and changes. My singing was fine for a kid, on pitch, in time and a bit more interpretive than most eleven-year-olds, and my acting was solid and unaffected. I had four or five agents in my seven years of professional performing before *The Mickey Mouse Club*, but my mom decided to become a theatrical agent in 1952 and then added me to her list of clients. She had submitted me for one of the leads, Marty, in the *Spin & Marty* serial and I read against Tommy Kirk and others. When I did not get the role, my mom called Mitzi Stollery, Dave's mom, for he and I had competed for a number of roles that were similar to what was considered our type.

Peter Votrian was caged in this same type and when earlier I turned down the role of "The Ugly Duckling" in *Hans Christian Andersen*; he shaved his head and played it while I had a much smaller role in my weeks on the film. My mother and I refused to shave my beautiful blond locks not knowing what would replace them. I had red hair until three, then to reddish blond, then a very light blond color. The role did not lead Peter anywhere so, in hindsight, it was a wise decision. Thus, along with Votrian and Stollery, I was typecast as an intellectual, wealthy, snobbish boy, the Black Hat who is an antagonist of the White Hats: wonderful, all American, normal, not too smart, frequently overwhelmed by freckles, "real" kids—the Moochies, which we were not. I played Oliver Quimby, the intellectual, know-it-all next door neighbor on the early sitcom *The Ruggles* (1949-1952). I had my first recurring role as a foil for the two young, "real" twins of the Ruggles family and Oliver was very like Marty on the MMC *Spin and Marty* serial.

David was British and I was well spoken, he had red hair and I had blond hair, both of us would be required to wear glasses now and again which translated to being bookish, ergo, not a real kid. In film and TV this made us both sort of aliens, or character actors, in America in the '50s.

Neither my mother nor I have ever claimed any credit for Dave getting the role but we will never know if he would have been submitted or not without Mom's call and timing—the timing of when you are submitted can be everything in the business of show.

A number of guys were seen for the two leads in *Spin* but the Mouseketeer auditions were "cattle calls," the pejorative phrase still used for hundreds and hundreds of actors, dancers and/or singers vying for a role or roles sometimes for days, in this case weeks, and, in this instance, for amateurs, not professionals. I had been getting paid for acting or dancing and singing for seven years: commercial spokesboy for two years, child lead on a radio soap, recurring sitcom role and directed by Cecil B. DeMille.

I did not find out for sure until my mid-fifties that there was also a large pay gap—the Mouseketeers were to get $185 a week, SAG minimum. *Spin and Marty*, at least for Tim and Dave, were getting much more. We were told at a SAG meeting for the arbitration in the late 'nineties that they made $450, about $50 less than Annette made after receiving all the pay upgrades via six-month options at the end of her seven-year Mouseketeer contract, which is the same that we all signed the first season.

Annie was the only Mouse to complete all of the seven years with the studio. Subsequently I learned that the $450 was for the last filming of *Spin and Marty*, but they still started at a much higher rate than we did—and they could not sing or dance on or off horses. They shot a total of 76 episodes while we, at least according to Disney, shot 360 episodes, although no one was in every episode on the MMC. I can only assume that the kids on the serials and other non-Mouseketeer segments and the Mice hired for seasons two and three got residuals for six reruns built into their contract as we had in ours since SAG set the precedent with the first season Mouseketeers.

Walt's main project was Disneyland and he needed completion money for what some typically brilliant people in the industry called "Disney's Folly"; they did not know it would be a coup like "Seward's Folly," the U.S. acquisition of Alaska, and make them, rather than Walt, look foolish and small minded.

One of the reasons that Disney has lasted independently beyond the other major studios is its diversification: not just movies and the then-new medium television but parks and music and merchandise. Another reason is their concept, whether from Roy or Walt or both of them, of cross-pollinating, which by the 1980s was labeled "synergy," with the TV advertising the movies, merchandise, music, parks and, when possible, vice versa, like a plug for an upcoming movie or TV series on merchandise, at one or all of the parks. For instance, I taught Moochie, as a guest, how to tap dance on one segment of the MMC that was publicizing the upcoming release of the Disney flick *Westward Ho the Wagons* in which Kevin Corcoran (Moochie) played a role.

ABC was pleased with the successful "Disneyland" television hour Walt had premiered in 1954 so they gave him over $1.5 million to complete and open Disneyland on the condition he create a one-hour-a-day, five-day-a-week show for kids and early teens. The necessity for moola was the mother of the invention of *The Mickey Mouse Club*

The show was seminal in many ways such as the varied approach of the four segments per hour, showing kids AS THEMSELVES, growing up along with their buddies (the children watching), who were always included, and a unique use of the amazing new medium, television. It was not until the 1960 Presidential debates that the power of the tube began to be fully comprehended. In many ways taken beyond our series, *Sesame Street* accrued a lot of ideas from *The Mickey Mouse Club* and the producers and writers have acknowledged this.

More importantly, there were now identifiable kids who linked together with Mickey Mouse and the entire world of Walt Disney. Other shows at the time only had real kids in the "peanut gallery" or child actors hiding behind the identity of fictional characters on some sitcoms except for the occasional pro child guest on a variety show.

Our series quickly became the number one ratings hit and "completely dominated daytime TV" according to the Nielsen rating system. It knocked off other children's shows like *Howdy Doody* and was only beaten out by the World Series' numbers the first season according to Lorraine Santoli's 1995 book on the MMC.

The original MMC had four fifteen-minute entertainments: segment one was the Mouseketeers singing and dancing and exchanging dialogue in our five theme days of the week—Monday - Fun with Music Day; Tuesday - Guest Star Day; Wednesday - Anything Can Happen Day; Thursday - Circus Day and Friday - with the cowboy outfits, Talent Roundup Day.

Segment two was the didactic quarter with "newsreels" and short documentaries on animals, many of which were in the Disney library, and other material, some original and filmed for the series, that taught kids about things like life in different countries or in situations that they had not encountered such as living on a farm, celebrating Christmas in Thailand, seeing how schools operated in South America or how to become an airline stewardess.

The third format was a cartoon from the large Disney collection introduced by the Mouseketeers. The fourth segment showed original teen serials like *Spin and Marty* and *The Hardy Boys*. Although soap operas had been on radio for years and moved to television, none had been geared to kids and teenagers before. Other than the cartoons the segments of the MMC were all firsts: no one in television had yet created a group of kids like the Mouseketeers casually displaying their talents - and sometimes being caught on camera in mistakes due to the chockablock schedule—having fun as themselves and teaching children through entertainment in the new medium. All of this was original.

Since the Disney producers were not sure how to get that much "product" on screen at 5 hours a week for 44 weeks even with the plethora of cartoons, it was decided they would hire 24 kids (plus four fired early on) the first season. The total for the three years we filmed was 39 children ranging in age from 8 to 15, not counting the many child actors and adults on the segments other than the Mouseketeers. The show was an hour format for the first two seasons then cut to a half-hour in the third year losing Guest Star Day, Anything Can Happen Day and Circus Day. The serials and the Mouseketeers' Fun With Music and Talent Roundup were alternated and a Mousecartoon or a short newsreel appeared here and there. The third season was much less of a hurry, hurry panic. The fourth season reran episodes culled from the first two years and made into two segments for the same half-hour airing.

The MMC premiered on October 3, 1955, the same day as *Captain Kangaroo*, starring Bob Keeshan, who was formerly the first of three Clarabelle the Clowns on *Howdy Doody*. The original MMC first re-

Mickey Mouse Offer I Could Not Refuse 119

played in re-cut half hours in syndication in the 'sixties; then in the 'seventies, prompting a short-lived MMC 2, *The New Mickey Mouse Club*; and again from 1983-89 to lead off The Disney Channel, which brought forth a third version called by some the "no Ears" MMC from 1989-1995. Finally (perhaps), the original MMC's last run was 1995 to September 2002 on "Vault Disney," again on the Disney Channel. Currently there are rumors of plans for a fourth version of the Club and there is a possibility it will be one of the series Disney has mentioned that will be run online along with the serials.

An interesting note is that Dick Clair and Jenna McMahon, who are in my 20th century comedy team book representing teams that moved from performing to writing, wrote for *The Facts of Life*, a sitcom that starred the only kid to make it after the '70s second version of the MMC: Lisa Whelchel. Everyone knows that the 1989-1995 third version brought us the fine young actors Ryan Gosling and Keri Russell as well as Justin Timberlake, Christina Aguilera, J.C. Chasez and the notorious Britney Spears.

Nine of us original Mouseketeers lasted the entire filming: Annette, Karen, Sharon, Doreen, Darlene and Cubby, Tommy, Bobby and me. Cheryl did not make the cut in year one but was cast for the last two seasons and is frequently included in our group because she made more of an impact than those on for one season or, for that matter, the only other Mouse on for two seasons, Dennis Day, who is not related to the tenor Dennis Day who sang on *The Jack Benny Show*.

The Mice first appeared on TV on July 17, 1955 on the television special for the opening of Disneyland with all 24 of us riding in a parade on Main Street and later doing a Talent Roundup dance and song, some in our cowboy outfits, which included me, and some in our ears, short sleeve turtle necks and slacks or skirts. Our first roll call and the number were performed outside in Fantasyland in front of what was then the Mickey Mouse Club Theatre, which later became the Fantasyland Theatre. It was the only roll call in which all the Mouseketeers were included.

The three hosts of the special were Robert Cummings, Art Linkletter and some B-movie actor named Ronald Reagan. Linkletter was there again for Disneyland's 50th Anniversary on July 17, 2005 and that evening I exchanged dialogue, danced and sang for about twelve minutes, along with three other original Mice, in a much longer, already rehearsed, live Disneyland Anniversary show for a private audience. The four of us received the only standing ovation.

For the 50th Anniversary of Disneyland they completely refurbished Walt's apartment, above the Fire Station as you enter Main Street, to its state on July 17, 1955. I signed the Disneyland Distinguished Guest book in 1955 and again in 2005 joining Presidents, stars and foreign rulers.

The MMC was canceled after the fourth season, allegedly because ABC demanded more commercials and Walt refused. There is much conjecture about this studio version of what happened. The numbers on the audience had fallen off and despite the studio line Walt was never as involved, nor interested, in the MMC as he was in Disneyland, his now more diverse and much larger Walt Disney World, which was already in the planning stages, and ongoing or future animation projects and films. You will hear disclaimers to the contrary and, indeed, Walt did not personally confide in me, but a little common sense and first-hand experience will yield this conclusion.

It is true that the only real criticism of the show among the stellar reviews the first season was that there were too many commercials that indoctrinated kids into holding their moms hostage at stores, visions of sugar-coated logos prancing in their heads. Even though the ratings had dropped the fans were still there, which would explain the first syndication of the show in 1962, only three years after the demise of the original series in 1959, and beyond the grasp of ABC which leads me to speculate that Walt felt too confined by his literal ties to the network which, ironically, Disney now owns.

The series completely captured the first Baby Boomers, before they garnered that label, was translated into five languages and played in eighteen foreign countries, which is one reason there is a Disneyland in Tokyo and another park in Paris. The longest first run was twelve years straight in Australia; France was second with seven years.

The kids were a varied lot and unusual at the time because on the surface we seemed to be all white, middle-class kids, but we were actually more diverse than almost all TV shows in 1955 even though black and Asian children, sometimes accompanied by adults, only appeared as performers on Talent Roundup Day.

There were distinctly ethnic types, like Annette, which was not the norm and even two Hispanics on the first season: Mary Espinosa and Dickie Dodd (no relation to Jimmie) whereas everyone else on TV was white-bread (unless you make a case for an American-Armenian adult, Danny Thomas, or the rarity of crooning Nat King Cole or the Indian organist Korla Pandit in the afternoon). Annie and some others were Catholic and there were three or more Jewish kids, including Doreen, on the MMC.

Mom took this snapshot when Annie and her boyfriend at the time were signing autographs in 1955.

People forget that JFK was said to be unable to win the presidency in 1960 because he was a Catholic. The film exposing anti-semitism, *The Man in the Gray Flannel Suit*, came out in 1956. America in the '50s had obvious prejudices and they were not confined to the South. There were no black kids at HPS, nor in my neighborhood. Even more liberal and progressive show business cast minorities stereotypically. Why else did Rita Hayworth (Margerita Carmen Cansino) and Anthony Quinn (Antonio Rondolfo Quinn Oaxaca) change their names to disguise their ethnicity and black actors play only maids, butlers and other banal, Stepin Fechit characters?

The national furor over desegregation when Supreme Court Justice Earl Warren struck down the "separate but equal" doctrine in the Brown v. The Board of Education of Topeka, Kansas decision was only announced in May, 1954. Not much later one Governor was toying with the idea of defying federal troops. Then one did.

The first black and Asian Mouseketeers showed up on the '70s *The New Mickey Mouse Club*. The original MMC pushed the postcard along but it was not an ethnically ground breaking series.

Annie Funicello was seen by Walt at a ballet recital and she was the only Mouse cast by the main man. She was also the single Mouseketeer who became a star as a child and as an adult. I am sure this was because Walt sensed in her an unusual quality. I did, too.

Since I was established in the business—in show business you do not go back but only move upward—my unique accident after eschewing the "cattle call" for the Club came from a phone call from another mother of a child performer to my mom. I was rushed down to the Capitol Recording studio on Melrose a block from Paramount to sing songs for a kid who had to be replaced immediately at a record session. One of my Mouseketeer colleagues has been claiming a similar story now for a couple of decades but it actually happened to me.

I believe it to be a pre-recording of the first MMC record but I have no distinct memory of the songs or the lyrics. I quickly rehearsed and sang along with the other kids and one adult, Jimmie Dodd. When we wrapped up, Jimmie asked me if I also danced and acted and I responded, "Actually, I act and dance better than I sing."

I was given a private audition, avoiding the hordes of amateurs. My mom/agent and I figured having a pro audition on the Disney lot, getting seen and found being 99% of the battle before you achieve more than a chance at day player bits, would not hurt for future submissions even if it was for a low paying role in a small mob that I most likely would not take if cast, so we grabbed it. I happened to be up for a lead in another series, but this was sound showbiz practice.

I went to an office on the second floor of the Animation Building on Dopey Drive, across from the theatre inside the studio, and entered a small room, accompanied by my mom the agent. I sang and danced for Jimmie, Hal Adelquist, who we were told was an Associate Producer but the Disney people later described as a General Coordinator, and Bill Walsh the Producer, who today would be the Executive Producer and main mover on the project or the guy just under Walt. It went well. They contacted my agent/mom a week later and asked me to sign a seven-year contract.

I was simultaneously up against Johnny Washbrook for the solo child lead in *My Friend Flicka*. In this series the pay was much more, I believe somewhere between $500 and $750 a week, and you did not have to compete with 23 other kids, there was just you, the character's mom and dad and a horse.

Mom and I agreed to refuse the Disney offer and it did not help that no one knew for sure what in the hell the neologism a "Mouseketeer" was going to turn out to be; in truth, it sounded a bit goofy to me—sorry about that. In addition, I had my own horse and had ridden since I was eight. Being a cowboy was definitely cooler than being a mousey something or other.

My mom called Lee Traver who was casting along with Jack Lavin, and told him we declined to sign. Traver then told her that if I did not sign I would be black-balled and would "never work in Hollywood again." Her agency and all of her other clients would also become *persona non grata*, according to Traver.

Mom the agent was as angry as Mom the mom, but the former was cautious; she did not know what to do and she discussed it with me. We were both frightened of the threat. Although not the behemoth they are now, Disney was still one of the six major studios, along with MGM, Warner Bros., 20th Century Fox, Goldwyn and Universal. It was an old boys' private club and the reverberations of McCarthy and blacklisting were facts of showbiz life by then. Writers could write under different names, but actors had no alternative except overwhelming plastic surgery or finding a new profession.

So I signed on as Mouseketeer Lonnie and never ever discussed this threat with anyone but my family and those few very close to my life. I certainly never alluded to it in anything I have written since the late 'sixties when I was first published, nor on any of the nearly one hundred national and local TV and radio talk shows, print interviews, live and internet interviews I have done in the last fifty plus years.

I wrote my mom in 1999 to confirm this one last time as well as asking for some earlier addresses I had lived at while a child; it never hurts to corroborate memory. My mom had multiple sclerosis for over forty years before her death but she was stabilized after the first six or seven years, which also was the time it had taken numerous doctors correctly diagnose the disease. Unlike Annie's more common progressive MS, Dot retained her ability to walk but was unable to use her right hand, arm and leg, which she had to drag behind her. As a result of her MS, mom typed and signed letters with her faltering left hand. Mom wrote in April, 1999: "I will answer a little of what you asked several months ago. First, it was big, old, fat Traver that told me you would be blackballed if you took *Flicka*, but I should have taken it." (see Appendix)

Signing the seven-year contract under these circumstances was a very damaging experience for me in many ways.

When by the second season I seemed to be boxed into being just one more Mouseketeer, although always in the big or harder dance numbers, and watched other Mice, who had no experience as actors, do roles on the serials and hosting newsreels when I was not even asked to read for them, I was depressed and unhappy.

Along with Sharon and Bobby, I was always considered one of the three best dancers out of the 39 kids even though I was much younger than Bob and a year younger than Sharon. But Annie got her own series, Darlene got hers, they both cut albums, and a number of Mice were on the sequel to *Spin and Marty, The Annette Series* and others did their parts and narration as well as appearances for the newsreels. Four were cast in the feature *Westward Ho The Wagons!*

In hindsight the MMC was a unique phenomenon that everyone remembers in one way or another, from cartoonist Gary Larson to filmmaker Stanley Kubrick in *Full Metal Jacket* to John Updike in his Rabbit Angstrom novels. Even Elvis sang one of our songs which is on CD. The original MMC is a favorite childhood memory of many millions, which I find very flattering and pleasing even though I am just one part of it. The show seems to represent much better times to almost anyone who saw it originally or in reruns.

There is no way to know if I would have beaten out Johnny, who got *Flicka*, but not a lot of people have recollections of that horse opera, which had a short run. So the frightening force used against us worked in my favor over the long haul, which is positive. The opposite possibility would be that *Flicka* could have been more of a hit with me in the role or it at least might have led me to another series or a significant movie role subsequently instead of becoming type cast as a tapping boy with ears as opposed to a solid young adult actor when I returned to the business in

Looking for acting work, 1968.

my early twenties. The last is not probable but in the entertainment industry possible is a very meaningful word.

After being myself as a Mouseketeer it was difficult to be cast as this character or that character. After receiving my M.A. in theatre arts in February, 1964 I returned to the business in 1965 and was Mouse pre-cast. I could still sing and dance well but I was intent on an acting career.

One or two of the girls had some success after the series, particularly Cheryl, but she had not left the marketplace and she was a beautiful young woman blooming. I was not and I had disappeared for over six years, which, in show business, is like being dead for six years. The same thing happened when Diane and I moved to the Maryland/D.C. area in 1998 and then moved back to California—*not* living in the Valley, which is a major reason we moved—but to the beach city San Clemente which is an hour-and-a-half south of Hollywood and the Valley.

That does not mean that I absolve Mr. Traver of guilt, nor any others that might have been involved with my being forced to do the series as a result of his threats. No one had any idea of the long life and enormous effect of this germinal children's television series. It is impossible now to deduce if someone above Traver was calling the shots but casting people did not have the same power they have had for about three decades.

Nor does it mean that I carry this around with me, for I left off being concerned about it decades ago. Like the other Mice, I made the lesser salary, as opposed to Johnny W's take or the larger pay and residuals of the boys that shot *Spin* out at the ranch, but the Mouseketeers had and have many more fans than Tim, Dave and Johnny.

The world could not believe that people would want to see shows for decade after decade, generation after generation. One original core member avers in interviews now that our six run residuals were a gift from those wonderful folks at Disney rather than something fought for by SAG. Even though experienced in the business, she fails to grasp that this is about as likely as you and your family getting into one of the Parks for free. It is show BUSINESS, not show magnanimity.

The residuals were the issue that Disney defeated when SAG brought an arbitration against them in the late 'nineties even though they had paid us beyond sixth run for the 'seventies and 'eighties usage, although they were not major amounts.

Prior to that, I was inevitably the Mouseketeer who contacted the Guild to point out the date and use of film from the MMC, for reruns after the 'sixties syndication in the 'seventies, 'eighties and 'nineties and for retrospective TV specials and other programs compiled from the original series. I note that not one of the Mouseketeers has ever thanked me, nor inquired about the checks—when I got paid every other Mouse in the clip or segment got paid.

This also occurred when we made a few appearances not under Disney's management, like in this century at Flicks Gallery, a company that used to sell Disney items just outside of Chicago. I got us all more money and a tiny cut of a totally new item they made for our appearance; not only was I not thanked by the others, but Flicks excluded me from the Mouseketeers' next two appearances. After meeting the other Mice I assume they concluded no one would negotiate like professionals as I had. None of my Mouseketeer buddies protested my exclusion.

When our series returned for a fourth time in 1995 and many actors in television were making a solid living off of residuals, even though ours would have been miniscule comparatively, Disney decided to spend the millions necessary to permanently stop this intrusion on their earning potential, hence, the arbitration.

After all, Disney, according to their showbiz accounting, never made a penny off the MMC nor the merchandising, which has numbered in the hundreds daily on eBay since its inception. Hollywood accounting is known for writing the net as being eaten up by costs, hence, nothing is forthcoming to anyone but our 2.5% was of the GROSS, in which accounting cannot massage things. The studio still puts out new merchandise in 2009, and most likely will in the future, that relates to our original *Mickey Mouse Club* from which we get no cut either.

Why they have seemingly never done very well at all on those hundreds of millions of Ears! Fess Parker once confided to me that Walt had given him a piece of the coonskin caps that sold almost as well as hula hoops. That is how he started his wise business investments. On the surface, it appears that the Ears the Mouseketeers are known for wearing, which Roy Williams took from an early Mickey film in which he tips the top of his head with the ears, like a hat, to Minnie Mouse, have no relationship to the kids who made wearing them a national pastime. It is a miracle that the various Disney enterprises, which earn billions on a yearly basis, have survived at all.

All of our seven-year contracts were kaput after 1958 except Annie's. She later sued to be freed from her contract. When she was working for other studios, like the beach movies and TV appearances, Disney would negotiate high salaries to loan her out and then only have to pay her the minimal amount accrued, somewhere in the area of $500 or less a week, since she was still tied to the Mouseketeer signing.

She lost the suit, but later won her freedom with a second suit that most likely had something to do with her first husband who was a somewhat powerful agent who handled such stars as Telly Savalas (*Kojak*). It was and is almost impossible to even bring, let alone win a contractual suit against Disney but being a star linked to a name agency has its advantages.

As to our 2.5 % of the gross on merchandising in the original contract, which was blocked by the confines of the arbitration, this huge lack of payments has never been looked at, nor challenged.

Another example of the Disney business ethic is characterized by Tommy Cole's situation in 1956. He was fired after the first season due to his clumsiness as a dancer. He immediately took numerous classes with the first-year choreographer, auditioned a second time for season two and was hired back, becoming one of the four boys surviving for the entire filming. Instead of getting the contractual bump up the other nine of us did (which includes Dennis for his second and last season), Tom returned making the same $185 as he did on the first season as he averred on more than one occasion.

I ran into Johnny Washbrook in Manhattan at a Broadway audition in the early 'seventies and we exchanged friendly hellos and conversation. I was still recognized as a Mouseketeer by many even before the third series of reruns whereas no one associated John with *Flicka*, which only ran one season shooting 39 episodes, unless someone told them or he put it on his resume. I excluded the MMC from my resume since the association had stymied me for more than three years when I returned to acting for a living in the mid-sixties.

Lee Traver later moved to casting at MGM and used me in the film *Live A Little, Love A Little* starring Elvis Presley in 1968. No mention of the coercion ever came up, as it has not until this writing. He knew I could easily do the role in the Presley movie and perhaps he felt guilty.

Despite working with and being around stars seemingly all of my life, it was fun working with the King. Elvis was not constantly surrounded by a retinue of hangers on, was in good shape and in no way appeared to be using drugs or booze. Elvis had striking jet black hair which, given Hollywood, was unfortunately augmented with dye so that every single hair was unnaturally the blackest of black and although we all had makeup on—I have refused makeup as an actor except to alter my age or to attain a large visual change for over two decades to achieve a more real look—he had a great complexion, too.

Elvis and I jived off camera, particularly when we did a scene in which another young actor and I entered the inevitable, huge party scene inside the house and by the pool, had dialogue, and then Elvis came into frame and the camera tracked him through the bikinis.

I liked Elvis. He did not seem negatively affected by his enormous stardom. It was clear he knew he was the man, the star, and that women were constantly drooling, but he did not make a big deal of it, nor project an attitude that many in his position, usually much more forgettable stars, are guilty of displaying. This would appear to have changed later before his desperate times and untimely death but I saw no signs of trouble.

Ignoring all my angst in 1955, I arrived on the Disney lot and we started rehearsing and learning what was expected of us. There were twelve boys and twelve girls and we each had a mother or guardian, required by law, on the lot with us all day. The adults were quickly rounded up and told that except for lunch they were to stay in the lobby of the Burbank studio's screening theatre across from the Animation Building. There were long couches there, immediate male/female lounge access and chairs and tables were brought in to accommodate them.

After some experience with stage moms and the rare stage dads like Mr. Gillespie, Disney was not going to have parents or protectors on set or at rehearsals obnoxiously promoting their kid's abilities and need for more screen time and bigger roles or at least one more line. They chatted and played cards but the majority knitted or crocheted. I don't think Mr. Gillespie knitted; he was not football great Rosie Grier. We would join them for lunch in the cafeteria and then after our hour off we went back to our school trailer, rehearsal or to refresh makeup before shooting.

Dik Darley, by whom I had been directed when I did a commercial on *Space Patrol* years before, was our first year director. He was an easy-going guy who looked and dressed a bit like Johnny Carson and he maintained his cool in spite of the challenge of dealing with twenty-four kids, twenty-two of whom were amateurs who frequently found it difficult to pay attention, remember their lines, dance steps or lyrics and to not jabber incessantly. Only Sharon and I were vets and knew the drill.

Darley's first and second ADs, Assistant Directors, who had to coordinate everything and had to find and get everyone on the set and ready to shoot and much more were constantly sweating profusely and looking as if wolves were snapping at their heels (or loftier body parts) as they sought missing and unruly kids.

Bill Beaudine, Jr., the First AD, was the most berserk and beset; his father, William Beaudine, Sr. directed *Spin and Marty* the first season, dropping out due to illness part way through the second year. Beaudine, Sr. also directed the Mouseketeers, Dali moustache in tow, for a TV special on Mickey's 40th birthday in 1968 in which I appeared with some other original Mice. The original MMC credits list Erich von Stroheim, Jr., presumably the son of the early film director, as an AD whom I do not remember, but AD Vince McVeety directed me decades later on a *Hunter* episode. The Oscar winning screenwriter and famous, prolific novelist Sterling Silliphant is listed as a production supervisor but he actually came up with the "What I Want To Be" segments, the first on Airline pilots and Air hostesses but it got a lukewarm reception and Disney fired him and cancelled that series on the MMC.

Much has been made of the fact that there was never any swearing on the sound stage because of the kids. I did hear a muttered "damn" or "hell" or "shit" now and then, but it was pretty tame for any show business venue. People in the business have a tendency to be profane but whether it is a way to relax in a stressful situation or because they are artists and different from everyone else, or some other reason I have not an inkling.

Once there was a sign when we came onstage and it was a joke given that Darley spelled his name Dik instead of the more common Dick. The sign read: DIK IS A PRK. Many of us got it, of course, and while it was not like listening to the offensive rhymes of oxymoronic rap music things were not as pure as Bambi's undriven snow, as other Mice describe it.

Sidney Miller thought I was terrific on The Colgate Comedy Hour; *but that is not the way he acted on the MMC.*

The first choreographer, Burch Holtzman, was a dour-faced, unpleasant woman who could have been related to Mrs. Burke except for her pedestrian steps and combinations. She may have been the inspiration for what passes as tediously simple and recurring over and over again choreography—hands up, kick; hands down, wink—at Disneyland and the other Parks. None of her dances impressed me and I fear she was irrevocably damaged in her youth by Martha Graham. Realizing it was a show for kids, to me the dialogue was still very boring.

I do not know how Sharon presented herself because she had done a lot of dancing on TV and in films, but she had very few outings as a character and has never really been an actress. Although I danced and sang when a paying job came up, I considered myself ostensibly an actor who *also* sang and danced very well. It always helped to be a triple threat. Even though Walt stated he wanted no showbiz kids, Sharon and I somehow slipped under their screening process. While researching for this book, I have also found online that two or three of the original group seemed to have done one or two appearances for pay.

Dik, who was not a prk, was replaced the second year by Sidney Miller whom I found to be a prk. He had started in the biz as a kid and partnered with Donald O'Connor in movies and other venues and was a vaudevillian type jokester, who could sort of carry a tune and danced as what dancers call a mover, in that he was not good but could fake simple staging. He seemed constantly harried and irascible, possibly because it was his first job directing. He did not seem to like kids and I certainly did not like him and avoided him whenever possible, even though I had his autograph from a *Colgate* I had done with him and Don O'Connor in the early '50s.

Cubby has said that he just laughed at Sid because he was so outrageous and overbearing but Cub was not a pro performer, nor an actor—he was a drummer and just moved on to the next measure. Musicians are always a little different than the rest of us. I took rude criticism personally. I made sure I always did the best job I could and it hurt and exasperated me when Miller gave me an unnecessarily bad time, sometimes for something that was not a mistake of mine, but of his.

We were dancing in a Swiss number once and the guys had to wear weird hats with large feathers and appalling leather lederhosen shorts festooned with edelweiss and other crap. I was partnered with Sharon and we were always one of the front couples. We started the number and

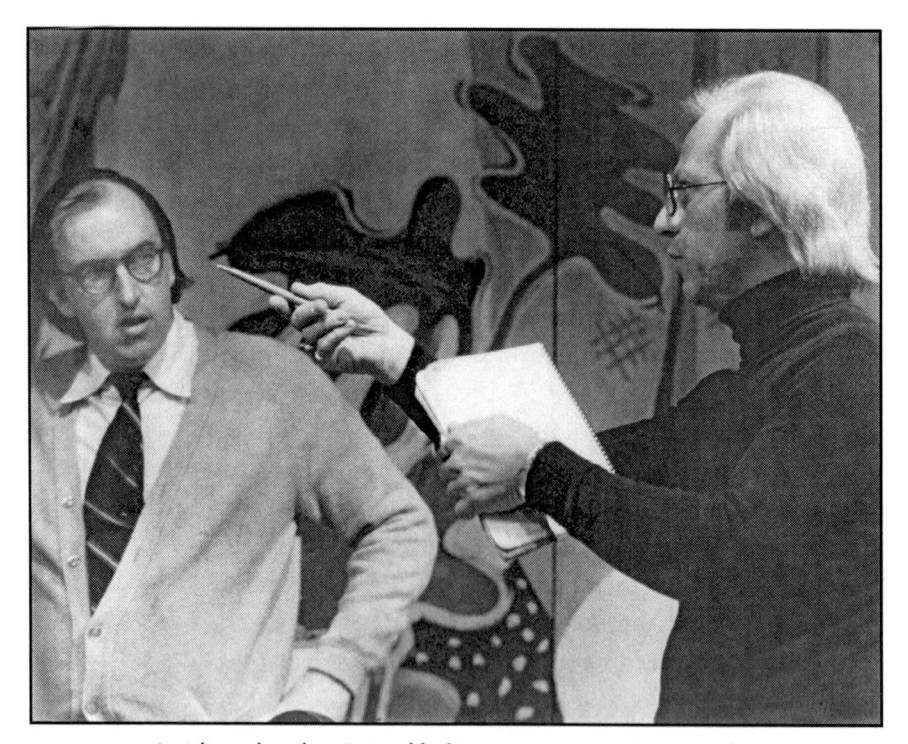

Avoiding absurdity, I give blocking notes to actor Britt Leach in
The Bald Soprano, *1978.*

my pants ripped from the bottom of the zipper to the waistband in the rear. I was mortified that my underpants were showing on camera and Sid did not even notice!

Despite my embarrassment, I finished the take but when I came over after Miller called, "Cut!" he was dismissive. When I persisted and he actually listened to what had happened, he was extremely angry and acted as if I had done something awful and on purpose to him personally as well as ruining a take. He was not a nice man and he should never have been directing kids, pro or amateur.

Decades later I shot a short-lived TV show, *Equal Justice*, which had such young actors as the aloof and self-consumed Sarah Jessica Parker before she became a television star on cable. A somewhat odd-looking young regular named Miller played an Assistant D.A. in all of my scenes as a detective. When I inquired if his dad had directed me on the MMC he conceded that it was a fact but that he wanted nothing to do with discussing the man. I understood his point of view and even where he got his ill-mannered attitude.

I'm giving Cubby advice in 1956 at the Burbank (Bob Hope) airport before we depart on a personal appearance tour with other Mice.

Choreo Burch was replaced on season two also and the new Balanchine was an openly gay guy, not the norm in 1956, named Tom Mahoney. He terrorized the Disney lot by wearing loose slacks and no underwear so he could move "more freely"; thus, his penis swung around very openly. He probably would have been fired today since he had other habits that would now be considered inappropriate for children.

When on the sound stage recording once he was singing on the track with Tommy and me and was between us on one microphone. He had his arms around our shoulders and kept pinching our nipples, which neither of us cared for. It was not erotic, or at least did not seem so, and we kept hitting his hands away, but nobody seemed to care or notice.

He was a much better dancer and choreographer than Burch and he restricted his nipple pinching, with me at least, to that one occasion, so there was a definite positive side to our dance routines which pleased me. Numbers like "A Whale of a Sailor" that I did in a sailor costume with the two eldest boy Mice, Larry and Bobby, were much more complex and rewarding to do.

Then there was Annette.

I turned twelve after we had just started working on the series and had been dating girls for some time. I was going into the tenth grade in September, having completed my quick scholastic ascension prior to that year and I was as lasciviously inclined as Cubby, three years my junior, but I was more socially subtle and restrained than he was, keeping my romantic moves private. Given his nine-year-old cutes he got away with sexual mayhem.

Cubby had not dated yet but he would innocently but coyly fall or lean into and, if possible, accidentally touch or grab a developing breast and/or ass of the little girls who would slap his hand, giggle and *not* tell their moms. The first Mouseketeer Bonni of two Mice with the same first name comes to mind as one of his accommodating prey. There were also two Dons and two Marys in the three years we filmed but never the same season, which is why Dallas' replacement by his brother John Lee made him Mouseketeer Lee due to the conflict with Mouseketeer Johnny Crawford in season one.

Annie and me on the cover of the November, 1957 Children's Playmate Magazine.

Many girls were careful when the tiny drummer's digits were close by and Cub sagely restricted himself to the older girls who would not turn him in. It reminded me of my much younger accidental falls to pursue visions of femininity. I swear I never did that as a Mouseketeer. Maybe Cubby did that too and I just missed it.

I looked over the twelve ladies and immediately focused on Annie. I was in love, pursued her and after a few weeks she fell in love with me. Our romance lasted most of the first season and through the Disneyland Circus gig from November, 1955 through part of January, 1956, but then she moved on to crushes on adults, like one of the cameramen and then Guy Williams, the actor who played *Zorro* for Disney. I returned to girlfriends outside the show, although I did have some minor romantic involvements with other Mouseketeer girls due to propinquity, desire, a demanding schedule and hormones on the prowl!

Annie and I actually went steady! I presented her with my ring on a gold chain at a Mouseketeer party. She accepted it, put it around her neck and all the girls began screeching and running about as they whispered to others and celebrated this racy item. HEY—it was 1955!

Unfortunately, Annette's dad Joe found out and the ring and chain were returned forthwith. If car mechanic's looks could kill, I never would have seen thirteen.

I was very happy that Annie was very caring in mentioning our romance in interviews for her autobiography in the 'nineties. I learned from reading her book that I was her first love and gave her her first kiss. There has never been an era in which young girls or young boys announced such a thing to their very first love. I have never alluded to the fact that it was by far not my first kiss, nor my first love, for that would have been rude and ungentlemanly.

I believe that I inferred something about this lady before anyone else except maybe Walt. Despite her success as a child and adult acting star and vocalist, Annie always maintained that she was not the best actor, not the best singer, not the best dancer. She was talented, of course, but she is honest and correct in that assessment. What she has always been is charismatic.

This overused and misused word charisma is something that very few people can actually claim. Annie entered a room and everyone noticed and gravitated to her, just as the camera has done for all of her life. It does not hurt to be beautiful but charismatic goes beyond beauty and does not necessarily require it. Humphrey Bogart was not hand-

The doctor was one of my roles in 42nd Street, *1983-84.*

some, nor was Fanny Brice beautiful but they were both charismatic. I think Walt recognized this quality as Annette danced in the ballet chorus and that is why he wanted her on the screen for his new children's show.

Annette was the "it" girl, America's sweetheart, for the 'fifties and 'sixties and some subsequent years. I discovered in my twenties that I was driven to her just before turning twelve for that ineffable quality and I feel fortunate to have been a small part of her growing up. I am also the only Mouseketeer to work in front of a camera with her as an adult. Until her illness precluded it, Annie did join us for some appearances at WDW and Disneyland.

She and Martin Mull starred in a made for TV movie titled *Lots of Luck*. I played a pivotal character as Sid the newsstand guy where she buys the winning lottery ticket. I was doing a principal role in *42nd Street* in the L.A. company and if we shot late my understudy went on for me.

More importantly, I beat out Paul Anka and millions of red-blooded American boys not to mention infatuated young fellows from eighteen other countries!

Our gig in the circus at Disneyland, after wrapping the first season, added additional time to our normal work week because it took more than an hour to drive from the valley to Anaheim and another hour back at night. Normally we had three hours of school five days a week and homework which made up for time we missed in regular school and a sixth full day with no classes. The series shooting, personal appearances and the Circus cut us out of our school social life and neighborhood friendships, playing sports, going to parties and just about everything else.

It also affected our eating habits since lunch was at the cafeteria on Mickey Avenue or you brought it in a bag, which I was not about to do. The saving joy of home-cooked meals was not really something I could look forward to when I got home either—my mom had discovered frozen dinners. Mom was never much of a cook except for simple, salty, over-cooked southern dishes like fried chicken and dumplings, ham and lima beans, damn near cremated steaks and mashed potatoes, but now she got home from the studio or her office and merely popped a frozen dinner into the oven. The worst was the bland, limp turkey, miserable mushy dressing along with acrid gravy, wrinkled, overwrought peas and pasty mashed potatoes. My dad was inconvenienced greatly by this practice, too, and objected loudly at least once a week.

While shooting the series a kid's life was totally on hold except for the hiatus time in which we were not working, nor paid. Since our contract guaranteed twenty-two weeks of pay out of twenty-six for each six-month option, they made damn sure we were used all twenty-two weeks and all six days, which gave rise to our performances in the Disneyland Circus. Our work also involved promotional or publicity appearances and road trips, but the most time off we got was eight weeks a year. My memory is that these few weeks were never during summer but always when I had to go back to school five full days a week.

After we finished the first season I embarked on my short and only circus experience as an employee and it was definitely not by choice. I liked

Mom's snapshot of Cubby, Karen, Doreen, Lonnie and Darlene losing in the Kentucky Derby, 1956.

The Greatest Show on Earth as a child audience member, but not as an adult. The sometimes humorless, sometimes hilarious clowns, the death-defying aerialists, the ladies in revealing outfits, the beautiful but terrifying large cats, even the seemingly controlled tawdriness of the environment no longer pleased me, maybe as a result of propinquity at twelve.

In addition to our mandatory pay weeks, Walt's love of circuses, calliopes and carousels that were added onto a traveling circus were surely the motivation for this venture as well as to make sure our pay was not wasted and to both enhance the Park and our own show for fans—Disney synergy in action.

I learned things about this milieu that I never knew. The smells of the animals and the feel of the big top was nothing like DeMille strutting around in his jodhpurs on the set of *The Greatest Show on Earth*. The fake film circus sets were, at least in some ways, more like a real circus. I found that riding on an elephant's or camel's back was fun, but their long, tough hairs would poke through most costumes or clothes and hurt. And the camels sometimes spit at you. YUCK!

I gained insight into the toughness of cowboys from owning a horse as a kid. I have always found it something other than coincidental that I read for Marty, who could not ride, and I was one of the few kids who owned a horse, rode well and did not get cast in *Spin and Marty*. Real cowboys are rough. In addition to knowing Rex, the cowboy who managed the Hollywood stable where I kept my horse, I took a date dancing one weekend with my mom and dad at Corriganville, owned and named for cowboy star "Crash" Corrigan. A lot of westerns were filmed there in the then-undeveloped northwest San Fernando Valley. The men *and* the women were rough-edged and tough.

The circus people, men and women, were the same as these very dangerous cowboys and how I imagine Hell's Angels and other cycle gangsters are. Trust me, none of these three groups are people a sane person ever wants to offend, nor be near anywhere, anytime. We never returned to dance at Corriganville.

Perhaps the atmosphere was an additional motivation for the only known Mouseketeer fistfight to occur during our filming for it was at the circus location behind Fantasyland.

I enjoyed the long drive to our circus interlude because, as Annie wrote, we sat in the back seat and furtively held hands and occupied ourselves with conversation and other young love pursuits which were much more enjoyable on the ride home in the dark of the night.

We opened in the Circus on November 5, 1955 and closed on January 10, 1956. They were 75-minute shows but only about ten minutes involved the Mouseketeers performing our semi-aerialist act; before our act we joined the opening costume parade with everyone else. Jimmie did more as the ringmaster as did Bob Amsberry as Bob-O the clown in full makeup who was on the cover of the show's program. I heard of Cubby and Karen doing a small bit with one of the cat acts—Keller was the name I believe—but I never saw it and I have no idea what Roy did as the Strong Man other than appear in the parade.

My only real buddy during the show was Mouseketeer Tommy Cole. He would stay over at my house and I at his. One time I was taking a bath at his place and he somehow opened the locked door and came in with a bucket of ICE COLD WATER which he threw on me as I pleaded for clemency. His mom, June, laughed uproariously in the hall.

This amusing—but not to me then—practical joke was a mini-betrayal that later registered big time as the actual thing after I returned from living in New York and Diane and I became close friends with Tom and his wife Aileen, and their adopted kids, Lindsey and Casey. Tommy's betrayals continued and became too substantive to take ever again, but during the show we were buddies.

Friends in 1955 (and before and after) did argue and I had a very quick tongue, a mandatory defense mechanism that I had developed without malice aforethought at a young age. Being around older guys, having my blond hair and good looks, as well as being intellectual and talented, caused lots of problems.

It particularly offended Darlene because I inevitably beat her verbally. She had a constant need for attention and daily performed her club act, usually starting with her tedious Ed Sullivan imitation, which she actually used on one or two of our Mouse segments. She got extremely distressed when she was not the center of attention that she obsessively demanded. I believe this to be the main reason we did not get along as kids on the series. As an adult her desperate necessity for all eyes present and the limelight continued and seemed to grow so that she became crushed by anyone who was not mesmerized by her patter or singing or anything. When I was forced to be around her, inevitably by Disney appearances, I said little and stayed away as much as possible, but it was always unpleasant. I never want to be in her presence if I can avoid it and I assiduously have followed that precaution.

Besides, my defensive, aggressive humor was really only kidding but it was more like a pint-sized Don Rickles than Red Skelton for I have always had a knack for seeing people's vulnerabilities and if they aggressed against me I aggressed right back and enough so that they would think twice before repeating their attack.

Meanwhile, back at the Circus, I was "chopping" Tom, the term then used for brittle, sardonic exchanges—more current versions go, "Yo' Momma is so…"—in the dressing room, which was a medium-size tent with the boys separated on one side and the girls on the other and both about thirty feet from the back entrance flap to our much larger one-ring circus tent.

Tommy was getting flummoxed and red in the face so he ordered me to knock it off. I surely had touched on, among other sore points, his pitch pipe. He was mainly a singer and he constantly went around carrying and blowing into a round, plastic pitch pipe, annoying everyone, including musicians. It also made a strange bulge in his pants which I frequently referred to: "Is that your pitch pipe, Thomas, or are you just glad to see me?"

Stealing from Mae West was not only done by Milton Berle.

Bulges in the pants were a constant threat for boys our age, particularly when we ended a number with our crotches thrust against the girl's bums, which was far too often. Somehow, it never seemed to bother Dennis.

Tommy would compulsively whip out his prop and toot away for no reason whatsoever. I did not desist in my jibes and he pushed me. Not being a big fan of the fight game but understanding the gauntlet brandished, I pushed back despite his being older by close to three years and heavier.

We then proceeded to push back and forth for a minute or two: I pushed then he pushed, he pushed then I pushed, and finally Cubby said, "If you guys are going to do that then why don't you get out of the dressing room."

So we exited the tent and then resumed pushing, first him then me or me then him—no fists to the face, we had a show later or a reporter or fan might take a photo—for a few minutes attracting a couple of the girl Mouseketeers, who probably thought we were rehearsing some bizarre dance they had not heard about. One of the ubiquitous mothers looked up from her knitting and said, "You boys shouldn't be pushing each other out here. What if a fan came by? What would Mr. Disney say? You're liable to get fired. Go behind the tent if you have to do that sort of thing."

So we moved to our third venue behind the tent, attracting more girls and some boy Mouseketeers, who were intent on seeing this innocuous 1955 exercise in limited fisticuffs. We started pushing each other again and probably would have kept at our fevered choreography until

I'm next to Tim Considine, agent Steve Stevens, Tommy Kirk, David Stollery and we're celebrating Tim's birthday at his Beverly Hills home in the late '80s.

lunch, but then Tom accidentally caught me on the chin, which I found unfair. Doreen actually said, "Look, Tommy's fighting dirty. He hit Lonnie in the FACE!" Dodo has always said things like that.

I impulsively started fighting dirty myself and caught Tom a good one on the ear which knocked him down. I smiled in victory. The sad case was that my mother had been told I was fighting behind the tent and she rushed in and hustled me away from any victorious diatribe as she shouted unpleasant rebukes.

So even if the Mouseketeers were always considered the perfectly behaved children of Disney, at least two of us were capable of having a normal kid's fight on one occasion over three years. Of course, Tommy recalls it quite differently, with him winning, but the last time it was brought up in a Question and Answer situation in front of an audience in the mid-nineties he started his inaccurate version and, at a pause, I commented on mike, "Apparently I hit you harder than I thought." The audience cracked up loudly. I savored this victory almost as much as the first physical one.

By late December the daily long drive time to and from Disneyland, even holding Annie's hand, was getting to be a drag for me but, fortunately, the circus was not a hit.

There were some perqs from December through January working at Disneyland that were terrific and unique. On breaks or when not performing, rehearsing or going to school, we got on the rides before the Park opened FOR FREE! In addition to no lines we could sometimes go for more than one time on the attraction. My favorites, like most of the guys except Bobby, were the Autopia and the Cups and Saucers.

I could not wait to own and drive an auto. The strange little vehicles on the Autopia in Tomorrowland were not hooked into a track as they are today. They had to be warmed up before Disneyland opened so the guys who worked there liked that we would do some of their work by driving the cars around the track. Adults got no bang out of going slowly on a tiny course. However, the governors that kept the cars to about six miles an hour were not engaged during the warm-up and they got up to speeds of about ten, maybe twelve miles an hour! To a pubescent guy this was excellent.

The Cups and Saucers in Fantasyland are worked by turning the wheel in the center to spin them faster as your cup was also spun round and round by the machinery and they could be spun first one way, then the opposite way. The goal here was to get four guys to make it go as fast as possible with one guy doing it as long as he could then passing off to the next and continuing until you were totally dizzy, and the ride stopped. You also really hoped that somebody else would puke and, most importantly, not on you. This did happen, of course, but I managed to escape the hurls. This was not the girls' favorite ride.

But back at work, after the opening parade around the ring, we changed costumes and midway through the circus acts we did our insipid specialty—the girls struck various ballet poses on a suspended ladder which the boys carefully swung back and forth. Not very creative but nerve-racking since the girls could easily fall and be hurt badly. They would mount the ladders and then be pulled up to about nine or ten feet to do their routine.

I found quickly that the circus life was not for me. A real fight happened between two of the circus roustabouts, an extremely short guy and a huge, muscled guy. They both were pretty banged up and the bloody fight was over before we got to work but it had started hours before. They used no gloves and no weapons but just pounded each other over and over. These are scary individuals and the little guy seemed no more injured than the big guy; even if he was he would not have shown the effect of his injuries. It was like being around a lot of convicts without guards.

Although my pugilistic skills have never been one of my strong points, I was involved in one later struggle that was misconstrued as a fight but this was not with fists and became a myth that I heard about in a twisted way in my second year of college, then again when I was tending bar at twenty-one.

In our last year of filming, Tommy and I were playing ping-pong in a serious match, at least for us, on one of the permanent tables set up outside the cafeteria on the Disney lot. Mischievous Cubby and two new young boys, Don Agrati (Grady, later on twelve seasons of *My Three Sons*) and Lynn Ready sauntered over to our game.

They started kibitzing and irritating us and we kept telling them to go away but they were giggling like fools, slurping on ice cream cones and having a hell of a time. Lynn grabbed the ball during a feverish point. Tom and I were very displeased and as Lynn tossed the ball back on the table and as the three amigos dashed off I managed to grab Lynn's ice cream cone. I threw it at him and it landed on the back of his neck. He said, "Ouch!" but was not hurt badly—IT WAS ICE CREAM—and continued running while Tom and I resumed our ping-pong game unharried.

The next day Lynn's mother saw one of the executives and tried to get me fired for attacking her son. Lynn's much older brother, I believe nearing twenty, called me at home and threatened to beat the mousekashit out of me. Nothing came of it. Lynn and I avoided each other for the rest of the last season but by this time there were a number of cold shoulders between different Mice, particularly Darlene and Annette, and there had always been cliques and loners.

Annie was especially feeling duress (she later confided to me at her home in the 1990s) because by now Darlene and her father were consumed by Annie's success and Darlene's sputtering trip to nowhere despite having her own series and making solo records and albums, and they both took it out on Annie more than previously. Annie said they were constantly berating her verbally and they were very cruel.

My ice-creaming incident was brought up in college by a fairly drunk gay fellow at a theatre arts party after we had closed in a Shakespearean play. He told me he had heard about me and Lynn, implying that I was gay. This shocked and annoyed me but I downplayed my anger, denied it offhandedly and chalked it up to some gay bashing of straights.

The second hint of a gay shot at my heterosexuality came after my M.A. when Tommy Kirk was getting further into his drugs and booze and finally had come out of the closet. He turned up with some friends at an over-crowded bar where I was the bar manager and after a while, feeling the results of his ingestions, accused me of the same thing in connection with the same ice cream episode. This really riled me and hurt much more since I considered Kirk a friend.

He and I always gravitated towards each other at parties well after the MMC stopped filming; we had almost no interaction while on the lot together but knew of each other. In my teens, he was the closest intellectual peer I found. Only a year or two older than I, he was quite smart, had a fast brain and mouth and clearly had more erudition than anyone else. We seemed to be at odds but we were simply chopping each other and trying to win an intellectual, verbal game.

We even got together in Paris in 1961 when I was in Europe for the first time and Tom was shooting *Bon Voyage* with Fred MacMurray. I was with a tour group and JoAnne, a pretty, young, somewhat intellectual girl with whom I was considering marriage but fortunately, after this adventure and a formidable argument just off the Via Veneto in Rome, she returned to California and found a rich, older lawyer and I was saved.

Finding that we would be in Paris at the same time, Tom and I met at my hotel and had a night on the town. He insisted on using his Disney

Among our other adventures in Montmartre, high above Paris, Tommy Kirk (middle) and I had a charcoal sketch done of myself by this street artist while a bag lady looked on, 1961.

expense account as we dined at the *tres* expensive Henri Cinq, did Montmartre, where I got a charcoal drawing of myself that I still have hung along with a black and white snapshot of the artist, Tom and me plus the world's first bag lady lurking in the background hoping for a handout.

We walked down the hill to the shady Pigalle section and a seamy Parisian promptly opened up his long coat to display fifty or more watches for sale, which surprised me for I always thought that tons of merchandise dangling inside on the lining of a long coat was a comic bit not what actually happened in real life.

The next stop was our *scène à faire*. We entered a small estaminet that was peopled only by two presentable hookers and a madame/bartender. We ordered drinks, talked for a while and settled details with the madame. Soon we were strolling and chatting with our ladies *du noir* and arrived at a small, seedy hotel. Tom had not yet come out and was never effeminate so I can only assume that he was still having sex with women or they talked a lot while I had the most clinical sex of my entire life thrust upon me.

With all of my assumed eighteen-year-old sophistication, I fumbled with my vest, tie and shirt as she whipped off her dress to reveal panties and bra that looked like a vivid, print bikini. She then snapped those off and squatted on the bidet to cleanse herself thoroughly. I fumbled more furiously and then was jumped upon. Some of her dialogue included, "You want suckee?," to which I animatedly nodded and later as she pumped away and looked down at me she inquired, "You from Calleefornee?" Clinical with a capital "K," but I somehow managed to stay the course.

Tom Kirk and I then wound up merrily drunk in Les Halles, where all the produce and food used to come into Paris in the morning, as the sun was beginning to show itself. We drank beer at an outside table and began throwing peanut shells at each other from the table provisions. It was a memorable night.

I followed up the next day in London getting the most painful shot of my life. This British doctor seemed to enjoy my anguish as he inflicted the requested penicillin and blatantly stated his disapproval of what I had done with a Parisian whore. Maybe, like other Brits, he just hated the Frogs. Walt always seemed to me like a regular guy and may not have been put off by the use Kirk and I made of his money, unless, of course, it somehow was made public.

Apparently Kirk forgot our camaraderie when he brought up the faux gay Lynn Ready incident later. But I never heard this gay myth again so I just let go of it and thought that since both of the perpetrators were into that life it was something they made up or grabbed onto when it was passed around in their circles.

There are only three gay original Mice that I have ever been aware of. One is dead; the second, Dennis Day, came out in 1980 and the third, a female, has remained secreted in the closet all of these decades. She is also in the closet about something else just as substantive but I have never heard of anyone confronting her with it, nor even daring to verbalize it and that is how I plan to leave it.

Given my previous success in the halls of academe, it was strange that I had problems with two of the three teachers we had on the lot over the years. Our first teacher was a female and was the best of them. The second one I remember was Mr. Stark and he was just that—a tall, thin, balding, stark fellow with an aquiline nose that took over much of his face. His beadle-like attitude and attempts at education were self-defeating.

Mrs. Seaman (whose name gained smirks from me and some of the guys) who is revered by many Mouseketeers, did not like me and made it apparent immediately. I believe she had an animus toward me because I was three years ahead scholastically and singled me out for snide acrimony and tough times. My grades dropped and I lost enthusiasm for subjects I actually liked. I would reverse this course when I was back at HPS during the filming but not at school on the lot.

I had the bad fortune to see Mrs. Seaman and get a further negative attitude over thirty-five years later when she showed up in Palm Springs for Sharon's fiftieth birthday party in 1992. Maybe the London doctor after Paris with Kirk had contacted her. I remained polite but she made it clear she could not stand me and could carry a grudge for many decades. It was obvious that my assessment of her was accurate.

Most of the wardrobe people and makeup folks were fine, but the friendliest individuals on the series were the musical people and Jim the sound man, who was the only person who did Mickey's voice except for Walt and also did our live sound effects, just like radio, when we shot. He also played in the Dixieland Five New Orleans jazz band on the lot. In that capacity Jim actually guested on our show more than once.

Buddy Baker put all the music together and in much later contact Diane and I really liked him and his wife. Marvin Ash, an unfiltered cigarette always dangling from his mouth as he played and continually dropping ashes all over himself just like Bob Fosse did later, was our pianist for rehearsal. He performed on the set for our first season because we used live music, not lip-synching to our own playback music. The use of the live music and a three-camera shoot the first year gave way to a single camera and canned playback, just as fewer kids were needed after our first year to get the shows done on schedule.

The legion of song writers, with Jimmie Dodd the most prolific, included big "Mooseketeer" Roy Williams, Bob Amsberry (our third adult the first two seasons), Cliff Edwards, known as Ukulele Ike and the voice of Jiminy Cricket, Buddy Ebsen and, believe it or not, Fess Parker.

There is confusion among fans about who Bob Amsberry was but every time you see an "old geezer" or another bizarre character like the soda jerk at the Malt Shop, who is not Jimmie or Roy and definitely not a kid or a guest, it was Bob. He was much younger than Roy and Jimmie and was a disc jockey who was cast as our resident character man playing various roles usually with moustaches, beards and/or wigs. He seemed much older to all of us because we were kids. Later I found out he was only in his late twenties.

He gave me a bad time about my chubbiness; the first season I still maintained some baby fat and I shot up about five inches and remained the same weight, ninety-five pounds, over a year later. We joked around a lot and I liked Bob a lot, just as I liked Hal Adelquist the most on the production side. I think Bob responded to my chopping at which he was swift as well.

He was crushed when he was fired after the second season and died the next year at twenty-nine in a car accident returning from Vegas. This was my first experience with death that involved a human I knew well. It bothered me a great deal and I did not know how to handle it. The other kids were hit hard, too, and the girls wept a lot. Guys were not supposed to weep and so I kept my grief and shock mostly to myself.

The next person close to me to die was Jerry Dodge, by his own hand, after we opened on Broadway in *Mack and Mabel* eighteen years later in 1975. Jerry was unusually sage for an actor and had been a burgeoning Broadway star creating the role of Barnaby, along with Charles Nelson Reilly as Cornelius, in the original production of *Hello, Dolly*, also for Gower Champion. Jerry was a very private person and was a gay man who was not in the closet but whom you would never think of as being gay.

He read the lead in my play *Occam's Razor* at the Dorothy Chandler Pavilion rehearsal room while we had *Mack & Mabel* on the road performing, rehearsing and changing pre-Broadway in Los Angeles. I got to know him some and we would sometimes have a drink at a bar in the Watergate between matinee and evening performances when we played right across the street at the Kennedy Center in D.C. I was also his understudy as the camera man and later a director who was along for the ride during the rise of Pres as Mack Sennett.

Jerry was a loner and I sensed he was depressed a lot, which I understood for I have dealt with that most of my life. I knew he was not pleased by *Mack & Mabel* nor the role which Gower, his former mentor, had thrust upon him but I am sure there were other issues that troubled him.

I was surprised and saddened by his suicide after *Mack* opened at the Majestic Theatre on Broadway. The hideous David Merrick, who produced the show, attended the services at the small but well known Actor's Chapel near our theatre in Manhattan and was heard muttering "I'm at the services for a suicide!" as if it was a personal affront. I later wrote one of my better poems about Jerry's death.

I had the misfortune to work for Merrick twice—*Mack & Mabel* and *42nd Street*—and even won a disagreement about pay on *"Mack"* with the help of my theatre union, Actor's Equity, and that ain't easy. Unlike the other cast members who would hang out in the hall to be seen and to greet when Merrick made one of his rare backstage appearances, I would rush into my dressing room bathroom, lock the door and remain there just in case he decided to open the door to the room I occupied, naturally without knocking. I disliked him and the horrible way he treated everyone and, unlike many in life and particularly in show business, I am not as good as I could be at being hypocritical.

Merrick even gave prominent, Tony Award-winning, star choreographer/director Gower Champion a bad time. We had to rehearse in the upstairs lounge of the Dorothy Chandler on the day of our Los Angeles opening because Merrick would not pay the $1,000 it cost for a stage hand to raise the curtain. The IATSE (International Alliance of Theatrical Stage Employees [and Moving Picture Machine Operators—U.S. and Canada)], nicknamed IA, is so much tougher than actors' unions. The stagehand had only to press a button to raise the curtain so we could put in script, dance and blocking changes on the sets where we would be performing. Pre-Broadway on the road is a nightmare of constantly-changing work.

Once the late great Pres, Robert Preston, had a new set of lyrics put in that afternoon for the Keystone Kops number in *Mack*. We were playing the Kennedy Center in D.C. that night and Pres had a rare moment of "going up" meaning that he completely forgot the new lyrics. Shortly after the number began everyone in Kop costumes fell flat to the ground, in this fifth or sixth version, while Pres sang, so no one on stage could do anything to help him.

Pres had an unusual habit on stage, but not in film, of emphasizing points by stomping. He hummed most of the lyrics he had forgotten and stomped like mad. The rest of us could be seen doing a version of the wave as our prostrate bodies rippled with laughter. As far as anyone could tell, the audience did not get the gaffe, for Pres was ever the excellent pro. They just thought it was a very bizarre number as far as anyone could tell.

Gower ranted and complained about needing to put in the new number on the set onstage but Merrick was not putting out the 1K and just said no, so we rehearsed in the bar area of the house. The nasty producer is one of the very few people who, upon his death, cast members and crew members made immediate jokes about his demise. He was not well liked; he was not liked at all.

The next substantive death was my grandfather later the same year, 1975, and that began a series of family deaths followed by my dad in 1980 but both of these two were predestined: John had a stroke in 1973 and my dad was diagnosed with pancreatic cancer in 1978.

But Amsberry was the beginning of my finding a way to cope with this formidable reality of final loss. There was much speculation among the kids about Bob's death being a possible suicide since he was so damaged by Walt's decision that he was no longer pertinent. To my knowledge, no reason was ever given for his dismissal so it would seem Walt just did not feel he added anything to the show any longer so he was dumped. Unfortunately, the same thing happened to Adelquist.

Roy had been an artist and gag guy for Walt for years and had to be forced by his long-time employer into doing the show. He hated the idea of being in front of the camera but Walt knew his huge, rotund body, distinct features and bald head as our only Mooseketeer would be good comedy relief opposite Jimmie. When on the road Roy could be found in the men's lounge on the train with a bottle inside a brown paper bag. He could be irascible and he was a somewhat coarse and uneducated man but generally he was fine with the kids and was the only person involved with the show to invite us to his house on more than one occasion. His pool was permanently done up like a Tahitian village.

I have heard that Jimmie had a party but I did not attend or for some strange reason have no memory of the event and I know I would have been invited. Jimmie would have invited anyone but Beelzebub if they had been part of the family.

We went to a party at Jerry Lewis' house because his kids were fans and wanted us to come over. I had worked with Lewis and Dean Martin on the *Colgate Comedy Hour* but my mom had told me then to be very careful and if possible avoid Jerry since he might just pick up any nearby kid and throw him through a set to get a laugh.

What was interesting when rehearsing with Dean and Jerry was that the comic was somber and nervous and Dean was relaxed, loose and funny. When the director told Jerry to make a cross from stage left to stage right, Dean shouted out, "He can't make a Cross—He's Jewish!" Everyone laughed but Lewis.

Jimmie has always been revered and the fantastic truth is he was exactly like he was on screen as he was off. He was a very caring man who was a born-again Christian without being obnoxiously fervent. The religious homilies he wrote for the show he really felt and believed. He even recorded separate religious albums after the series. Sharon always mentions something I was unaware of and never witnessed: the Mouseka-Martinis he and his wife Ruth would have in the afternoon but I, for one, do not consider that an un-Christian thing to do.

Jimmie and Ruth were putting together another children's show in Hawaii when he became ill. He did have heart problems but he actually died young, age 54 in 1964, of a staph infection. As I got older I really appreciated that Jimmie, believing deeply in his sect of Christianity, never brought that up in a solicitous way. He would bring up God and ethics and the right thing to do at times, but not his specific God. Jimmie acted as he believed a Christian should and did not proselytize for his flavor of deity. If more religious people in the world were like Jimmie some of the manmade strife, killing and terrorism that has occurred since recorded history began and is again rampant throughout the world might just go away, or at least respect some boundaries.

But, my Tristram Shandy meanderings about death appeased for a while, I return to the early days of the Club.

While we were shooting the first season every day on the lot we rehearsed or shot new scenes and song and dance routines. We might begin with a costume fitting, then school, then rehearsal or shooting, depending on which

Jimmie and Ruth Dodd's Christmas card the year we stopped shooting the MMC, 1958.

group we were in, but there was never any regularity to it and they always had to allow time for eight or ten or more kids to get into makeup and costume.

This was uncharted territory for everyone. Even though we only had one of the four fifteen-minute segments, it was a struggle. We also did the cartoon intros (*"Meeska-Mooska-Mousekteer/ Mousekartoon Time Now Is Here!"*) and other bits outside of our own fifteen-minute segment.

Spin shot separately at the Golden Oaks ranch in Placerita Canyon about forty minutes northwest of the studio in Burbank. Walt bought the ranch and used it for other shoots and rentals to other studios. The real segments (like milking a cow or kids celebrating Christmas in a foreign country) also shot autonomously, sometimes on location, and only occasionally involved any of the Mouseketeers' time. I got a postcard from Annie when she and Sammy Ogg, a buddy of mine from HPS and one of the boys on *Spin*, were shooting *Adventures In Dairyland* on a farm in Madison, Wisconsin. She was very discreet about our relationship and made no reference to it. She would say the word "love" to me, write it for an autograph hound, but not write it to me.

At the outset the producers divided us up into three teams: red, white and blue. While one team rehearsed another took class and the third shot film on Stage 1, a huge sound stage, but the smallest one on the lot. On rare days we might also use another sound stage to film two segments. One team only was used in roll call. The production bigwigs learned during or near the end of the first season that all this could be accomplished with fewer kids. They fired fourteen and kept the nine of us who lasted all of the filming and Dennis for a second season.

Dallas Johann was hired first and dropped the first day; he just could not handle the stress and tension and cried so he was replaced by his brother John Lee; Paul Petersen, who went on to *The Donna Reed Show* had an attitude problem before that phrase was coined, including socking the casting director, Lee Traver, in the stomach and calling him "Fatso" (I probably should have thanked him for that given Travers' draconian threats to me and my mom.), which got him promptly dumped; two of Mickey Rooney's multitudinous progeny, Tim and Mickey, Jr., went a few weeks longer than Paul before getting into the paint department and doing a Picasso on some finished set flats—they were banished to oblivion that same day.

As I have mentioned earlier, I was not happy and really did not want to do the third season but I was only thirteen and, unless you are a true outlaw (which I have never claimed about myself) you do what your mom wants you to do. I usually was a rebel, but I was not obtuse.

I join Doreen and Karen in front of the original 1955 curtain for the MMC, being interviewed by Leonard Maltin behind us for the 2004 DVD of the first full week of the show. We gave Leonard his first ears as an adult since he was a huge fan of the show as a kid.

My disillusion was manifold and some of it I discussed in a front page newspaper piece I wrote and was published in L.A. and Santa Barbara in two different rags in 1980. This piece also shows that after thinking of the show as boring, puerile drivel for years, I had come to an understanding of the MMC after the renascence in the early 'eighties as I approached forty, as the joyful, memorable entity that so many cherish.

Concisely put, by the third season I was not pleased with doing the "same old, same old," of not being offered more than continuing as one of the main dancers and singers and speaking lines here and there but never getting a chance to use my acting ability and hard-won experience. The grinding schedule and separation from friends and schoolmates took a toll, too. I also was going through the adjustments of being more sophisticated in many areas than even the eldest of the Mice since I had been in the business and around adults so long and hung with older guys while dating older girls.

I brashly thought of myself as a dashing, intellectual young adult finishing the last year of high school and looking toward college. I did not want to be weighted down with childish mouse ears. Perhaps a bit grandly, as is the wont of the early teen years for many, I viewed myself as a burgeoning Cary Grant-Fred Astaire in the making, who was too mature for this kid stuff. In a few short years I found out that I was going to be neither Cary nor Fred.

Cary and his new wife Dyan Cannon attended Mouseketeer Cheryl's marriage to Lance Reventlow, who was Cary's stepson from a brief marriage to Barbara Hutton. I had arrived in a new blue suit and with Brenda Benet on my arm. I was pretty cool but I was no match for Mr. Grant. I am also a damn good dancer, but Fred was unique. But life is not about being someone else, nor, much more to the point, about competing with other people. Life is simply doing your very best.

I did find out later from a few of the guy Mice that I was looked up to for a number of elements of my eleven- to fourteen-year-old style: the way I dressed, my courtly attentions to the ladies, my professional demeanor and experience, an occasional covert cigarette, my intellect, my wicked, dangerous tongue, and so on.

But I had had it and I did not stay on for the later tours with Jimmie to Australia after we finished filming. I wanted out and my mother, perhaps in anticipation of her divorcing Ham and moving to Vegas, allowed me to at least get out of this extension of the show. Maybe that is why I was the only one to go straight through a B.A. and M.A. directly after the series and pursue a Ph.D. I had not yet come across the 1941 quote from television writer Harry Miles: "No one in movies has a higher education in anything. Education is the last thing you want."

Much later in life two of the girls, Karen and Mary Espinosa, went back for their Bachelor's degrees and Karen later got her M.A. in a psychological field; she works as a counselor for women in trouble. I have recently read online that a couple of the others at least achieved undergraduate degrees. Bob alleges that he only lacks a few units for his B.A. Karen and I are the only two who have graduate degrees.

There were some swell times but the onerous schedule over three years was getting to me. I had only done one TV series in a recurring role before and I did not have to work every week. I did do the radio soap for a long time but that was much less exacting—we aired live one night a week, about a three-hour gig; we read the new half-hour script, worked on any problems in the text and/or the live SFX (sound effects) and then went on air, live.

The West Coast plays I was involved with did not run for years like many Broadway shows do—two or three months was a long L.A. run then and that still is the case whether you are paid or they fall under the Equity-waiver contract (in ninety-nine-or-fewer-seat theatres, unpaid but union-sanctioned).

I later played over a year in two plays. No matter how good your technique and craft, for part of theatre is maintaining the same vividness in every performance no matter how many times you have said the same lines to the same actors in the same play, it gets very difficult after six or seven months. By the same token, the MMC became drudgery. If I had been more challenged or worked as an actor or used better, perhaps I would have felt differently. I still would have not liked the childishness of what was, by definition, a show for children.

Before the bizarre building with pixilated little dwarves decorating it was built across from and west of the Animation building on the Disney studio lot, the playing field for employees was much larger. The adults played softball at lunch close to the ping-pong tables outside the cafeteria. I tried to get the Mouse guys to play football in another area but whether to protect their faces from injury, fear of being cut out of a segment or just being scared of physical contact—I would have played touch but I preferred tackle football—no male mice wanted to play. A few got good at ping-pong and we played some baseball once or twice, but that was it.

Fans are unsure about who was in or not in roll call. Usually it was the "first team," which in film usually means the actual actors rather than the stand-ins used for lighting, camera set up etcetera, but for us it meant the kids who were featured. I was in roll call for seasons one and two but cut from the third year because of a facial injury. I still did featured parts and dances during that last season.

I found online in 2005 that Bobby stated in a live interview at WDW that I was replaced by Tommy in roll call that third year, which is not true. I politely wrote Bob explaining his faulty memory but he did not, as usual, show me the courtesy of responding, nor has he apologized when we worked together subsequently. I have heard he is pleasant with his fans but then I am not one of his fans, merely a long time, always polite co-worker who finds it rude to be lied about and ignored by other people. He also made a DVD later and cut both Tom and I out of the nine saying he and Cubby lasted the full filming with seven of the girls.

We are now officially in a period of mouseka-senior moments, of which Bobby is at the head of the class.

I missed the third year roll call simply because I fell doing a handstand in rehearsal and it took off a part of the skin on my cheek about the size of a silver dollar. Maybe the guys were right about not playing ball, although the handstand was for a show number. I was introducing the guest winners with Jimmie on Talent Roundup that week so they added a lame line about my walking into a "mouseka-door," which was the precise word I was given to use, but the powers above reasoned that they could not have me with this abrasion, which could not be covered by makeup, showing up for the whole season openings and closings and any reruns, so I was cut.

No one would have predicted that a series that only lasted four years, one of which was not new film, would be rerun in every decade and into the new century but that is why I am not in the last year roll call and the singing sign off: "Now it's time to say goodbye/ To all our company...."

Furtively exploring the Disney lot and underground tunnels that run under buildings, was something that most of us did, even some of the girls, when we thought we were unobserved. It was fun, a little scary since Mouseketeers had to be paragons of virtue, and it changed a grueling schedule into exciting explorations. I was also drawn to privacy which would allow making out with Annie and later any of the girls with whom I had brief encounters. After the show the only two I dated were Doreen and Cheryl, the two prettiest ladies in my eyes—except for Annie.

However sophisticatedly I may have talked the talk, I was still a virgin and had not "poked the poke." Although relentlessly seeking the touch of a young breast and related matters, I still accommodated my religious teachings, so things were very innocent compared to the too unrestricted times in which we presently live. Somehow I eventually decided at about fourteen or fifteen that oral sex was acceptable as long as actual copulation was avoided. To this I only add: AMEN!

At an appearance at Disneyland for which we stayed, with our parents, overnight, we had a TV watching (MAKEOUT!) party—no parents allowed—sometime in 1956-57 at the Disneyland Hotel. Annie and I were no longer an item and Mouseketeer Charley (Chuck) Laney was with

Annie. I decided that it was a swell idea to revisit old flames and told Chuck that Cheryl wanted to talk to him. I then sat beside Annie and rekindled our former ardor as Cheryl and Chuck enjoyed each other's company. My last romantic revisit with Annie was at a party at Doreen's house after Dodo, as she was called, was the first Mouseketeer married and we were in our very late teens. Doreen soon became the first mouseka-mom.

Some of us were drinking. Bess Tracey, Doreen's mom, was usually somewhat scattered and she wandered in and out in her dotty fashion, taking care of the food and either did not care or did not notice. Actually Doreen's husband Bob got so wasted that he passed out in some bushes in the backyard and was missing until the next morning.

Bess suggested that some of us perform; being an old trouper she felt performing was what life was about for everyone. This did not appeal to me or most of the others but, predictably, to our dismay and strained looks, first Darlene and then Tommy felt compelled to sing. That is probably the only reason either one of them attended. The majority of us did not take to the concept of performing for free for people with whom we had performed with for years not too long before. We had diametrically opposed concepts of fun.

Annie and I started making out on the floor during these boorish displays. My performance with Annie eventually seemed to agitate Bess, so we moved into another room.

When the party broke up I offered to follow Sharon and Annette back to Annie's house to make sure they were okay to drive. I also secretly sought to further my activities with the beautiful teenaged woman I had loved as a girl. I walked them up to the door in Studio City and mom, the late Virginia Funicello, opened it to greet us. All was cordial until she pointed to my neck and asked what that mark was on it.

Being bright, I realized in a second that she must have been referring to a hickey Annie had given me that I was unaware of since I had never had a mark on my neck except on just such occasions. It could be nothing else but a hickey, so I instantly explained.

"It's a birth mark, Mrs. Funicello."

Her smile slackened and she said, "Lonnie, I've known you since you were a young boy and you never had a birthmark."

I instantly and suavely claimed, "That's because it's very unusual. It only comes up and shows under rare circumstances and the doctors have never been able to establish what those circumstances are."

"JOE," Virginia called off to her squat but thick husband, Annie's father, "Come here now!"

I had experienced a little of the wrath of stocky, Italianate Joe the mechanic/gas station owner, Annie's father, when he found out that fast Lonnie was going steady with his virtuous daughter. There was no violence at that meeting other than vocal belligerence and bulging eyes but I though it best to beat a retreat rather than try to convince Joe that I had a sometimes birthmark on my neck that looked like a hickey. I waved goodbye, made it to my 'Vette and peeled off laying a large strip of rubber.

It is quaint and innocent in terms of the 21st century, but that was almost five decades ago. By the same mores, I am sure that none of the Mouseketeers had coitus during the show—making out, canoodling, holding hands, feeling up, sure, but no actual sex. Dennis describes guys having masturbation parties somewhere or other but perhaps that was just his imagination. I surely never saw, nor heard, anything about it.

After the show, after everyone turned seventeen or eighteen, all virginity is off the table and the bed. I do not know, and I would not say if I did, who did what to whom, but I am unaware of anyone but me being later involved romantically with any of the other Mice, except for early teen crushes. Long after the show I had some intimacies with more than one Mouseketeer lady, but that's all I have to say about that.

It is better to be Forrest Gump than Gerry Rivers. You may know Gerry Rivers by the name he used after eschewing his Jewish parentage and focusing on his Hispanic as Geraldo Rivera, whom I had the misfortune of being superciliously interviewed by in the '80s.

Whatever my personal experiences, the MMC gave us all marvelous and always rewarding chances to meet and/or perform for kids who were living with diseases, were in post surgery recovery or burdened with severe disadvantages. We did an appearance and performed a show for the kids at the Tracy Clinic in 1956; Spencer Tracy had a son who was hearing impaired and founded this nonprofit facility specializing in hearing and vocal impairments of the young. The smiling faces and devotion of our fans were much more meaningful than fame. That proved just as true when I made appearances at hospitals solo with Mickey in 1983.

The opening of the refurbished Fantasyland at Disneyland, which cost millions of dollars, was tied to an Amtrak tour of about thirteen states. It was just Mickey Mouse and Mouseketeer Lonnie with a Mickey wrangler—the person playing MM in the outfit cannot see nor move

Mickey Mouse Offer I Could Not Refuse 159

Mickey, Lonnie and the Mayor of San Antonio during the 13-state Amtrak/Fantasyland tour in 1983.

well and is vulnerable, thus, needing a helper. The fourth person was a Disney coordinator. I have a little of the tape with Mickey and the kids on my DVD and how they relate to Mickey is thrilling every time I see it. I had fans too but I was more interesting to the adults, although the kids liked me too for they believed we are all just Mouseketeers.

This also connects to other experiences I have had on more than one occasion. In one of our adult appearances at Disneyland to sign autographs for fans, after a hundred or so signings a tough guy swaggered up looking very much like someone just out of the place: levis, armless T shirt, black leather vest, tats, a couple of scars. He asked for my autograph. I thought I might be in trouble and tried to be cool and impervious to his appearance.

He spoke up and said that his life, "was going the wrong way..." but he had listened to Jimmie's words and lyrics and he continued, "...that helped me turn it all around." It was moving to me but I carefully hid my feeling about being a significant part of this tough guy's life. I merely smiled, talked and signed, hiding my sensitivity, as my father and grandfather would have.

Encounters of this kind have never ceased being wonderful over the fifty-plus years I have experienced them. It is difficult to see what others have to contend with when you are healthy and well, but their bravery and honesty and joy at connecting to you as a Mouseketeer makes you feel as if you are actually doing something of value, not just being an entertainer.

There is no way of denying how important the show was to millions of kids in various ways, but I really did not realize how much our series had affected so many until the renascence of interest for the MMC in the '80s. People's faces are authentic and pristine in showing their pleasure. Seeing their feelings makes you feel very, very fortunate to be associated with the show.

There are still stalwart fans in the 2000s and they have pleasantly surprised me since it would be easy to assume that adults who are parents and grandparents might not have interest in such childish dallying. There are also young fans in this new century for we reran from 1995 to 2002. The age range is smaller due to overexposure to more adult programming on TV, computers, cell phones, iPods and the wretched, violent, demeaning lyrics of too much pop music, for the MMC has run for six decades—so far.

The first time we all realized the Mouseketeers' effect on folks in a concrete way was flying into Oklahoma City after our first season. We had all been told that we were a success and we got fan letters and had fan clubs. I was one of the ones, along with Annie, who had fan clubs just for me, not for the whole gang. I went to a meeting of one of my personal fan clubs and it was very flattering to see and hear all these lovelorn young ladies who were infatuated with me. I was friendly and accessible.

Being quite experienced I was not in awe like the other Mice anent the show's success, but when we flew into Oklahoma City there were thousands of people waiting to greet us. I had never seen anything like it. I had read about Sinatra getting fan adulation years before and there were those crazed ladies for Elvis but this was 1955 and the days of the Beatles and mass lunacy had not yet arrived. At first I thought something horrible had happened locally or nationally with so many people milling about.

We waved and shook hands and were helped to wade through the throngs smiling from ear to ear and shouting our names and singing our songs. We were escorted to a TV station on a bus by motorcycle cops with their lights and sirens on! My surprise at these greetings was exactly the same as my colleagues. It is one thing to HEAR you are hot, it is something else to SEE it and FEEL it, despite being a showbiz vet.

I have always been glad that this happened to me so young because I am not a public person and would very much object to the constant attention celebrities get. I could not deal with the paparazzi, people staring and pointing, meals and shopping interrupted by fans asking the same questions over and over and assuming that I must make time for them because it is part of the job. It could be even worse and require bodyguards and an entourage, which means you never have any privacy. I really value privacy.

I am fine today and have been for years if it is a planned occasion when I agree to show up to talk to fans and sign autographs or perhaps to perform or, in another medium, like exchanging on my web site or being interviewed on TV or radio, but my private life is private; I do not want it invaded. It is just as well that I have been a character actor and only get recognized if I am supposed to be recognized or I bring it up myself, which is very rare indeed. This recognition is based on work done as a child, so I am not instantly identified.

There are other Mouseketeers who would have loved it. At least three, maybe more, would have much more meaningful lives with this recognition and they always identify themselves as original Mouseketeers, but I am not one of them. However, the love fans show makes me feel wonderful and humble.

We made a number of road trips, one to Oregon for the Parade of Roses, a rival of Pasadena's Rose Parade, where we caused a big traffic jam when we visited a hospital; another time it was a charity show in Houston and I remember an elementary school we visited in Evanston, Illinois. In March of 1956 I joined Jimmie, Annie, Sharon, Bobby and Darlene at the Linda Vista Elementary School after being at the Shrine Auditorium in L.A., then Disneyland earlier in the day. We did not take all twenty-four kids or however many were on in any season when we made appearances except our first TV outing at the opening of Disneyland.

We sometimes traveled by train. I think this was on the Chicago/Evanston journey that some of us snuck into each other's berths and messed around a lot, but quietly. Those of us who were found out would hear, "Doreen! You get down out of Lonnie's bunk!" Bess Tracey knew precisely what her daughter might get up to if left to her own—and my—devices.

We were responsible for our Ears and the price mentioned has varied but most remember it as $50 if we lost them, which was a bundle in the 'fifties—close to a third of our weekly pay before taxes. On one of our tours some kid grabbed Bob's Ears and was chased down and tackled,

Doreen and the gracious host as she tells a Mouseketeer Mensch [Mensch, n. decent, mature and responsible person, Yiddish.] story at one of our parties at the Seacliff beach house in 1981.

or so Bob tells it, by casting director Jack Lavin or some other member of our retinue. Given Lavin's girth, he must have busted his ever-present bulging suspenders. Doreen recalls that she and Annie lost theirs more than one time but found them eventually; once Dodo did not find hers and paid the fifty bucks.

When we were told that the show was history there was a lot of crying and sadness among the girls, and worse, sobbing on the last day of shooting. I was pleased and more than ready to say goodbye to this part of my life. I was a star and turned up in magazine photos for a number of years after the show and the first reruns, but I did not think that was going to be a hindrance for any long period of time, since I was only fourteen and still changing visibly.

Very few people have a bad memory of the MMC, just as few have an animus toward Walt Disney. Some object to what has happened to the Parks and the movies and the television shows since Walt died in 1966 and I understand their grievances, but most humans have a positive smile when the animation, films, Disney, Disneyland, WDW or the Mickey Mouse Club is mentioned. The only people outside of show business who hate Disney are usually hard cases in one way or another, moribund about many things in life.

On one radio show I did on the trip with the Mick in 1983, the DJ, in the few seconds we had before we went live on the air, told me he hated Disney and their incessant promotion of products and the Parks. Since I was promoting the refurbished Fantasyland at the Anaheim Park, I asked him why he had me on the show and he averred that the station boss forced him. Mentioning synergy as a business tool that many people used after Disney originated the concept was not going to help matters. I

The final season Mouseketeers at a formal dinner at the now vanished Moulin Rouge in Hollywood. Left to right: Bonnie Lynn Fields, Linda, Don Grady, Cubby, Karen, Lynn Ready, Bobby, Cheryl, Tommy, L.B. and Annie, Darlene, Doreen and Sharon, 1957.

prepared for an onslaught of nasty verbal anti-Disney abuse, but whenever he intimated he was going that way I would redirect and move on and, fortunately, it was a short spot.

Positively, of the thirty-nine original Mouseketeers, the eldest (Larry Larson, second season) born in 1939, the youngest (Bronson Scott, first season) in 1947, only one is a convicted felon and those problems began in her late fifties and did not involve drugs nor weapons and, as I have stated on my website since its inception in 2000, that is a darn good average since the positive outcomes of the Helen Hunts, Ron Howards, Jodie Fosters, Sally Fields, Jackie Coogans and Shirley Temples are the exceptions, not the rule.

As I turned fourteen you could have described me as Mouseketeer Candide. We were finishing the last season of the MMC and I soon found out I did not have to return. I was going into my senior year of high school and would have time for dating and friends and parties and then proceed through college. I was a star and had everything going for me monetarily and otherwise. I told Mom my agent and she acceded to my decision. I stopped being a hard-working adult six days a week and returned to being a fourteen-year-old with an older perspective and fewer responsibilities. I decided to find myself and the world and do it on my own.

Not only was the world not really interested, I found that there were many pitfalls along the way as I began to explore and read and learn and love. There was something lurking beneath the surface of my many toys, stardom, success with girls and my easy proficiency at school. I was only vaguely aware of whatever it was but I could not identify it.

Like Candide, I found that much that was glittery and inviting was fake when you got up close to it. In some ways I went through some of the same experiences as Candide did. I had no idea if I was ready to contend with them all but this is what happened.

Chapter 8
No Matrix For Matriculation

As I began my senior year not all was sweetness and light but I knew I would soon never have to say, "Look, Jimmie, we made a Mousekadrum from an old smelly shoe! Play it, Cubby!!" I was fourteen and I resumed my A grades, dating and partying at every opportunity.

I went out with blonde Gretchen, who used beer to lighten her hair, and Rosie, my first Hispanic girlfriend. I also got my girder glided by the notorious Barbara. I hung with my buddy Dave and we listened to jazz at his pad above the Sunset Strip, where he lived with his Brit dad, the Jag mechanic, and his mom. We went to the nearby Renaissance Club for jazz across from Ciro's (later The Comedy Store) below on the strip.

Dave was an odd fellow and, like all my friends and dates, older than me. We were both enthused by sports car and attended races and I worked pit for him once in an amateur race with his hopped-up, beaten down MG. I had two youthful career desires as a kid: 1) to be a football player and 2) to be a sports car racer. The former was quickly nixed since it was clear that I would not even be large enough to be a "Me kick-kick" extra point guy, which I would not want to do anyway. I did keep my QB or WR roles in street play and once on an actual football field.

In my late teens I decided not to pursue racing because while my double-clutching and downshifting was excellent my toe-and-heel screwed up on me on Mulholland en route to Malibu when I hit the brake instead of the gas and almost went over the precipice. My P-1800 ended up front half hanging over a dirt mound that ran alongside the road and, like my dad's jockey career, my race driving became a dead issue.

Dave and I also managed to get into jazz clubs. My style, clothes and actions helped me and he was 6' 1"+ and dressed as an adult on such excursions. I saw much less of Dave after entering college. He went on to teach art at a small school in L.A. We did get together for jazz outings, but that was it. To put it simply, Dave was fun but weird. I encountered him in the late 'seventies when I moved back to L.A. from NYC and he had not progressed one whit from his bizarre mentality. He was a big Nazi fan when I knew him at HPS, which we did not discuss since I objected vehemently.

I was in some form of teen love with Rosie and Gretchen, and later with Barbara, but it was not the depth of feeling I had previously had for Annie, nor would soon have for Sharon in my sophomore year at Valley College.

I attended two proms, my own at HPS with Eunice because of her excellent dancing ability and large accoutrements and Gina asked me to hers at Van Nuys High. Gina gifted me with a huge set of blood-red lips on my expensive shirt which would not come out, among other gifts from flailing about in a car. As much too frequently in these early teen years my left pant leg was stiff as a two-by-four afterwards.

Finally, I had problems at my graduation with the despotic Mrs. Mann. As Student Body President I had to write and give a graduation speech. I took it seriously, researched and came up with a solid speech that avoided the usual hackneyed dullness. Elements of my work were not to Mrs. Mann's liking and she cut and rewrote some of it. She insisted I read it as rewritten. My independent nature would not allow me to do her trite, obvious, sentimental version, so I refused to give voice to it.

I cannot be definitive in memory but what I recall is that I lingered in the background as much as I could and watched the ass kissers and characterless do what they needed to do. It mattered little to me for no one showed up to watch me graduate. My mother was frolicking in Vegas, my dad was somewhere unknown and had no contact with me and my grandparents shunned leaving their home for much of anything—they never went to a movie, ever, and my grandmother's vegetarianism had her terrified of eating out for someone might have used a pan to cook meat and not cleaned it well enough before they cooked her vegetables. They clipped coupons and John drove them to shop for food because they had to eat but they only ventured out for mandatory practical items, not entertainment, except to go bowling. John maintained a steady 200+ average and Glade enjoyed seeing the other bowlers and their wives as the amazing whiz score keeper for her husband's team.

Later, after much cajoling, my grandmother came to something I was performing in at a club, but she refused even drinking water at their table. I could only guess she was afraid someone had put some meat in the glass. My surrogate parents for my mid-teens until twenty were in their sixties in an era when most folks that age looked, dressed and acted like very ancient, life-is-over types, as opposed to mature people in the current era. Gram, except for gaining some weight, looked pretty much the same at one hundred as she did at sixty-five; the no meat, restricted vegetarian diet kept her from as many wrinkles as others I have seen at over one hundred years.

I turned fifteen on May 31, 1958, received my diploma six days later. Prior to that I was given a choice by my mom. She was finally divorcing my dad and going to Las Vegas immediately for a quickie divorce, but she also planned to reside there. She sat me down and said I could join her or stay in L.A. and live with my grandparents in the apartment building they owned in North Hollywood on Whitsett Avenue.

I did not know if it behooved me to stay with the Burrs or to trek four-plus hours northeast to the hot, glitzy town of Vegas where almost every breath is synthetically air conditioned. When people go from car to building or building to indoor tennis court they hold their breath.

I had no idea what to expect but would immediately loathe my soon-to-be stepfather Don. Our first meeting in 1959 was a disaster and our second near Yosemite was worse. When Dahrlene and I exchanged vows in Vegas in 1968, we were invited to dinner the next night at my mom's house near Lake Mead. During our meal Don casually referred to the assassination of Martin Luther King, Jr. as being "a damn fine thing."

I reviled him. I had been as broken and angry at Dr. King's wrongful assassination as I had with JFK before him and Bobby two months after MLK. Despite my mother's protestations, Dahrlene and I left right then. He and I would have been tooth and tong daily. He was a crude, alcoholic, uneducated, violent woman chaser.

Even though it was the right decision for this reason alone, I do know now that no matter how sophisticated and intelligent a fifteen-year-old is he should not be given this much freedom. It is premature to leave a young teen to his own devices, which was close to the case with Gram and Gramps. As it happens, there was not much of a choice.

My mom was stridently strict and frequently difficult. The stress of having to be perfect every day in everything would continue to be my role. My grandmother did pressure me to be perfect but she was not as zealous, nor rigid as Dot. I could also get around her.

Vegas had only a two-year college in Quonset huts and it was then a small, dreary oasis in the middle of the Nevada desert unless you were on the strip or the downtown drag. The latter had not as yet struck me as a modern Sodom and Gomorrah with absolutely no redeeming qualities. My friends, familiar places, my overly generous grandmother, my new Corvette, places to hang, my girlfriends and the whole package was in North Hollywood and over the hill in Hollywood. I also was sure that my mom's limited funds would thrust us both into hand-to-mouth living very shortly and since I was not yet sixteen she would most likely sell my Corvette. I voted for this much more promising life of staying home and voted against what I later found to be agons with Sweeney Don the bartender.

Gram posed for this formal portrait in the late '50s.

As whimsical fate would have it, I wound up at a two-year institution, Valley College, in North Hollywood in the same type of Quonset huts in early November, 1958 after the problems with ROTC, no license to drive and humongous classes I encountered at UCLA. Gramp drove me the couple of miles to school but not too many years after I got my license I refused to ride in a car he drove, including his own, unless I drove. He was a "nervous nellie," always below the speed limit and had a very slow reaction time.

My buddy George would pick me up sometimes which was much better than college guys and girls seeing my grandfather drop me off. Sometimes, if George was not available, I walked or hitchhiked home. Hitchhiking was not as dangerous as now, particularly during the day; people still did not lock their doors at home in the Valley and a lot of the U.S.

The classes were not difficult and, as a theatre arts major, I immediately began reading for plays. I was noticed on campus because of my independent haberdashery style but few, if any, noticed I was Mouseketeer Lonnie despite the MMC running through 1958 and part of 1959. My grandmother gave me a healthy allowance and with no other expenses except gas for my rarely driven Corvette (when I could entice a buddy to drive for me) and any entertainments I wanted—from a film to an album or clothes without my grandmother's accompanying me with her check book. I was insouciantly solvent and in much better shape than most fifteen-year-olds. Besides, if anything financially challenging came up, I would just ask my gram for it and inevitably I got it without much ado.

I continued to see Barbara, who remained at HPS, thus being one of the rare girls I dated who was closer to my age. She was a brash, tough, ribald chick and that was enticing—at least when she was not in a frequent snitty, foul mood, or worse, when her palpable evil arose. I dated a few girls at Valley but no one of any significance until fall of '59 when Sharon entered my life.

In addition to George I had buddied up with Pete and attended T.A. parties at which I began to learn to drink a palatable, sweet concoction of bourbon and Coke, which my father also drank. Pete did most of the leads in our campus productions, like the Kirk Douglas role in the film of the Broadway play *The Detective Story*, while I played one of my early menacing character thugs, Lewis. Pete went with the lady who played the fem leads in most of our shows until Sharon showed up. It was only in writing and researching this book that it occurred to me that I did not become a character actor during my mid-teens in college but by doing all the roles I had done at four and five on *The Enchanted Lady* radio show just as my first professional, paid gig was ostensibly in vaudeville at five.

I had also become pals in my first year of college with Tom G., a buddy from the Witnesses, who would drive me to pick up Barbara and the three of us would go out or find Sonja and mess around, much to the dismay of the Jehovah's Witnesses when our racy foursome showed up at one of their parties and seemed way too worldly, something they intensely preached against. Our style of dancing was particularly threatening and *de trop* to Witness adults and kids our age.

The first time I actually got drunk was at Barbara's house on Franklin, a block north of Grauman's Chinese Theatre. I was fifteen. She and I, Tom G. remaining wisely neutral, had argued while drinking and I sneaked out with a few extra of those tiny airline bottles I had spied at her house. I roguishly staggered down to Hollywood Boulevard near Grauman's where Tom G. and Barbara chased me down and brought me back before the constabulary snared me. The streets were not as fraught with cops then, nor was the boulevard yet as minatory as Times Square.

Another friend was Ed, a drummer who was married and had an autistic son named Tod. Ed was a huge jazz fan, which allowed me another rare person to share my jazz love with; we would boozily sing Four Freshman songs, Ed harmony and me on melody, at parties. This friendship, although Ed maintained an emotive distance, was significant to me and to him. It lasted until a small argument turned into a confusing, silent ending in my fifties.

I had smoked grass furtively once or twice but it was Ed, and then Doreen's husband Bob, who introduced me to weed as the precipitating key to joyous, meaningless laughter—hours (or so it seemed) of no stress and the munchies. Eddie collected motorcycles, racy cars and weapons, the latter being quite foreign to me. No one in my family hunted or owned a gun that I ever saw or heard about.

Ed took Diane and me out to learn to shoot my Mossberg 12-gauge when I decided in my forties that society had changed so negatively that if you gave what was asked when your home was invaded you could just as easily die as if you fought with your attacker. This was the first weapon, after two switch blades in high school and a Bowie knife later, that I owned. I needed a way to defend myself and those for whom I cared. An off-duty cop, acting as security on an episodic (*Hollywood Beat*) I was shooting in a jewelry store just north of Hollywood and Vine later in the 'eighties, suggested that the shotgun was impractical around corners in a house and I should saw off the barrel. I never went that far.

Eventually I noticed that there were some undercurrents to my sociability in the T.A. department at Valley and one night Pete's lady, in her cups, made a slurred slur to me that both shocked and confused me. Pete hurried me out to his car and we took a drive. He pulled over to talk to me and confessed that he was gay and she was jealous of me because he was hung up on me.

I was a very shocked fifteen-year-old whose close friend, about thirty, was in love with him. I literally had not a clue; Pete showed none of the tells of most homosexuals and he had never put a move on me, nor slyly said anything that would indicate his sexual choices. Being sharp at fifteen in some areas does not mean you are sharp in all areas; of course, that is true at any age.

Soon after hanging with Tom G. I figured he was gay but he was in the closet and never talked about gay things, nor suggested anything sexual between us. The gay people in the business whom I had encountered for years were pretty obvious, at least the ones I knew about. I realized that many would think I was involved with Pete as his girlfriend apparently did. I did not condemn him, although I was hurt that he hid this reality from me, but he drove me home, for I still could not drive, and his betrayal—not of caring about me, but of not telling me the truth—led to my decision that we no longer would be friends.

As to my school work, I was taught some things but not inspired by any of the very fumbling quasi-educators in all subjects. I did manage to begin reading novels on my own; it would take a solid teacher much later to bring me to an understanding of poetry and, soon after, start my verse writing which shortly led to being published and then winning poetry awards.

It has always seemed terrible to me that none of the novels I was forced to read in high school, nor in my first college years, interested me. I had read *Silas Marner* and other tedious crap of that nature and, outside of the halls of academe, *Hot Rod Gang Rumble*, for obvious reasons, before college. Thus, I had no motivation from school or from my home, to read unless it was a compulsory class assignment and, unfortunately, the books I was forced to read bored me.

It took my own curiosity to bring me in my sixteenth year to Dostoyevsky, Faulkner, Joyce, Hemingway, Flaubert, Fitz, Proust and many others. I have been an avid reader since, probably going through about forty or more novels every year since this time. No matter where I live I always get a library card and go to the library every week or so although the search for literature has been meager for the last three decades but the McCarthys, Harts, Smiths, Bankses and LeCarres are still out there as well as some genre writers of merit like Hillerman, Burke and Martin Cruz Smith.

Some classes were quite impossible to be interested in, like Geology, and two semesters, that my idiot advisor wrongly told me I had to take, of South American History. This subject translates into a lot of bananas and *coups d'états* with the one interesting element of politically focused and active college students, which was the antithesis of late 'fifties and early 'sixties teens in U.S. colleges.

College life was much more about beer parties, Greek groups and getting laid (or in my case, close) in spite of memorizing drivel and getting grades good enough to glide past the parents, in my case, the grandparents. Very few college students showed any interest in the world outside of their own entertainments and needs. Except for not getting caught or put in jail, no one cared about much else except having fun. We took our freedom and unusually unfettered lives for granted. The late 'sixties—the assassinations and Vietnam—changed all that, at least for many of us.

My one absurd fraternity experience was being pledged by a frat, going to smokers, drinking suds and watching grotesquely bad porno films, hanging out and so on my first semester at Valley College. I knew that group mentality had never been for me; I am not a chorus member nor happy in that role while most people are, including the other Mouseketeers with the exception of Annie, for they need to belong to something. I was not going to wear Bermuda shorts and watch "F" films at every opportunity while guzzling far too much beer, using matches to ignite my passing wind and being a nameless cog in a social machine. When I was asked to join the brothers I politely told them I could not. I found out a while later that the fraternity was all-Jewish. This was never mentioned and I could only infer that they must have thought I was Jewish or thought it would be cool to have a *shagetz* for a mascot.

The South American history professor was a homey yokel who took Will Rogers sans humor and wisdom as his model. His stymied thought process led to horrid jokes with worse puns as he laughed at his own funnin' and bulged out his suspenders. I imagined he was always dying to stick some corn silk or other farm edible in his mouth as he pontificated. I managed to get a B from him, which damaged my grandmother and knocked out my $25 bonus to my allowance for every A, even though I loathed going to the class and memorizing meaningless crap I would absolutely and categorically never use or think of again. Paul Simon wrote, played and sang the apropos lyric a few years later but too late for me.

In my second semester on campus I almost got beaten up by a gym instructor I had never met. The geology teacher, a young woman with no feminine appeal and no concept of interesting students in any subject, noticed that I sometimes left class quietly and a few minutes early. It seemed obvious to me that this was her first teaching job. She apparently had this thug from Phys. Ed. sit in. I surreptitiously departed before the bell ending class and he stopped me outside and shouted at me regarding my rude and unacceptable behavior.

Without the uniform and badge, he was more fascistic, and physical, grabbing me hard by the arm to get my attention, than the anti-pea shooter cop in Pasadena. I explained that I was a theatre arts major and had a rehearsal for a scene I had to get to, which was not true but impossible to verify. He became more belligerent, his face raging red, and threatened to take me out to the football field and beat the shit out of me if I ever did it again for any reason. So much for academic enlightenment.

As much as I hated this young woman's execrable efforts as a teacher in a subject that I probably could have liked under other circumstances but have loathed ever since, the Neanderthal gym guy leaning on me kept me in the dreadful class, although the grade was, again, a B and not my usual A. I was also obliged to the head of the T.A. department who took this galoot down when he complained about me via inter-departmental phone call. My department head advised that I had best stay in the rock class and so I did.

And here I thought that by maturing to college I would be graded on my work and abilities. To these feckless teacher clones the rules were much more significant than getting students actively involved in and knowledgeable about the subject matter.

A surprising, unexpected problem crept up on me my first semester in a small role in a one-act play, *A Young Lady of Property* by Horton Foote, on the stage of our tiny theatre, the size of 99-seat houses in store fronts that debuted later. I had not performed since the MMC in mid-1958 and for three years on the Disney series I had been playing myself. I had not tried to become a character in a play in front of a live audience since I was ten, five years previously, and these are quite different ventures.

I was petrified much more than in my first professional appearance before an audience at four and my mind kept flashing to stories I had heard about Robert Preston, a film and Broadway star, who allegedly vomited because of nerves before every stage performance. Once he puked, he was fine. When I worked on Broadway and became friends with Pres I never witnessed, nor heard anything about this necessity of his to appease his fears. I thought I was going to hurl before and during my small scene near the end of the one act.

I entered tremulously down left with palms awash in sweat and my legs shaking so badly that I was convinced everyone in the audience could see the tremors in my slacks. I managed to get through it and get my lines out, surely not at the highest level of which I was capable, but having gotten through it I found it was easier each performance and I improved more each time. By my second play as Alan Seymour in *Picnic*, with Sharon in the female lead, I was okay, and as Sebastian in *Twelfth Night*, with Sharon as my twin and Penelope as my lover, I was pretty good.

It took me until my senior project in college portraying the lead, Jerry, in Albee's definitive one-act *The Zoo Story* in the second L.A. performance of the work to know that I was much better than just pretty good. I had worked very hard for no money, just desire, to build my acting craft and skills. I actually wrote to Edward Albee about ascertaining the film rights so I could write a screenplay and star in the film and I still have his polite letter of refusal. Unfortunately, no film was ever made of one of the best one-act plays, including Chekov's works, that any playwright has created.

The now legendary ACT San Francisco regional theatre sent a director to see the senior projects and she gave me very complimentary and encouraging words in the role of Jerry, including likening me to, "…with the proviso that I could be understood," an older actor who was doing pretty well in 1962: Marlon Brando. I improved further whenever I got the chance. I have only wished that I could get a larger, substantive role in film or television; most of my leads have been on stage, doing supporting work on tape or film, but I am confident about my abilities. There are actors who are capable of more than I am, but I am a good, dependable actor and better than most.

I have had little problem with theatre or any other performing since this regression rocked me in my first semester of college and I began learning not to take for granted the many things that came easily to me. I always check my stage props at half hour and film and TV props before

At 18 playing Jerry, the lead, in Edward Albee's drama The Zoo Story, *1961.*

shooting, and I always go over my lines, cues and key points of the performance beginning, middle and end even when I do a lead in a heavy book part, before each of the eight performances a week or the shooting of the scene.

When a stoned prop man demanded I return the actual cash I had used in a scene in *Lionheart* with Van Damme, I knew I had sought him out and returned the money as soon as the final take was over. There is a lot of drug taking on film sets. That is not to say that everyone is using but might explain some of the terrible problems and accidents that occur. The close-ups made the usual fake prop bills impossible to show in this scene which is always shown in promos for this flick. As the bookie who travels with the fight circuit, I say to Van Damme, "You know the rules. There are no rules!"

The prop man was adamant that I had kept the money and began getting unreasonable with my denial. He later remembered through what I assumed was his drug haze that the other bookie, an old Borscht Belt comedian, had also been given cash and he had kept the real gelt. Being at the level of too many of the supporting workers in a film, those involved in less creative efforts like driving or serving food or providing an actor's tools, this bullying cretin never apologized. I knew that my reporting him would cause me more problems than it caused him, so I let it go.

Except for sitcoms which are shot live like a one-act play but can be stopped for a huge mistake, TV and film always shoot in spurts, short scenes or parts of scenes, and it is not the end of the world if someone goes up on a line. However, if you are jobbing in and want to come back as well as protect your reputation, you leave mistakes or cracking up to the regulars or name actors that guest.

In these filmed or taped formats the hard part is getting to the pitch needed for that scene and maintaining it as you repeat it over many takes and reverse shots (showing the other actor or actors with whom you have dialogue). In theatre if you lose your lines you better know your character well enough that you can adlib and get back to the playwright's words and continuity or things quickly become worse than embarrassing.

I learned this at six in my second play at the Pasadena Playhouse. I played Rudy, a smaller role than my first stage role, amidst many other children most of whom had no lines, just adlib agreements or denials. In *The Pied Piper* there was one boy who had the kid lead and I just spoke up here and there in sundry scenes. The only memorable things about the experience were that it was co-directed by Gilmore Brown, the founder of the Pasadena Playhouse, and that my mom, since she had to be there due to my age, played a town woman, her only appearance as an actor.

One night the child lead did not make it to his entrance for the final scene and the Piper picked up the closest male child offstage, me, to

Van Damme is the fighter and I'm the head bookie in Lionheart, *1991.*

deposit in an audience box close to the proscenium but in the house of the theatre with the actress playing the kid's mother. It was my first experience that close to an audience since in a proscenium theatre there is a "fourth wall" and some distance. Of course, later in stock in the round and most intimately in *Tamara* audience members were always within touching distance, but at six it was very different than being onstage and having at least the convention of separation.

I was not the boy's understudy and only vaguely knew the scene, which I was not in, and I certainly did not know his lines. The actor playing the Piper wisely took the import of the lines and used them as his own, merely asking me if I agreed, which I did with very large and meaningful shakes of my quaking head, for I was scared you-know-whatless.

This frightening experience taught me a great lesson about knowing who you are, where you are, what you want and what you really want and really mean in any role. Being comprehensive about a script and your character is much more effective than one aspect of acting like Stanislavski's sense memory concept—recalling an emotion in a situation in your own life to use for a similar feeling in your character's life—and other thumbnail posits of effective ways to bring a name on a page to life.

I turned sixteen in '59, began driving my 'Vette to school and became instantly more popular. I picked up Dave one night and we went to a drive-in restaurant that no longer exists and we made a move on an attractive lady in the car next to us. She followed us back to the Renaissance Club and she refused to choose between us but took our phone numbers. She called me and it was my first experience with a call girl.

Later Christie moved to an apartment a few blocks away from the drive-in and up the street from the Whiskey a Go-Go where I much later shot my first segment of *Falcon Crest*.

Back at Valley College, it was hard to not notice Sharon for she won the school beauty contest as well as taking over all lead female roles. During *Twelfth Night* with my much older buddy Mike as Duke Orsino, I asked her out and, being a couple of years older than me herself, assured and a school beauty, she put me off for a while but I ingratiated myself, we dated and fell in love.

Or so I thought.

She did care about me and said and wrote "I love you" to me so I was more than a beard for her illicit affair with Mike, who was in his late twenties then and married with two children, but they were definitely rutting away whenever possible. Connie, Sharon's rotund and somewhat butch friend covered for her. Mike had notoriety as a child and young actor before the service, as one of the kids in *Gone With the Wind* and later the young sailor that Vivian Leigh talks to as she descends from a New Orleans streetcar that was named Desire in the film of Tennessee Williams' stage play. After leads in college Mike never made any headway in the business. Eventually, I understand he found a career in the airline business.

I was a veteran of various sexual maneuvers, but still a virgin. Naïve enough not to know Pete had a thing for me, I also did not pick up on the subtle interactions between Mike and Sharon until it was too late and I was consumed by my fifteen-year-old romance and my first consummated love. Well, *sort of* consummated.

Mom had married the crude, oafish bartender in Vegas, and my grandmother had bought them the small resort that my mother had found, asked for and received: a gas station, diner and about ten small rental cabins high in the mountains at the Bass Lake turn off, the last stop before Yosemite National Park. Mom offered to let me come up and stay for free with a girl, not being prissy about my sexual habits. She might have assumed that I had still avoided the missionary position by my sixteenth year, which was fact, but, whether due to our long separation or something else, she no longer delved into my private life.

I had taken Barbara up the year before and had good times and bad times. The good was getting to the not-yet-overrun-by-tourist-geeks beauty of Yosemite after my one experience with my parents as a kid and getting off with Barbara but not having actual intercourse. I also managed my very successful first and last water skiing experience on Bass Lake. I got up pretty easily on the skis and even managed doing some feats on one ski on that first outing. Subsequently, I learned of a young fellow who lost a leg and another who was killed both by being run over by speed boats so I never returned to that sport. Later my snow skiing became a one-time event in St. Moritz, Switzerland but it had nothing to do with mortality, although later Sharon's son died in just such an accident.

The bad was Barbara's unpredictable mood and nasty streak and my second meeting with my onerous step-father Don who would later be the bar manager at the Stardust for roughly twenty years. In our first terse, one-on-one conversation he invited me out back to watch his dog capture cats and literally tear them apart. Not my kind of guy.

I drove Sharon up in 'sixty and we were having a marvelous time. Our second night I was ready to thwart my and the Witnesses' god and give up my virgin penis for the first time for the eighteen-year-old beauty queen I loved. This was the fulfillment of all of my relationships from before Annette until this point in my life, sixteen and almost done with my second year of college. We had been drinking and we became more and more passionate in our love making. As I ardently thrust myself inside of her, Sharon was so overwhelmed with love that she called out, "OH, OH, MIKE!"

Not the way I would have written it.

I managed to hide and stifle my urge to cry from anger, threw on my clothes, jumped in my 'Vette and screamed down the mountain on the very winding two-lane road away from Yosemite. I tried at least three times to head off into the long plunge into the dark night and the long fall to the bottom of the mountains, but each time I steered that way I would pull back to the road at the last second. I finally pulled over and stopped at the first place that allowed it. I lit a cigarette and realized I was not going to kill myself—at least not on this dangerous, sinuous path on this lonely night of betrayal, shock and depression.

This was my very first attempt at suicide.

I drove back to the mini-resort, passing Don in his pickup looking for me, and I improvised through the reprehensible minutes of explaining away what I could, lying because it was necessary, and certainly not revealing what I had tried to do. The rest of our stay was cut short and was most unappealing to both Sharon and me.

We did not see each other for some years. Mike, who was about ten or eleven years older than Sharon who was two years older than me, divorced his wife and married my first lover but, of course, it did not last long at all.

Soon after returning from Yosemite, I visited Christy, who I found was in her early thirties. In our previous encounters she cared enough about me to not have penetration but to introduce me to many other exquisitely delectable sexual endeavors, some of which I had never heard of, nor read about before. She also introduced me to poppers—amyl nitrate—which at the right sexual moment can make everything very stimulating indeed. I have never used them since but they are in my memory bank.

She was surprised and pleased to learn that I had chosen to give over my religious holding back and go all the way. I saw no reason to keep myself pure for women who were screwing me only figuratively while screwing another guy or guys literally and continuing to tell me how much they loved me.

I graduated with an A.A. degree from Valley but did not attend the graduation ceremonies. I had learned from my HPS graduation. I later did not attend my B.A. or M.A. grad rigmarole nor any other such formal, pretentious waste of time. I was never excited about graduating, I just assumed it would happen. That fall I started classes at Valley State College, later to be known as California State College at Northridge or CSUN, in the same boring, useless major.

You learn to act by acting, not by text books. It helps to read a few books by Stanislavski, Michael Chekov, Boleslavsky and others but they are only able to open you to ideas that you must make your own, if you have not discovered them on your own, by actually acting. I have a very poor opinion of most acting teachers who tend more to be untrained, lay shrinks and actors that cannot make a living rather than instructors who can help novices to learn about their craft. Lee and Uta and Herbert and the rest may have been effective for some actors, but the ones I have encountered and seen are not of this ilk even if whatever method is viable.

The late, great actor Paul Scofield (*A Man for All Seasons*) felt that it was "…a great relief to be inhabited by somebody else." He felt that acting "…has something to do with being completely removed from oneself, which doesn't necessarily mean one is uncomfortable inside oneself." I do not agree thoroughly with this excellent thespian's take on the process, but perhaps in some way I found getting into some other character than Lonnie became, as Scofield said, "…a tremendously liberating sensation…" for I no longer was burdened with any form of depression, anxiety or the fear of not being the perfect boy.

When I was playing *Mack and Mabel* in Broadway's Majestic Theatre, whose back door leads into Shubert Alley, Anthony Hopkins, not yet Sir, took over the lead role of the shrink in *Equus* from Richard Burton and was quite excellent. I was convinced the boy playing the sociopathic other lead role was a method actor for he continually showered the closer rows with tears and snot for long periods of time. Acting may be being, as some teachers describe it, but too much reality shatters the illusion of the reality of art.

When my Cockney accent could not be understood no matter how authentic when I played the lead, Cocky, in the musical *The Roar of the Greasepaint, the Smell of the Crowd* in 1969, I altered certain words and lyrics, softening them enough to be understood by American ears, no matter how unauthentic they may have been.

I took very few acting classes, save those required by my degree, in which I learned not much at all; it merely helped, like dance classes, to exercise and improve my craft. My last experience was in 1970 in Greenwich Village with acting teacher Gene Frankel who was known for his Broadway directing.

I have the same opinion of bartenders who did not learn behind the stick, as I did. They merely memorize a lot of rubbish and have no feel for what making a good drink and serving people is all about and since I later tended bar for income from 21 to 24, I know of what I speak and drink.

At CSUN I was not the straight A student I formerly had been but I maintained more A's than B's and a rare C in something I was totally uninterested in and that was made much worse by yet one more wretched facsimile of an educator. It was a very rare class that forced me to labor.

These two years at CSUN led to my worst grade ever. A pixilated Brit teacher—obnoxious, demeaning and downright rude—gave me the only grade below C I have had in my life: a D+. However, the only grade higher in the class of about thirty young people was a C- that soon became an F when it was ferreted out that he had plagiarized. My D+ was then the highest grade in class, but the brain-challenged fop who expounded in front of the blackboard learned nothing and refused to change his clearly inefficient stabs at teaching. He was not new at the profession but should have received an F- from every student in the class. Despite him, I managed another B.

I met the young ladies Sue, Karen and Laura. Sue was mesmerized, she later confided, when I came to her class at the teacher's request to do a seduction scene I had done for my class with him at the opening of *The Life and Death of King Richard III* with an older and very good college actress playing opposite me as Lady Anne. I was wearing tight-fitting pants, which were new for guys in that era—most guys wore blousy, loose, over-sized pants, which again became fashionable in the early '90s when sloppy gang styles took over youth apparel. I liked the way tight pants looked and wore this style. Most guys were terrorized and suspicious of such outfits but girls, who were my focal point, were fascinated.

"I could not take my eyes off of it!" Sue said at seeing my dick halting around in my street pants in Richie III's disfigured locomotion that I used in the scene done close up in the classroom. We got together sexually very soon at a T.A. party. Sue was a caring young woman, the first I had met who had been abused by her father.

Karen and I met in competing roles in my only children's theatre production. I was a night person and my seeking sex, parties and booze was not well juxtaposed with getting up to do early morning kiddie matinees. They are a fun, reactive audience but I need to wake up more before emoting, even when not hung over, with the emotional demands of stage work. Film can be early but it does not last for two acts.

I played the fumbling, comical king and Karen was the terrorizing wicked witch. She was always trying to upstage me, despite our not being onstage often together, and I was very good at thwarting her attempts in a game I believe we both enjoyed. At a party during the show we made love the first time outside in the back seat of my new '61 T-bird. We fell into some sort of sexual love that lasted until after my M.A. and my second trip to Europe, more than three years.

Karen was blonde and sophisticated sexually, having had affairs (I later learned) with a leering, pipe-puffing dirty old man of a professor in the T.A. department and with a former college leading man, Pat, who left to teach at Valley College. Only Christy surpassed Karen's oral proficiency and interest in the same, which was not always the case for women in the early 'sixties—or today.

She introduced me to one of my unmet poetry mentors, T. S. Eliot, and she was very neurotic, erotic and dramatic. These things are attractive to young men but are qualities that I have found are best to avoid. Our last meeting was a disaster for me and apparently some kind of revenge for her.

Somehow we came into contact in the late 'seventies after Diane and I had moved from the Apple to L.A. and she invited us over for dinner with her husband. She spent the night belaboring me with indirect and direct insults. We have not met since that unpleasant attack. But then, from seventeen to twenty, she was my most important female relationship, and that I remember in the fervor of it rather than the diminishment and demise.

Laura was her best friend and when she and Karen were on the outs, then split, Laura had had her eye on me so we quickly became intimate. I liked her very much and she had a fascinating habit. She said she had never done it with anyone before but she loved falling asleep with my penis in her hand. Until middle age I was not an easy sleeper and how I managed it I do not recall but I do know it would never happen again, nor could I ever again achieve any sleep being held in this intimate and, in some ways, comforting manner. I actually do need my space.

I found my ultimate subject in my junior year: philosophy. It was taught by a very sardonic Mort Sahl-like professor who amusingly was built and looked very much like Jackie Gleason. It was quite a combination for imparting the love of thought. I went on to take philosophy whenever I could, read outside class on my own and in my thirties, well after my work on my Ph.D., returned to college to take non-goal-nor-degree-oriented units due to my interest in Western philosophy.

But after considering changing to a philosophy major in my junior year, I decided that my five invested semesters would string out my college years for an even longer period. I was already bored with most classes and this major would be as impractical as theatre arts, both leading to nothing but teaching the subject.

I only wanted a general liberal arts education and the option to fall back on making a living as a teacher if I did not succeed as an adult actor, so I stayed with my major and took mandatory entrance exams to return to UCLA for my master's degree.

I did encounter Dr. Frank Morgan in my studies at CSUN and he had quite an affect on me for he was a true teacher and educator. An overweight, bald man with reddish, round cheeks, and stuffed into rumpled Brooks Brothers type apparel, he had the seldom-experienced ability to enthuse a student, and this about dramatic literature. Enthuse, when examined by its roots, means "to give breath to," and that he did.

When a very old woman who had returned to college ranted about the heinous act of Haemon, the brother of Antigone, who kills himself in despair after his sister Antigone is slain, Morgan said, "Anyone who reaches adulthood and has not at least considered suicide once is not worth knowing."

He also once said that he read at least fifty pages a day and I have done just that ever since he blithely uttered the sentence in 1962.

He was a sad man, drank too much although never visibly drunk but he was the very best teacher I ever had in many years of college and all the years prior to that. I have more than once felt badly that I never connected to him and told him how important he was to me and my forming and have always assumed he just continued to enthuse students and drank himself to death. I wrote a poem about Dr. Morgan a few years back and likened him to a mentor, particularly as a writer, and the father that I never had.

I became best buddies with Conrad at CSUN, like Mike before him a guy back on the GI bill who was about eleven or twelve years older than me. He was even more of a con artist than Mike with much less of the charm and hair and when he attempted to put me on, as he did every one else including all the professors, I looked him directly in the eye and was having none of it. He immediately decided I was to be his best friend for that would prevent me from exposing his social skullduggery, which in essence, is his only contribution to life other than fathering children.

I ran into him in a bar about twenty-five years ago and his solipsistic braggadocio had not changed, as he told the attractive female bartender that he could take some pro shots of her if she wanted to get into commercials. He maintained that he was a pro photographer which I knew to be a lie. He wanted to get into her pants, pure and simple, and she gave him her phone number. He bragged that day about putting two kids through college but since he was untutored for someone who had attended college, I have always assumed that his meager acting career was merely a front for his actual business dealings. The last time I saw him at his home in the 'seventies he offered Diane and me some coke. She said no while I hit a line, but it did not do much for me. I had tried coke one other time with Frank, a guy I knew from my first *George M* run, in the bathroom of the star house in Tahoe. Frank was in Debbie Reynolds' act at a hotel there and I came up to visit my friend Broadway conductor Jack Lee who was orchestra conductor. After the show I attended a party with Frank and Jack that was thrown by Debbie. I did not get off on the coke, although I know that drinking and/or smoking grass before doing it can change the effect but that was the case both times so I have never returned to it.

I have always resisted habit-forming drugs like heroin, coke, sundry pills and, for different reasons, peyote, acid and other mind-altering drugs. I prefer liquor and from time to time, although quite rarely in the last thirty years, grass; mixing the two has not been provident for me.

One night in 1969 I was thoroughly juiced, while touring the country in *George M* and I smoked some weed that I found out later was laced with angel dust. It led to the worst drug/booze experience in my life and I was fortunate to have my lover Janyce there to minister to me on the large, very cold, tile floor of my hotel room in Milwaukee. I was much more careful from whom I took *ganja* after that night in my twenty-fifth year.

Conrad and I were involved in many wild escapades in my junior and senior years of college which always involved parties large or as small as four, ladies and booze. One of our most scandalous took place with no women but lots of booze at the Harbor House, an upper class motel directly above the Pacific Coast just north of Malibu. He was friendly with the manager of the place and the club had very good jazz entertainment. We also got some free drinks and, after closing at 2 a.m., we now and then were given access to free food from the oversized fridge.

Ben, the manager, was gay, and in my senior year Conrad and Bob, Doreen's husband, met through me. When a new, paying roommate was needed Bob, separated from Dodo, moved in with Conrad. One night the three of us drove down to Harbor House and proceeded to get wasted. Bob disappeared with Ben, for he had two ways about most things, and Connie and I drunkenly went into the kitchen and ate.

When we came out we heard the sounds of sexual congress and decided to investigate. We had noticed earlier in the evening that an attractive older woman at the piano bar was inebriated and coming on to the black pianist and the white bartender. Not being sober enough to consider that we could get in some major trouble, Conrad and I climbed up to the second floor via outside trappings of the building and were watching through a sliding glass door and a diaphanous curtain as she was being serviced in the rear by the bartender as she simultaneously was servicing the pianist—his organ, not his piano.

We began to laugh and one of the guys looked toward the window, although they could not identify who it was since they were in the light and we were not. We both jumped down but escaped without too much damage to ourselves.

Bob had disappeared, just as he had at Doreen's party; this time, most likely after doing what we suspected with Ben, he had wandered off and had fallen down a hill to the beach. Ben, Conrad and I finally found him and helped him limp back to our vehicle. We made it home very slowly and carefully.

On another occasion out drinking, after I had sold the T-bird and bought my P-1800, I let Conrad drive and the stupid S.O.B. rolled it by taking the corner to his rented house much too fast. We wound up upside down, wheels in the air, in our seat belts and not hurt much at all. We were very, very lucky.

The car was just this side of totaled and it was an era when drunk driving was not considered as dangerous, nor as deadly as it has been for thirty or more years. We were not even tested for booze. I was not pleased that I could have been permanently injured or killed, nor that my P-1800 was in for major repairs. I got it back seven weeks later and after causing the accident Conrad would not even pay the $200 deductible, which more or less covers the extent of his friendship and his character. It also taught me that no one but me drives my vehicle except in an emergency.

There were many other episodes at Conrad's rented house, like when my buddy Cliff (later one of the leads on the TV series *The Name of the Game*) and I woke up, both with hangovers, we enthralled someone else's lady outside as we played badminton, nude. She said she found new, delicious nuances to the game.

I learned some female-seducing techniques from Conrad but I preferred being direct and honest. It took me about two years to realize how unreliable, solipsistic and selfish he was to everyone, even the very few people for whom he cared. His mutually alcoholic, shifty older brother the lawyer who flew planes was actually worse. I backed out of actual and future betrayals by Conrad and his pathological, onanistic, con life at the end of my senior year at CSUN.

I moved on to my master's degree at UCLA, all in very small classes, unlike my first experiences there, and to more theatre arts tedium and boredom and a singularly unusual, now that I was no longer a virgin and intent on sexual merging as often as possible, outlandishly pristine relationship with Marlene. My love for Karen still hung around me but it had waned, we went to different schools and could only see each other now and again. Frankly, I had found then and until my forties that having more than one female involvement at a time was more to my liking.

I was only cast in supporting roles at UCLA due to an unspoken scholastic theatre system much like actual show business, in that people cast what they know and David Birney, then at the Westwood campus in his fourth year before his TV fame, was always the first choice. The same was true of other actors who had been there for a year or more, like George Takei, later on *Star Trek* with whom I shared an agent at one point, although casting Asians, blacks and Hispanics was extremely atypical at the time unless the role demanded it.

I did manage to do my first company of *West Side Story* in the L.A. Youth Theatre production in Hollywood in 1963 the summer in which I turned 18 and in September began my M.A. degree. I played the leader of the Jets, Riff. I cut my first album at eleven in 1955 before I auditioned for the MMC. After becoming Mouseketeer Lonnie I cut some others along with a few other Mice. The album for this production of *West Side* gave me two solos as opposed to a solo line here and there. My next and last album singing was for *Mack & Mabel* in 1975. I did a song for *Hook* with some solo lines as a cockney pirate but the section was scrapped by Spielberg, so I am not heard in the score.

Marlene was in the theatre department at the Westwood college, but she was engaged to Mel Blanc's son Noel, who was in the military, which prevented her from the quite often procreative if not properly defended against act and left us the alternatives I had lived with for too many teenage years. Marlene was working on her B.A. and was a year or two older than I. She had marvelous hair and skin and was bright, if not a comprehensive intellectual.

I had a good relationship with Dean Melnitz, a star academic for *The Living Stage*, a mandatory text for any T.A. department that he coauthored with Professor McGowan. I had to write the first paper in his seminar and I had only one week to research and write a close to thirty-page work, with footnotes, on the last half of nineteenth century French theatre. I brought the paper in, he gave me an A and exhorted the other students to read my paper and follow my example.

Dr. Selden, however, was the ancient fellow I wrote about earlier who was known for his set designing in academic theatre, not professionally. To my dismay he was teaching playwrighting and had written a paltry book on the subject. I believe that constraining any art form is wrong. Art is not science, nor is science always what most people think it is, fact.

My first play, a one act titled *N'aboutir a'Rien* [*To Come to Nothing*], was a satiric parody of Beckett's *Waiting for Godot* and other Absurdist playwrights, even Albee in *The Sandbox*, although Sam goes farther than Ionesco and the others. Selden deemed it a near-plagiaristic work. That was inaccurate but I could do nothing about it except explain that it was indeed a satire, and he would not accept that.

Grading me down as much as he could, I still got a B from him and I have already discussed the extra unit and semester he put me through to show me who was boss by rejecting my first two-act play as my final project. As stated, Dean Melnitz bailed me out but I also had to take a lengthy written test—essay questions, three hours in the morning, three after lunch—which was the same as Ph.D. candidates took, the only difference being they also had to take lengthy oral exams. I did manage to avoid any class time, while agonizing over books for the written essays with essay questions like: "18th century British theatre: extrapolate."

I had not yet decided if I could face any more theatre arts sterility in classrooms even at Cambridge. I wanted to get on with my life as an actor, an emerging director and choreographer and a writer in the initial stages of playwriting, poetry, and the novel. I decided to travel and enjoy Europe that summer and then to go to Cambridge to see what was what on campus and in their doctoral program in theatre.

What I found in Europe on my second visit to St. Moritz, Paris and London was anomie and despair and loneliness and, when I returned, a situation beyond my ability to contend with at the time. In the loneliness of a less than palatial single room in London near Paddington Station, I finally convinced myself that my unfocused love for Karen, who was still a part of my life, was what I truly wanted and needed most in the world. I gave over the idea of pursuing a Ph.D.—I wanted to act, not teach. I also wanted to go home.

    I found on my return that while writing love letters back to me Karen was screwing and would later marry a pool hustler and wannabee actor. This led me to the heart of my troubling despondency and depression and to the night of Scotch and knives.

Chapter 9

The Rest Was Almost Silence

One of the most important things to come out of my first European trip was to convince me that I preferred acting in theatre over film and television. I became much more intense about stage work and it would eventually drive me to New York. I have been fortunate to see many stage stars, also known from film work, like Sir Alec Guinness, Jessica Tandy and Hume Cronyn, Sir Anthony Hopkins, Maggie Smith, Sir John Gielgud (known by friends and coworkers as Surgeon, as in Sir John), James Earl Jones, George C. Scott (with whom I filmed *The Hospital*), Sir Michael Redgrave, Alan Bates, Hector Elizondo (with whom I worked on *Chicago Hope*), Henry Fonda, Frank Langella and Glenn Close. I have missed Meryl Streep and will see her work on a stage at the first opportunity. These great actors move you and make you laugh with no two-dimensional or three-dimensional tricks.

I witnessed Chuck Heston, who surprisingly to me, started in theatre, do a play as Sherlock Holmes and found his acting, as on screen, wooden; Diane and I left before Act II. The worst professional work I have ever seen in my life was Robert Vaughn at the Pasadena Playhouse in a most foul attempt at the lead in *Hamlet*. He even lost some of the lines the entire audience knew by heart.

After months of the pain from Sharon's rejection, I reconnected, much to her mother's dismay, with the pretty, flighty blonde JoAnne. We spent hours on the phone since it was difficult to get face-to-face time together. JoAnne had been inculcated, as had Mouseketeer Cheryl by her mom as well, to find and marry a wealthy man. JoAnne did well with a lawyer but Cheryl hit the jackpot with Lance Reventlow, who died prematurely in a plane accident, leaving her a young heiress. I reconnected platonically with Jo after her marriage and realized what a termagant, unhappy life and divorce would have followed our marriage. Jo's husband Lester died fairly young some twenty-five-plus years later after a self-defense gun battle with one of JoAnne's lovers, according to a newspaper account I found online.

The year after breaking up with Jo I began my first novella, *Off to Europe with Mr. Pond*, which detailed the wondrous and tedious failed love affair I had with her. My next writing was my first novel *Scooter, Or All for Love*, which was a satire of a male's coming of age sexually— a retort to Terry Southern's *Candy*, which was a retort to Voltaire's *Candide*.

The trip to the foreign countries started merrily for I drank legally in NYC at eighteen as well as in Europe, mostly wine with a few extremely expensive Johnny Walker Red Scotches on the rocks—not my favorite, but the most common in Europe at the time. One double on the Via Veneto in Rome cost me $10! I complained to the manager to no avail, but $10 for a double call Johnny Red on the rocks in 1961 was extreme. In a tiny Parisian estaminet I paid little for my first cognac as I stood at the bar. Just a sip of the liquor hit above my eyes and soared downwards scorching my throat and then streaked to my toes. My eyes were close to tearing and I avoided cognac until I discovered the smoothness of Remy Martin VSOP a few years later.

I encountered my first nightclub hookers in a walk-down bar near Times Square and eschewed the choice. My former college teacher and the tour leader, Bob Rivera and I, in a rare moment away from the tour group, got held up for expensive drinks by two call girls in Heidelberg but our objective was not sex. During the seven-country, five-week excursion any sexual endeavors were confined to JoAnne and my one unpaid professional dalliance in Pigalle the night I met up with Tommy Kirk.

I maintain great visual memories from the Rijksmuseum in Amsterdam, even after the Metropolitan and MOMA in Manhattan. I had a marvelous afternoon being enhanced by Vermeer, Hals and most especially the iconic chiaroscuro of Rembrandt Harmenszoon van Rijn. I believe this was the birth of my museum searching throughout my life, for my family had no interest in art and I never had a school field trip of that nature, actually, no field trips at all. I only really saw the Louvre and other exquisite Paris museums and their art in 2006 on my third visit to the city after a week in Firenze, Italy. It was a wondrous two weeks for Diane and me.

While on the road with a show, my primary pursuits (after finding a woman) were museums and excellent food. I discovered the largest collection of Matisse in the U.S. in Baltimore, the frontispiece of an Elizabethan house and many fabulous El Greco paintings in Toledo, Ohio, the sister city of Toledo, Spain, and an excellent triptych by Bosch, in addition to a wonderful sculpture by Kahlil Gibran. I had not taken to Gibran's overrated writing and was unaware what a good sculptor he had also been. This epiphany was at a small, obscure museum in Norfolk, Virginia.

I remember the Rijks much more than the canals and the rest in Amsterdam. My only memory of Cologne, Germany, was that I saw two young women walking down the street; one had her arm stretched above her head and I was shocked to see a great patch of dark hair displayed. Women did not do such things in bourgeoisie 1961 North Hollywood nor anywhere else in the U.S. that I was aware of at eighteen.

Venezia was extremely humid on my only visit, which should be no shock, but I hate humidity. I bought some exquisite 14 karat gold-rimmed brandy snifters with an inscribed N for Napoleon Brandy. This was after I opened the metal louvers covering my window in the hotel room and had one snap closed on my finger leaving me with a black fingernail for some time. Before the telltale fingernail occurred, we had a fine time in a casino and I lost a few francs the only time I played roulette in Lucerne, Switzerland.

Jo and I were getting along for a while and then arguing fitfully. We had taken to buying a bottle of chilled white wine, cheese and a baguette every other day or so at our mid-morning rest break from our tour bus. I have been a cheese lover all my life. An argument in my room just off the Via Veneto led to Jo slapping me and my returning her slap, my first striking of a female since attacked by Tammy's fists in the second grade, and she was so shocked to have a man respond in kind that our interaction was cooled for a while. It was merely a light slap and she had boasted that I would not dare to return her violence. I was unable to condone that kind of overbearing demand and challenge.

We rekindled in Nice, where we saw a local carnival and I ordered the worst martini on the rocks I have ever had. I surmised later they did not understand my classroom French and served me MARTINI & Rossi vermouth on the rocks. So much for my youthful *soignée*. We came close to consummating our relationship in Nice that night, but no cigarillo. Hence, my aforementioned foray with Tommy Kirk in Paris the next night and the winding down of the tour and my relationship with Jo at Stratford-on-Avon. The hotel was ancient and lovely, with wood floors very warped by time. We saw a pedestrian *Romeo and Juliet*. Back in London we saw a Chekov play and *A Funny Thing Happened on the Way to the Forum*, one of Sondheim's less complex works.

I was picked up at the airport by a long-time girlfriend (now deceased), Sandi. My grandmother thought she was the best female I had ever been involved with but I knew she would not do for me, although I cared a great deal about her for years; she expressed her love but always seemed as closed as Eddie and later my former friend Tommy. I believe she hid or drifted toward women later, which could explain why she never married. She also played my grandmother like a Strad.

JoAnne and I no longer saw each other as lovers, yet we became friends a couple of years later after she married Les. We double dated and went away for weekends in my early twenties when I began dating Sharon after her marriage to Mike dissolved. Eventually, JoAnne became an alcoholic, surely inherited from her mother, and moved from the Bobby Darin/Sandra Dee house Lester and she bought above Sunset to a lovely home on the ocean near the village in Montecito, California. It had the first swimming pool I had ever seen painted black.

I drove up a few times but it was uncomfortable and she seemed to have switched to Quaaludes and other drugs to augment the constant white wine. My last meeting with her was in 1980 when I was living at Seacliff, a small beach colony due west of Ojai, California. After warm initial greetings, it dwindled into a sad and final goodbye for both of us.

Karen and I had matured our relationship but we were distant in many ways. We still saw each other and I assumed she dated others as did I with JoAnne then Marlene and still Sandi.

My second European experience in 1963 was definitely quite different. A student I knew at CSUN was going to St. Moritz, Switzerland to meet up with a friend. I did not know him all that well and had never heard of his buddy. They were then going to drive to Paris and I wanted to return to the city of lights, where cars used only their dims, which is no longer a tradition.

Rob was a bit of a geek to me but seemed affable enough despite copying me like Don Little at HPS: I got a horse, Don got one a year later. I had an Alfa Romeo and Rob got one the next year. I bought a pair of unusual shoes and Paul G. bought the same shoes. Maybe the worst copyist was Dale Babcock, a tap dancer at HPS, who in his second year at the school changed his pro name to LONNIE Dale Babcock. Since I could do nothing about this sort of thing, I squashed my frustration and tried to view it as what it was—a compliment.

Soon after arrival in St. Moritz my intuition about Rob was proven correct. His offensive whining and pettiness did not make things pleasant. Geekish qualities do make the geek. His buddy from somewhere or other, Jack, had just gotten out of the service and, ostensibly, had not much more than a few *sous*, absolutely no higher, perhaps no lower, education and was on the sleazy side, but seemingly not dangerous.

I discovered fondue and *fleisch* (meat) fondue in St. Moritz before it became a vogue in the U.S. and one day Rob and I attempted to write a song, for he played the guitar and I wrote lyrics. In the 'eighties at a BMI workshop at the Dorothy Chandler Pavilion in Los Angeles, I wrote the lyrics and book to a musical titled *Fantasies* but the ditty Rob and I wrote was sub-par, and so we put an end to that.

We did drive to Paris after about two weeks but our threesome became a foursome in Paris, now joined by a French girlfriend of Jack's who stayed in the small room the three of us shared in a one-star hotel with three single beds—they were on a budget and I voted to stay with those I knew who spoke English. To my distaste and sleeplessness, they screwed like bunnies every night and I have never been a voyeur—nor a coitus audiophile.

In a short time I had cut myself off from the world becoming a lone being, more acutely aware of the isolation and depression that had been developing in me throughout my childhood and teenage years. In those earlier times I would hole up in my bedroom, door closed to the world, after a hurt or slight by some female. I played Sinatra's *Only the Lonely* album or other laments by Bennett or Mathis, nursing and indulging my somber view of my life at that time and into the future. I had no music with me in Europe, so I merely stared. Obtuse, self-pitying and puerile it may have been, but I am guilty of it and no one, including me, realized depression was a distinct and serious disease.

Both in St. Moritz and Paris, where I could barely do more than order a *jambon et fromage*, I was lumbered with two unpleasant strangers and the giggly, erotically vocal girlfriend of Jack. I became the most isolated that I had ever been in my life. Being unable to communicate with other humans except on an extremely limited level exaggerates loneliness. My only other outlets were a few letters from Sandi, which were very innocuous, and my growing love and missives to Karen.

I did not analyze it until much later but I had arrived at twenty successful in show business, having a meaningful amount of blings and no financial worries, a stellar academic record through my M.A., a new Alfa, a huge wardrobe, jewelry, the atelier/bedroom I designed atop the home I shared with my grandparents for no mortgage, nor rent, as I drank from my Venetian glass snifters, looked out on the pool and entertained ladies. I had no health problems and was in Europe for the second time. I was a very lucky, well-off young man. But I was indomitably unhappy and depressed. My only solace was Karen and I fell back into a deep love for her.

I became unsure whether I wanted to go to London and finally decide about my Ph.D. and Cambridge. We drove Jack's old Volkswagen north to Calais, stayed overnight and took the ferry to Dover in order to proceed to London. On board we were given a very hard time by the extremely insulting and nasty British immigration officer. We were low on money and both Rob and I were expecting money at American Express in London. The immigration dictator preferred not to believe us. I had my clothes, jewelry and so on, Jack owned the Volkswagen and other personals, the same with Rob but, at the moment, we only had about three hundred cash between us, most of it mine.

We were stopped by this immigration schmuck and I politely and appropriately questioned his choices. As a result, we were kept as prisoners overnight on the ferry in Dover, locked in our rooms with only a cheese sandwich and milk. I hated milk, and as you recall, was allergic to it. The next morning we were put on the first ferry for a return trip back to Calais which we had to pay for, which seemed to me to be a bit much even for Brits.

I was livid and had my grandmother wire two thousand dollars of my money to Crédit Lyonnais in Calais. Rob got a thousand from home and muttered something about a distant relative who was in Congress and we paid a third time for the bloody ferry and after rocking and rolling tumultuously across on the extremely choppy channel waters again, we entered England and entrained north to London.

Soon after our arrival I got my own room near Paddington Station, although we did not know it was a disreputable area, and they shared a room. I could usually understand and be understood in English so I was sure things would be better. I did a good Cockney accent in a cold reading without preparation even then but downstairs in the "Whatever and

Chips" place there were Cockneys that I could not comprehend except for a word here and there as they chatted me up for a cigarette and commented bitterly on Liztyler's loflife.

I decided to forget Cambridge and get back to Karen and home, so I booked passage on the *S. S. France*, which left in three days. It was my first ocean voyage. I moved to a nice room at the Hilton, near the U.S. Embassy, and was pleased to bid a final farewell to Rob and Jack. I walked about seeing pilfered Elgin Marbles and other sights, ate well and enjoyed the few days before the ship's departure, at least when I was out and about and around other humans.

There were two attractive British girls and a middle-aged American male at my dining table and the voyage was enjoyable, but I wanted to get back more quickly and realized too late I should have taken a plane. The man tried to get me to sneak some booze through customs, but I refused to put myself in a compromising position.

Sandi dutifully picked me up as she promised but I did not want to hurt her even more in this context and held off telling her of my resolve about Karen, whom I saw the next day.

Karen and I made marvelous love. I asked her to marry me and she asked for time to consider it. I did not find this a problem—it is a big decision; I had been away for six weeks and we had not been as close as we were for some time. My memory is not as clear as I would like, but some time in this period of waiting for her response I heard that she was seeing someone else.

What I heard more precisely was that a snide and untrustworthy friend, David from CSUN, had turned a friend onto Karen because of her gifted oral talents. David was an egocentric user. He was the son of a screenwriter, who got him into the business, and I have only heard of him as one of the many producers of the *Alien* film series, although I have never seen his name on a screenplay, nor a teleplay.

The last time I had seen David two friends from the nightclub act I had done in the 'sixties were coming over and I asked him and his date if they would like to drop by. The female performed in the nightclub act I did and also directed the written dialogue that linked the songs. Her pleasant husband did not perform, but was not William F. Buckley, Jr. David, who should not be confused with Dave from HPS, came over with a girl from CSUN who later became famous and unfortunately contracted MS—Teri Garr. These two entertained themselves, I assume after smoking too much funny stuff, by patronizing and belittling my two less intellectual friends. It was impossible not to see and I would stand no further cruel impoliteness. I asked them to leave and they did so.

In response to my proposal, Karen asked me to come over and said she could not marry me; she was in love with someone else. I had no idea at the time, but if we had married, our mutual depression would have become vitriolic and soon terminal. I acted as if I could deal with it. I was disappointed, naturally, but able to "move on." That was a testosterone saving of face, a lie.

I began about a week of serious daily depression and drinking until one night I had started on a second fifth of scotch. Mike had introduced me to scotch and told me that at first it would taste like dirty socks, but then I would never touch sweet drinks again. He was right on both counts and I have disliked the taste of bourbon and liqueurs ever since. Now I was twenty and drank J & B.

I needed someone to talk to, perhaps it is more appropriate to say someone to *vent* to, although the usage of the word was not in fashion then. I called Tim. We were not close friends. Actually he was Karen's friend, but he was an intelligent, likeable acquaintance of mine. David pretended to be bright, but Tim was actually sagacious and that was rare even in the hallowed halls of memorization at HPS, Valley, CSUN and UCLA, and that included almost all of the faculty to whom I was exposed.

I continued to drink and voice my monumental angst and raging hate for being betrayed and abandoned by Karen. It is hard to believe and disclose here how deeply I felt all this for it sounds like someone else who is tragically deluded, or a character in a soap opera, but it is an honest truth of who I was that night.

All the earlier abandonment, rejections and betrayals were now joined by yet one more female rejection after my mom and dad, Sharon, Mike, JoAnne, Conrad, God and any others I could come up with, all of which added up to an enormous sense of not existing, not only not being perfect but being so loathsome that no one gave a damn about me and whether I lived or died. I believe I felt I was going to get back at all of them by making myself literally nonexistent.

In many ways what happened next is the most positive thing in my life for it led me, against my family's wishes and without their aid or that of any friends or lovers, to seek the clinical help I needed. At the time it was just a physically abusive shock and a more shameful episode than when my mother slapped me at the Masonic Temple or insouciantly left me for Vegas and my gross stepfather, Don. There was actually something even more decimating that I would not bring back from my subconscious until later.

I had never wanted anything to do with guns; the only time I had as yet used one was with Karen and Tim in the hills when he let me fire the .22 revolver he had. But I had begun carrying a knife when I was about eleven or twelve to be a tough guy and for protection, even though my mom had prevented me from having one when I was younger. My grandmother had gotten me a very tiny gold pocket knife, with a half inch blade, for a watch fob at about seven, but Mom took it away. The first small pocket knife I bought was in Evanston, Illinois, when the Mouseketeers trekked there for a personal appearance. I was twelve, but Dot kept it for me until I was fifteen. I soon bought a four-inch switchblade on my own.

I was smaller and younger than all the guys in high school and there were always bullies and gangs even in the 'fifties; they just were not as prolific, did not have the same notoriety, nor weaponry. The only known name was the Hispanic White Fence Gang. In addition to fists, their weapons were knives, bats, pipe lengths and a rare zip gun, as opposed to the assault rifles and automatic weapons that have been standard in L.A. for twenty years or more now.

My drunken anger and depression led me to take my Bowie knife, much bigger than the switchblade, out of a drawer. Tim just stared at it and I began slashing at my wrists. I found out later that you don't cut across the veins but along them but I was so boozed up the multiple hackings caused me little pain.

Tim attempted to dissuade me, but aided by my depression and alcohol and rage, I was determined. He tried to leave, less from fear of me than to call the cops or get aid but, to my most profound shame, I threatened him with the knife if he did not stay until I completed my death act.

I had shown violence only toward myself and objects previously. In moments of drinking and anger and/or depression, I had put my fist through doors and walls, but the only death attempt was in the car—not with a large blade—and I had *never* threatened another person.

The blood did not flow quickly at all, so I continued to chop at the wounds to get it over with more quickly.

I had been playing music and talking loudly at times, shouting off and on, and it was about three or four a.m. My grandmother came up the stairs, saw what was going on and pleaded with me to keep my voice down. She did not want my grandfather awakened. I told her to get out and she did. I did not threaten her with the knife but kept it exposed. It appeared to me that she cared more about John being awakened than my bleeding to death.

I continued chopping and eventually, very fortunately, passed out from some blood loss and the liquor. I was lucky not to impale myself on the blade.

Tim took me to an emergency unit at a hospital and I was sewn up by a disgusted physician who commented that I was like too many fools who are too stupid to succeed in taking their life. I responded that it was my first time and I had not read enough literature on the subject.

The scars were formidable, for he did nothing cosmetic, and for years after they healed I wore long sleeve shirts to cover the shame I still felt for my rage and lack of character.

I asked Tim to drive me over to Karen's rather than back home. It was about 6 a.m. and light by then, and since he could not convince me to go home, he drove me to my former lover's apartment in Northridge. I do not recall seeing Tim after and know I have never seen him since I recovered. I owe him an apology and a sincere thank you for being with me during this night of lunacy, liquor and too-close death.

Thanks, Tim. I might have succeeded if you had not been there for me.

Karen was asleep and surprised, but she let me in and Tim left. I told her what had happened. She was kind enough to make love to me, but I knew from her lack of intimacy that it was totally ended, dead.

I also knew I had to stop drinking and see a psychiatrist for I remembered my reaction to Sharon's rejection with the car and my lonely bouts in my room that my grandmother never attempted to assuage or even acknowledge and absolutely never discuss. I did not want to kill myself and I needed to find out what motivated me and how I could stop it.

When I mentioned this to my grandmother, she was appalled. Being uneducated, she felt that seeing a shrink was more shameful than whittling away on my wrists. There is no question in my mind that everyone else in the family felt the same way. My father remained incommunicado and my mother, told of the events, offered nothing in the way of consolation or interest except for predictable, hollow, sentimental words. I am no longer sure she even did that. She certainly did not leave Vegas to see me.

It occurred to me later that it was major serendipity that the police were not called, for attempted suicide, the act many existentialists believe to be the only possible human act of freedom, is against the law. Later, while in therapy, my attempt was noted at my induction and physical for the draft, with a smirking remark from the soldier to whom I spoke.

There was nothing of my shameful act in the news and the MMC had begun replaying in its first reruns in 1962, the year before. I believe that Disney somehow used its power to quash any knowledge of my suicide attempt because it would not fit their image if an All-American Mouseketeer tried to off himself. That might impair money made off the MMC being reissued and, of course, the synergy tie-ins with related products and other film, television and Park entertainments.

Oddly, the second original Mouseketeer to die, Charley, committed suicide in 1997 and the studio Mouseketeer liaison, Lorraine, put me in touch with his son who was seeking help. It is interesting that she thought of no other Mouseketeer who would be able and willing to take on the responsibility to help him.

Lorraine and I had a problem that has never been resolved, although I have at least made the effort. For one of our early live shows at Disneyland after the 1980 revival and TV special, I reluctantly agreed to attend the auditions for kids as a casting person, choosing one to appear with us as a Talent Roundup winner. After about twenty minutes of seeing primarily terrified children who were obviously forced to perform by their parents, I left—after explaining to Lorraine that I could no longer take it. She was mortified and enraged. The show could go on for there were other Mouseketeers doing the same thing in other places; the rest of my auditioning would simply be split between the other auditioning Mouseketeers. I was depressed by what I was seeing and this is really a symptom of another disease.

Lorraine never forgave me for this even though I took pains later to explain how devastated I was to see what the parents had done to their kids. All she cared about was Disney. My feelings and apology, and the obviously pained children, were of no significance at all to her. She is not typical of all Disney employees, but more than one or two that I have encountered. Some Disney employees, particularly at the Parks, are very kind and polite and helpful. They are usually not executives.

Chuck's son told me that he had tried to get an obituary in the Orange County paper where they lived but they would not run it, nor tell him why not. He explained that Chuck had been depressed for two years over the death of a daughter; hence, his suicide.

We talked about the matter and I gave what help I could. I said I would make some calls and help him and the family. Although I had written for the *Los Angeles Times*, they did not print an obituary. I contacted *Variety* and *The Hollywood Reporter*, but they did nothing. Nothing ever showed up where they lived in the Orange County issue of the *Los Angeles Times*, nor other Orange County papers, nor in Los Angeles. Could it be possible that Disney was repeating what I suspected from my unsuccessful attempt at death more than thirty years earlier?

A couple of weeks after my suicide attempt in 1963 I made an appointment with a psychiatrist and had two meetings with a fellow in a white lab coat and a four-in-hand tie who was so coldly objective he seemed to be an precursor to R2D2—with a less perky voice. If I got near anything Oedipal, he would grunt to himself and write more feverishly, and so I played some other Freudian clichés.

I dropped the clinician and found a human, Lou Leveen, a therapist with an MSW, working on his Ph.D. to become a psychologist, a goal he attained during my years with him. Lou was incisive and effective. I saw him for five years and he wanted me in group therapy also soon after I started; I participated there, and it was quite efficacious as well, for three years.

The next phase of my life was recovery. I learned, sometimes fitfully, about my problems, their roots and how I could better contend with them. I also began the long hike of moving beyond merely earning a living tending bar and returning to acting, dancing and singing. I continued to write and finally was published after returning to college for a Ph.D. in English literature. Most importantly, I no longer dwelled on the edge of Camus' precipice.

Hamlet's last words before dying are, "The rest is silence." I have never been a man who furtively thinks but does not speak about his ruminations. I railed against the dying of my light and, along the way, I eventually discovered a new mental illness.

I named it Showbizaphobia.

Chapter 10
Showbizaphobia

The redolence of White Shoulders perfume, a Bogart twist on a wise crack, the lovely touch of velvet, the nose-tingling fizz of a root beer float, a spine-arching riff by the Kenton band—they all bring a smile and a sigh in an instant but we seem to experience them only when they accidentally surprise us.

We must learn to open ourselves to these meaningful frissons, take a small amount of time to sense the orchids in all ways instead of focusing on the need to deracinate the constant weeds, instead of hurtling into the next problem to solve, the next chore to perform, the next prompt of the cursor. Most of us do not do this and we must.

Showbizaphobia, which has eluded the psychiatric text books, is a disease characterized by many symptoms, all of which coalesce into a reversion to a childlike state of overwhelming submission and fear of what people will think of you or your abilities. This ultimately leads to rejection, failure and not being loved. If you are rejected, which by the law of averages will happen most of the time for sundry reasons that have nothing to do with your worth or talent or heart, you will be found out as not perfect—a failure.

Thus, if the agent, casting director, director, producer, network or product people or just about anyone rejects your abilities, you, as the victim of showbizaphobia, cease to exist. Your parents' and friends' and lovers' faces and attitudes say more than a mere one thousand words, they say everything. Most importantly, in this illogical, negatively emotional cosmogony, you do not get the job, so you not only do not exist, but you also find it difficult to subsist.

In a 2008 interview in the *Los Angeles Times* successful child and adult star Jodie Foster was quoted as saying, "Being a child star is inherently lonely."

I muttered to myself, "and then some."

Even though my experiences were more positive than negative, I have always been against and written negative pieces about children and young teens being in show business. Performing in any way in front of people is frequently positive even if the early attempts are shaky or miserable. Taking classes in music, dance, singing and—less efficacious but acceptable—acting, is fine. Doing any of these things for money is simply very wrong, very dangerous, very misleading and very cruel. (see Appendix)

I believe that being in the entertainment industry is the key reason that so many former child actors and child stars have extremely difficult problems that they are unable to overcome, frequently leading to liquor, drugs and/or crime-filled lives that often drive them to rehab after rehab, to prison, or more often, to premature death by their own hand.

Some bypass this majority to transcend youthful emotional burnout; I guess it may be possible a few never experience it. The mass of those whom we read about have misinterpreted acceptance, success and appreciation of what they do as lasting, deep, all-encompassing love. It is quite like familial love is supposed to be and sometimes is, as not being for what they do, but for them, individually, uniquely. This is not the case.

When what is identified as success, acceptance and love is instantly withdrawn, no matter how much they intellectually understand, the series—or limelight or career—stops shockingly dead and they are emotively scarred for life.

Child actors and child stars have the unmitigated audacity and temerity to change. It is impossible to be what you were when your mind and body have gone through enormous transitions and alterations in a short period of time and you lack the maturity and wisdom of tragedy and joy that life visits on everyone, the only variance being degrees of either. You no longer look the same, act the same, sound the same or are the same as you were as a child or teenager. The loved, successful child is tossed out of the home for doing nothing wrong but growing up. He or she has naturally metamorphosed into a different person and can no longer be the tiny, youthful captain on *The Good Ship Lollipop*.

All of this tragedy comes from one primary source: the parents.

Usually the mother is the instigator, although fathers hang back as enablers or care so little about the kid they do not realize what is going on or simply refuse to do anything about it. Less often dads are the instigators, for they are in a position to be supported in their role as providers by the child's income or for other vicarious reasons. Both parents are sure that they can always win the showbiz lottery, despite the lottery odds against that outcome.

The minute that money comes into the equation of a young person's life as the most important element, the child, whether successful or unsuccessful as a child performer, is on a road to failure.

THE CHILD HAS DONE NOTHING WRONG.

He or she has merely tried to please the first, most important givers of love, the parents, and everyone else from relatives and neighbors and friends to sleazy agents or managers or casting people whose only purpose is the BUSINESS of show. In an article Jodie Foster wrote around the same time as the interview, I read, "...us actors still plagued by people-pleasing;....". The choice of the word "plague" is absolutely accurate. There is no such thing as show nurturing or show loving—there is only show business.

I discovered later in life that being in show business as a child, and being successful at it, had caused my having this then undefined, unnamed disease, showbizaphobia, which is a major contributor to the disease I have had since my childhood: depression.

In my case, undiagnosed at the time, I ceased to exist. I was uncovered as the imperfect child that my mother, grandmother and others from Miss Anderssen at HPS to an arbitrary casting director mandated that I be. Ergo, I was blithely discarded.

I began my life with my dad ignoring my existence and my grandfather disliking me. My two saviors, it seemed at first, were my mom and grandma. I came to learn that they would shame me and dump me in a second if I did not get straight A's, did not get the job, did not give all of my life to the goals Dot and Gram deemed to be my essence. I even had nightmares in which I was imprisoned and because I was such a failure and an embarrassment they did not bother to find out if I was guilty, which I was not; they just left me there.

I discovered that in addition to god's betrayal that sundry humans like Sharon, JoAnne and Karen found it just as easy. Indeed, Dot went off to Vegas a year after the MMC stopped filming and my grandmother seemed to think I was only interested in her money.

Through vulnerability and tears that she displayed or were clearly just below the surface always, Judy Garland would smirk wryly, have another drink or pill, and understand thoroughly that she was a victim of showbizaphobia, too—and *she* transcended childhood stardom and became an adult star. Been over the rainbow, been there done that, and unable to escape—except in death.

After all, what horrors and nothingness would follow if Lonnie did not give more than 100% and much more always, every single day, every single opportunity, every single moment? This literal metaphoric paradigm was true not just in the desperate world of entertainment but in all things deemed worthy by the despotic duo of Mom & Gram: school, decorum, my appearance and the entire package. Lonnie is perfect, ergo, he cannot fail—at anything on any level—ever.

I excelled above most other children in many things, even sports and studies and politeness, but if I failed it would be a bona fide tragedy and prove the unthinkable: Lonnie is imperatively, categorically, by Kantian dictums, not perfect. This is unacceptable. The sun always rises, even if you cannot see it. Lonnie is always perfect. It is worse than unacceptable. If you are perfect by definition and make only one mistake, you not only lose all worth, but there is no you.

It took me decades to analyze, formulate and begin changing this emotional equation, although it took less time to think through the

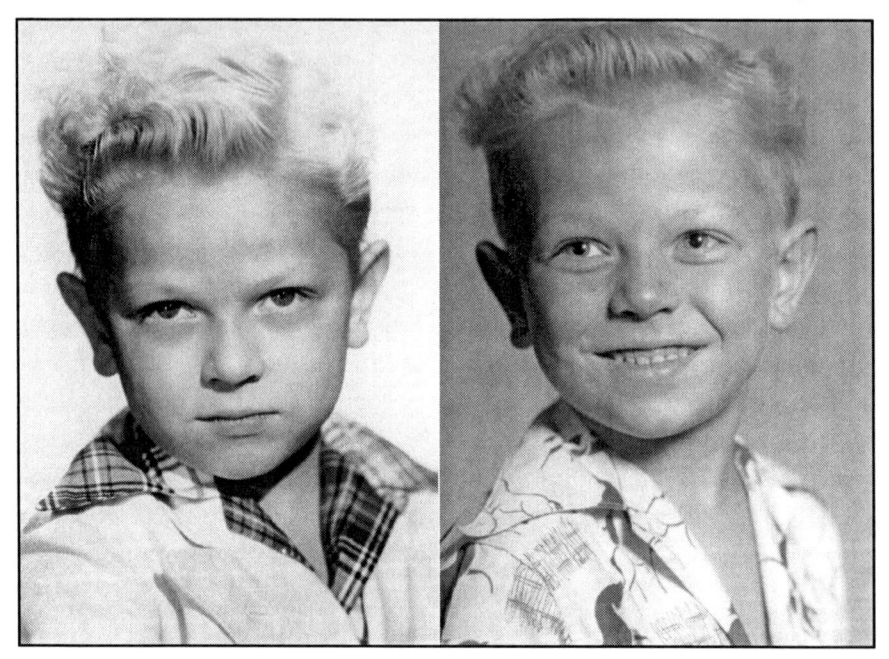

Professional headshot at age five and snapshot at age five. See any difference? 1948.

premise, and things do set in concrete in a child's mind, however much later understood and changed by behavior, feelings and thought. They do not ever go totally away but they can be held in abeyance.

This is one reason that when I clean a toilet or deal with any other meaningless endeavor, I do it just as I audition, perform and write: with full concentration and more than 100%. I have, in the later stages of this life, mitigated my self-punishment for my allegedly criminal acts of failure but, once in a while, I am unable to realize the desperate negativity of this; I am unable to forgive myself again for not being the unattainable perfect boy.

By sixteen, acting and dressing appropriately, I imbibed in better dinner house bars like one of the Belgian haute cuisine Frascati's chain, this one across from the more mundane Pandora's Box, one of the first coffee houses of note in Hollywood, as it sat on a small triangle of land across from the restaurant.

Sherry's, the jazz club, was across the street to the right looking back up Laurel Canyon from Pandora's near Schwab's drugstore at this intersection where Laurel collides with Sunset Boulevard and, in Hollywood fashion, is absorbed suddenly and becomes Crescent Heights. To the left of Pandora's, across the street in this mangled traffic jam of a design, was the notorious showbiz den of iniquity, the Garden of Allah, which was later replaced by the Chateau Marmont farther along on the Strip as the Vegas-hip, hell hole vacuum where many Hollywood types lived, partied, got into trouble and died. This triangle, like a discarded matte shot or deleted pixels, disappeared in time.

I was greeted by a foul stench when I opened the bar for my first lunch gig as a bartender at twenty-one but these *noir* riches still remained somehow mystifying and inviting to me as they had for years before I was legally allowed inside the insider's circle—unless I was on the other side of the stick and employed there—for they meant I was no longer a child but an adult and in the cool.

I later hung at Sherry's near Cosmo Sardo's styling salon and the cool rags at Zeidler and Zeidler. Don Randi ivoried Monk for me every once in a while for I had a fake temporary license, which made me twenty-two. I was never asked to show it.

Being accepted as an adult when you are an emerging teen, however hip and educated you seem, cheats you out of significant, basic, life lessons that need to be comprehended, understood and engaged. Without these lessons it is close to impossible to make sense out of yourself and of what you are in the process of becoming—in order to make coherent the arbitrariness of life itself.

Something as seemingly useless to everyone who lives in a city as having a basic understanding of nature can cloud the very meaning of life, leaving you grounded only when in a civilized, urban, dependent situation.

I had owned two horses as a child and rode in the hills of Hollywood, more than once going over the hills to the Valley in small groups and another time, surreptitiously, alone. I had visited Yosemite more than once, killed tons of ants and snails as a predatory child, but I could only name a few flowers and was completely inept at knowing the difference between a sapsucker and a chickadee, between a woodchuck and a vole. I had not an inkling of what to do to survive if left alone in the mountains or the desert, on the ocean or any body of water or even late at night in the city when everything is closed. There were no viable text books and no PCs, cell phones or iPods.

From minor childhood remorse over dead, stiff chameleons, tiny turtles, fragile white rats and one Boxer dog to becoming a star, nothing had taken me out of the urban prison that without electricity and all our other multiple, assumed amenities leaves almost anyone extremely ill-equipped to survive and defend themselves. We are all too reliant on others to provide everything for us from food to light, transportation to firefighters and police officers.

This became a life and death situation on a night in the mid-1970s when Diane and I were stranded on a 36-foot boat without a functioning rudder in the black vastness of Chesapeake Bay.

The onerous, actor-unfriendly Equity contract for a pre-Broadway show allows thirteen straight days of work before one day off and in addition to six evening shows and two daytime matinees, rehearsals continue on every one of the thirteen days, in other words, two days off a month—with no extra pay.

We were performing *Mack* at the Kennedy Center and Gower was crazed with the problem of emulating screen chaos for the Keystone Kops number on stage. After five versions, the enigma was never solved.

Ray Dickey, my late father-in-law and D.C. poobah attorney with whom I never got along, took Diane and me out on the Chesapeake Bay for my one day off in two weeks. Unannounced, he brought along his mistress of a decade, Ms. Peggy, for whom he would soon desert his wife of many years and their four children, then young adults, to be regularly titillated and misused until his relatively early demise. At this time he was separated from Hilda, but not divorced.

After a sun filled, enjoyable day on the waves of the Bay, we stopped off at a small island inlet to picnic. On negotiating out of the shallow waters, Ms. Peggy, an attorney with "upper drawah" credentials, attitude and demeanor and a ruthless singularity, had requested and been allowed to become captain. She deftly beached us on a sand bar and snapped the rudder.

I was given the splendiferous opportunity to sit in an uncovered hold near the rear of the 36-foot craft for hours and attempt to steer port or starboard on command by pushing or pulling a large wrench Ray connected to the rudder. We were isolated in the middle of a huge extension of the Atlantic Ocean that afforded no view of land. Then darkness was upon us.

We should have radioed a mayday to the Coast Guard immediately, but Ray refused for he feared it would then become public knowledge that his mistress was with us and he had told Hilda that she would not be. I believe Ray was also concerned that this could hurt him in divorce proceedings if Hilda became more angered at him. She was aware the three of us were bound for the Bay. Only it was the four of us.

The dark became black and we eventually saw a ten-story high, or so it looked, ocean-going vessel that would not, could not be our savior. The behemoth was outlined by its own lights which made it huge even though a quarter mile or more away from us and its denizens could not see us despite our small craft's lights being on. They would be unable to see or hear us if we signaled either as they sliced through the night sky and the threatening depths. Ray had not thought to bring flares.

After reasoning and arguing with Ray for hours, Di finally jumped into a unique fit of hysterical shouting, crying and throwing things about. She threatened to jump overboard and try to swim to land if he did not act to get us out of this desperate situation.

This fit moved Ray to finally radio the Coast Guard but there was no rescue vessel nearby and the Bay is vast. It was clear to us all that we could easily be crushed by any large ship and they would not even feel the bump. Other frightening possibilities included drowning, freezing to death in the water or becoming a savage great white's tidbit. This did not sit well with any of us. Ray, of course, never fully apologized.

I had no knowledge of the sea or boats; it would have been the same in an airplane of any size but that seems more acknowledged when you choose to fly. I should have been able to do something besides wrench the rudder back and forth. I could not even use the radio. It never occurred to me to clunk Ray on the head with the wrench because he had the only knowledge that could save us.

We were finally rescued by the Coast Guard at 4 a.m. and I managed to get back to the Kennedy Center for rehearsals at 9 a.m. much worse the wear—and terrified for hours. I managed to act attentive and nonchalant to avoid any pixilated behavior from the oddest choreographer/director for whom I have ever worked, Gower Champion.

Even strutting around with his tiny whip and shouting at everyone or merely to himself, Cecil B. de Mille was no match for Gower. I have auditioned for more peculiar individuals, like John Kenley and John Waters, but did not work for them. Despite making some excellent documentaries, when I auditioned for a commercial Michael Moore was casting and directing, I found him, of course, very overweight and slovenly, but unable to describe what he wanted. He became extremely agitated and rude. He believed and acted like he was a genius and because I could not comprehend his incomprehensible description of something not in the text he superciliously treated me like a boob.

I had another very odd audition with Peter Falk for a *Columbo* special. Why he would spend the time to audition an actor for a day player role as a bartender with a couple of lines not with his character, wearing his Columbo trench coat, straggly tie and suit, and sitting behind a huge, executive desk about thirty feet away from me, I will never quite understand. I also found it weird when I was photographed in costume, without makeup, for a single scene on *Murder, She Wrote*. For some reason that was not explained, the show's star, Angela Lansbury, insisted on having pictures of every actor in costume before she worked with them.

In the aftermath of our rescue, Ray was exposed and he had to deal with another betrayal of his estranged wife after cheating on her and hiding it for a decade or more. Since he almost got us killed, which augmented the polite but unrelieved antipathy between me and Ray, I had no sympathy for him at all. Ms. Peggy, whom I thought of as a nouveau riche, bulimic Miss Piggy in more than onomatopoeia, surely continues today as an extremely egoistical, unpleasant female dragging around another Ray. I was not pleased at all about being with her in this situation.

I came to love Hilda in time, after we skirmished and tangoed around her attempt to incorporate me as the fifth eldest child in her brood and under her thumb and other digits. Eventually she allowed me to be who I was and, after her death, this led to another poem.

Unlike the stereotypical mother-in-law, she was one of the very few humans in my life who seemed to accept me and care about me for who I am rather than all the various social formats of metaphorical and literal tap dancing I executed as second nature, with a plethora of teeth bared inexorably, in order to be liked, accepted and loved.

We all want to be liked even if we say and act like we do not, and as a child it is easier to please adults, no matter what it costs you later, if you are what they want, or at least *say* and *act out* what they want. This continued for me into adulthood, as it does for all of us in varying degrees, more so for the professional child performer, but ultimately you become less as they become the dictators of who you are.

Thank you dearest Hilda. I always remember you with warm, nostalgic feelings.

A knowledge of nature and the real world might not have saved me out on the Bay, but it may have given me some help, some clues, some support. The point is I was ignorant of many practical, simple things but none of this bucolic, pragmatic and exquisite knowledge would have been allowed by me in my convoluted, urban, showbiz world.

I had grown up thus far not having been raised with, nor taught, what life's values really are, which would have helped me escape the speeding cars on perilous winding roads, the *soignée* of alcoholic haze, the jail of cigarette addiction and the many tantalizing, destructive women. The world outside homes, restaurants, bars, museums, gas stations, Macy's and Broadway and May Company, cafes and the lot of city life was for senseless, backward buffoons, Beverly Hillbillies and rural clowns, not the cool elite of my engrossingly stressful, dangerous life as a young city cave dweller. Despite Plato, I thought the shadows on the wall were merely there for effect, a sort of philosophical matte shot.

I began correcting my unnatural lack of nature in my forties by indoctrinating myself as a docent at Descanso Gardens, a beautifully preserved 135-acre park in La Cañada, north of Glendale, west of Pasadena in the San Gabriel Valley. This oasis of flora and unthreatening fauna, once in a while interrupted by a frightened, errant dear leap, was one of the last places Walt considered for locating Disneyland before opting for what were then the lonely orange groves of Anaheim.

I knew enough about myself that if I committed to taking mandatory classes to become an unpaid guide I would learn about the natural world in order to escort, inform and interest third to sixth graders for an hour and a half once a week. Once I commit it is very rare indeed for me to waiver for any reason. It would have been too risky to merely buy some books and find excuses not to read them. I would also make use of my tools for educating, and to a much younger group than ever before, to enthuse other deprived city kids about the real world which I had not understood.

It took only one young boy in those six years to make it worth all the effort and weekly duties even if I had not benefited in opening up my *weltanschauung* at all. He was from the "inner city" and remarked in wonder at the quiet at Descanso when we were not exchanging. We had been out for over an hour and he was introduced to and awed by trap door spiders but not quite as much by the "jigsaw puzzle-like" sycamore trees, which is how I described them to make them more easily remembered on sight.

He blurted out, "Wow—I haven't heard one gun shot."

It was sad, but it made me feel better than applause or an award. At Descanso, in my forties, I realized I had changed diametrically from my sometimes too self-consumed, urban-isolated childhood, teens, twenties and thirties.

Later I taught writing at UCLA, tap at the Debbie Reynolds Dance Studio, and directing at Montgomery College in Maryland and auditioning and acting for TV, theatre and film at Learning Tree University. The acting I taught was practical, not about Lear's preference for the color orange or the effects his birth sign had on his progeny. I heuristically imparted knowledge about the more practical aspects of auditioning, acting and related topics. All of these teaching experiences were short term engagements that had a definite end in sight before I would take them on. I could leave at almost any time, or find a replacement, when acting or other related work was offered to me.

My college degrees were achieved not just for general enlightenment but as a fall-back option, another way to make a living. I was trying to circumvent the problems in which so many child actors and/or stars find themselves in after leaving the cul-de-sac of acceptance, "love" and success we all thought would last forever. I did not really want to teach. I needed to learn more of myself and the world and to mature.

Discovering trap door spiders with the kids during a Descanso Gardens tour in the mid-1990s.

    I knew in my early twenties that there was absolutely no way I would be able to repeat the same things over and over again for any reason whatsoever—not even what I heard twenty years later from the little boy who was amazed at the lack of gunfire. That kind of experience does not occur every semester. After six years of four-monthly docent tours with some vacation, I welcomed my move back to the East and stopping the peregrinations around the natural woodlands and pond. I also realized that going to the same place of work and interacting with the same people five days or more a week for years would not be acceptable to me.

The longest I have been employed in acting, other than the three years on the MMC, was a little over a year twice in theatre. It was difficult after nine or ten months despite doing what I wanted to do and making a good living. I managed not to let my craft be challenged by this enervating situation so the audience had no idea of my negative feelings, but it is difficult to hold back encroaching depression when you are unhappy in what you are doing on a regular basis.

The longest I maintained a workplace job, as bar manager of a dinner house in my early twenties, was even more difficult and did not last much longer than a year and a half.

Never having children, I had avoided teaching pupils younger than eighteen prior to Descanso. I thought I would feel constrained having to translate down as I tried to captivate the students' interest. I found that I did not have to talk, nor translate down but to simply change my approach. I reached youngsters by relating to their interests at the time, in my last Maryland classes in 2004 by referencing the subject to Muggles and at Descanso, earlier, by co-mingling natural wonders with *Star Wars*, Disneyland and *Jurassic Park*.

The ginkgo trees at Descanso were around in the Jurassic Era, for example, and my improvised script, never formally written out, would draw the kids in from things they knew and liked into things they would discover, understand, relate to and look upon with interest. The trite playing field was leveled and I was charmed by the sometimes halting letters they wrote enthusiastically in thanks for their visit with me to the Gardens.

I also became a bird watcher, as did Diane, during my years in La Cañada educating amidst the anti-city quietude and the red eared slider turtles and hummingbirds and oaks and camellias. California's large amount of quercus (oak) trees, too many now consumed by homes, are still abundant enough at Descanso to be beautiful and provide some of their gifts for all species.

My late transition to an understanding and love of the natural world, beyond simply looking at a rare, extraneous sunset or, less often, inhaling clean air and scents that were not fouled, led me to discover a part of myself that was totally new: that one of the two very different lives I should have pursued and would have pursued was working with animals in some way. I prefer animals to people much of the time.

I became a part of the pecking order at the San Diego Zoo, 2005.

Opportunities have been offered to me, which I have jumped at, to pet and be close to a number of wild animals that most people have not. My most recent is now common on a special tour of the San Diego Zoo in 2005 when we were able to feed and touch giraffes and rhinos. My first encounter of this close nature was the MMC circus 1955-56 riding on the stiff, harsh hairs of elephants and spitting camels. At another time I got to be with different types of penguins. Appearing on *The Merv Griffin Show* in the early 'eighties along with Joan Embry from the San Diego Zoo, I got to pet a koala bear she was bringing out for Merv.

In 1995 while appearing at WDW a kind Park employee, Dawn, took us to the now disappeared Discovery Island and I was able to pet Stu, a large monitor lizard, wander with some capybara running free to beg for food and touch a huge Galapagos tortoise well over 100 years old. I also held a hedgehog, let an owl sit on my gloved arm and petted an opossum.

The other virtually undiscovered country which I have been involved with since a child as a dancer and singer is music, but I cannot read music, although I am a very fast learner and have always had excellent instincts. I have little understanding of musical composition. If I had taken this path as a child or in my college years I believe I would have had a more enjoyable life as a musician and, I believe, a composer and conductor.

I was dissuaded by an ill-chosen instrument, the most odious one I have come across, an accordion, and an inept and uncaring instructor.

With no music courses, nor lessons in piano, when my mother (grandmother's money) bought a French Provincial grand piano for our living room on Bluebell I sat down one day and managed to plunk out the main theme from what is still one of my favorite pieces of music: Debussy's lovely, simple "Clair de Lune." Eventually, I managed some acceptable, inaccurate left hand chords that seemed to fit, but that is as far as it went. It is quite possible I would have resisted piano lessons, but if my mother or father had insisted I would have complied and gained that option and asset for my whole life at a young age when learning is much easier and meaningful.

Having worked with some famous composers and conductors, like John Williams, Jerry Herman, and my good friend Broadway conductor and Professor of Musicology at NYU, Jack Lee, I am sure it would have been a life that was much fuller.

Mouseketeer-then-actor Don Grady had a hit with a musical group he formed during *My Three Sons* but he continued acting as an adult. Don told me at our 1995 fortieth Mouse Reunion at WDW that he returned to his musical roots midway in life. As a result, he has become a very successful composer and conductor who is never out of work. Don is a much more content fellow since making this decision and finding out this truth about himself.

For allegedly ultra-sophisticated Lonnie in mid-teens, the concept of camping out or searching aimlessly for feathered warblers or studying the musical composition and chord adventures of Ravel would have received a dismissive, knowing smirk and a negative head shaking. The thundering silence and unspoken tumult and sublimity of the natural world was not a reality that I had been gifted with by either family or schooling and so I did not understand it, care about it, nor seek it until after three decades of wandering aimlessly about in big cities like L.A., Paris, Chicago, Toronto, Manhattan, London and Rome.

Now I had gone fishing once with my dad. Dad scattered onces throughout my childhood. He showed me how to hammer a nail once, we played catch once and he took me out on his truck once to show me where he worked and what he did, which was load heavy metal ingots on his truck, drive to Ontario, California from downtown L.A., unload the ingots and then return to L.A. He then drove home to the Valley for frozen dinners. It kept him in shape after giving up dancing, which he still did but much less often. In addition to his minimal pay he got free car repairs from the company's truck mechanics and he made a modest living from doing things that would have sent me screaming to the hills in less than a week. There are better, free ways to keep in shape.

He took me once, with large, crude, tough, uneducated Scotty, his street-Scots, Catholic-driven, Scottish-accented buddy from work to a soccer game at the Coliseum. For about three hours two groups of ant-sized men ran around chasing and kicking a ball, when not chasing, clouting and kicking each other, making for many very red jerseys, until finally one team made a goal. I have never become a fan of this game.

Scotty was not an individual that I saw often and I preferred it that way. I had taken responsibility for my dad and his affairs for over a year. His cancer was in remission but began attacking him more fiercely again. Dad's divorced wife Paula did not visit him. Dot found a way down for a family holiday on Thanksgiving and Dad was there two months before his death, but she did not come down prior to that, nor was she there specifically to see him.

As Dad lay dying an uninvited priest showed up at Mame's apartment one day when I was there. He was overbearingly rude and zealous, insisting on seeing my father. He started in and I stopped him, saying my father had not asked for a priest. I told him I would ask my father if he wanted to see the man. I never asked who sent this nasty messenger of god but I am sure it was Scotty who was a strict Catholic and an extremely physical, violent bully who had been a rugby goalie before moving to America.

My father said he did want to have the Last Rites even though he converted and was re-baptized decades earlier. I allowed the priest access, for which he did not thank me, and left them alone to do their mumbo jumbo. The man left without saying a word to either me or Mame. Not the kind of representative I would want to have for a religion.

Dad had also taken me as a small child for another once and we stopped on the way back at a bar. He walked me inside for my introduction to these dark, smoky venues. He had two quick shots at the stick while I sat alone at a table with a coke and felt definitely out of place and a bit threatened

These onces accounted for about one percent of my childhood time, another nine percent were Dot/Dash/Virgule taking a meal to a drive-in movie or going to a café for dinner. In the latter Dot would invariably find something in the food or service or ambiance to complain about and Dash would unavoidably become embarrassed by her way of dealing with the problem and they would argue, sometimes volubly, in public. It was as entertaining as being eaten by a bear.

I did savor the one percent with just Ham but no bond was ever formed, no worldly wisdom disclosed, no emotions discussed and no touching happened, whatsoever. My memory is that my dad, like everyone in my family, had never been on an airplane so he actually hugged me once in my life when he saw me and my mom off for a propeller driven plane flight from the Deco Burbank, now Bob Hope, Airport when we left on our first MMC appearance tour. Fear of flying for my family was more than a title for a novel, so this was a different first.

I recall my first fishing event on my first visit to Yosemite with the chilly, shivering son washing up with his dad and many other men in my only communal bathroom experience, watching the campfire and then the multi-colored fireworks exploding high in the night then down the Bridal Veil Falls or some other precipice, the wild animals not confined by iron bars and the total absence of houses, factories, apartment buildings, gas stations and stores, i.e. civilization. The city boy was awed.

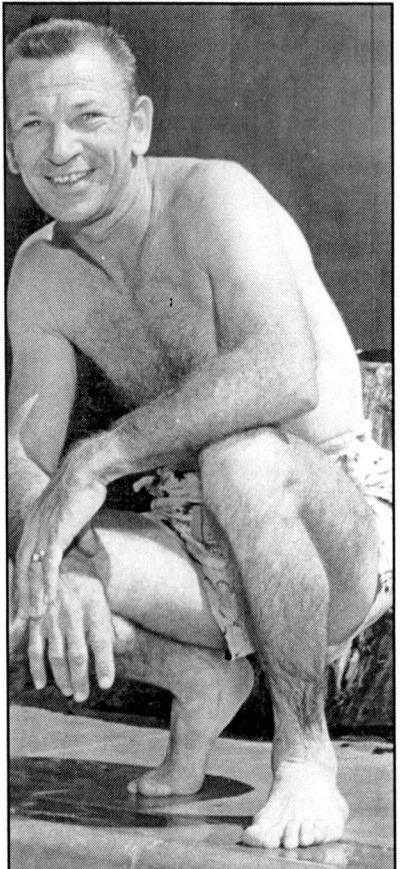

Dad had only a faltering grasp of fishing but he did show me how to bait a hook and sit around for extended periods before catching nothing. He, too, had little schooling and no interest in the outdoors beyond Dot's insisting we visit this national treasure once so he could make some fitful efforts at fathering with the boy from whom, at three, he had divorced himself.

My dad at Big Mooseketeer Roy's pool party, 1957.

When I was nine my second and last fishing expedition took place at a private, stocked pond in Monrovia. You rented a reel and bait, cast and were almost assured of catching something. Dad had to go off and do something, most likely get a beer, which he drank daily after work. Mom was having trouble and asked me to hold her hook before she threw her line out. She then cast without alerting me and shanked the hook through the meaty part below my thumb on my right hand.

I was whisked off to an emergency room where they had to cut a second hole to extract the jagged, curved metal. Fortunately, it left only an inch long scar which I retain to this day, but I incurred no disability. However tasty I find fish, the act of fishing has ever since seemed to me only slightly better than hitting and chasing a tiny ball around a primly manicured rug of grass with sand traps and water and holes with flags stuck in them. I was given a new set of expensive golf clubs as one of my high school graduation gifts. After a little putting and some driving lessons, I was convinced this slightly more-athletic-than-walking diversion held no interest for me.

My mother was the substantive influence in my life, given that Dad ignored me unless to carp about something or other, until I wrested it from her, leading to my ultimate escape on my fifteenth birthday. Her psychological punishments, as she called them, to guarantee my adherence to her perfect child ordinations were more damaging than the physical pain of Howard's violent hands.

I vividly recall our dog Donnie introducing fleas into our home. Mom may have scoured him after learning of the infestation but she did not bother with exterminators. I was not that worried about getting the plague. The nasty little buggers infested the carpets throughout the house and I could not sleep at all due to the bites and itching. Dot insisted I stay in bed. This convinced me that she was maladroit at raising children and showing empathy for me. Finally exterminators did their deeds. The fleas were more intimidating than one enormous pain and some more in the ER from the fish hook attack.

Much earlier, in my seventh year, while auditioning for my first of a dozen *Colgate Comedy Hour* TV shows, this one starring Eddie Cantor, I learned the lengths she would go to in order to succeed vicariously through me. We were in the large, downstairs lounge leading to the bathrooms in the Masonic Temple on Hollywood Boulevard just past Max Factor, west of Highland. This is where the musical/comedy show cast and rehearsed prior to being performed to a live audience at the El Capitan Theatre at the opposite end of the Hollywood Strip. Thus, we rehearsed almost directly across from Grauman's Chinese Theatre of footprint note.

We were waiting among other mothers and kids who were auditioning and she slapped me very hard. Tears came to my eyes, not from being hurt but from embarrassment and anger at her. I went through a period as a kid where I would get into such a rage that I would break out crying, rather than lash out physically or have a fit. This caused a great deal of trouble for me since most people see a boy or a man crying, certainly in the 'fifties, as a weakness.

Being able to cry without drinking too much alcohol when I need to express my grief, loneness or empathy is still a struggle for me on a rare occasion. I am now able to cry at music, films, plays, novels, poetry and even a few genuinely moving shows on Oprah. To hell with my dad, gramp and the generations of testosterone absorbed and scarred males.

I instantly regained my professional demeanor. After all, I was not a child. I was a tiny professional adult in showbiz.

I had taught myself how to stifle my emotions to circumvent this character flaw, just as I corrected my easily tickled sides by finding a way to shut off my sensitivity to tickling by focusing my mind against the sense of touch in vulnerable areas. My crying from anger and my ticklishness were shunned by my self-imposed, stoic mental defensive carapace. Much later I would work to regain my honest vulnerability in order to cry or let out held in emotion that this defensive, seemingly necessary ploy had locked down.

My crime at the audition was that in this my sixth year I had an extremely painful belly ache which had made me queasy. It was an anomaly but I desperately wanted to go home and be in bed. I had requested the same from Dot more than once. The third time she struck me hard, in front of everyone.

Mom's ambition did not allow for compassion; the show, audition, whatever MUST go on. The opportunity was rare and the only thing of importance. She was right, of course, in terms of showbiz. There may not ever be a second chance. And, as it happens, I aced the audition, did the show and that led to all the other *Colgate Comedy Hour* shows I performed on and, I can only assume, other work was due in some degree to these notable credits. But I still look back in anger at this scene.

About this same time I was up for a good film role that required me, not a stunt double, to fall in front of a speeding car that would stop

RIGHT BEFORE my head was squashed. Dot asked me if I wanted to read for it and take the chance that the stunt driver was competent. I answered NO instantly. I have always wondered if she would have let me do this dangerous gag if I had said yes. I believe she would have. Remember the late Vic Morrow and the two Vietnamese children who were killed by a helicopter propeller while filming? Remember Bruce Lee?

Accidents, like death, happen.

On one rare occasion, when I was about ten, Dot left off her pre-Gitmo psychological approach to punishment when she was overcome with rage. I had responded with a smart mouth to some order she gave me and it resulted in an accident that she shamed me for almost as much as the premonitory malice I had shown in my criminal embryo state when I forced her through a painful caesarean section to bring me forth.

The cheek thwacks had long been held back but I saw in her eyes and heard in her voice that she was going hit me *whacko*. I lunged for the breakfast room exterior door and opened it to escape corporal punishment.

She bolted across the small room and lunged to grab me, violently breaking through one of the four, small panes of glass on the upper part of the door as I opened it. The glass cracked into jagged edges. She spurted blood instantly but had not severed an artery.

She shouted, "LOOK WHAT YOU'VE DONE TO YOUR MOTHER!"

Mom ran, crying, to the kitchen and staunched the blood with a towel. I lost all professionalism and ran after her, crying tears of guilt and regret to see if I could help. She staunched the blood with a towel, picked a few shards out of her arm and rewrapped it. I apologized over and over but she left for the bathroom and I doggedly began to try and clean up the glass, blood and other detritus on the floor of the breakfast room and kitchen. This is another image that I will always retain. As a boy I saw with clarity that Jewish mothers are not the only mothers who can instill guilt and create shame.

The grossest rejection for me as a child had nothing to do with being in the entertainment industry. I had hidden this one away for years in my subconscious and only reclaimed it in my thirties without a shrink dragging it out.

When I was about six or seven, Dot decided to bless us with a foster brother "for me." I am sure that Dash had nothing to do with it and I am surprised he went along with it. He did not seem to want one son so he certainly would not be thrilled by a second one to whom he did not even contribute sperm.

I rationalized as an adult, but this was never spoken nor discussed, that she arbitrarily added foster brother X, for his name eludes me, and Dash agreed in order to fend off Glade's controlling, oppressive financial weapons, for there is compensation for taking on a foster kid. If that was not the reason, it hits too accurately at my unvoiced fears then—that I was never actually loved for who I was; I was just told that I was loved and served as an excellent agent for my mom's showbiz zeal and dad's lack of earning power.

My understudy could always go on for me, even though he had neither talent nor training as a performer, no marked intelligence, nor social charm, but he could absorb my life into his role so that the reality of my life would make me a supernumerary in my mother's, and everyone else's life. However inaccurate, everyone in Hollywood knows that if you do one day of extra work your acting career is over forever.

My emotions staggered through the following maze: getting straight A's, being one of the best actors, dancers, singers for my age, rarely getting into trouble and never substantive acts of unlawfulness, constantly being complimented for my looks, deportment, intelligence and talent, and being incessantly polite and proper were simply not enough. My desperate acuity at attempting to be the demanded, assumed "Perfect Boy," was miserably inadequate; after landing the job as son, I could not keep it and was fired. My daily efforts were of no value, nor was I.

Constant rejection, à la showbiz or parents or teachers, becomes a way of life, a way of living and thinking, unless you have the tools and maybe help to contravene these feelings of inadequacy. The successful in entertainment, those very few who survive until their break through role, their big chance—the vast majority never get this opportunity—still know that hovering around them constantly are the questions like, "What have you done for me lately?" "Did your last film/play/series/performance tank?" "Do we need someone younger?"

And so it goes.

There are millions of extremely talented individuals who give up and find another way to work, pay their bills and live their lives, thus opting out of being incessantly threatened and asked to show their abilities time after time, decade after decade, even though their talents have been established for a long time. After all, Brando did have to audition for Coppola's *The Godfather* even though the director went to Brando's home and no one else was present. There is also a large group of actors who eke out a living for ten or twenty or more years, adding to their income with other noncreative labors to live—the most obvious being waiting on tables—and do not get the break, the opening they need. Talent has very little to do with it. Who you know and/or are related to, when and how you are seen and by whom, accident and luck matter much more. You do know that Nicholas Cage is Francis Ford Coppola's nephew, right?

The respected Broadway director Jose Quintero, who also suffered from depression among other problems, titled his autobiography, *If You Don't Dance, They Beat You*. I had been making those clacking sounds with my taps at triple time and it afforded me only replacement by a foster brother who finally was expelled for stealing from my stamp collection.

I had told my mother that he was stealing from me but she confronted him and he denied it. She then set a trap and caught him. My feelings of not being loved were not discouraged by her disregarding what I told her until she trapped him in the act.

It is quite likely that I was running away from home, as I did after the milk incident and the kitty-tossing gaffe, and away from my mother when she dumped Dash and moved to Vegas. I had had enough of her broken dreams, for she was never successful in a big way as a dancer, nor as an agent. If I had been given this choice at three I would most likely have moved into the under side of the dining room table, staying with my grandparents. Who knows? I might have turned into a composer or a zoo keeper.

My therapist made it clear that Mom psychologically abused me. She went through the motions of love and did not punish me every day but the threat of what might happen after the foster brother and other negatives were now a permanent part of my world. It was a bit like living in paranoia-for-cause forever.

I shunned it, ignored it, hid it and it took my brutal suicide attempt and my own seeking of help through psychotherapy to get some relief from feeling criminally imperfect and unloved. I did my damnedest, was not a horrid fellow, only rarely difficult and not incorrigible. I made mistakes and the fact that they were fewer than those of many kids did not matter. This confusing, extremely negative paradox remains with me.

In the 'nineties the shrinks found that chemical imbalances in people with depression can be helped by pharmaceuticals. They had passed MAO inhibitors and their negative side effects and found SSRIs—or selective serotonin reuptake

Mom and son in happier times, 1989.

inhibitors—that improved the movement of the neurotransmitter serotonin between nerves in the brain, which is a problem for depressives. These pills do not end the struggle, they do not cure the disease, but they are substantive tools. They have helped me but are not a final solution anymore than behavioral therapy has been, but they both are good implements to employ even when you know you have to build the life that holds your values yourself.

In the mid-seventies I became a runner, until my first of two right knee arthroscopies, and unknowingly began supplying myself with endorphins that helped mellow me. After I had stopped running in 1993, Prozac provided a different but similar calming effect. The memory of having been one of the best and brightest was no consolation at all to my healing.

None of my troubles with life, love, depression and other conundrums describe a tragic childhood. They do not compare to being raped, abandoned, nor beaten badly. My problems with depression are nothing like what children in Palestine, Iraq, various countries in Africa, in India and all of the third world must endure.

The truth, which Nietzsche said we would be destroyed by if we did not have art, is that we truly feel only our own pain, not the pain of others. With the decline of most art formats in America for the last thirty or forty years, the alleviation of the brute force of the truth is harder to achieve.

I have had difficulties finding effective, evocative authors and artists but not dreadful poets who merely rhyme trash at "slams." It is even a workout finding humans who can correctly and interestingly speak to most subjects in appropriate English. Bill Buckley is deceased and Gore Vidal will not be around forever. Will everyone wind up like George Bush the Second sounding like an ill-educated hick for whom a metaphor is some form of sweetmeat?

We are capable of empathy but empathy will not stop a tooth ache or a permanent injury to the heart nor the mind. Empathy does not last all of your waking moments.

I display my emotive scars in a number of ways but the most obvious and worst is in my compulsive acceptance of truly nasty, cruel, rude, insulting things from people who have power in show business. I somehow endure injustices that I would not take from anyone else at any time unless they were bullies larger and badder than I am, or sociopaths with a weapon, or in order to save Diane's or my life. I might not even take it then, at least not when younger, except for this inculcation of fear and dread as a boy via my mother's need to vicariously succeed through her perfect, intellectual, multi-talented son.

My decades of struggling with depression and showbizaphobia have been healthier and less termagant in recent years. I do still fight the symptoms for they can, Phoenix-like, rise once more and I can, without blinking, refer to myself as an asshole, an idiot, or worse, "Leonard," the fellow who never existed, when I make a simple, obtuse human error that is truly without any meaning.

My disease is likely the basis, after being spoiled with none of a kid's predictable chores or duties and easy money until I moved out at twenty, of my tidiness and responsibility. I frequently succeed at insulating myself from minor or major failures. It helps me, on my own, to make and find some sense in the constant unpredictability and turmoil of life. I conceived of a way to do everything within my limited power to stay away from the stress which surpasseth understanding.

Acting, performing for an audience in any way, is not brain surgery, it is not giving birth, it is not dropping a hydrogen bomb, it is not life. It is simply a craft which in some instances attains to art and it is a desperate business. Art is not life either. If you are playing Hamlet or Lear at the Old Vic it is still just a PLAY no matter how revered and moving the performance or the writer.

The concept embedded so deeply in me that the "show must go on" is an insidious falsehood perpetrated by those to whom no god is before Mammon: producers, agents, managers, venue owners, lawyers and stage moms and dads. It is also true of far too many soccer moms and dads; only in their scenarios "winning" replaces money.

As a younger man I refused to call myself an artist but later in life it became clear that I was an artist and dedicated my life, resulting in a lack of affluence, into making people cry and feel and laugh so that they could transcend the humdrum repetitiveness, sorrows and failures that we all encounter. If I had been committed to my life in art so that nothing else mattered, it still should not overwhelm every other aspect of living. I have been committed but I am not Van Gogh, and even if I thought I was it would be solipsistic to sacrifice, as I was taught to, everything and everyone else.

To make the impersonal, gambling of your life in an uncaring business because you feel your efforts transcend the pedestrian work of others is supremely obtuse and snobbish. It is impossible when after many years of showing your worth you must go on tedious, often sub-literate commercial auditions with others who have not a hint of what acting and dedication to acting is beyond loose memorization and taking a shot at the obvious meaning of the copy. You need to make a living, you have to do it but it is not pleasant even if you view it, as I taught, as a free class that allows you to exercise your acting skills.

This is mitigated if the job is for a meaningful role, even just one scene that is more than being an unnoticed plot mover for a major film or on Broadway, although the commercial may pay much more. The entertainment industry average is thirty or more auditions for one job lasting a day or two. Stage work is usually for less money and there are no residuals, or "back end." Most actors are not even considered for anything other than small roles or bits, particularly since names and stars took to guesting on television shows in the late 'eighties.

Unless an actor is seen in a focused role in something with some success it is just paying the mortgage or more often the rent. The business becomes more difficult and there are fewer opportunities and auditions when actors are at their best, seasoned with years and experience. Women are discarded earlier than men for reasons of age, but wrinkles and lack of hair and other youthful accoutrements work against men too unless they are established, adult stars. The number of lucky, successful actors that land a running role on a TV series is small. Many of them never work again, or certainly do so fitfully, not making enough to live on.

The approximately three percent of the 125,000+ members of SAG who make more than $100,000 a year, and lesser numbers under AEA and AFTRA and AGVA, are the ones considered for roles first. Only if they do not match up to demands—and often these demands are changed to accommodate them—are journeymen actors even considered. Casting breakdowns now are filled with independent films and television casting memos

In my dressing room as Behman in my first production of George M, *1969.*

stating that only "name actors" should apply. Having tons of credits, being an established, solid actor, having been a star, doing leads in theatre—these facts do not make you a name. You will be ignored in the manila dumping ground or deleted online before being given a chance.

This leads, of course, to almost incessant failure and that leads to depression and eventually despair. But still, the show must go on.

My audition at the Masonic Temple, which now fittingly is used to tape game shows, drove me to perform when ill on many occasions. The first time I refused to do so was in *George M.* It was 1970 and after having a very bad flu for four days and continuing to perform I had to stay in bed all day and night. There have been only a few other instances when I did not do what all actors must do: keep the show running (so the money comes in always).

When I tried to work and continue but could not on October 1, 2005 at Disneyland for the live show, appearances, autograph signing and assorted media events in conjunction with the Fiftieth anniversary of the MMC, I was badly used. We were in our early sixties and were treated like chorus performers, not the stars of a series that attracted and charmed millions of fans for six decades. We were not given enough rehearsal time, despite going two hours longer than scheduled on rehearsal day. Disney found a totally new way of underpaying us, as opposed to a union minimum. They used the terminology honorarium—"A payment given to a professional person for services for which fees are not legally or traditionally required" (American Heritage Dictionary). By using innovative terminology that had not been used before in our contracts and agreements they also bypassed the protection of union rules and even minimum pay for ANY performers, not unique individuals, in the three days of work that were each much longer than eight hours. The term itself was insulting, implying they were giving us approximately $330 a day because they were so generous. All of this was not new but typical. It actually worked out to about ten dollars an hour.

I knew none of the others would care, nor look up the word. They would do it no matter how they were treated. I arrived with a feeling quite different than the others, which I hid completely until things started turning badly and my suffering and ire advanced. We had been misused for too many decades.

The schedule: DAY ONE was costume fittings and other technical matters and three hours of rehearsal; DAY TWO was four performances of a half hour+ live dialogue, song and dance routines plus an early morning dress rehearsal and media Q & A and other duties, about a twelve+ hour day with time off for fast food and a few minutes of rest; DAY THREE was more appearances, a formal dedication and more performing, about a ten or eleven hour day.

Knowing the others would agree without a thought, I went along because a fiftieth anniversary in show business is rare; it is rare in most things. I had a physical problem that I explained to "writer"/"director"/choreographer Marilyn, but thought I could get through it. I was suffering from an extremely painful left shoulder, rotator cuff problem that my orthopedist said required immediate surgery. I convinced him that the fiftieth anniversary appearance took precedence so he gave me medication to help my constant pain.

In addition, Marilyn called me to run ideas by me and I mentioned some errors in her derivative script, which named a Mouseketeer who did not exist, quoted Bobby's age incorrectly and so on.

Marilyn was dismayed that Cubby and Don Grady were not going to be able to join us because of very heavy schedules, Cub playing drums for the musical *Chicago* and Don with his composing and conducting. Since everyone else had failed, she asked me to try and sway them. I contacted both of them and made successful arguments about the uniqueness of a fifty-year reunion and anniversary. As a result, they both did the show. I also called Mary Espinosa, gave her the producer Martha's phone number and suggested she call her. I thought it would be nice to include Mary for once. She was one of only two Hispanics on the MMC, which is a great public relations plus factor for Disney. I knew this reminder would appeal to them.

All of this was done for free because I wanted to be helpful and I always seek the best performance by everyone involved. This would be a once-in-a-lifetime performance and the better everyone else looks the better you look. If you are great in a miserable show or with bad performers it brings down your talent as well.

On the first day we began rehearsing and we were casually told that rehearsal was extended to five hours. Changes of this nature happen inevitably with Disney. We were invited as guests previously for "100 Years of Magic," a WDW celebration for what would have been Walt's 100th birthday in 2001, and we were told that at most we might be involved in a parade when, indeed, we wound up working the entire time for no money at all.

For the MMC fiftieth, we arrived at Disneyland at about eleven a.m. and broke at about nine p.m. We had no food break at all. After costume fittings and other matters we began the five hours of song, dance and dialogue rehearsal; we received only two breaks, five minutes each. No union would allow this—it is five minutes an hour or ten every two hours, but even though I belong to four performing unions, most of the others to at least one, this was ignored.

It was clear during the rehearsal that I was not going to be able to do the show. My pain was major and incessant despite my judicious use of my orthopedist's drugs, and during all the dances, songs and dialogue we had to hold our mike in our left hand, thus continually stressing my stinging left shoulder. If the billion dollar company had paid for clip-on mikes I would not have to hold a mike, thus, obviating my problem, but that would cost more. I resist showing much in the way of suffering due to the role of males in the era in which I was brought up along with the brain washing that the show-must-go-on and personal discomfort and health are meaningless, but anyone could see I was in trouble.

I was further distressed that Marilyn suddenly changed things she had promised me so there were other negative surprises as well. I would have done the show in spite of being displeased by these, as opposed to my aching shoulder, but I would not have been a happy camper.

First, Marilyn had given me a difficult patter song telling me by phone that I was the only Mouseketeer who was capable of doing it. It was similar to *You Got Trouble* that Pres did in *The Music Man* on Broadway and in the film. Mine, however, was never written out with music; it was simply words grouped in no particular order on a page, so it was impossible to do until I was given the music and learned the appropriate accents in conjunction with the melody. To make it worse, it was not rehearsed separately, nor would it be. This is impossible and could not have been done by the late great Pres either. Second, except for "move it along" rubbish, I had one meaningful line about Walt and his magic in the entire script. Marilyn, giving no reason, arbitrarily cut it.

Third, it had become the Bobby and Sherry show. It is true that Bob was one of us four males who lasted the entire filming of the MMC and did the same steps in different order, with different partners, in different peculiar costumes for twenty-one years on Lawrence Welk's shindig, but so what? Sherry was only on the second season and was not remembered like Karen, Doreen, Sharon, Darlene, Cheryl and especially

Jack Lindquist is wearing my ears on July 17, 2005 at Disneyland for the Park's 50th Anniversary. Jack is a Disney Legend. He started at Disney in 1955 as a marketing executive and was Disneyland's president from 1990 until he retired in 1993.

Annette. Very few fans recall Mouseketeer Mark, Mouseketeer Judy, Mouseketeer Sherry or Mouseketeer Lee.

For the NBC 1980 twenty-fifth anniversary TV show, before I was hired on staff, Sherry convinced the producers she was well known and eligible to replace Doreen who was then in ill-repute with the Disney people due to two vulgar nude layouts she did to help the single mother pay for raising her son Brad.

Since Sherry did the 1980 show as the only host Mouseketeer not part of the series for three years but only one, she has managed to push herself into the lead female position opposite Bob. We all had lines here and there, but the focused and substantive dialogue all went to these two. The other seven Mice of the original nine on the entire filming plus Cheryl act as if Sherry was always the nonexistent eleventh Mouscketeer and are never surprised by this phenomenon. I can only assume they are so thrilled to be one of the bodies included that whatever happens just happens, pay or no pay.

While it is possible that the prescribed medication and darting pain affected my mood, I would have been very unhappy even without it regarding the unfair and unjustified way Marilyn had rigged the show after seeking my help and advice. After all, I was the only one present who actually has been a professional writer since the late 'sixties and wrote the first show for the original Mice as a live performance at Disneyland and worked earlier in 1980 as a writer on our NBC Twenty-fifth Anniversary TV special.

My shoulder kept getting worse so I was not in good spirits at our provided dinner after rehearsal at 9 p.m. I ate because I was very hungry and then went straight back to my room. I called Diane. She convinced me I was an adult who needed to make the right choices for my health and that I was too old at sixty-two to be playing "the show must go on" as I had for over five decades. Diane drove up, got me and brought me home.

She then called Martha, the producer, and Marilyn, the director/choreographer, to explain the situation. She could not get through but left them phone messages. My pain was so intense that Diane gave me a larger dose of pain pills as my orthopedist had suggested and I was finally able to fall asleep.

Neither Martha nor Marilyn returned the calls and they did the show without me; I am sure they had to cancel or greatly alter my patter number. In both her messages Diane said that I was able to do all the media events, be at all non-dance, non-performing venues, including signing autographs with my unaffected right hand and arm but they chose not to call me. Both Diane and I thought it best to let me recover from the five-hour rehearsal ordeal.

I had surgery on my shoulder shortly after that day.

Neither Diane nor I had told anyone the agony we were going through then after just moving, in July, from Maryland back to California. Our eleven-year-old kitty, Syny (Mnemosyne, Greek goddess of memory, nicknamed SIN nee) had been diagnosed with lymphoma and was undergoing debilitating chemotherapy. We have never had children and our animals mean a great deal to us. I hasten to add we do not dress these animals in cute costumes, nor do we act like puerile idiots; we truly loved Syny like a daughter and our daughter was dying, disoriented and in pain. The chemo weakened Syny, changed her personality and made her even more ill. When it was clear to us and our great vet Jack Mannix that she was suffering, we held her as she was put to sleep right before my shoulder operation.

I was still aching and remained in bed on the Monday after that debilitating rehearsal and Diane deposited the Disney check, given to us all the first day, along with other checks of mine and hers. On Thursday Martha the producer called and asked for the check back. Diane explained she had deposited it and Martha became quite angry. I found out two days

Syny and her dad like watching Animal Planet together, 2003.

later that she had stopped payment. So after all my contributions, including managing to get Cubby and Don to appear, and my painful rehearsing and the rest of it, I was stiffed by Disney via Ms. Martha.

I understood and would have had no problem in not being paid for the second and third days of appearances and performing, but I thought it only right and fair that I be paid for the day I was there and working as hard as I could under a number of difficulties. Ms. Martha did not see it that way.

Early in 2006 I learned a new fellow was hired as head of the Parks and I wrote him a polite, professional letter explaining the situation. I asked for one third of the one grand because I had worked one of the three days. I was sent $500 with a terse note from Martha, but if I had not gone above her I would have received nothing for my contributions.

My first run-in with this person was also very unpleasant. It occurred at the Fortieth Anniversary show at WDW in 1995. After we finished one of our autograph sessions and were exiting "backstage" to an adjoining room, I openly picked up one of the small boxes of then-and-now photos that they provided for us to sign. We gave Disney current photos of ourselves and these were added to one of their copyright 'fifties Mouseketeer photos for autograph signing events.

Martha stopped me, accused me of being a thief and grabbed the small box of photos from me. She did this in front of some FANS/GUESTS who were still hanging around. First of all, I am not a thief and I get unhappy when I am falsely accused of stealing. Secondly, she was violating Disney policy by doing this in front of the remaining fans and park visitors.

When behind closed doors a few feet away, which she could have availed herself of if she had acted according to Disney policy, I explained to her that in every past experience we had been given some of the photos that had not been used since they would be anachronistic and incapable of being used again, as was the case ten years later in 2005 with these specific then-and-now photos. She did not apologize, nor did she return the photos.

I explained to her at the time that I had signed no legal papers, as none of us had, for using my copyrighted current photo as half of the small box of then-and-now pics of me she was holding. This did not make any difference to her. The next day the car that was to pick Diane and me up for the long drive to the Orlando airport did not show up. When we contacted them we were told that an anonymous someone had cancelled it. We managed after some time to get a cab and barely made our flight. I think I know who cancelled that car.

I wrote Mike Eisner and a couple of other of people about this rude, false accusation and incident and received apologies about what happened but apparently Ms. Martha maintained and enhanced her position with the company but did not forget our negative interaction even though she had caused it.

An individual who has contributed to the promotion of the company in multiple ways, usually with no compensation, as we all have for more than fifty years should not have to fight for what is nothing to a billion+ a year corporation for work done in all good faith under duress and pain. Many would say, "But that's showbiz," just as they might say, "That's the law," when a person that everyone knows is guilty is found innocent due to amoral lawyers and judges. Too much autonomy or power makes things morally questionable and frequently much worse than reprehensible.

The showbiz law still remains that the show must go on. You can always be replaced by an understudy, or just someone taking over your lines, songs and dances. As Sherry once put it to me, Disney only really cares about having the necessary number of Mouseketeer bodies and she is correct. Everyone can be replaced by another body or a foster brother.

The showbizaphobic automatically assumes a self-defeating mindset as an instinct, like a knee when hit by a rubber hammer. It is like being brainwashed as a showbiz *Manchurian Candidate* showing up on *Groundhog Day* to relentlessly pursue the goal of doing absolutely anything asked of you.

The defining evening for my insight into showbizaphobia came in the early 'eighties when I had dinner with a lover from my first two years in Manhattan, 1970 and 1971. We met in acting classes in the Village and she had moved into casting and eventually became a prominent television casting director. This second Karen was never a beauty, but she was bright. In the time we had no contact her orthodonture challenges and her large girth had grown apace. Her redeeming oral virtues in our short-lived affair were history for me and I much preferred keeping it that way.

She caught me playing Billy Early, the younger lawyer that Bobby Van performed in the Broadway revival of *No, No, Nanette*, during which I received a gratifying note from an audience member telling me I had more than matched Bobby Van in the Broadway revival she had also attended (see Appendix). During this show I finally met Mike Hoey, my future friend, and Ruby Keeler.

As suave, nonchalant dancing lawyer Billy Early in No, No Nanette. *The tie was my dad's from the '30s, 1982.*

Karen Two came backstage and invited me for a drink at Yamashiro's, an old Japanese restaurant isolated above Highland and Hollywood and between Grauman's and south of the Hollywood Bowl. Karen Two complimented me and we talked about the intervening years since we saw each other in Greenwich Village. Finally she asked me to dinner the following week, which I accepted. Our conversation after a long separation was pleasant and amusing and I looked forward to further reminiscing and learning of her journey from actress to CD. It was also significant to be on a friendly basis with a casting person who liked your work and liked you.

Ruby Keeler, who starred on Broadway in the 1971 revival of "Nanette," in the bar at the Masquer's Club after seeing our production, 1982.

I drove to her West Hollywood house and she had decided where we would eat. Her attitude seemed to have changed and after we ordered drinks she became adversarial and proceeded to rant on various subjects that had nothing to do with her move from actress to casting. She brought up a film I had not thought much of, *Mad Max,* and insisted it was a "fag film." I saw some elements of what she said but did not agree; it was not *The Boys on the Bikes.*

I offered a wonderful film I had seen recently, *The Unbearable Lightness of Being* and she scolded me because the book, which I had not yet read in translation as she had, was so superior. I later found it was a very good novel but that did not change my view of the film. I was the one who had reviewed films and theatre professionally for magazines and newspapers, although I did not point that out.

Usually a film from a novel is badly translated to the screen, as in *Catch 22* with all those talented stars and Mike Nichols directing. Films like *Being There, The French Lieutenant's Woman, The English Patient* and *The Wings of the Dove* in which a work of art is translated into a different work of art, are really quite rare. For me, as with *Unbearable Lightness,* both the novel and the film are legitimate works of art in different modalities. Karen Two would abide no opinion but her own on any subject we discussed and continued in this vain vein throughout the meal. I began to wonder if she was on something other than a couple of drinks.

When I offered to buy her dinner, she denied both that and my further attempt to pay for my half. She haughtily refused and insisted on using her card. She wanted to return to her place and have another drink. I did not like the way things were going but I was still a victim of showbizaphobia regarding her position and the long-awaited goal of getting THE role so I could move beyond just making a living. The truth is that as an adult the only leads I have done had been in theatre and one NYC student film and this short opus was no Lucas *THX 1138*. The majority of my other roles were supports or day player bits.

If I offended Karen Two she could keep me from being auditioned at her cable company, the most respected in the industry, and perhaps elsewhere; although unvoiced, it seemed a bit like the Disney threat when I signed the MMC contract. Karen Two had always jockeyed for intellectual superiority with me and most others, but she lost more than won with me and that seemed to have some part in what was going on. She now had power; I did not.

Having a drink back amidst her Mission furniture, which she overbearingly bragged about, she suggested we smoke some weed. We had taken a hit now and again years ago in New York but I preferred not to just like Bartleby. In addition to wanting to cleanly and amicably extricate myself from the situation and not wanting to have sex with her ever again, I have never enjoyed smoking dope with anyone I was not close to and did not trust. Having not had a doobie for some time, I did not need clairvoyance to know that things would have progressed further negatively if we both smoked.

Karen Two used intimidation and cajolery but she took tokes alone which made her close to livid, so the conversation became more and more aggressive on her part. If I had not been showing symptoms of my phobia I probably should have told her to screw off and left much earlier. I managed as quickly as I could to extract myself after swallowing more abuse and assumed she would never read me for anything.

A couple of months later she did have me in for a day player role and I gave one of my very rare questionable auditions. I later inferred that this result was a hangover from my disease. Her attitude at the reading was cold and very like we had left off the evening of our dinner and this threw me to some degree.

I have no vanity about wearing my glasses, although I started with vanity that my mom superimposed on me. I wear my contacts only when I audition, am on a talk show or actually doing a role in which it can be deciphered that I do not see well without an aid—when eye squinting shows on a movie screen or when I need to dance or do a piece of business that requires good eyesight.

I use monovision with contacts, meaning one eye is set up for distance viewing, waylaying my myopia and astigmatism and the other is set up for my presbyopic reading lacks. Thus, I do not read, nor see in the distance with nearly the acuity that I do with my glasses, which correct both eyes for my three visual difficulties.

The troubling issue is that anyone in a casting capacity has incapacities in translating a person in front of them for a role wearing glasses, which carry many typing qualities (intellectual, snob, geek) that can interfere with your goal in obtaining the role. The fact that you have the glasses off before you read and a picture in front of them without glasses does not seem to help them enough.

It was too dim in the room, whether unnoticed or on purpose, for me to see the lines and cues as well as I needed. If I had not been reacting to her power position, a possible money job and our recent contretemps at dinner, I would have politely requested more light. This is the actor's few minutes of opportunity and, as learned in Acting I, you must make the most of it. Instead, I forged ahead like an abused child and read falteringly for I could not see the cues, nor my lines, clearly enough.

Even giving your all and more, you may not get the job. You learn that there are countless exigencies and reasons that control your success or failure. You could remind someone of an enemy or ex-husband, you could have the wrong hair color, you could be a stranger and not a relative, lover or friend, you could just be wrong for the role, whatever that means, and they are frequently not sure themselves, despite the author's words and the director's descriptions of whom or what they want.

It later occurred to me that Karen Two's transition from realizing she had not a chance as an actress due to her looks and talent and moving to casting small then larger theatre roles in Manhattan before moving to casting for TV in Hollywood had changed her for the worse.

I had not been in love with her during our trysts and acting in scenes together in the Village. The sex was relatively good and her intelligence, humor and education were a triad that too many young women did not have. In this unusual audition all I had to contribute was my showbizaphobia victim persona responses, which may have been what set her predatory side off on me from the beginning at this time in our lives. I only hope that we never encounter each other again, which does not speak well for my being cast by her, nor anyone with whom she works.

Positively, it has kept me from perseverating in my showbizaphobic way, too much like going on "It's A Small World" over and over and being tortured by that insipid, repetitive song for the rest of your life.

After first writing this chapter I found something in Al Gore's 2007 book *The Assault On Reason* in which he takes on the far right political teamwork coming from extreme religious beliefs underlying Bush II's many negative acts leading up to declaring war on Iraq, without the sanction of Congress, and the years of war that have ensued. He briefly mentions an interesting discussion of findings by neurologists and psychologists. Fearful, anxiety ridden, traumatic events, e.g. the slap at the audition, the foster brother, being forced to sign the Disney contract, and the rest I have encountered, move out of the realm of time that our memories normally keep. They speed to the forefront and seem present in the present, in the now, when they are triggered. Surely the episode with Karen Two, as well as hundreds of others, are indicative of showbizaphobia occurring in the now again and again.

I only add that I remember from Al's book that the media is Medusa, the worst snake being television's one-way grasp on the mind of the individual. In an early graduate school essay I was asked to write about what I thought was the most important change in the 20th century. This was before the first moon walk but I believe I would have written the same thing even after it.

My impromptu essay came to the conclusion that TV is the most important thing to happen in the 20th century, not the atom bomb, not space travel, nor anything else. I added that we all knew that television could be used for good or evil. What would have happened if Hitler, or Stalin or Mao's propaganda machines had the full understanding and use of television for their attempts to rule the world? If you read Al's book you'll know what he would think.

When I was younger my need to be perfect also drove me to unconscionable actions in order to always win an argument or contest. Sometimes I would be in the middle of winning a disagreement and realize that what I was supporting was wrong. I had the arsenal and facility to continue to pursue and win while knowing my winning was simply being able to reason and argue better or to just outlast the other person or persons. I lost some of these controversies but not many. I stopped myself from doing this in my thirties.

As a result, I was asked why I did not become a lawyer but I knew that such an anti-ethical need to win at any cost and by whatever duplicity was not something I would be capable of doing, even for a short or limited period of time. Certainly not for child molesters, rapists, killers and other odious people but even for the righteous. I truly believe that in most, if not all, situations there is good and bad, right and wrong, fair and unfair. My late father-in-law, the second name in a recognized D.C. law firm, truly believed and stated that everything, including the colors black and white, was gray. In the law, showbiz and Vegas there are only winners and losers.

I grew up thinking, as most do, that Vegas was a glamorous, adult Disneyland but I learned to hate the city when I lived there for about nine months while onstage in *George M*. The only choices seemingly allowed in Vegas are to be either a predator or a victim, just as in nature.

I refused to take on either role and, therefore, did not fit in at all, which seemed to confuse and anger everyone. Of course, there are residents of this neon desert resort who simply live in a small town in Nevada, as my mom did, but they are not the norm on the street or in the hotels and casinos.

We all must make judgments for which we are required to suspend our beliefs, to look only at the final result, the bottom line, whether in degree or worse, in order to function. We all compromise but it does not have to be on a weekly, nor even on a daily basis. As a lawyer you must do this always.

My obvious signs of depression during my college years living with my grandparents were never addressed, nor brought up for discussion in any depth by anyone. Anytime I approached the subject no parent, friend or lover inquired further, nor offered me counsel. Depression had not yet come into its own as a distinct disease so I viewed my emotional tussles as only one more nail in the coffin of the failed, imperfect pretender.

I have been convinced for most of my life that every person must take responsibility for his or her actions and life. Having depression as an illness does not exclude me from taking steps to obviate the disease's inbred negativity, inner and outer aggression and self-destruction. I began taking on this battle in the 1960s and continue into this century. I have made enormous changes in my character and life. I still sometimes lose—but not nearly as badly as I continually used to lose. I pick myself up, brush myself off, sincerely apologize if warranted, and start all over again. The pharmaceuticals help, the therapy and lessons learned help, but in essence it is still always up to me.

Attempting suicide, learning I was replaceable even as a son and other emotional battle scars were not the best ways to begin my adult life, but this does not make it a monumental tragedy. I did subconsciously find liquor as a medicine to alleviate the pain by drinking myself into a stupor, but booze only works, if at all, for one or two drinks, then you are dragged under by one more form of self-imposed depression. At fifteen I had moved onto what seemed an unalterable trek to exacerbating and never dealing with my inherent problems. This less traveled path began with Dot and Dash, John and Glade, but picked up momentum in search of something to hold onto in college after my family was no help.

After the night of Scotch and the large Bowie knife and my search for help outside my life, things became better and worse. Subsequent to my second European venture and my wrist slashing, my weekly therapy helped me through over three years of working at mundane jobs from 1964-67+ and then my more unfortunate first marriage.

I never met Studs Terkel, but I think he might have found me interesting enough for a paragraph or two in his enormous quest for the experiences and tales of working stiffs.

Chapter 11
Chilling Draft/Snake Eyes In Vegas

In my twentieth year I suffered a number of shocks and difficulties that I managed to overcome but then I turned twenty-one and a monstrous problem that I thought I had covered and that scared me badly came at me like a tiger burning bright: the DRAFT.

The worst threat my mom ever came up with was sending me to military school, even though this was directly opposed to the non-violent teachings of the Witness religion she believed and inculcated in me at six.

I was no longer a Jehovah's Witness so I had no bona fide religious reasons for being a conscientious objector, and by this time COs were being forced into service in ostensibly noncombat situations—but clerks and medics get wounded and killed, too. In 1964 no one would have suspected that Vietnam would become, perhaps, the worst war that Americans have fought, excluding the ongoing bloody Iraq debacle, but it was certainly minatory to anyone with a world view.

I had finished college, was not married with an expected, nor actual, child and I was in great shape physically except for wearing glasses. Burning draft cards had not yet become a fad and I was not the type to take off for Canada.

I was commanded to present myself at the induction center and was immediately nervous and afraid of the way we were being dealt with as numbers rather than humans by the uniformed oppressors. Individuality no longer existed. We were part of the system, the lowest element, and we were made to feel this way every second. It struck me as being quite communistic or fascistic or what I imagine being in prison would feel like. Individualism, the hallmark of American democracy, was not allowed.

During the physical I had one of the most embarrassing experiences in my life as I stood naked in many lines of nude men and someone I never saw spread my butt cheeks and jammed a large finger or something else up my ass. While I never had any doubts about it, this confirmed to me that I was not a homosexual, nor would I ever be. This graphic invasion made it clear that I could not be subjected to this kind of psychological and physiological treatment, not to mention injury and/or death, for a minimum of two years.

I knew that as a staunch individualist I would be in very serious trouble if I was drafted. Thirty-five years after the draft disappeared, the inevitability of this Orwellian world is just as hard to understand for young men today as it would be to find something growing in your stomach for months that kicks, causes nausea, problematic mobility and discomfort and after nine months you have to somehow push it out through a very tiny aperture.

I was also blond, good-looking, notable due to the MMC which was rerunning, neither tall nor a weight lifter, not a pugilistic expert and I refused to go along with the crowd on most occasions. Unless significant forces make it too much to my disadvantage, I have always stood for what I believe to be right morally, ethically and by my principles, which always seem more consistent than those of most folks who delude themselves into believing they are paragons of virtue. This meant that the only worse place for me to be would be prison. I most likely would not get raped in the service but I sure as hell would be picked on by noncoms and officers daily, so physical and mental abuse would be inevitable.

I have always been proud to be an American. I love and respect my country although in the last thirty or so years I believe the American ethos has changed dramatically from the country in which I grew up and held far above others including Switzerland, Canada, Sweden and other nations that are not violently set upon world domination. I am no longer secure in this belief, which saddens me greatly.

I almost got into a very nasty situation in a movie theatre as a teen. Right before this WW II epic began they played "The Star Spangled Banner." I did not stand and sing the national anthem, much like I refused to recite the pledge of allegiance at HPS, but not just for religious reasons. I knew we were being manipulated by the movie makers and it pissed me off. I received some disdainful, inciting words but kept silent and no one moved on me. My date was not too thrilled.

This was in my late teens and I still believed that Jehovah, like all gods, would have no bronze animals, nor flags mucking about with his primacy. I had also read of Nietzsche's hatred for any kind of nationalism that supersedes the individual's morals and ethics, which is why he lived most of his life as an expatriate German. This is absurdly ironic since the Nazis convoluted his *ubermensch* (in correct translations, overman, *not* superman) concept for their Fascist German nationalism. I would not follow the other lemmings over the precipice because it would be more socially acceptable, more politically correct.

As a young liberal I was for predictable causes and, later, against the Vietnam War. Naturally, I canvassed door-to-door as a volunteer for people ONLY to register and vote just before I became voting age. At no time did I say positive things about my candidate, McCarthy, nor anything negative regarding the dreaded Goldwater. In going door-to-door I discovered how few people actually voted or even considered registering. But I was beginning to come to the conclusion that voting is always a pejorative Hobson's Choice, at least since 1964 when I turned twenty-one and was able to vote. The alleged choice is to pick the candidate who is the least evil liar and least dangerous to the world and yourself and our free, to some degree, way of life. Indeed, we appear to have more freedom than other countries, except perhaps Canada or a few other open societies, but our freedom is more one of appearance than fact.

Even as a liberal, I was an independent and on some issues I had conservative views, which is still my credo. It comes down to judging people and issues individually and adhering to your own beliefs, principles, morals and ethics. To alienate both groups at once, I am for a woman's right to have an abortion and I am also for capital punishment.

My aversion to the allegedly democratic system became more pronounced when I realized that what I deem to be the uselessness of voting really comes down not to having a voice and caring but merely personal and business reasons. If you are a property owner or have children who go to public schools or pay taxes or use the sidewalks and streets and so on you want to have a voice in what the local, regional, state and national government does. In America you have this choice via the vote—or so those in power would have us believe. Whether you actually have a say in any of this is easily arguable, if not a complete crock. The phrase "eminent domain" comes to mind.

In 2009 there were more than three hundred million Americans. If you check the Presidential race figures even cursorily you will see that the percentage of people who take the time to vote is comparatively tiny. Even with the upsurge in voting for Obama, will they remember in four years? This could be for many reasons but two, I am sure, are apathy and anomie because voting appears to the majority of individuals to be useless. Voting is supposed to mean that we have a free society and every person counts. Al Gore was not defeated in 2000 by one vote, he actually won more votes, but some very tricky uses of judicial and legislative legerdemain forced our worst President upon us. All Americans' rights have been under a deluge of radical attack for almost eight years and it will take much work to change these violations of the constitution that set America apart from the entire world over two hundred years ago.

I was registered as a Democrat for one reason only: to vote in primaries. Indeed, I still tend more toward a Democratic viewpoint than a Republican on many issues but neither party is a stellar example of ethical politics and, more to the point, right and wrong.

Being registered as a voter for any tiny, independent alternative party is useless except as a personal statement or to impress others because this choice is not going to be effective in our system. I remained a Democrat of sorts for years because it was, for me, the only logical choice I had. I have not done that for some time but I gained hope from Barack Obama, registered once again, and voted for the man with the possibilities of change and hope.

The non-choices for President and the rest that have existed since I could vote are fictions to me. There are conspiracies beyond the assassinations of JFK, MLK, RFK and the latest Bhutto and none of us will ever know who is actually guilty or what happened except, perhaps, those in power.

I still read the paper daily as well as watch the repetitive, mispronounced, interminably pedestrian TV précis of news, getting appalled more on some days than others, but it is a daunting pursuit. There were examples of Mammon as the only true American god long before I was born. The difference is that the world and its history are rampant with this greedy god but Americans have hypocritically acted as if none of that pertained to us; we are for humans, individuals, rights, not just financial success.

Read Arthur Miller's 1947 Tony Award winning play *All My Sons* in which Joe Keller, an American manufacturer, is so fixated on getting rich "for his family" that he knowingly sells defective airplane parts, resulting in the deaths of twenty-one American WWII pilots. He then frames his business partner for the crime and engineers his own exoneration. His tragedy lies not in his being discovered but in his own evil, selfish actions. It is an American tragedy and unlike classic Greek tragedy it has nothing to do with mythology. It is fact, history and reality. Things now are just more obvious and much, much more common, much, much worse. Names like Halliburton and Cheney come to my mind. I tend to think of Cheney's motto as, "See it, Shoot it, Spend it."

The ME generation was exactly that long before one group got the label, and has become all generations in America for much more than just the majority of Americans. There are still good people out there. Among them I do not include oppressive, sometimes dangerous, religious right wing or left wing maniacs and zealots. The majority of good people in my America, the society in which I grew up, now appear to be the minority. In 2009 the plurality of people are so self-consumed that they care about and respect only themselves, their family and their friends. They believe only their beliefs are valid.

My reasons are manifold for believing that the positive, humanist American ethos that existed when I grew up is gone. I can only hope that the possibility of resurrection exists. We all experience rude, solipsistic behavior daily on any freeway, on any street, in every neighborhood, even in the supermarkets where most leave their carts in the middle of the aisle so no one can get by. A recent news story far from California or New York or Washington, D.C. showed a man mangled by a hit-and-run driver being ignored. Cars drove around him, a small crowd gathered and perhaps someone dialed 911 but no one approached him to try to help, cover him with a blanket—they did nothing.

Some acts are more blatant than others, but hordes of seemingly average people like this are present in almost every city in America. It is sad and frightening, as is the abyss of existentialism versus believing in one of the myriad gods is, but both must be recognized and reconciled in some way in order to live a life that is more than just existing, getting by, trying to avoid the increasing dangers outside your cave.

Long before moving to Manhattan in 1970 I said, "You're welcome" to women and men, of any age, ethnicity or religion when I opened a door for them and they did not say thank you. Having grown up in upper middle class, surreptitiously segregated communities in Southern California, when I initially began living in the Apple I carried an umbrella around all the time, day or night, to have some kind of weapon to defend myself with. I gave up my bumbershoot toting after the first few weeks.

In broad daylight, people passing right and left and a police officer on a scooter checking meters, a junkie stuck a knife into Diane's stomach and demanded her money. She gave it to him instantly, worried because she never carried much, but he left and she was not harmed, which was purely good fortune. She had just left the theatre where she worked in midtown Manhattan in the early 'seventies.

We all know about or have experienced difficult to dangerous incidents regarding the rights to a parking place and minor, no-injury auto accidents. We have all seen people cut into lines, cut off another motorist without signaling, push around someone smaller whether their own children or a defenseless elderly person or just another adult. Behavior like this has been commonplace in third world countries and even some first world countries like Japan for too many decades, but this is not the way America was when I grew up. In the culture in which I grew up there was, as in *It's a Wonderful Life*, an old, nasty curmudgeon, but he or she was an anomaly, not representative of the majority in any given town.

There were things that were wrong in America in the 'forties and 'fifties; there have always been rude people, bullies, thieves and killers, but this type of behavior has grown almost as quickly as our so-called beneficial technology. As billions of people bring forth billions more, everything declines. For some time I have been convinced that this festering situation as it exists in 2009 will only get worse as people have children, crowding the globe further, making things more difficult and complicated, only because they think that they are not whole if they do not propagate, and I am only addressing those who comprehend birth control but do nothing about it. The more people are overcrowding and competing, the more conflicts will occur and will be unsolved—except by violence.

Education in America is presently an immense, deteriorating system and that is certainly true in many other countries. Most children receive an inept, hardly adequate education, a worse upbringing at home given the now common self-as-religion style of their parents' quests for more and better. Parents' work and drive time allows very limited quality time with youngsters. Then, of course, everyone wonders why everyone else is so uncaring, unable to satisfy THEIR personal needs. Everyone is concerned that it is so dangerous everywhere, and thoroughly do not understand why no one is aware of THEIR rights.

No one remembers Schopenhauer's porcupine parable. Artie proposed that a passel of chilly porcupines gathered close together for needed warmth but, due to their quills, they had to keep a certain distance to avoid being injured. That distance for humans is accomplished by "loving thy neighbor" which translates to being polite and formal. But the social contract of Hobbes or Locke or Rousseau was shredded sometime in the 'sixties and into the 'seventies, even though the 'sixties appeared to promise a move toward equality and striving for what is right, not just what is profitable only for the individual's and their chosen ones advancement. We have become socially unconscious toward our fellow humans; they have become objects.

One conclusion I have reached about military service is that I believe I would have gone into the service if I had been born twenty years before WW II, the last "clearly good versus clearly bad" war. This does not mean to say that everything about any war is done altruistically, nor with the lives of humans as the most important factor. Now almost all wars seem to be related to economic supremacy and control of major world resources, which has been a traditional format but used to include violent aggression by an oppressor, as in World War II or the Spartans attacking the Athenians or Alexander, Charlemagne, Napoleon and Stalin-Hitler-Mao out to conquer the world and make it their own.

Dangerous conflicts, which are politically correct mishmash for wars, frequently carry the seed of civil wars like the North versus the South, Jews versus Arabs (both of whom are Semites), Arabs versus Arabs, Sunnis versus Shiites, Hutus versus Tutsis. Human rights, although manipulated as propaganda, have nothing to do with any of these dreadful massacres. The noncombatants always have more humans killed than the combatants and live under desperate circumstances during and after the onslaughts, however long they last.

There has been a resurgence in the zealotry of organized religion that excludes all other points of view and which prevailed in many if not most previous wars in history—everyone who does not believe is an infidel and, thus, should be killed. After having been crusaded against centuries ago and defeated, the prevailing factions of Islam have reignited the crusades. There is no victory in revenge. Victory in war can have positive results when the conquered are not oppressed, enslaved or forced to change their religious beliefs but are aided in recovery financially and in other ways, of changing the lives of all people in the specific country positively.

Germany and Japan and Italy attempted, at the instigation of Hitler and his cohorts, to conquer the world. Japan and Germany are two examples of what victory is when it is positive. Italy is not quite as formidably successful as a nation but it also never became a subjugated, slave society by the conquering forces it fought.

Former warlike peoples enslaved the entire population when they conquered another civilization and religious zealots would do the same thing. Imagine the world if the Nazis, who came much too close, had been successful.

In this era of global-affecting nuclear accidents or attacks, perhaps worse biological warfare or errors, it is a good time to be at least in your sixties. I hold out little hope for the youngsters who are being ineffectively educated and improperly raised. Will they be able to take on what the deadly heat of the near future holds—if they survive school massacres, gang warfare and drive-by shootings, global warming, deadly air, food and water, slavery to machines and all the other negative elements that appear to be growing exponentially in 2009, will they be able to cope with what appear to be overwhelming catastrophes whether man-made or from nature?

I hope so.

One cannot live without hope and I reject Camus and Sartre's gloomy forecast. I do have hope, but one is a fool to ignore what philosophers and religionists call the abyss and, further and worse, the seemingly overwhelming but avoidable dangers that are not created by anyone's god, or nature but by humans beliefs and actions particularly when they are accompanied by, as in Nazi Germany, complicity through silence.

My problem with the draft was solved by my therapist without really explaining it to me. The gang tough sergeant at my induction attacked me verbally, but I held my anger in because I knew he could have me incarcerated and I would accomplish nothing. I explained that I had other personal reasons that caused my suicide attempt that had nothing to do with avoiding the draft.

Lou, my therapist, saw that Vietnam was becoming a nasty imbroglio and had sent the induction board a letter after I told him about my draft notice. He would not tell me what he said in his epistle except that he gave part of my diagnosis as depression. Given what they seemed to want, you would think a person whose violence puts his fist through walls and doors and who attempts to kill himself with a large Bowie knife would be welcomed to whatever wet unit was in need.

In essence, Lou Leveen kept me from killing or being killed; without him I might not be here. Thank you forever, Lou.

Whatever actually happened, I nervously awaited my notice, got through it and I received a letter classifying me 1-Y. I have never known what that meant but I inferred it meant that I would be called up for review again in one year but that did not happen. Lou was incisive in realizing that I would not function well, probably not at all, in a military environment.

As Vietnam progressed Lou sent another letter a year later. He truly believed I would have imploded or exploded if I was made to become a slave of the service and any cretin above me in rank. He also was concerned about what my fury might cause if I was put in a position in which I could not control my anger and that the person or persons who had "diss'd" me might just become dead. I have become better and better about controlling my anger and I have almost always resisted physical violence, except as noted herein. My private therapy with Lou and within my group offered me alternatives to a life begun in pain, isolation, anger and depression.

My struggle with the draft came almost a year after my suicide attempt, my argument with my grandmother and then moving out on my own. Taking care of everything at twenty without the net of my grandparents' money still left me with what we all have in common: coping with life and its vicissitudes, health problems, love entanglements, car accidents and coarse abusive strangers, family, friends and coworkers—those maladies of the quotidian. I was quite the virgin to much of this due to having been so spoiled financially and some basic good luck but I was up to the challenges presented.

I quickly found out that I was not made for sales, the people with whom I worked, particularly those in power, and the grind of nine-to-five meaninglessness. My one highlight at my first job, about six weeks at the May Company, was a young co-worker. She explained before leaving after our one-night sexual adventure my last day of work there that she was engaged, soon to be married and wanted a last fling. I never saw nor heard from her again, nor do I recall her name, after she dropped by my apartment for a cocktail and intimacy—but then, it was the 'sixties. We had rarely spoken until that one afternoon and night.

I then tried teaching ballroom dancing, which I had been paid to perform many times but had never studied. I found the strident strictness of formal ballroom very different and unpleasant, much like a stilted ballet formality versus tap and jazz, from being able to cha-cha, swing, rumba, samba and tango in my own style, rather than like everyone else stuck with a ramrod up their butt and that eternal, false, teeth-baring necessity.

Meanwhile, I had taken a series of real estate classes and when it became clear to me that the ballroom classes were more about being close to and hit on by old, not very attractive women rather than forcing myself to dance clone-style steps, I joined a real estate firm.

This is another form of salesmanship that some actors I know take to with ease but I felt it was a lot of sitting around and then acting, not lying but carefully avoiding the truth and forcing people to like things that you disliked, sometimes intensely. I was not good at smilingly conning people and pointing out the great things about a house while standing on rat droppings.

To start my students thinking, on the rare occasions I have taught acting, I have offered a very simple maxim as a definition of acting: Acting is lying. Of course, it is much more than that, but in essence you are lying to an audience, however truthfully baring part of yourself, to make them believe you are a Medusa who kills her children to get back at her betraying husband or a benign Gump fool or Dostoyevsky's Prince Myshkin. There is an accepted convention at work whether you are on a stage, in film, on TV or just a voice on the radio.

The conventions of acting, from the *cothurni*—tall, platform foot gear that Greek actors wore in their tragedies—to huge faces on a film screen or tiny ones on TV, give you the freedom to be as evil or righteous as you want. It is not you; it is acting. The more convincing the lying within the convention, the better you are at it. It is a craft that attains to, and sometimes succeeds, as art—it is not being.

I have always found it difficult to lie credibly in life. It would be impossible for me to be a con man or thief or conspirator or spy. I would not be able to pull it off. I can, however, with the accepted convention that we all know I am acting, accept Coleridge's "willing suspension of disbelief," do it quite well and convincingly and have done so in all the above mentioned modalities.

Many humans other than actors and con men and con women lie all their lives about liking a boss or loving their emolument-producing yet sterile work, not favoring one child over another, on their taxes, to a cop, keeping a secret sex life, having two families without living in Utah and billions of other lies that are passed along daily. Sometimes it is necessary to lie in life to function, but most of the time a lie is an individual's selfish need or evil desire and has nothing to do with sparing someone's feelings, saving one's face, being a kind, tolerant person, nor any other righteous reason. No one seems to comprehend the difference in the formality of conventions that suspend the truth. I could not be a real estate agent or any kind of salesman, just as I could never be an attorney—although I would be much better off financially.

An acquaintance from Valley College managed a bar his parents owned in a bowling alley, the Corbin Bowl, in the depths of the Valley and I decided to become a bartender. I actually started as a bar boy, cleaning up for two bartenders on the club side, separate from the bowling alley, working primarily beer orders from the bowling lanes but memorizing bar recipes and learning how to build drinks when they were too busy and I jumped in to build a cocktail. Not the preferred first job for someone with an M.A. at twenty.

In two weeks I took over for one of the bartenders and soon was the head bartender in a very busy bar that had dancing and a small band in the evenings and was an early version of a meat market. There were two places for waitresses to order, one for the bowling alley side and one for the fairly large dance and booze room.

I became more knowledgeable about the work and more adept than most and made a lot more than at the other working stiff jobs I had tried previously. I could also ostensibly be myself, except for intellectual palaver which I avoided to not offend people who might tip. I was polite and friendly, but I would not take much guff at all. The worst work time in a bar is when you are not busy pouring or cutting fruit or cleaning and there are only a few customers with whom you are forced to converse. I was not making excellent money including the tips but in my situation with no car to pay off and few other needs it worked out for me until I started getting more work in entertainment.

I met Betty, the most efficient and attractive of the cocktail waitresses, who had short brunette hair with blonde highlights and a petite and excellent figure. She also had a fast, salty but not profane tongue. She would take no bull from any barfly and could leave an order for seven drinks and give the correct addition to confirm my mental math, while picking up eight cocktails she had ordered previously. We were a terrific team, exchanged quips, flirted and laughed a lot.

We only met at night in the bar dimness and she thought I was older than twenty-one, just as others assumed when I was younger, and I thought she was younger than thirty-nine. I asked her out and she put me off for a while.

Eventually, I broke through Betty's no sex with co-workers policy, for it was clear that a sexual tension existed between us, and we began dating and fell in love, before she found out my age and I found out hers. She was the oldest woman I loved and made love to, being eighteen years my senior, but we both knew and accepted that with her eleven-year-old autistic son and an eighteen-year-old daughter from a first marriage, added to our age disparity, we were having a marvelous affair that would not go on forever, nor lead to marriage.

Her daughter objected to me since her fiancé was the same age that I was. Once, out with Betty and her offspring and the fiancé I had a rare instance of being carded in a restaurant, no doubt due to being with a kid, an eighteen-year-old female and a much bigger guy who had just turned twenty-one and looked eighteen, but it was embarrassing, especially after all my years drinking under the age limit.

I was quite proud of my first meeting with Betty's eleven-year-old autistic boy for I had little knowledge of children and no knowledge of how to react to autistic behavior, which was true of most people in this time frame. I went to Betty's house, he opened the door and hugged me and said he loved me.

To most men of any age in 1964 this would have been a confusing moment and would have frozen them stiff, but I simply went to my knee to get on his level and hugged him back, telling him that I loved him, too. Betty beamed behind him.

My first Betty and I had a wonderful relationship that lasted about seven or eight months, and then we parted but on friendly, caring terms, without a hint of rancor. I saw her much later at a jazz club near NBC in Burbank where she was still serving cocktails, and she looked great.

I remained at the Corbin Bowl bar but had hired as second man a bartender who was much older, and eventually he showed that he objected to my authority. He would show up late having not cleaned properly the night before and would not perform his responsibilities like cutting the lemons and limes, and when I talked to him about it, he got irritated and acted like a wiseass.

There were now new owners and so I talked to them and told them that he had to go or I had to go. When the bartender heard this he threatened to knock my teeth out and he was a lot bigger than I was. They fired him but I decided to move on, to the dismay of the owners and after giving them a two-week notice a month or so later began bar work at a Mexican dinner house, Santana's. I soon learned that I had a problem on the night shift. After dinner I was left alone with one waitress, who left early when there was no business. I was stuck in the separate bar area, away from the now-closed dining room, separate and in the front. I was alone in the back of the building where cars parked with a separate entrance and a full register, thus, vulnerable to a stick up or just one or two rowdy drunks.

I complained about this but nothing was done and so I gave notice and moved to a Jolly Roger franchise in the Topanga Plaza Mall, the first huge mall, we were told, in Southern California. Here I was taught by the head bartender (who worked nights while I did lunches and afternoons) how to pre-mix the martinis that were the mainstay drink of the extremely fast lunches for mall employees and customers. It was a very busy venue then almost deserted after lunch until the late afternoon.

He took three bottles of gin or vodka and a fourth bottle with an inch or so of vermouth filled to the top with water and poured all four bottles into a large gallon jug. I was told to do this when I came on in the morning if there was a lack of pre-made martinis. Obviously this was done before opening in the small back room and the premixed jugs were kept very cold in a freezer—alcohol does not freeze. Arte Johnson told me he kept his vodka in the freezer and poured it into a glass with an anchovy wrapped around a caper, much more L.A. than Manhattan.

In the months I spent there, not one person complained about a watered-down drink. I saw no profit from his pilfering from the register with his form of thievery, nor would I have accepted any—he later could either take money from the register or comp big tippers or friends and still make his PC, meaning percentage—the amount of profit the house makes from the liquor doled out according to the register. I objected, but said nothing. I was not proud of my taciturnity but I needed the money until I found a new position, which I began looking for soon after starting there. I certainly feared being considered a co-conspirator, whether profiting or not.

I also did not like many of the patrons, which had also been the case at the Corbin Bowl. It was not just unruly drunks, who are relatively rare, but the type of guy who comes in and starts telling racial jokes or becomes loud and vulgar. I stopped a guy working on an "N" word joke as soon as the word was uttered, which was premonitory for society in 1966. I took his drink away, refunded his money and told him to drink elsewhere.

He grabbed for me and I quickly backed away, the ice mallet in my right hand; he mouthed violence while my other hand rested on a bottle, which makes an effective weapon. These two failing, I always had the ice pick. He blathered some expletives and then left. I was fortunate to never to have to use any of these weapons in my years behind the stick. I knew then that due to these dangers and other reasons this would not be a life long way of making a buck when not acting, writing, dancing, choreographing or directing.

Violence came very close once when my future wife Dahrlene visited me at the Mexican bar and the only patrons were three sailors getting drunk. I had already told them after two rounds that I felt they had too much and would not serve them anymore but I held off ordering them out to avoid contributing to a dangerous problem. Dahr happened to stop by for a drink; she was attractive and they began hitting on her until I lied and explained she was my wife prior to it being a fact. Somehow the subject of Vietnam entered the conversation. We were in the war now and they were on leave. Oh, brother.

Dahr's brother had been killed in 'Nam, and the sailors acknowledged his death. Dahrlene originally had been gung ho for the war to get those "slopes," her word usage, for killing him. I had slowly and gently explained what I knew about this shamefully pursued war, very like the current one in Iraq, and had converted her to realizing the invalidity of our presence in Vietnam and the futility of her brother's death. She was now very anti-'Nam. She stated her strong dislike for the war and this, not surprisingly, hit the sailors badly. I was afraid of what was about to happen, but I managed to cool them and her down and they took off. This was a very propitious night for me and for her.

It was not luck but my thin slicing that kept us from being badly beaten or worse later at the Century City march against the Vietnam War when LBJ was visiting at a hotel there near 20th Century Fox studios.

The thousands and thousands in the organized crowd were ecumenical—seniors, parents with kids, young couples, singles of different colors, ages, religions but there was a contingent of SDS and cohorts, that none of us in the march was aware of, at the front of the innocent thousands who wanted to show President Johnson what Californians felt about this evil war that was killing our military men and women and civilians. Our march ground to a halt and was stalled for about half an hour. The police, using bull horns that made it impossible to understand what they were saying, told us to *yadda-yadda*, which actually meant disperse or you will be forced to disperse, which indicated they could and would attack us.

Even if we could have understood their orders, they made no sense since we knew via the tube and papers that there was an accepted marching permit and more police than I have ever seen, except on TV at the near-massacre at the 1968 Democratic Convention in a corrupt cop fraught Chicago. These shade-wearing-solid-wooden-baton-brandishing L.A. cops, some mounted on horses, looked and acted much more than aggressive.

I grabbed Dahr's hand and led her down an embankment that would afford us escape back to the golf course parking lot where we had joined the other marchers. We drove off for home. About ten minutes later the cops rushed the thousands and began indiscriminately hitting old women, children, preachers, nurses, businessmen and anyone else in sight.

It was only after seeing the bloody melee later that night on TV that we learned that the radical and criminal SDS and some followers sat down at the front of the march and would not move, thus stopping the masses and giving the police a reason to break up the march. Breaking up a march and breaking people's heads are very different pursuits.

I had always resisted the idea of special prescience, like the proverbial and sometimes literal women's intuition, but much later in life I have learned that I have something quite like that myself. Diane has always insisted that I have it and now we just follow it whether convenient or not. I have been well served whenever I have listened to my non-linear, subconscious self rather than the outward Lonnie who like all of us—as Shelly Berman pointed out in one of his comedy routines when he allegedly sat watching an engine flaming outside the window on his plane but was too embarrassed to mention it to the flight attendant—would rather die than be thought of as a fool. It is better to be a fool and much easier to recover from than death or even a mere concussion.

I got away from Santana's by finding a position as the second bartender at a German dinner house: Hans Hoppe's Old Heidelberg on Oxnard Street in Sherman Oaks. It had a European, old-world atmosphere with a nice bar area separate from the main dining room, although they also served dinner in the room. There were many German doodads, glass beer boots and other trappings as well as German beer and gin like Steinhager. I did not appreciate the German musicians with accordion and whatnot in the evenings but then my grandmother would have preferred Lawrence Welk to Bill Evans or Segovia.

Hans, the owner/chef, who, like many Germans I have met, was a little too proud of being German was generally pleasant when he was not in a temper. He liked me and my blond hair and thought I looked Germanic and, indeed, I have some German blood on my dad's side, which I mentioned. I did not tell him that my blond air came from my Danish genes. I was the only non-German employee except a snippy, officious Swiss *maitre 'd* and one Scottish waitress. Everyone else, including the dour, extremely rotund, cold woman, Hans' wife, who handled the register up front, was German. She could have been Mrs. Mann's German sister.

I stayed there from 1966 through 1968 and soon became head bartender and bar manager, hiring my own second man and handling the bar while my second handled the table orders for the waitresses. I bought the needed booze and overlooked everything for Hans. It was only slightly better money and side money. Unless you are in Vegas or are a thief the side money is always variable but best in Vegas despite San Francisco, for some reason, having the highest union bartender minimum in the country at that time. This was the only traditional union I have ever belonged to although I belong to seven creative unions: four for acting and performing and three for writing, some of them since childhood.

The advancement in pay did not make my car payments on the new Impala go away, but I managed to get by. I also resisted credit cards, except for gas, until 1975 and never paid interest after it was taken away as a tax deduction some years later. Before then I almost always managed to pay off my balance on time and never have interest added on.

After my M.A., my first one-act and then two-act plays written and the latter given an unstaged reading, some dreadful poetry and some promising short stories, my writing became more important to me.

I was already writing my first novel, *Scooter or All for Love*, subsequent to finishing some short stories and my first novella. *Scooter* was never published, but one editor at Fawcett recalled it favorably when I sent him a manuscript later, although it had not been right for them when I originally submitted it. The editor asked who had finally brought the book out and was surprised when I told him that no one had. Contrarily, I recall a literary agent in Canada who wrote and accused me of being a Jewish pornographer, neither of which is accurate.

I began looking for an agent again in the hope that the Mousekaboy-tapper image was no longer a problem for me. I went to a party at CSUN and ran into Nora, who had played Maria in my first *West Side Story*. For whatever reasons, we had not made much of an impression on each other then but at the party we seem to belong together, left early and made wonderful, intimate love.

Nora was beautiful, with long black hair and a superior soprano voice. She was a fine young actress as well. She was more Audrey Hepburn than Mamie Van Doren, but I felt that was an improvement. I have only rarely been impressed by or drawn to overly developed females. Many people thought Nora looked like Liz Taylor and she was asked if she was related to the child and adult star. Her dark looks came from her Italian dad and her mom was Irish so she predictably had a feisty temper that went with her glowing, dark eyes and her very sexy demeanor.

I saw Nora as Eliza in *My Fair Lady* and she was marvelous; later, in San Francisco, she played the ingénue in *The Fantasticks* and I have never seen, nor heard, anyone do this role better. She was closer to my age and still working on her undergraduate degree from CSUN and I remembered how good she had been as Maria when I played Riff in *West Side Story*.

Nora was the most talented young woman I knew intimately and it has always saddened me that she did not continue plugging away. When I did my second version of the Jets vs. Sharks she was doing chorus in *The King and I*, with Darren McGavin in the lead; I had done many of my scenes in

A few pieces of MMC memorabilia, 2006

my first film, *Queen For A Day*, with Darren as my adult male antagonist but we never worked together again. Darren was very good at his craft.

I had moved deeper into my depression and drinking which was exacerbated by doing a working stiff gig and getting no work in the business. This hindered and eventually overcame my love for Nora and hers for me. I came over one night, too full of scotch, and argued with tiny Benny, Nora's loud Italian dad who would not let me see her. I remember this, but for years I did not acknowledge to myself how much my drinking drove Nora away. I hope wherever she is she knows that I truly loved her and thought she was the one.

I was almost never a loud, obnoxious drunk. I did not stagger around in public, become belligerent, get into fights or spew scatology. I hate public drunks. I am not fond of private drunks but at least no one else is subjected to the irascibility and snide double-entendres that a drunk exudes. I was desperately depressed and I knew not why.

I was in therapy when I fell for Nora but I would still fall off the sober wagon and beat myself up with liquor, bruising others psychically along the way. I would make infrequent, lonely, desperate late night calls in useless attempts to get some kind of validation that was not forthcoming. I learned that the only meaningful validation comes from me but it was a long, hard journey. Consolation is good and helpful but it is difficult for the amateur— a word that describes most people—and it does not solve the problems. In time I found only I can do that. I stopped this rare but abusive late-night calling, even to my therapist Lou who would not condone it, making it even rarer, but it was a factor in my life, however rare, until my forties.

There is no question that my failure to get back into the business after my graduate degree and my pedestrian jobs exacerbated my difficulties. Except for one night in 1973 as a waiter at the Upstairs At The Downstairs and later that year doing research for a public relation firm's industrial film. My twenty-first birthday, in 1963, until I left the Old Heidelberg in 1967 is the only time in my life I did not act, dance, sing, write, choreograph, direct or teach.

I did a nightclub gig while at Hoppe's but not from an agent—on my own. I have played a circus once and a nightclub once. The show was called *Broadway à la Carte* and played a large dinner house and cabaret in Panorama City. My second bartender covered for me. The producer, who has been my friend since this first meeting, Marty Wiviott, cast three males and three females. The hour-long act was a series of Broadway musical numbers from four or five well-known shows that were linked by a few lines of lead-in dialogue.

We did three half-hour shows a night on the weekends, dressed in two small closets, one for each sex, and made very little money, but it built up my bar pay and I was performing once more. Clubs can be awful and one night late in our run, we were playing to a table of six drunks, three female, three male and no one else but the waiters, busboys and bar staff. They interrupted, threw small things on stage, sang along off key, and made rude comments in the blackouts.

Although I later denied it, in the last blackout before our finale, as they were uproariously supercilious I shouted out, "SHUT UP AND BE POLITE!" They were stunned into silence as the lights came up and all six of us stood a few feet away, onstage smiling hugely, singing and dancing as if nothing had happened. Marty was not pleased, but I continued in the show.

I met Dahr there. The slick, older head bartender was hitting on her too but I managed to cut him out; later I found out that Dahrlene was five years older than me. She was a cute, brunette coloratura soprano with a solid voice and a terrific figure. She had won awards as a ballroom dancer but had no other dance training. Since I was not ramrod stiff, nor did the same steps as everyone else when I danced socially, we refrained from that for it led to some discomfort for both of us.

Marty later began producing theatre, which was always his goal. I ran into him after a few years in Milwaukee when Leonard Nimoy's one-man show as Van Gogh's brother Theo opened at the Pabst Theatre. Marty had become the producer of plays and star nights at this theatre. It was the only time I have been somewhere that had a tornado warning and I was much more than concerned.

I visited because the best stage manager with whom I have ever worked, including on Broadway, my wife Diane, was filling that role for a heavy call show with constant projections and light changes to accommodate all the slides of the work of Nimoy/Theo Van Gogh's brother Vincent.

Eventually Marty became the producer for the Nederlanders overseeing all the shows that have been seen since for decades at the Pantages theatre just east of Vine on Hollywood Boulevard. The Pantages, originally a vaudeville house, then converted to a movie theatre, was readapted in 1977 for stage use. Marty also hired me later, after he returned to the West Coast and before he began his work at the Pantages and I had moved back from Manhattan in the late 'seventies.

As tap-dancing gang leader Spats Palazzo in the musical Sugar, *1981.*

He was casting for summer stock in Sacramento in the 'eighties and I played (with excellent billing) the role of Spats Palazzo, the tap dancing gangster in *Sugar,* the musical made from the film *Some Like It Hot.* Spats was played in the film by George Raft, a former dancer who did no dancing as the gangster in the movie starring Jack Lemmon, Marilyn Monroe and Tony Curtis. *My* Spats had a larger part and danced his bullets rather than shot them and I got "stopped the show" reviews.

Arte Johnson, playing the Jack Lemmon role, and I became friends; TV actor Monte Markham played the Tony Curtis role and was not a theatre person.

As in most stock, we had to put this production together in a little over a week with a very weak director and a choreographer who could not tap, nor even describe accurately what he wanted us to do. Many choreographers are inexperienced with and lack knowledge of tap, although they are fine with jazz and ballet. That is why Gower Champion had someone else choreograph the one tap number in *Mack and Mabel* and Twyla Tharp did the same in the film I did for her starring Nick Nolte, *I'll Do Anything.* No tap number could save this film which was very close to being as bad as my second film, the corny *Queen for a Day.* I found out later that most of the musical numbers were cut from the Nolte/Twyla film after screenings for audiences.

Fortunately, for all of Spats and his gang's numbers are tap, I had some good hoofers in my gang and I saved my own ass, as well as my gang's and the show's, by choreographing our numbers with no billing and no extra pay but at least we did not look like the five Stooges in tap shoes.

Our opening number, *"Tear The Town Apart"* was lauded by the *Sacramento Union* as "…a show stopping number and Lonnie Burr, accompanied by the other gangsters, brings it off." The *Sacramento Bee* reviewer wrote, "The most inspired addition [to the film *Some Like It Hot*] is the figure of the head gangster, Spats…Lonnie Burr raps out the role with convincing force, and when it falls his lot to die, he falls with style."

Arte and I were appalled at Markham who would ask insipid, Actor's Studio questions when the director would give him some blocking instructions.

"But why would my character cross over there?" Markham would inquire.

Arte and I, plus the director and everyone else in the show—and the theatre and showbiz—knew the answer: *because that is where the director wants you to go.* After all, we only had a week to put an entire musical together.

Subtext and natural acting need not stymie stock acting but you never take meager rehearsal time for anything other than learning your lines and blocking (movements, crosses, sitting, entrances, exits), songs and dance steps and the props with which you work and become comfortable. Then, on your own, you do any interpretation and soul searching you need if that is your style.

After two plus years on my own, I moved back into my grandparents' apartment building, which was next door to the house I had lived in with them before starting at Hoppe's. They did not come over and they would not accept rent from me. I took the few steps to their house to say hello and talk for a while one or more times a week and Gram preferred that to seeing me much more rarely when I was at my first apartment.

Being back also led to my saving my grandfather's life one night. He awoke choking and could not breathe. Gram called me and I ran over, helped him into the car and drove madly to the closest emergency facility. She never learned to drive and was frantic. He had medical insurance but did not have the card with him and I ranted loudly and forcefully enough for them to take him in and save his life. We would both probably be rejected by security and arrested now, and he would have died.

I was cast in my first stock production, my second *West Side Story*. This is the first time I performed in the round with the audience surrounding you in a circle. The residuals from the MMC had dried up in '65 and I had sold my used Alfa for cash a while back and my savings were close to gone so I had to buy a cheap, used car to get back and forth from Anaheim, where we rehearsed and opened. After the Melodyland theatre-in-the-round opening across the street from Disneyland, we moved to another round house in San Carlos, just outside San Francisco.

In this stock version, Tony was played by Pat Boone, a gregarious, pleasant man who actually did wear white bucks most of the time and puffed frequently on his pipe. His pop voice was not strong enough for Tony's powerful songs, nor was he much of an actor but he did draw audiences and was a very nice, clean-cut guy. After we closed, Pat invited the cast to his nice but unpretentious house in Beverly Hills, just north of Sunset near the Beverly Hills Hotel for a closing party.

After Betty and Nora and then Marty's club revue, Dahrlene and I began living together while I continued tending bar at the Heidelberg, but we had a number of issues that seemed unsolvable so after more than a year she moved out.

I then fell in love with a new German waitress at Hoppe's named Renata. She had an evil husband, also a German, who had become a United States citizen and brought Renata to America from Germany, which made her an American citizen, too. He worked as a *maître d'* at the main dinner house at the Dorothy Chandler Pavilion, the largest of the theatres in the downtown Los Angeles complex.

Renata was so beautiful that she wore her auburn hair with blond highlights much shorter than mine and would have given Audrey Hepburn a run for facial beauty. Renata's body was lithe, small and waif-like but very lovable. I loved her quite fully and she loved me, finally breaking away from the husband who inflicted mental and physical pain to live on her own with their son Oliver.

After leaving him she saw only me but Dahr contacted me and we began seeing each other again. I loved them both and this was not my first, nor my last situation of duality in my love affairs. Dahr began working on me, telling me about a guy even younger than me whom she was dating. She threatened to have sex with him. I suspect she had sex with him anyway but she used it and it was clear to me I had to make some kind of a decision or lose her.

I was twenty-five and had been some adaptation of an adult since my childhood. I feared that I would get too set in my ways to ever be able to make the adjustments mandatory for any long-term living arrangement. In all candor, I loved Renata more than Dahr even though Renata still had problems with English, was unable to express herself as well as either of us wanted, and was even less educated than Dahrlene, which would always be a problem for me. Worse, she also had Oliver, her six-year-old son. This made our relationship more than problematic; it was impossible.

I have never wanted children and that has never varied in my life. First, no matter how good or kind or loving or knowledgeable I could be, and there was always a chance that I would not fulfill what I thought I was capable of as a father, I was not going to take the chance of inflicting on a child what had been inflicted on me.

Secondly, I knew I could not pursue my dreams and careers as an artist when the reality of meeting the rent, food, insurance, taxes, vehicles, and a child's many needs all the way through college were hanging over my head. Third, my drinking problem, which was better but still evident, would be a bad influence at the very least. My violence to myself and objects had stopped but would I continue to control it? Finally, I had none of the seemingly compulsive need others show in wanting, in some way or other, to clone part of themselves to obviate their death or have something of theirs still around after they are dead. Nor did I have a need to follow tradition: school, work, marriage and mandatory progeny.

I had begun to make some progress in the business, shooting *The Beverly Hillbillies* and other TV shows, doing a couple of films and being cast as one of three male leads in the six character Dos Passos play *U.S.A.* in which everyone plays many roles, one of mine being silent film star Rudolph Valentino, in this historical panorama of the early 20th century.

While separated from Dahr I also landed the lead, Cocky, in the musical *The Roar of the Greasepaint, the Smell of the Crowd* as a Guest Artist at a college. The vocal range was a stretch for me but my acting and added dance talent, that Anthony Newley, a child star who succeeded as an adult, lacked, allowed me to do a good job. Over the years, more than once a stranger has stopped me and mention my work in *Roar* quite favorably. I knew now, before *George M* and New York City, that musicals were a natural for me.

The academic choreographer/dance teacher for *Roar,* an oxymoron in most cases, began by having me dance, "… a fluttering step on the toes as if being moved forward and back by the emanations of a street lamp at night", which is how she described it. This woman had been seriously disoriented by Martha Graham at a formative age just like the first MMC choreographer.

I went to Les, the director, and said he should have her do the chorus numbers and I would do my own choreography. That is what we did and it worked quite well—again.

People who do not understand dance have very bizarre ideas about what it is. I once did a Carl's Jr. commercial with one other guy and the late Carl Karcher himself, who was gracious enough to give us both a card for a free hamburger—we were both in our late thirties and I never ate at any fast food place if I could possibly avoid it but I graciously accepted Carl's gift.

We had auditioned doing improv, which is how they save a bundle on commercials and we found when we got on the set to shoot that there was no choreographer. We had not rehearsed, also odd, and showed up to shoot and found we were to dance IN UNISON to music—not simple 4-4, nor 3-4, nor 2-4 but 5 against 4, Spanish Flamenco—we had never heard before.

They were obviously ignorant vis-à-vis dance/choreography and very fortunate that the other dancer was also very good and had been a regular as a dancer on Carol Burnett's variety show. We listened to the music over and over as they set up, came up with some great looking Flamenco steps (it was for the introduction of their Guacamole Burger) and it looked swell and aired for a long time.

I did immediately call my agent and got us both a double fee for our choreography and principal appearances which helped the residuals. My colleague thanked me, but I have always fought for my rights and that frequently affects those with whom I work.

A jump for my solo number "Shipoopi" in The Music Man, *1973.*

The director and the ubiquitous and pushy "product people" must have assumed that dancers just get up and dance. One of the reasons Fred Astaire was great was that he rehearsed forever and, thus, looked like it was all just happening at that very moment. It never happens that way unless you rehearse or are very, very accomplished.

I had had it with not acting, performing or writing to make my way so I quit my bar managing job at Hoppe's. I think Hans was genuinely sorry to see me go. He knew I was honest and his customers liked me, some coming from long distances for my way of making a very non-Germanic Singapore Sling or a French 75—the correct way.

Hans was a rotund, jolly, red-faced fellow who, like many chefs, fought off the heat and furor of the kitchen by tippling beer and wine during the day and evening and we had some interesting conversations when the place was not busy. We disagreed about many things but we enjoyed the banter.

Knowing I could not make it with Renata and her son, I made a very bad decision for my life; I broke up with Renata which was very sad for both of us. I bought a ring and drove over to Dahr's apartment just off Riverside Drive. She was ill, looked like hell and after letting me in returned to her bed. Having seen too many movies and too much TV, I actually got on my knee and proposed at her bedside. She was shocked and did not believe me at first, then she cried and accepted immediately.

So in late 1968 we drove to Vegas, were married in a civil ceremony downtown with no Elvis Impersonators allowed, saw Mort Sahl and the boring musical *Fiddler on the Roof* and celebrated with the regularly excellent chateaubriand at the House of Lords at the Sahara. We lost a little of our not too large savings. Dahr was pretty good at craps and won; which surprised me since the game is a mystery to me. I lost less than $100 at blackjack before the boxes made it ludicrous to play this card game. We also had the insulting dinner with my mom and the slob stepfather Don.

Since she had only second-hand bits and pieces of furniture, Dahr divested herself of these items and moved into my larger two-bedroom apartment with pool and that is where we lived our short married months.

Soon after our marriage, Dahr began to change. It was noticed by others before me: I denied the change at first, but I began to see it too. Acting as if I could do no wrong after we got back together and were married and after having achieved what she wanted, a second marriage with no children required, for she had no interest in becoming a parent either, she became sour and rancorous on an almost daily basis.

I was out of work and collecting unemployment and she had a number of low-paying jobs outside her talent in show business, one of which was as a used car saleswoman, which was unusual for the late 'sixties. I did not find enough work acting, nor a new bar job, and I also felt being in a bar job would be negative for my drinking.

We agreed that I should return to college to work on a Ph.D. in English literature, thus improving my possibilities of teaching college; I had no interest in teaching high school or lower grades. I would now be able to teach two different subjects if that became necessary; I also would not be bored silly with academic theatre, which usually has very little to do with professional theatre. I received a 4.0 my first semester and only one B the second, which was a result of the negative interaction with the professor for the Romantic Poets who was against protesters of the Vietnam War. It is likely he was pro-Vietnam, but he steered clear of stating it. He stopped class once to denounce some very quiet protestors, as they passed by the window behind us, even though they were not interrupting his class. I politely inquired what his position on this current issue had to do with the poet Blake. I began writing on staff for the school paper, articles and drama reviews, and I continued getting my poetry published, winning my first verse awarddespite the actions of the ultra-right wing pedantic prig.

Dahr and I, however, argued often about the usual: money, sex, money, the other's objectionable habits and other mundane matters. She began trying to force me to hit her to stop her from being literally in my face. I have never been a hitter of women, nor did I get into many fist fights with other guys. Physical violence is something I avoid. I was guilty only of the depressive's self-violence toward inanimate objects and a suicide attempt. But Dahr would push me and push me and then push me further until I told her to leave me alone. Once I attempted to get into my car to escape her violence-inducing harassment and she, having a key to mine as I did to hers, jumped in the passenger side and continued her harangue. I made it clear that I was very, very close to losing my temper, losing my control and if she did not leave me alone I would blow up. This is patently what she was trying to force me to do.

Dahr's aggression kept building and one night I could not take it any further. She would not leave me alone. I threatened her and she persisted so I hit her in the upper arm. That stopped her attack and began her sobbing. She bruised easily and she shamed me with it for a couple of weeks. A month or two later I told her I could take no more of her nagging, whining and insults once again and she spewed forth more vitriol. I hit her in the thigh, realizing in that moment I could not allow this to go on. I was afraid I might one day do something worse and I did not want that to happen.

I am still ashamed of what I allowed her to manipulate me into and I have never done this with any other woman. In truth, I have come close a very few times but I have always resisted this violent side of my temper and my depression and my liquor. My other relationships with women did not ever come to such an impasse.

Naturally, my drinking had picked up during this mess with Dahr and my lack of work added to our money problems. I had begun calling Renata who always gave me a sympathetic ear; she was still in love with me. We were not having sex, but Dahr was a very jealous woman and when I went out to drink alone or to get away from her hollering and baiting me, she accused me of screwing Renata—or someone else.

She scoured the phone bills for something to use against me, and finding Renata's number there she confronted me with it. I explained that I needed someone to whom I could talk without being verbally and psychically abused. Someone who would not continue compelling me by any means to verbally and eventually physically abuse them as Dahrlene did.

One night I was depressed and drinking alone after Dahr had gone to sleep. I drove to Renata's apartment, knocked lightly on the door to not disturb Oliver or the neighbors. Just seeing and talking to her calmed me. We did not wake Oliver for more than a second on my entry and we drank tea and talked and smiled for over an hour.

Dahr had followed me and thought to catch us *in flagrante*. She made a huge row, knocking on the door and shouting at three in the morning outside Renata's apartment. Renata let her in and Dahr berated the two of us for having the sex we were not having and terrified young Oliver. Then she stormed off into the night.

I apologized to Renata and Oliver, drove home, and quietly asked for a separation from Dahr. It took me a couple of weeks and finally a demand to get the separation accomplished and Dahr caused me a number of problems. She took 100% of the 50/50 dishes and cutlery given to us by my grandmother and most other wedding gifts, none of which came from her family. They were old country Hungarians from the Buda side of the river in Budapest. They had objected to our living together and because of that had even refused to come see their daughter when she had pneumonia and came close to death. They maintained their disdain even after we married.

I had given Dahr a few pieces of my furniture since she no longer had her odds and ends, one of my couches and so on, but she took some very distinctly male jewelry of mine when I was not home. After this violation, I changed the locks so she could not get in unless I was present, correcting the mistake of trust I had made previously. She came over, found her key did not work and I let her in and explained the new policy—she had access only when I was present. Knowing we had about a third of a lid of marijuana left, she called the cops on me and did her tearful, misused wife act, the best acting that she actually was capable of on or off stage, completely oblivious to the possibility of going to jail that we both could have faced even if she denied having knowledge of the grass.

The male cop, easily manipulated by female tears and not knowing the law well enough, ordered me to give her a key. Wanting them out as soon as possible rather than taking a chance they would stumble on the dope, I gave it to her. As almost always, my rare interaction with officers of the law was predictably negative.

Our separation maintained and I auditioned for and landed a role in the traveling, first national company of the musical *George M*. It was my first long gig on the road and fortunately not a bus and truck, which I have never had the misfortune of doing. In a B & T you travel by bus at least once a week from theatre to theatre to theatre and I know it would be very unpleasant and unacceptable to me. In a first national company you go from Phoenix to Cleveland to Boston to Toronto by plane every three weeks or so. I did have to buy my first trunk since suitcases are not enough when you are away from home for six or more months.

I needed the time away from Dahr to see if there was anything salvageable in our relationship. I sold my Playboy bed far below its value. I gave the other items to my relatives, who occupied two other apartments in the complex, and I stored a few things.

I then learned what life was like on the road, fell for Janyce, saw a lot more of the U.S. and returned to L.A. I met with Dahr and it was clear that she could not or would not change; she was vitriolic and harsh. I made plans to move to the American home of theatre, the Apple, and hoped to never have to film another *Beverly Hillbillies* gig again for the rent.

I never saw Renata again. I have tried to search online for her or even for her son Oliver, but I have had no success. She probably remarried and changed names; she may have moved back to Germany. My last apology did not have the substance that it should have. She, like Nora, I truly loved.

Dressed in wig and Native American outfit as the hippie Medicine Man between my chick and Max Baer, Jr. on The Beverly Hillbillies *in the "Hot Rod Truck" segment, 1968.*

I am very sorry, Renata, but I would not have made a good father for Oliver, nor husband for you at that point in my life.

Before I left town for over six months, I discovered that Dahr had left me with one telling gift. Her first husband had been much less than a gentleman, which she harped on often but she did not tell me what he had passed on to her. I noticed a lesion on my penis and, in a panic, went to emergency at the closest hospital I could think of, St. Joseph's, directly across from the entry to Disney Studios in Burbank. Sometimes I really resent irony—more so in real life than in literature. I instantly thought of Ibsen's play about syphilis, *Ghosts,* and pictured my dick growing green, then black, then falling off just before I went raving mad. The doctors were not tragedians and I was diagnosed with herpes simplex before it became the leading STD. It has never been a big deal for me, unlike the folks on the frequent TV commercials. I took medication and avoided sex until the lesion was gone. I have never given it to anyone because I always follow the prescribed course of pharmaceuticals and no sex. A virus like herpes can never be cured but the problem lessens with age and for decades an occurrence could run three or four days at most, cause no pain and occur only once in two or three years. It can be brought on by stress as well as other factors.

I never really had an opportunity to thank Dahrlene for leaving me with this token that will last my entire life and is much more unpleasant than the two body bruises, for which I am still recondite, that I gave her.

Romance in musical theatre, in which the majority of males are gay, leaving all those lovely ladies to the only, or one of very few, straight guys, is a much more inspiring subject, so I will move on to that part of my life and my years of risky propinquity with the hoodlums that constantly roam the streets of New York City.

Chapter 12
On the Road (or, Not a Kerouac In Sight)

My family took very few vacations and the farthest we went was from L.A. to San Francisco. These trips, no matter the time and distance, seemed endless to a young boy who was easily bored and who did not read much outside of school except comic books—I had a large collection including Scrooge McDuck, one of my favorites, and all the Classic Comic books. I donated these nearly 1,000 comics to a children's hospital when I was about eleven.

I did not appreciate being imprisoned in a hot car with no air conditioning or bathroom. Besides San Francisco, we drove to San Diego once and Vegas once. That was it except for the MMC personal appearance tours; my first airplane flight was in 1955 on a DC-4 (four propellers!) with the other Mouseketeers. We visited a lot of places but there was no time to see sights because we were working.

Away from the family, I added my two trips to Europe, both after a few days in Manhattan, and one car trip to Tijuana. The long drive to TJ was to watch a bull fight. I had read most of Hemingway, including *Death in the Afternoon,* his tribute to *tauromanquia*. I found that bull fighting, probably even in Portugal where the bull is spared rather than killed after being tormented, was not beautiful, nor an art. It is not even a sport, unless you like cock fighting or pitting dogs against each other, which I hate. I did get to see one torero, El Cordobés, who was much better than the other toreadors that day, but this bloody experience confirmed to me only that Hemingway was an overrated author, except for a few of his works, and also was a testosterone lunatic.

George M, the musical based on the life of American writer/director/performer George M. Cohan and the film which won James Cagney his only Oscar for playing Cohan as the *Yankee Doodle Dandy,* starred

Joel Grey after his triumph in *Cabaret*. When not at the theatre I had vacation time on the tour during the day or on our one day off to learn more about Phoenix, Cleveland, Baltimore, Dallas, Boston, Toronto, Washington D.C. and other cities.

Theatres are always downtown, even in L.A., and that meant I was introduced to the dirty, unsafe, decrepit parts of cities that one avoided where I grew up. My first street rat, a huge bugger and not anything like my tiny, white pet rat, crossed my path while walking back the few blocks to my hotel from the Morris Mechanic theatre in Baltimore, which is only slightly less well named than the Nixon Theatre in Pittsburgh. Rats exist in Southern California, but only some of them are in show business.

In 2000 I shot a segment of the last season of the Baltimore TV cop show *Homicide: Life on the Streets* but fortunately I lived in Maryland then and drove home at night to Sligo Park Hills, about a half-hour south and just outside of D.C., with nary a rat sighting. The Sligo is a well-known river in Ireland which I found in a few of Yeats' poems in rereading all of his work in 2002. Of course, there are hordes of rats in Washington, D.C., more than any other city in the country, some of them literally rodents. For *Homicide*, I shot inside a bar, playing the bar manager whose female employee had been whacked the night before and lay dead behind the bar. Rats, like cockroaches, are more furtive in daylight hours and none intruded during the shoot.

The *George M* tour had been on the road a couple of months and I replaced another actor/singer/dancer by auditioning at the Dorothy Chandler Pavilion in Los Angeles. My long time friend later in life, Jack Lee, a noted Broadway musical conductor and later an NYU professor, was heading the orchestra and had a role in the casting. Jack and I originally met on the film of *Sweet Charity*, for which he was the Choral Director.

I left town soon after and our first stop was in San Diego where I got a few hours of rehearsal, after watching the guy I was replacing do the show in L.A. I went on that first night only partially secure in two musical numbers. After that premiere I was put into more numbers every night until my singing and dancing assignments were complete. Lines are easy, the intricacies of dancing and singing with others is hard. But I had to do one scene that first night with Joel, just the two of us onstage, with only a verbal run through at half hour.

The character I played was Behman, the stage manager, who fires a loud-mouthed, smart aleck young Cohan. I was nervous but managed to get through it well and unscathed; neither Joel nor the director had any comments to make. Obviously, I improved quickly in all of the areas required with more rehearsals and performances.

Soon after this first experience I learned that Joel, at least with me, talked under his breath but in character about things that had nothing to do with the dialogue, which was very distracting. Why he had this quirk was never discussed. It was selfish but I managed to block out his muttering and the audience could not hear him.

Dahr came to visit for an overnight stay in San Diego and we managed to get along but it was a bit less than pleasant and indicated the final outcome of our relationship. We "made sex," for there was little love attached to it.

I had no time to see anything in San Diego since I was working full time to get all of my bits and lyrics and dance steps together in addition to performing eight shows a week, not to mention the 20+ wardrobe changes in the two acts of the most multiple costume change show for me and everyone that I have ever done. We added locals in each town as dressers and opening nights could be very hairy. I was grateful that this was after Velcro had been invented; I did not have time-consuming zippers and buttons to contend with and I got the hang of the routine quickly.

It took me a while to realize the onerous craft necessities of acting the same words and scenes and singing and dancing the same lyrics and steps eight times a week, every week for months. Theatre requires much more of actors than film or even a regular TV series, for the series at least goes on hiatus for a few months and even though the sitting around twelve or more hours some days on a movie shoot is tedious even if you read, knit or play cards, it does not take the same toll.

Plays can run for years. I have known people who have done *Fiddler* or *Dolly* or *Grease* in different companies for over a decade and I wonder about their sanity, for it is extremely difficult to go out and do the same things over and over and over and find ways to make them fresh for the audience and for yourself. Of course, not everyone does that but some do and that is the *sine qua non* in order to make a regular living and raise a family in the theatre. I have known career chorus singers and dancers, but the dancers do not last as long as the vocalists.

I got some help midway through the tour when I lost my contact lenses. I did the show without clear vision and managed to get through it until replacements could be sent to me by my optometrist in L.A. Being nearsighted, things were fuzzy from a few feet away and my focus changed; thus I noticed things that other characters were doing from a different perspective. It is like rising from your seat to view a chess board in a new way. I have used this technique of looking at things with "new" eyes ever since in long runs, which does not mean that I literally take my contacts out.

Our next stop was nearby Phoenix which seemed quite dull, but I did get lucky our last night with a very attractive cocktail waitress at a watering hole near the theatre. She drove me to the airport the next morning and we corresponded for a while, then lost touch.

Denver was better because I had managed to get close to a beautiful young chorus girl in the show, Janyce, who was a zaftig lady, a very fine tapper, a flirt who had short brunette hair and a distinct resemblance to Kim Novak. I invited her to meet me midday at a nearby hotel bar in the dining room and bought us Ramos Fizzes, having already acquired a single rose that I asked the bartender to put in a highball glass with some water before her arrival. I have always been more romantic than the women with whom I have been involved. I am a strange man. The only other conclusion is that all of these women were strange women and that seems much less likely.

Vegas is the only city that is known for and that pushes Ramos Fizzes. They taste great but are made badly or not at all in many places in the U.S. and hardly anywhere except Nevada. Fizz drinks were quite the rage from the 'twenties through 'fortes, if you discount the speakeasies when all that was managed was straight liquor and simple mixes rather than cocktails.

Janyce was not completely a girl of the 'sixties so we tussled with consummation at first, many other sensual adventures leading there shortly. She also was naive about sex and a few other things but I brought her along and we maintained our relationship throughout the tour and afterwards when we both returned to California.

In Cleveland we had the opportunity for low price tickets from one show to another show playing the same city. I had the pleasure of seeing *The Great White Hope* with James Earl Jones and he and his sonorous voice were excellent as was the fine actor, underused and underrated Jane Alexander who played the boxer's lover. Ms. Alexander was later the head of the NEA, the National Endowment for the Arts.

Janyce and I hit a number of nice restaurants and I continued my search for museum treasures. LACMA, the L.A. County Museum of Art, had always been superficial to me; I summed it up by their one, tiny Douanier Henri Rousseau, the atypical Primitivist being one of my interests, with the plate underneath giving the title, the date of the work, the artist and, in much larger letters, the name of the donor: BURT LANCASTER. It has improved enormously since then but it still does not match the Chicago Art Institute, MOMA, the Louvre and many other museums in D.C., New York, Europe and even Cleveland!

My primary periods of interest, which Diane shares, are Impressionism, post-Impressionism, some Expressionist and Surrealist work and the amazing Bosch and the fabulous Flemish artists from Rembrandt von Rijn, Hals and Vermeer through Ensor and Magritte and, of course, Botticelli, Caravaggio, Michelangelo Buonnaroti and the other Italians. Picasso got boring and repetitive for me and I loved the fact that his bravado was stymied frequently by Matisse, who was the only artist that he feared. There are many other periods of European art and 19th and early 20th century American art that compel me but from Mondrian forward I am harder pressed to find beauty except rarely, like the Brit Francis Bacon. Warhol, to me, is a sly illustrator at best. Dali, despite his blatant circus self-promotion, did some much more interesting work, which we saw in the Dali Museum in Montmartre in 2006. To my mind, Christo is a con artist as are many ersatz, yclept artists in the last fifty years.

Despite some good art visits, it was always a struggle to stay at an affordable hotel on the road even though our union compels management to provide a list of acceptable ones within our pay range. Actors on tour foot their own bills for housing, transportation and food. At least the IRS allows these as deductions.

When we closed a town, the costumes, sets and other necessities, plus our trunks, were picked up and shipped by truck to our next city. We were driven to the airport to board planes. Each new venue required a look around to make sure that there were no hookers, junkies, or thugs nearby or doormen who spent most of their time drunk and kicking away rats who sought shelter and food. Every three weeks was "check-in then check out the environs time."

Janyce's continual flirting with stage hands bothered me. Then the company was joined by fun-loving Betty, my second Betty.

I have never lied about my status to women and I explained to her that I was married but separated and most likely to get a divorce when the show closed and I returned to California. I also told her I was involved with Janyce. Betty, from Omaha, was then a permanent resident of Manhattan. Naturally, I did not say, "Hi, I'm Lonnie and I am married and sleeping with Janyce." When the appropriate time arose, I just told her what my status was so she could decide to get involved with me or not. She was okay with that and we had some very fine sexual hours together and a hell of a lot of laughter. She was very socially hip and funny. The gay guys all loved her and she was sexy in her own, petite, lascivious, always smiling way.

The rest of the tour was a delicate balance for me because both young women dealt with the duality fairly well but there were jealousies and disappointments. It is difficult enough to keep one woman happy for a while and this situation obviously involved some separation and, in addition, a traveling show's cast is just like living in a small town—everyone knows everyone else's business.

I did not feel that I could require either Janyce or Betty to see just me because I was involved with both of them. They did not see other guys much at all but our most difficult times were holidays, like Thanksgiving in Pittsburgh. I found the best cheesecake I have ever had at a deli across from the hotel there and Janyce and I had Thanksgiving dinner in a wonderful, haute cuisine restaurant that overlooked the city and the three rivers.

My love for Janyce outweighed my feelings of love for Betty but I was in a swell situation. Even the gay guys, who merely had to stroll in the park or go to a bar to get laid before AIDS became a factor, thought me fortunate. The straight guys were really irritated, particularly those who wanted to get to Janyce and could not or to Betty for whom it was not as easy as she sometimes made it seem.

I had always felt I would do much better with two women, rather than one. Not five or six or many, like Mormons and sheiks, just two very different, lovely and loving women who were not consumed by jealousy and possessing a man. I would not be a man who would possess either of them. Now that situation was at hand again.

Boston was covered in snow and even though our hotel near the Commons was quite close to the theatre, sliding across the ice at every corner was dangerous and scary. Our sad, ancient hotel, the Avery, known to all in theatre as the Ovary, was a bad face lift on an obviously aging facade and we actually had a fire while I was staying there that required a hasty run down some flights of stairs, but it was put out quickly and no one was injured.

The oldest theatre I played on this tour was the second oldest I have ever worked in—the Shubert in New Haven—which was built before 1900 and had not been refurbished. In this new century I played my oldest theatre—Ford's in Washington, D.C. The Shubert was almost completely wood and was one of the few theatres in 1969 in which no smoking was allowed anywhere inside ever. Every room had a bucket with water in case anything caused a spark or you snuck one past the fireman who was backstage every performance—and some of us carefully did sneak a drag. Most of the time, even during the show, we would slip out the backstage door and light up no matter how cold. Soon after all this smoking was prohibited everywhere, at any time, in all theatres in America.

This theatre was around the corner from Yale and I saw Woody Allen's *Take the Money and Run* in a nearby movie house and seemed to be the only person watching who found it hilarious. I frequently laugh at subtler humor in movie houses and in theatres, but I thought that close to Yale more people should have gotten the Marxian (Groucho & Karl) absurdist humor on the screen.

I was a big fan of Woody Allen when he was still a standup comedian and on my 1963 Manhattan, pre-Europe, trip I saw him at The Blue Angel. Sometimes being a brash young fellow, I sent a note backstage saying I wanted to talk to him about comedians. He actually joined me at my table, declined a drink, and we conversed about Mort Sahl, Shelly Berman and mostly about Lenny Bruce, his extreme and hilarious satire and his trouble with the police. Woody was typically rumpled but was very affable and unaffected. I had no way of knowing he was going to become such a good filmmaker.

Dallas was a blur of dusty dull with strange drinking laws. Many places in the East had and have "blue laws" about not buying and/or selling liquor on Sunday but in Dallas in '69 you were required to belong to a club (the bar) before you could buy a drink. In Salt Lake City you went next door and bought one or more one-ounce bottles, like airplane liquor bottles, and went to the nearby bar and paid for a set up in the bar area—glass, ice, water or other mix, a napkin and a swizzle stick, to stir your drink. I collected swizzles for years, beginning with the S.S. France in 1963. Somewhere in the late 'seventies they disappeared from most bars and no longer exist in personalized form but as nondescript plastic straws. I still have over a hundred of the personalized swizzles I collected. London was just as weird about the club fee and the bars shut down for two hours in the afternoon for tea. Good grief! That all stopped in 2003 but had been in place for ages. I still found this silly but the British, not just the Pythons, are frequently pixilated.

On leaving Dallas the entire company almost got busted. Someone in the cast had connections there and most of the members of the company - actors, managerial and musicians - scored a lid of grass. Long before the terrorism threats on planes, meaningless, overheard comments could cause problems. One very obtuse, attractive chorus girl sitting with her lover on the road, one of our stage managers, made some comment about bombing as a joke.

When we landed our plane was taken away from the plane embarkation and debarkation area to an isolated strip away from all buildings. We were all kept on board and we were told that the FBI wanted to see us. We disembarked with officers around us and were shuttled to an isolated area at the airport. The girl and the stage manager were interviewed. We were all sweating because we knew if they searched the luggage the show would stop dead in Texas for they had—and have - very stringent anti-weed laws.

Fortunately, they understood and bought the literal goof she had made and our luggage was not searched. We moved on to Toronto, where our head SM was stopped for bringing in a hand gun, which was a jolt to me and most of us. They confiscated the weapon and we again got our show up, but traveling was more careful from Dallas and Toronto forward.

I had no grass in high school, nor much during college. I was an alcohol man. The first time I bought a lid was in the late 'sixties and I was never a doper—one who smokes daily or almost daily. I met one guy, a straight hair dresser, who smoked a joint after breakfast in the morning; had some tokes at lunch; arrived home and reached above the door and picked up an already rolled number to begin his evening. Like a functional alcoholic, it was difficult for most people to have any idea he was under the influence of anything, unless they understood certain tells and the dilation or diminishment of eyeballs. He just did all things, including driving, very deliberately and slowly.

I liked to smoke dope once in a while because it always relaxed me, made me frequently hilarious to others and sometimes even myself— and inevitably ravenous. I did not enjoy it as much with strangers, nor even acquaintances as with one or two or three with whom I was very close and trusting. I assiduously avoided habit-forming pills and harder junk and I never experienced acid or other mind-altering alternatives. I think I have enough things to deal with in this world and leave the hallucinogenic perceptions to others. In her young years Diane tried mescaline once and liked it, but never returned. If you met her today or even twenty years ago you would never believe her hippie era, which was waning when we first met.

One buddy in *George M* usually smoked a roach before going on for just about every performance. I was always afraid that I would not be able to maintain my concentration (mandatory for any conscientious actor) if I did that, but Frank was a dancer who could memorize a few words. I might have two or three drinks with dinner between matinee and evening performance, but it was not a regular habit and that is a very different state than the world getting small and slower and food driven.

Toronto was beautiful, snappily clean and fun. We played a very large, new theatre the O'Keefe. It was my first Canadian adventure; Janyce and I ice skated on an outside rink and it was a memorable winter and Christmas. I was seeing less of Betty and she was seeing more of others but Janyce and I went to some more great restaurants in Toronto, one having a window through which you could watch the chef. We found (at the suggestion of our captain) that Grand Marnier heated in snifters like cognac was an excellent thing to have after dinner.

By this time I had discovered Remy Martin VSOP. Unlike the rotgut I had in Paris and other well-known brandies like Martell, Courvoisier and Hennessy that start at lower levels and are more heavily advertised, Remy is a wonderful, extra-smooth cognac that would be abused by ice cubes. It disturbed me a great deal that after so many decades, to appease the masses and boost sales I assume, Remy added the lower level VS sometime in the 'eighties; of course, it gave them a viable reason to charge more for the VSOP.

I also went to a freaky, stoned rock club in Toronto and thoroughly enjoyed myself with various Canadian females on the dance floor with the deafening rock blasts of bass and shouting treble vocalists the DJ played and oodles of revolving crystal balls overhead. I went with some guys from the show and not Betty, nor Janyce. I would not be surprised if every single person there was stoned.

I found as a young adult on this long sojourn away from home and with the propinquity of the company, who become like your family, that I got along well with gay guys who were not screamers and did not hit on me. I actually liked some of the screamers, too. Since gay men truly comprise the vast majority of males involved in musical theatre, this was very helpful. The straight guys in theatre, at least far too many of them, seem to be self-consumed schmucks and I have no idea why that is. The late Mort Marshall, however, was a diminutive, funny, older, married character actor who also liked museums and we maintained our friendship after doing stock together in the early 'seventies.

Joel Grey and I had a row once when I was doing one of my many fast changes just offstage right in *George M.* His dressing room was right there, the door was open and his wife was inside. He made a sarcastic comment about my being down to my skivvies within her sight. As I rapidly responded while rushing my change, there was no necessity for his wife to stare at me while I was doing my job in the only place I could do it. Generally, we got along all right, although Joel was difficult and frequently flippant. He was far superior in all ways, not just as a performer, to his replacement. He also gave me my favorite star gift which I still use daily four decades later: a plain silver Tiffany money clip that reads: "jg GM lb."

It is much more of a theatre tradition to at least give opening night notes, if not gifts at closing. Indeed, it is a tax write-off but that is certainly not the point. Pres gave me a great vintage, name champagne. Ginger Rogers bought us all lunch at a Howard Johnson's; liquor was on your own for Christian Scientists do not drink. Dustin Hoffman gave me a black, cotton vest that is much like a photographer's vest; almost all film AD's wear them, too. This one was black and had the *Hook* logo on it and was stolen when I accidentally left it in a sushi house one night decades later. It also started me buying these same kinds of vests in different colors for they are very handy when bird watching or hiking. They are great on planes and I have never travel without one; all those pockets come in handy.

I thoroughly enjoyed Toronto and all of my interactions then and since with Canadian people have been better than with Americans, and, of course foreigners. All of my later trips to British Columbia convinced me that Canadians are the friendliest people I have encountered but then I have never been to Quebec and I assume they are more like the surly French or curt Germans, at least in my experience.

The National Theatre in Washington, D.C. was where we closed. I lived downtown near the theatre and the city was grimy, like a poor man's Manhattan. We were originally scheduled for other dates but they were cancelled, most likely because of Darryl Hickman, who had taken over when Joel left the show.

Dwayne and Darryl Hickman were child actors. Most people remember Dwayne, who played Dobie Gillis on TV, whereas Darryl is not remembered by anyone, which might explain the chip on the shoulders of his barrel chest and barrel ego. He was not good at faking the tap like Joel, who was not a hoofer but good enough to look credible to an audience not knowledgeable regarding dance. Hickman in the Cohan role dancing downstage of us, I averred to a friend in the show, looked like Smokey the Bear was in a white suit trying to get gum off his hind paws while flailing his forepaws to keep from falling.

Darryl was an aggressive individual. In our first rehearsal of the scene where my character, Behman, fires the young Cohan, Darryl adlibbed a line and I told him that it was not in the script. Being of the Monte Markham style of acting, given that we had five minutes for this one rehearsal, he gave me some guff about how I would have dealt with that in front of an audience. I explained that I would have adlibbed back but an audience was not there and we were rehearsing and had very little time for method superficialities.

At the National in D.C. we occasionally saw a rat run across the fire escape rungs outside our dressing room's never-opened window. If you opened it for air the rats would rush in and eat your snacks and makeup or perhaps a piece of *you*. At that time it was quite sleazy in downtown D.C. away from the political sites, but D.C. does have a plethora of good museums and a few tantalizing restaurants.

Betty asked me to live with her in her NYC apartment after I returned home, started divorce proceedings and made my move to Manhattan. This was very beneficial because it was hard to find an apartment and they were super expensive, so I agreed heartily. I would have preferred staying with Janyce in L.A. but I knew I had to get to my real love, theatre, and away from jobs that I hated but had to do because I needed to pay rent and buy food—that meant moving East.

Janyce and I stopped over in Vegas for four days after we closed in D.C. and before returning to our respective homes. We had a lovely honeymoon, just no marriage. Back in L.A. I saw Dahr, who, if anything, had become more unpleasant and aggressive, and I did the right thing. I filed for divorce on the relatively new basis of irreconcilable differences, so no further hassles or meetings were involved.

For some reason that was never voiced, Janyce's family did not approve of our relationship. Was it because I was not Jewish? Was it because I smoked and drank? Did they have some animus toward former Mouseketeers? Because of this and the distance between where she lived with her parents and my apartment, we saw less of each other than either of us wanted. She did not like losing me to New York but she was not ready to leave home. I really did not want to part with her but I did in May 1970 when I flew off to live with Betty in her apartment on 46th Street two blocks from Broadway.

In 1976 I danced on a TV pilot with Janyce after my return from NYC for my old teacher and the former choreographer of *The Perry Como Show* on TV as well as plays and films, Louis DaPron. It was a show built around Carlton, the guy who played the voice of the door man on the *Rhoda* spinoff of the *Mary Tyler Moore Show*, and Louis needed some heavy hoofers.

Hearing a lot of tappers, there were eight of us, sounds muddy and not clear, particularly on TV or on film, so Louis, known for the clarity of his taps, which he often dubbed for Donald O'Connor with whom he worked a lot, chose two of us to do the looping for the click/clack taps of all the dancers. He picked Janyce and me even though his daughter Diane DaPron, a good hoofer, was one of the eight. We both appreciated the unstated compliment.

This could also happen in a group number in stage work where the sounds are not on a track but live. Bob Herget was so disappointed in the sound of many of the dancers in the one tap number in *The Boys from Syracuse* that he had all their heel taps removed. A lot of the messiness of the tap sound is a result of bad tappers dropping their heels in executing a combination. I was not in the number and it sounded cleaner to the audience and to Bob and me as his associate choreographer.

Janyce still looked beautiful but did not seem to have matured much. She was not married and I, of course, had been with Diane since 1970, so we laughed and tapped and were friendly, but that was that. I tried to contact her online a few years back via her school but to no avail. I have always wanted to know how she is and how her life has progressed and all of the things true former lovers wish to know, especially if they leave on a positive sadness, not a screech of hate.

I did look forward to the hustle and bustle of fabulous New York City, working in serious theatre from Broadway to off to off-off Broadway to stock to LORT (Legion of Regional Theatres) and so on. I had no prescience about the startling frisson of fighting my first gang of cockroaches, meeting my partner for life, seriously thinking about buying a hand gun, something that I had never considered before, and getting cast in a Broadway musical after not being cast in the same show.

Chapter 13
Sour Apples Are Worse Than Sour Grapes

Being a tourist in New York City is very different than living in Manhattan, which is in many ways like a much more foreign country than an actual foreign country in which many of the people speak some form of English. Everything from people to walking to conversations are very fast and it is dangerous, rude, smelly, exciting, messy, always busy, humid, winter slushy and a much less wonderful city than New Yorkers think.

In May of 1970 I sent ahead my trunk and three boxes of books. The manuscript baggage was mandatory for reference books, dictionaries, thesaurus as well as plays, poetry and novels. I reread good books and since finding them on my own in my mid-teens they define my world to some degree. Even in the anti-Eden of PCiPods, I prefer the feel of a book to a machine on my lap and that will never change.

I brought my large Random House back to California, eschewing an aged Webster, along with the OED small print and latest update. For my birthday this year Diane gave me a new American Heritage and the Oxford American Dictionary. It was in Manhattan, after Di bought me a gift - #827 of 1,000, all that were printed, of the first edition of *Ulysses* by Joyce—that I started my collection of first edition novels, plays and poetry.

I was a serious writer by now and had published poems, some of which received awards, published newspaper and magazine pieces and was working on a two-act drama titled *Occam's Razor*. The Latin phrase *entia non sunt multipicanda praetor necessitatum* usually is translated to mean "things should not be multiplied beyond necessity." This is a maxim given to us by William of Occam (also Ockham), hence it is known as *Occam's Razor*. William was an English scholastic philosopher in the 13th and 14th Centuries. It predates McLuhan's obverted "less is more" by quite a few centuries.

Dressed for New York chills and with a new hair style, 1970.

I cabbed to Betty's apartment, located on the fifth-floor in a shabby building almost directly across from Joe Allen's, one of three or four actor and theatre hangouts in the city. I would soon learn that actors, unless wealthy, were frowned upon on the East Side. Remember in the 19th century there were signs outside bars that said "Dogs and Actors Not Allowed." There was no locked front door to her building as in all safe and decent apartments in the Apple, which alarmed me, and the teeny elevator took forever and reeked of junkie urine. This was a Disney nightmare: Realityland.

You entered her cave through the three-lock Manhattan system including the iron bar supporting the toughest dead bolt. Straight ahead was a door to the bathroom. Turning left, there was a small kitchen and the living/dining space and past that a separate small bedroom. But the rent was cheap for one of the priciest cities in the world in which to live and we split it.

At that time (and it may still be true) when you wanted an apartment in NYC you had to pay the current renter a fee, then the renter brought you (the new renter) into contact with the super (superintendent) of the building or the rental management company. This helped either of these two from screening hundreds of applicants for one apartment. You were only buying and selling in the sense that the occupant turned the lease over to you, as it was turned over to them. The rent went up for each new tenant; legally the amount was 17% in 1970, which may have changed by now. I know people with some money who acquired nice, large apartments and have lived there for thirty-five years or longer.

Betty had spruced up the apartment and I used what élan I could muster against my disappointment and skepticism because the approximately 300 square feet, the dingy rug and walls were far short of what I had been used to all of my life. We were happy to see each other and went out and celebrated that night.

It did not take much time for me to get oriented to buying the trades, the show business papers in NYC that actors must read daily to learn about auditions, which are far different than *The Hollywood Reporter* and *Variety* in L.A. These two rags are ostensibly for production people, agents and managers, producers and so on, not actors. Later there were similar trades on the West Coast but they did not provide much about paying, union work. In Manhattan you do not sign with one agent but many agents and whichever one sends you out on the audition gets the ten percent, as opposed to California where you sign a contract with one agent. If you are not too bright on either coast, you also hire a manager who takes another fifteen percent.

I was embarrassed once in Joe Allen's when a man came up to me, said hello and began talking. He soon realized I had no idea who he was and said, "I'm your agent." The fact is that most work in NYC theatre in the 'seventies, whether you work in the city or not, is from open calls you find yourself in the papers with no agent involvement. Now it is probably done online. It is difficult to bargain about your own worth, or at least it was for me and still is, although I am the only Mouseketeer who has done it for all of us. Saving ten percent is a worthy goal.

I landed a summer stock production of the musical *Irma la Douce* the second month after moving in with Betty. *Irma* was on Broadway before being made into a film with Shirley MacLaine and Jack Lemmon; I would work a little later with Lemmon in the NY filming of Doc (Neil) Simon's comic play *The Prisoner of 2nd Avenue*.

There are a lot of auditions for theatre in New York. When I lived in Maryland, Baltimore and D.C. had much more professional stage work than on the West Coast. Theatre for money in L.A., except for picking up a role from a touring company emanating from NYC as I did, is very close to nonexistent. On the West Coast there are prolific commercial auditions for journeymen actors, TV work is second and third is films.

I had only two stock experiences in California. The first was my second run with *West Side Story* which lasted three weeks after rehearsal and only played two venues in 1965 when I joined my fourth and last actors' union, Actors Equity Association (AEA), known as Equity, which covers only professional stage work. The second was in the early 'eighties in *Sugar*, which only played two weeks in Sacramento.

On the East Coast you rehearse stock in the town in which you open and I did four productions. My first was Devon, Pennsylvania at the Valley Forge Theatre and then we progressed to Latham (New York), Beverly and West Springfield (Massachusetts), and finally Westbury on Long Island. Except for the two theatres in Massachusetts, and the shorter drive to Long Island, we traveled by plane and it still beats a Bus and Truck tour.

Two or three weeks after I arrived Betty was cast in a Mickey Rooney stock version of *George M*. Mr. Rooney took a burlesque approach to theatre, stepping out of character to adlib jokes about his many marriages or Judy Garland or whatever came to his mind, thus making the character unbelievable. Musical comedy, now called musical theatre, is not Greek tragedy, nor *Macbeth*, but there are ethics, rules and traditions. When I visited Betty and Mr. Rooney in Waterford, Connecticut and saw the show, I was appalled by the veteran's disregard for professional craft and, although visible in the first row, which would never have been my personal choice, I was the only person who did not stand for his bows.

Ginger Rogers in *Coco* the following summer would not even think of breaking out of character. However, once, playing an outside round house tent, she lost her patter tune—a difficult, long, rapid fire lyrical song—the paradigm being "Trouble" in *The Music Man*—because the sound of a fierce storm on the top of the large tent we were performing in made it impossible for her or the audience to hear the orchestra.

Ginger stopped the orchestra and explained to the audience that we would have to wait a few minutes until the music could be heard again. She kept their interest not as Ginger but by staying in the character of Coco Chanel and telling stories about her (Ms. Chanel's) life that were not in the script. When the sheets of rain stopped, Coco cued the conductor and went right back to her song.

I was taken aback on my arrival by train to visit Betty when many folks met me at the station with placards welcoming Mouseketeer Lonnie. One or two had even fashioned some makeshift Mouse Ears. I had back-pedaled my involvement as a child star, left it off my resume and at that time in my life the MMC was something I thought of negatively, as black-and-white, simplistic kid stuff. This was to change in 1980 when the show was revived and I saw first hand how being one of the more recognizable Mice made many people very happy.

Being in my twenty-seventh year, I was startled by the group and a little put off since I was sensitive then about the childhood credit and I had no idea it was a joke by part of the cast, but I managed to smile through it and eventually accept it as a loving gag at Betty's instigation with some of the cast thinking it was a cool goof.

It had been clear prior to Betty's leaving that the spark between us had dwindled although we still felt things for each other and made love frequently. My trip made this separation more concrete and after I returned I started trying to find some other place to live which we both knew was best. It was not an easy task.

The beautiful Elke Sommer, a young film star (and much later an artist) who had never done stage work before, starred in *Irma* with two male co-stars, Al, who thought he was going to replace Alfred Drake and never got remotely close to that actor/singer's brilliant work and career, and Larry, a TV soap star who is still doing the same NY soap well over three decades later. He occasionally gets a strong support, such as a cop in one of Bruce Willis' films, but he is, or at least was then, a soap actor through and through.

I know I may alienate some soap fans but my limited experiences with soap actors have been unpleasant. My only regular role on any soap was a kid on the radio show *Dr. Paul*. A character actor whose face you would recognize, Willis Bouchet, played the Doc and everyone, including the SFX (sound effects) guy was pleasant. I played a prisoner in *Another World* during my New York years. In the late 'eighties I appeared on GH (*General Hospital*) in two different roles and in the second one, as a news editor, I had a scene with one of the perennial bad boys on the show who apparently was type cast from life, bored and may have been using some kind of pharmaceutical edge. His name was Will something.

On a soap the director works from the booth and is only seen face to face when the blocking movements are set, business is discussed and camera angles set up. The director then retires to the booth and is only heard over a speaker. We shot the scene. This is not live and can be stopped or reshot.

Without telling me or discussing it with me or the director, Will decided near the end of our dialogue to hit me in the head with the prop newspaper on my desk to which we referred. I memorize my lines and after the unexpected head blow I screwed up my last line and we had to reshoot; I am not a soap actor who is constantly reading off the teleprompter and I did not know where precisely to look. The director was annoyed at me, not the actor who had hit me. There was no direction in the script or by the director for the attack. The actor just thought it would be cute and extremely creative. If he had done this onstage he would have been brought up on charges by Equity.

Back at *Irma,* Larry would break out of character like Rooney only not as often and, not being a real star, he had less to say. I played one of the four French *mecs* (pimps), Irma being a prostitute. I was Roberto les Diams, Bob Diamonds, and I wore a distinctive yellow fedora which I bought from the wardrobe company after we closed and still wear on a whim. This distinctive chapeau was later part of a brouhaha in Le Petite Chateau, a French restaurant in North Hollywood, the day the Mouseketeers' live variety show at Disneyland opened in 1980.

My hair looked rotten after doing the dances in the three live, half-hour Mouseketeer shows so I had brought the yellow fedora from *Irma* to wear afterwards to cover my matted down locks. A friend of Tommy's whom I knew from HPS had come to see the show and joined Tommy, Aileen, Diane and me. We decided arbitrarily to stop off at Le Petite Chateau for dinner. The very snippy, supercilious French female owner stalked up to the table and demanded that I either take off my hat while we were there or leave. I began to reply but Tom's buddy rose and politely moved the French harridan away from the table. He returned and quietly explained that she would allow this breaking of her strict rules because he told her I had just had major brain surgery and that my scalp would not be what she wanted the other diners to see while they ate. It was quick thinking and we all found it hilarious.

In one scene in *Irma* the *mecs* are escaping from Larry who played the head cop and he discovers us from the top of an aisle—most stock is in theatre-in-the-round houses, some outside, and these become beastly hot, like when I played Sacramento. In both venues entrances and exits are made via the wider aisles. There is always a slight sound delay from the orchestra and, in a large outside venue this later caused me a major problem. This also makes things very tricky when someone decides to go to the restroom or lounges a foot out from their aisle seat.

This theatre was outside. Our characters had donned very long prop beards that clipped over our ears like glasses as disguises and we all wore distinctive chapeaus. The beards were obvious and intended to be funny for it is a light musical, not *Sweeney Todd,* and in the round there is very little but suggestion for sets and minimal props. The four of us were ensconced on a small riser—square or rectangular wood boxes 6" to 8" high of different sizes and used for sundry reasons. This one was relatively large and had small rollers so we could move it about the stage when we were supposed to be fleeing in a boat.

Mr. Soap Opera decided not to use his written line and shouted, "Look, it's the Smith Brothers!" For those who do not remember, long before ZZ Top there were brothers with very long beards who were pictured on the cartons of Smith Brothers' cough drops. It got a small, cheap laugh but made me indignant. As pros we ignored him and managed to get back to text.

Larry could often be glimpsed sipping his six pack of half-quart beers for most performances and, apparently, really hated what he was doing. How it could be any worse than playing the same character for well over thirty years in different outfits with lines that were almost identical and only slightly rearranged, which is a format that characterizes soap operas from early 20th century radio to television into the 21st century, is quite beyond my reasoning.

Elke was a tease. She wore mini skirts and see-through blouses and she had great breasts and a great body. As we rehearsed a scene onstage she would some times sit in the audience and casually cross her legs on the back of the seat in front of her. It was very difficult to concentrate on the work when you really wanted to know if she was wearing panties or not. She had one of the greatest female bodies I have ever almost seen in person; Mouseketeer Doreen was her equal in this regard.

I feared Elke was going to be horrible in the role but she was pretty good for not having done stage work before. She was pleasant, too, less full of herself than her two lesser costars Al and Larry. A local Mafia Don was impressed by Elke and invited the cast to a party at his club. No one was sure who the man was but, prior to figuring it out, he once offered me change to buy a Coke out of the machine when he was around during rehearsal. I sensed that it was best to do what he suggested and not disdainfully explain that I was in my late twenties, could manage on my own and did not want a soda pop.

It was my first, and (I hope) last in-person meeting with members of the Mafia and it was unnerving. I found it strange in this small Massachusetts town since I had always thought of New York, New Jersey, Chicago, Vegas and Miami as more likely places to find a bloodthirsty, nefarious organization thriving. This was long before *The Godfather*, earlier than most Cosa Nostra films and thirty-five years before the lovable sociopath and shrink-visiting Tony Soprano, but these guys actually acted and dressed the way they are depicted with dark shirts, unusual shirt collars, loud suits, much jewelry and some bulges under one side of their coats.

I had connected with Linda, the bartender across the street from our hotel, and Elke, being a film notable and the only woman in the cast, was slightly surprised and a bit miffed that I attended this party with an attractive brunette whose breasts were at least as big as hers. Linda and I were consumed by summer (stock) love.

The guys in our typical musical were all gay except for the two leads, me and two of the other *mecs*, one of whom was a good black club singer I liked named Rod. It was a pain that Rod had not done much acting and, therefore, copied whatever I did. This is more than annoying when you look and see that a character bit not in the script that you have devised is being done right after, simultaneously or slightly ahead of when you are using it. Even though older than me, I supposed he saw me as an experienced mentor and was trying to learn. No actor wants to be copied for it looks false or even comical-but-not-on-purpose to the audience when two actors are doing the same business, a term for anything that involves scripted or unscripted action onstage. The same is true for TV and film.

We also disagreed about my not wanting to go up to Harlem, which could very well be dangerous for blacks but much more so for whites in 1970. Rod maintained it would not be a problem; after all, he came downtown and mixed with whites. His reasoning was illogical for it was a totally different set of circumstances. He had a good pop voice and we and the other straight *mec* Larry—not beer-guzzling Larry, the soapy lead—would hang and talk, since we were not part of the majority gay coterie nor Al and Larry who felt special since their parts and billing were larger than ours.

I was the only guy in the show who got involved with an attractive woman. I found Linda by accident. We exchanged some banter and I returned the next day for a beer and asked her out. It was here that a wonderful occasion arose. It was very like a scene used in the film *Good Will Hunting* decades later in which the lead character is attacked by a bullying, upper crust, rich guy in a bar who rattles off some intellectual facts to belittle this poor, lower echelon new guy. The bully is decimated when the supposed victim retorts by showing the preppie geek how little he actually understands the subject he has chosen to use.

One day in Linda's bar three guys older than me and definitely not mafia types, had been giving Linda a bad time with suggestive comments and somehow a subject came up in which one of them said, "Beware of Greeks bearing gifts!" The three laughed and I inquired if they knew where the quote came from. They thought for a second and had no idea to put forward.

I extrapolated that it was line 29, Book II of *The Aeneid* by Virgil, (Publius Virgilius Marus the Roman poet who wrote about the Latin quest of Aeneas to found Rome which was the later equivalent of Homer's *The Odyssey* for the Greeks). The man warning the Trojans about a gift from Greek Spartans was Laocoön, a priest of Troy. The Trojans had just defeated the Spartans in a war caused by Helen of Troy, the much younger wife of their aged ruler Menelaus, who had an affair with the Spartan male Paris. The priest was cautioning the Trojans against accepting the fallen Greek's gift of supplication: a huge wooden horse.

The usual reaction to a war victory in this era was that the conquering army got completely drunk and passed out. The Trojans ignored Laocoön, opened the huge gates and helped the Greeks roll in their oversized gift horse. That night the Trojan soldiers, including the night watch, were passed out from drinking and the Greek soldiers inside the horse snuck out, opened the gates to their army and killed as many as they could. The few who escaped included Aeneas, Vergil's hero, like Odysseus in the Greek version, who travels a dangerous and didactic course to what is now Italy and, as myth would have it, founds the Roman Empire. Somehow, they give short shrift to Romulus and Remus.

I had actually read both in translation and I explained all this much more succinctly, not as above, and with no attitude attached. I wisely restrained myself from telling them I had in person seen a beautiful Hellenistic Greek sculpture of Laocoön and his two sons being consumed by snakes after being cast out of Troy for trying to warn his countrymen.

They grumbled some but did not take too much offense and this garnered more interest from Linda. I sensed she was not popular at the Mafia party and later found out she had formerly been involved with a high-ranking cop in the town. Since I did not want an accidental or any other kind of run-in with these dangerous, sociopathic fellows we left the party soon after arriving and went elsewhere to enjoy each other.

The last place *Irma* played was Long Island so the cast met our chartered bus in front of a midtown Manhattan deli and we were driven out to the theatre and returned to the same place after the performance. Betty was still out of town and I had taken to eating sometimes after the show at Joe Allen's across the street. Eventually there was a Joe Allen's established in L.A. but it was nothing like the restaurant/bar nor the crowd in Manhattan, although the interior resembles the original.

An act of fate occurred that changed my life dramatically and has continued until this writing.

Seated at a deuce (table for two) on the larger dining side due to my usual bar-side table being filled, I was next to a large, round table and two of the gay guys from the show came in with a young woman who was seated close to me. This was how I met Diane Dickey, now known as Diane Coleridge Dickey, who had an M.F.A. in theatre arts, like my M.A., and was quite fetching and dressed in an attractive hippie type outfit but not a granny dress. I distinctly recall she had on a short skirt and purple velvet sandals that had matching material that wrapped around her legs and were tied just below the knee. I found her quite enticing.

In addition to my rare seating, the fate part includes her having the flu and not feeling well at all; she had told her college buddy Ray she was not going to come to the show. He somehow refused to have her not see him for he was proud of his comedy cop schtick in *Irma* and almost bodily dragged her there.

I began talking to her and our personalities as well as our educational liberal arts background, theatre knowledge, interests and mutual feelings started sparking. Not many people can be witty about Hroswitha, a medieval nun, poet and playwright who was instrumental in restarting theatre productions when the church had them abolished in the Middle Ages.

The table filled with gay guys from the show, some with partners in tow, and eventually they were all laughing and talking and Diane and I were laughing and talking.

I invited her across the street for a drink and she accompanied me. We were quite involved in our lovemaking later but she refused coitus, which was unusual for that time frame in America and especially among theatre people; sex was indeed free and frequent. She also was not pleased that there was a cockroach on the bed when we entered that room. I had become somewhat inured, but not nearly as much as Betty, to the commonality of these creatures.

A couple of nights after I moved in with Betty I got out of bed to go to the bathroom and I turned on a light in the kitchen/living/dining room to get there. I was literally shocked to see maybe fifty or more—it looked like hundreds—cockroaches scurrying around trying to hide. I had heard of delirium tremens and I thought I was experiencing them even though I was not drunk. I began stomping them after making a shout—more profane and profound than EEK!—which woke Betty.

She rushed out, probably expecting a burglar with a bazooka, and calmed me down saving more messes on the floor and my gruesome bare feet, which I immediately washed, by explaining that this is common and unavoidable in New York. In the dark at night these bottom feeders come out to explore and dine. I had never seen a cockroach before this incident. I hated them and was leery of being there, but I had no choice. I checked the bed thoroughly thereafter every night. In my later Manhattan apartments they were rarely seen at any time. Recalling my bumbershoot weapon after arriving in Manhattan, I decided against being armed with toothpicks for the little scurrying vermin.

A middle-class guy who grew up in Pasadena, Glendale and North Hollywood, California was not used to passing junkies and thugs frequently on the street on a daily basis. Indeed, it was a cultural shock for me. I hated taking the subway but found there was more room to get away than on a bus. I wound up getting a lot of walking exercise in Manhattan and I walked at a brisk pace, never stopping to talk to, nor give a cigarette or money to anyone. Unless I knew you, I kept moving.

There are certain areas of the city you just do not go to at night. Wall Street, for instance, is desolate except for bad guys. This is also true in limited areas in L.A. and most major cities but no one really ever went to downtown Los Angeles at night unless they lived there or had to and so I was not instantly prepared for the constant threat of danger from just plain malice to mugging or stark violence.

One night in my early NYC stay I was coming home and thought it wise to spring for a taxi, despite the cost. We passed a group of guys beating up a man. I asked the cabbie to pull over; he was an unusual, verifiably American cabbie as opposed to someone from a foreign country with, at best, rudimentary English and worse driving skills.

I got out and shouted at them to stop. I wanted to go help but the cabbie said, "Get back in, man. It's not our fight and we don't know what weapons they got. Get in!" I faltered but returned to the back seat. I felt horrible then and I do now for not trying to come to this man's aid but it was the safest, smartest thing to do. At worst I could have been killed, at best I would have been hurt and also mugged.

Other near attacks and verbal aggressions of varying kinds occurred in my five years walking or riding on the streets of or below the avenues of Manhattan. I have already mentioned Diane's knife-wielding-junkie mugging. In my fifth year I sincerely considered getting a handgun, illegally because you may not own one in the city, and that was when I knew I had to move away. I had had no involvement with any kind of firearms except for being shown Eddie's weapons one time and shooting Tim's .22 once. I refused to acquire a gun.

In 1984, long after I rejected buying a weapon, Bernard Goetz was attacked by three or four young thugs on the subway. He pulled out a hand gun and fired, hitting one of them, and he avoided theft, injury and possible death. Goetz, not the thugs, was arrested and convicted of criminal possession of a weapon, not the shooting. He was sentenced to a year but served only eight months. One of the young thugs he shot was paralyzed, brought a civil suit against Goetz and a 1996 jury awarded Goetz's attacker 34 million. Goetz filed for bankruptcy and in 2004 said he had not paid one penny of the money.

The Law God did not think it wrong for the man to defend his life and shoot others but did think he was wrong to be carrying the gun that very likely saved his life because there was a law on the books. This is the same Law God to whom Charles Manson and Sirhan Sirhan are in debt and thank for being alive because executing a killer is not civilized. I did not want to get a gun and wind up like Goetz, even though I had not heard about him nine years earlier in 1975.

There are always mitigating factors but unless someone is wrongfully convicted, which is more difficult now with the use of DNA, there is one statistic that cannot be misused nor spun: a sociopath or an even more ordinary killer who is dead, just like a dead child molester, can NEVER kill again nor violate a child again and scar him or her for life—if they survive.

This is not a liberal point of view. This is not a politically correct point of view. It is my point of view. Now with drugs that merely induce sleep unto death as we do for the pets that many of us love more than the majority of the humans we have known, it is not the same as communal beheading, hanging or a firing squad. It is not torture. Yet these drug-induced executions are also being fought by dangerous people who are really nowhere near grasping what life is and is not from my vantage point.

Diane and I began dating and I learned she was the wardrobe mistress of *Oh! Calcutta!*, the first nude musical. As contradictory as this sounds, it got her on *What's My Line*, the game show on which the usual cast guessed a person's occupation (and they did not figure out what she did), *Calcutta* did not have nude people coming on stage, doing scenes and then exiting. They usually were dressed and then took off their clothes as a result of the dialogue and character interaction. If they came off nude they then had to put on clothes for the next scene, so Diane was very busy, helpful and nonplussed.

Actually a number of TV stars like Bill Macy, the husband on the sitcom *Maude* and Alan Rachins of *L.A. Law* were in this ribald play; they do not bring it up much on talk shows. This extravaganza was one of the first to have a resident shrink because the disrobing was unusual and the actors had problems with it. I saw the solid actor Hector Elizondo playing god in the comedy *Steambath* in which there was a nude woman and I believe *Hair* was the first show with everyone nude in one number at the end of Act I, but nudity pervaded every scene in *Calcutta*.

This play was a strange phenomenon put together by Kenneth Tynan, the British critic. The title came from the title of a painting by Clovis Trouille which is a pun on *"O quell cul t'as!"* which translates from French to "What an ass you have!" Tynan asked playwright/director/actor Harold Pinter to direct but he declined so Jacques Levy, remembered as the songwriting partner of Bob Dylan on his *Desire* album, took on the show. The script was a series of lubricious comedy scenes by such disparate writers as John Lennon, Jules Feiffer, Sam Shepard and Nobel Prize winner Samuel Beckett. It had a very long run. A lengthy run, though, is not necessarily an indication of being good; *Grease* ran for years.

I found out later that Diane had previously worked for the William Morris Agency in the literary department. Given my dim view of most agents, I am glad I did not know it the first night. At Morris she was an assistant to a later significant and powerful independent agent, Lois Wallace, who handled such disparate writers as Erich Segal of *Love Story* and the more literary Don DeLillo and Joan Didion.

I began taking classes in acting, my only serious attempt at this communal exercising of your skills, with well-known Broadway director Gene Frankel. Some of Gene's other students included Anne Bancroft, Morgan Freeman, Frank Langella, Eva Marie Saint, Rod Steiger, James Earl Jones, Viveca Lindfors, Lou Gossett, Jr., Lee Marvin and Walter Matthau.

The one real validity I have ever thought there was to acting lessons is they CAN offer actors a place to practice their craft in front of other people without the onus of auditioning for paying work for the rent and food. American actors are not given the same opportunities that British actors are. They go out and do work away from London and even if they get bad reviews it has no effect on their career. One can, of course, invite in family, friends and neighbors and perform soliloquies and speeches, but then one would lose family, friends and neighbors.

Gene liked my work and within two weeks cast me in two one-acts he had running: Brecht's *The Jewish Wife* opposite Karen Two, the later casting director previously discussed, and an original one-act titled *The Burden*. I realized I was not going to learn much from Gene when I was asked to bring in a classical scene and I reworked the *Richard III* opening soliloquy that I had done in my third year of college. I played Richard quite differently for the most part, making him less obviously the evil incarnate villain that Will created, although I did not make him comedically gay as Doc Simon did to Richard Dreyfuss' character, playing opposite Marsha Mason, then Simon's wife, in the film of Doc's play, *The Goodbye Girl*.

Gene's criticism was that he thought the interpretation wrong but he loved what I had done at the very end, which was a dramatic flourish that I kept from my original teen interpretation. I told him and the class, who backed Gene up, that I disagreed and without rehearsing I would come back for the next class and do the scene just as I had done it when I first took it on many years earlier and they would approve.

I did just that and Gene and the class thought it was terrific. I know what I can do as an actor and a class is supposed to be a place where you can extend yourself and do things that you cannot take a chance on when auditioning and usually not in actual working situations because too many people have predispositions about what the text is and what must be done, which can often be quite different from the subtext you create that the author only indicates or does not include at all.

When I landed my second stock job, Gene wanted me to continue paying for classes during the seven weeks I would be out of town and unable to attend classes. This was not in the agreement we signed and I considered it a rip-off. Gene loved chess and played with students frequently. He castled and I left, knocking over his king without bothering to declare, "Checkmate." That is the last time I have studied acting with anyone, but one must always be learning as an actor—the experience just does not have to include a teacher.

Knowing I had to move out of Betty's, Diane offered to let me move into her tiny apartment in a brownstone just off Broadway on West 82nd Street; that part of the long street named Broadway was called Needle Park for the many junkies who hung out there. Diane's place was even tinier than Betty's and had just been broken up into apartments with walls so thin that a guy snoring next door kept us up some nights. There was, though, only the rare, solo cockroach.

Just prior to moving away from Betty's, I met V on an interview, brought her back to the apartment and we made furious love. She had a beautiful face and singing voice but she was fatter than just zaftig; still I fell for her hard, not knowing that she would have puzzled Freud, Adler and Jung. The pheromone problem is shared by everyone, not just insects. V was the kind of young woman who spread her pheromones thickly and widely, just like L'il K, my short, final mistake in the late 'nineties.

After my feelings for V increased, I felt it incumbent on me to tell Diane that I was in love with V and even though I still cared for Diane I had to break it off for it would be unfair to Diane and to V. I also did not think Diane and I were ready for living together yet; in hindsight I may have presciently sensed that it would be my most important relationship and I wanted to avoid committing at such a young age. I told her at a sad lunch in the Village and she accepted it with great character, but I had to follow my heart and be honest.

So, I moved uptown from W. 82nd Street to W. 111th Street immediately east of Broadway and V's larger apartment in a big Sanford White designed building which was originally four apartments per floor then cut up into twelve. At V's there was an actual kitchen with a window, a breakfast table you could eat at and room in the corner for a small desk so I could write more comfortably. I was so excited that we made love standing near the table, the desk and the window.

The Upper West Side had not yet become as fashionable as it did, but it offered a lot of things if you did not venture to the east or north to Harlem. Some snobs believed that if you were not on the East Side or below 80th Street you were living in Frontierland. The locked front door of 545 West 111th Street was just off Broadway and two blocks east of the Hudson River, which made for pleasant daytime strolling and picnics. I later played my last game of football there when a guy dropped out from a group of teens scrimmaging and I was asked to join them. I caught a touchdown pass about ten minutes later. It was a great way to leave the game; I had wanted to be either a quarterback or a wide receiver as a kid.

There was a great Greek restaurant and Szechuan close by, a grocery on the corner, and it was near the subway and buses or I could just hike down Broadway. We were a couple of blocks south of Columbia and very near the beautiful Cathedral of St. John the Divine, where Louis Armstrong's funeral was held, and which 111th ran into at Amsterdam Avenue, the opposite end of our block from Broadway. Actually I learned all of this later from Diane; V and I were not privy to the history of this area during our short time together.

That Xmas V betrayed me but not sexually, although I know that happened with one guy and I suspected others. We were invited to spend Christmas with her family in Short Hills, New Jersey. Even though they knew we lived together, they would not allow us to sleep in the same room, for we had been asked for Xmas day and to stay that night.

I told V that adults in their mid-twenties who live together should not be treated as children and dictated to in this manner, so we could go on Xmas day and then take the last train back. I was not going to be a hypocrite over such puerile crap. I also offered the alternatives that she could stay and I would solo back to NYC or she could join her family and I would spend the day in our neighborhood alone and that was absolutely no problem for me. After the discrediting of the birth of Jesus on December 25th by the Jehovah's Witnesses, a date still argued over to set his birth from many critics' points of view, I have never been involved in the seasonal event and think of it as a nice time of year to give kids presents. My first Christmas married to Dahrlene, 1968, I painted the tree black and used only blue metallic ornaments. It looked very attractive and we received a number of compliments.

V assured me that both of us taking the last train back that night would be the best choice. I met her parents and both of her brothers and their wives. I must say that Short Hills was a pleasantly snowy, woodsy venue even though nouveau riche and quite lovely for a guy who since 1948 only saw a very small snow one year in L.A. after having his first three Christmastimes snow-filled in Kentucky.

V's family was friendly and even included me in their gifting; as a poet I was given another poet's work. They were unaware that Rod McKuen, very hot at the time, wrote some good song lyrics but was a horrible poet, which every person who had a vague concept of scansion and exegesis knew. I accepted graciously knowing they did not do it to insult me; very few people have any understanding of good poetry at all, considering rhyme the main object. Long after dinner but still at the table I reminded V about the train and her father said the last train back to the city had left a half an hour ago.

I looked at her and she smiled, thinking her pretty face and obsessive need for sex would make everything all right. I began to drink more heavily and was told where my separate room was but as they all drifted off including V, I stayed up drinking and my anger built. I wrote obscene things in the doggerel gift book, which they discovered for I left it there. I finally managed to get upstairs and fall drunkenly asleep.

I spoke normally but as little as possible the next morning and took the first train back alone. I knew I should move away from this pretty, seriously neurotic, perhaps pathologically ill girl/woman V who cared for no one except herself and that not very much, but hormones kept me with her—a story we all know and experience more than once and sometimes with much more dire consequences.

I spent that New Year's Eve out with V and before midnight she asked me to meet some of her friends outside in Times Square, which we all know is a very rowdy, crowded ritual, just as my later buddy Martin would meet his brother in Times Square once a year to get drunk on St. Paddy's day, but I declined. I have never liked crowds and rarely if ever go to big sporting events, rock concerts and the like. I will go to a theatre or club to see a master like Tony Bennett anywhere, Paul Horn in the 'fifties at the Renaissance Club, Cleo Laine at the Rainbow Room in the 'seventies, Shirley Horn in the 'eighties in Westwood or at the Hollywood Roosevelt Hotel, Miles—Bill Evans—Toots Thielemans wherever, Mel Torme, Peggy Lee, and now Diana Krall, but these are very different experiences with very different audiences—as opposed to combatants. I decided to stay in the bar alone and have my drink. V was fine with that and said she would return after the midnight hubbub and craziness. There are times when I wonder at my naïveté and faith in other humans.

I waited until 2 a.m. and then went back to the apartment. She returned at about 4 a.m. with excuses but I was beginning to realize after much denial that she was a nymphomaniac as well as a liar and many things worse. She had confided to me previously that she had sex with her two brothers in her early teens and still was doing it after they married and she was in her early twenties.

I explained the situations, symptomatic behavior and hurtful incidents to Diane who had, by this time, left her former apartment and found a much better place in the same, large Sanford White building on West 111th. Diane is one of the smartest women I have ever met, so I will not extrapolate further. Because of my ethics and Diane's acceptance of my ways, we were not having sex but as with Renata I had someone else to talk with about whom I cared and who loved me and was not the head case that was V. Diane and I had few friends in the city except for theatre cohorts at The Big Spender, a gay theatre bar at which we hung out in the Theatre District.

The Spender, named after the "Big Spender" number in *Sweet Charity*, belonged to Pat, a former performer who had been in the Broadway company and who was married to Linda from my company of *George M*. It was a theatre bar, more gay than straight, but straight people did frequent it for drinks as well as some limited fare. A hand-lettered sign hung above the bar mirror stated, "Hamburgers Available," which stuck me as quite whimsical. Diane and I would usually run into someone from the theatre world we knew at this comfortable bar.

I did see Jack Lee now and then but not that often. He was going through a bad time for his long time lover had left him for Juliet Prowse, whose Vegas act he had choreographed. Jack was quite devastated. A new musical to rehearse or conducting on Broadway or on the road helped as did his private musical coaching, but he had not yet made the move to teach musical theatre, singing and so on at NYU.

Diane had had enough of *Oh! Calcutta!*, so the well known Broadway producer of the show, Hilly Elkins, moved Di to wardrobe mistress of two newly translated Ibsen revivals of *A Doll's House* and *Hedda Gabler* off-Broadway starring his wife, Claire Bloom. They then took *A Doll's House* on the road to Toronto, Philadelphia and D.C. Chris Hampton (who is known now more for his screen writing than for his theatre work) was the translator and *A Doll's House* was made into a movie in Britain co-starring Claire and Anthony Hopkins. The same year, also in Britain, Joseph Losey, who had directed me as a child in the remake of *M*, directed a film of the same play, different translation, starring Jane Fonda. This doubling of films would never happen in America.

The parents Dickey and I had no problems when we first met. Diane's father Ray treated us to my all-time favorite restaurant, the Four Seasons, which I discovered alone on my second NYC visit en route to Europe at twenty and have continued to visit whenever in Manhattan. I had the same captain, Steve, for over thirty years and the service, food and ambiance have always been excellent.

Diane was cutting a lamb chop which, she avers under its own power, swan dived to the floor. The waiter quickly picked it up with a napkin, apologized for the dead meat's bad manners and went to bring her another one. She has this habit of making some kind of messy dining faux pas when we are dining out. There are a few occasions when she does not have to instantly thrust a napkin somewhere *tout de suite* but they are the less usual events.

The same problem of us sleeping in the same room when we went down to the Dickey's home in Georgetown, D.C. for the first time over the next Christmas was solved by Ray and Hilda springing for a room at the nearby, intimate and venerable Georgetown Inn, which was fine with us and only about a three-block walk.

Having previously told Diane what I had endured with V, she asked me to move in with her permanently; after all it was just across the air shaft and one floor higher in the building. I desperately needed to get away from the dead relationship and V's pheromones, but I was concerned about what it would mean for us. I did not want to hurt Diane any further than I already had when I left her for the dreadful V.

I believed and I told Di that I did not think I could live with one woman for the rest of my life without having sex at times with other women. I would not be out searching for sex as I had previously and as most men do most of their lives, but things do happen—particularly on the road or during long separations. I could and would guarantee that no matter what love I felt for another woman I would not leave Diane, and that she would not be blindsided if I was involved in anything other than a one-nighter that she would have no knowledge of and I always have come home to her. I also would make her aware of any serious involvement I had with another woman.

I did not think she would accept this for possession was what everyone still thinks, but does not say, is the most substantive element of a deep, lasting relationship. I also would not, nor could I, compel her to not have other involvements for that would be unfair, hence, wrong. I was cautious and eclectic and STDS, AIDS and the rest were not considerations in the 1970s.

She thought about my words and said she believed she could handle it and wanted to try. Diane said I was worth it. She appreciated my not being a hypocrite like so many men who promise fidelity and do nothing but go to great pains to not be caught. Some women do the same thing and that is one of the primary reasons that well over fifty percent of marriages do not last.

I moved my things from V's to Diane's and we have lived together ever since, although our anniversary we date from our first night of full lovemaking: September 27, 1970.

Of course, after some years, two last relationships outside my life with Diane in the mid-eighties and one short, meaningless six-week fling in the late 'nineties when we were bicoastal for nine months, I have not had sex with other women. That last person in the 'eighties, Susan, treated me so cruelly in breaking away after two years that I never wanted a serious involvement with anyone other than Diane since, and that was twenty-three years ago.

Ours is not the middle-class paradigm of a perfect marriage, but show me one, and if you do, tell me how fun and interesting and intelligent the couple seems. It is a solid, laughing, cerebral, sexy relationship we have both lived with for almost forty years which is much longer than either her parents or mine managed.

Diane's road trip was short and she got to know and like Claire and others in the small cast of the revival. Hilly had a party opening night after the off-Broadway premiere in NY that was catered by a sushi house and we enjoyed ourselves in their large and pleasant brownstone just off

1974 in the Upper West Side apartment Diane and I shared in a Sanford White building.

Central Park on the East Side. Both Claire and Hilly had attitudes but neither was close to being a monster like David Merrick.

The Ibsen revivals closed and Diane soon became the press agent and coordinator for the largest lecture bureau in the U.S. at that time, the Leigh Bureau, working for the couple who founded it, Mr. & Mrs. Leigh. Here she met and interacted with such disparate people as David Niven, Art Buchwald, Celeste Holm, Leonard Nimoy, Moshe Dayan, the always-ready-to-sign-for-a-fan Vincent Price, Hume Cronyn and Jessica Tandy, Betty Freidan, the creator of *Star Trek* Gene Roddenberry and Alex Haley who was just becoming known beyond his Playboy interviews for *Roots*.

I met Alex Haley in 1983 at the famous Peabody Hotel in Memphis, where the ducks are brought down every day by a handler via an elevator and paraded in the lobby to the fountain where they cavort for the pleasure of the guests. I recognized Alex as he read the paper in the lobby and I introduced myself as Diane's husband. He remembered her well and fondly. We exchanged for a while and he was quite the distinguished, refined, witty gentleman.

I was in Memphis for the 1983 Disneyland/Amtrak tour gig I did with Mickey Mouse, his handler and the Disney roadie who took care of our needs and saw that all ran smoothly. Actually, not all things ran smoothly and the roadie, dressed like a young exec, booked us into a hotel that was sleazy and dangerous. I insisted we move. If I had not we would have missed the famous Peabody Hotel and I would not have had the pleasure of meeting Alex. It is one thing to be Disney stingy and something else to be in danger.

Meanwhile, I continued doing stock: *Coco* in 1971; it was a kind of thrill to exchange lines and sing and dance with Ginger Rogers. She was still an excellent dancer and was adamant about her Christian Science beliefs. Wanting Ginger to be part of their group, some gentlemen invited the cast out for a day on the ocean in their large private craft on our Monday off and Ginger agreed as the rest of the cast leapt at it.

Ginger, at an advanced age, looked dynamite in her bathing suit but wore fish net stockings. Diane was visiting me for the weekend and we concluded that Ginger was hiding varicose veins in a unique manner.

Di had driven up in her brother's convertible Fiat and one day we were cruising some curves when I was pulled over for a citation. In New York one does not use a car because it costs almost as much to have a permanent parking place as it does to rent an apartment. If you do not pay for a permanent garage to park in and manage to negotiate the streets and dreadful drivers and accidentally find a place to park a few miles from where you live, the vehicle will be gone or stripped when you return. Hence, I never got a New York state driver's license and, by then, my California license, which I showed the officer, was no longer valid.

The cop decided to throw me in jail. As sincerely as I could and knowing the amount of money the show brought to the small town we were playing, I told him that if he arrested me then Ginger Rogers and the show would have to close and refund thousands for I had no understudy. It was not accurate, but he relented. I made the show. Diane did all the driving during the rest of her visit.

During this production, which has many beautiful female dancers who play models, I met Denise, the young, zaftig, beautiful French woman and Christine of the compellingly lovely long hair. Denise and I only had one night together during rehearsal and decided we would remain friends, but

In the boxer sketch for the TV special I'm A Fan *with Carol Channing and Dick Van Dyke, 1972.*

Christine and I became lovers during and after this musical and on return to NYC. Neither of us wanted, nor demanded, an exclusive relationship.

The choreographer Bob Herget hired me for the Kraft musical/comical TV special *I'm a Fan* starring Dick Van Dyke, who some young casting directors think is a Flemish artist, and Carol Channing. I played a boxer in one sketch and danced in a musical number with choreographer Larry Fuller and Ms. Channing, singing in her distinctive manner as a blonde chasing diamonds while we two hoods pursued her. Yes, she really sounds that way all the time.

Pete Marshall as Harold Hill. I played his buddy Marcellus in The Music Man *and, although Marcellus is not in the number, Pete thought it was more fun as a duet! 1973.*

Larry had not made it as a Broadway choreographer yet but he had choreographed me in *Coco* and later worked with Hal Prince as the Broadway choreographer of *Evita, On the Twentieth Century* and Sondheim's *Merrily We Roll Along*, which is definitely making the grade. We all have to eat, so he was a dancer and Herget's assistant choreographer on this special. He also had become the first and last Scientologist I have known. This group held a birthday party for Larry, who was an orphan, and he was told to invite all of his friends. Initially, it was convivial for Diane and me but soon the guests were isolated for individual proselytizing. I ended up with two females who were definitely rabid; the experience taught me to stay far away from these cult followers. I later had dinner with Larry at the L.A. opening of *Evita* and the subject did not come up.

In 1972 stock I played Marcellus, best friend of Harold Hill, *The Music Man* played by Peter Marshall whom I still consider a friend. Many people only know Peter from *Hollywood Squares* but he was a Broadway musical lead actor and vocalist prior to hosting the game show. Later that year I acted, danced and sang in a Pepsi industrial live show celebrating their 75th Anniversary. The show played at Disney's WDW in Florida. Donald O'Connor was doing his act at a club at the Contemporary Hotel where we were put up but I did not have a chance to get backstage to say hello to Don.

I then played a principal role in a revival of *The Boys from Syracuse* for Bob Herget and director Christopher Hewitt. Chris is also an actor; audiences know him best as the gay director in Mel Brooks' film *The Producers* and on television as *Mr. Belvedere*.

We played the Goodman Theatre on the lake in Chicago. It is part of and connected to the excellent Chicago Art Institute, one of the best museums in the country. I played Angelo the jeweler and understudied the two comedy twins, the Dromios. This Rodgers and Hart musical is taken from Shakespeare's *A Comedy of Errors* in which two sets of twins are separated at birth and accidentally run into each other much later in life through a series of unbelievable and absurd coincidences. Bob also used me as his assistant choreographer which added money and is much better than being the dance captain.

Bob and Chris had choreographed and directed the original Broadway production of *Syracuse* and hoped the revival, worked out of town in Chi, would lead back to Broadway. That did not happen but the show was so well received that it was extended and extended so after Bob and Chris left I recast the dancers as people left for one reason or another.

I found Chicago to be a great city, far superior to NYC in many ways except one. It can be bitterly cold with the wind coming off Lake Michigan even when it is not three below zero. The people with whom I came into contact were much less hostile and rude than the folks in Manhattan. I discovered the relatively obscure but marvelous Chicago artist Ivan Albright in the Chicago Art Institute, which I visited often. It contains the majority of Albright's work; he took the picture alluded to in Wilde's *The Picture of Dorian Grey* as the everyday, everyone, every thing in a decayed state. The Institute also houses wonderful pieces like Seurat's *Sunday afternoon on the Island of La Grande Jatte,* which inspired Sondheim to write *Sunday in the Park with George.*

I also found my second favorite restaurant The Bakery, which closed when the owner, chef Louis Szathmary, retired. After I returned to Los Angeles we exchanged our books, his with great recipes, and traded views on chef and restaurant owner Wolfgang Puck, who made himself into something of a Dali celebrity and had playbill credit for the included meal between the two acts of *Tamara* I did in L.A. in 1989-1990. I always went to The Bakery when I was in Chicago.

Puck started at Ma Maison and Diane and I came to know the *maitre d',* Claude Gouldar. One evening Claude and I found ourselves wearing the same, dark charcoal brown double breasted Ted Lapidus suit. Being men, we were not offended but complimented each other on our taste.

The only chef Diane and I got to know really well was Noel Cunningham, an Irishman who worked at one of the best and oldest restaurants in Los Angeles, Chianti Ristorante. It is a shame that this restaurant, which became our hangout in 1979 because it was just down the street on Melrose from where my two-act comedy *Over the Hill* had its world premiere, was bought by a chain and became just another pasta place. Before that it had great food, service and ambiance. When we came for dinner we just sent a Heineken back to Noel and he surprised us with whatever he felt like making; the selections were always excellent.

Punchinello's, a theatre restaurant bar in downtown Chicago, was better than Joe Allen's because it had entertainment and performers playing the town would get up and sing a tune or two. It also had the first bleu cheese burger that I had ever seen on a menu and it tasted terrific every time. Chi, which Chicagoans feel about as a name as San Franciscans do about 'Frisco, another good city but not on the level of Chi, is also a great city to walk in and is not as constantly filthy and littered as Manhattan.

Bob Herget was the most musically accomplished choreographer with whom I ever worked, and that includes Twyla Tharp, Gower Champion and Bob Fosse. All dancers and choreos must be able to count beats and accents but Herget really understood music thoroughly. He was also quite educated and intelligent which is frequently not the case with dancers, choreographers, directors or actors.

When I returned to NYC I was cast off-Broadway as the lead, Roy Lane, in a revival of the notable writer and director George Abbott, who also wrote the libretto for *The Boys from Syracuse,* and co-author Philip Dunning's drama *Broadway*. It is a story of gangster bootleggers, hoofers and chorus girls from the 1920s that originally premiered on Broadway in 1926. I had some excellent reviews in this drama including *Variety*—"Lonnie Burr does well as the feisty egotist and resembles Lee Tracey."

Tracey played the original lead and his understudy in 1926 was one James Cagney. Cagney was promised the lead in *Broadway* when the show moved to London. Instead, they booted him and it was the only time in his life that Cagney almost "caught the bus," which is theatre jargon for getting out of show business forever. Tracey went out to Hollywood, starred in a few films and vanished. James followed him and did far better than that. Most people do not know that Cagney, with no dance training, made his first professional appearance dancing in a chorus line in drag, thus, the irony that his long, celebrated career as a tough guy garnered only one Oscar—for playing George M. Cohan. It is the only role, except for a tap sequence in *The Seven Little Foys,* in which people could see Cagney use his unique, self-taught style of hoofing along with his singing and dancing talents. A number of people have noticed that my energy and approach as an actor reminds them of Cagney, which I consider a great compliment.

My favorite review for my Roy Lane was from the critic on the *New York Times* who wrote, "Burr is amusing and interesting in the oddly complex role of the club's leading hoofer. His arrogance and vulnerability, quick temper and sudden flashes of heroism add dimension to what might have been a stock figure."

Before my solid reviews in *Broadway,* I was cast in an original off-Broadway musical titled *Look Where I'm At,* adapted from a popular 1933 novel *Rain in the Doorway* by Thorne Smith, better known for the *Topper* series.

The director/choreographer was Wakefield Pool, who had been the associate choreographer on my *George M* tour and soon after this gig became known as one of the first successful porno film directors. At the first

Dancing as Roy Lane, the lead character in the play Broadway, *in the 1974 revival.*

reading of the script, at which hardly anyone laughed at the jokes but was in no way pornographic, it was clear that we were being paid for rehearsal and building up weeks to unemployment, which was more important in Manhattan than anywhere else, then we would close on opening night.

In NYC you could ostensibly earn over $100,000 performing in any medium over nineteen weeks, paying into the system the entire time as your employer would also, but if you did not have a twentieth week you could not collect unemployment. Quite an unfair system. Where did all that money for everyone's nineteen weeks go? In California and Maryland and D.C. and most other places unemployment is more logically based on the amount of money earned. If your earnings in the last twelve months are high enough you are eligible to collect unemployment.

I worked in this loser with Sherri Spillane, the then wife of tough guy detective novelist Mickey Spillane and I met him and saw him a number of times. He seemed pleasant enough but he also looked like he would be as tough as his protagonist, Mike Hammer.

We opened, were taken to the upstairs part of Sardi's, where I often went for drinks and which is the traditional place to watch the first TV reviews on opening night. We were not just panned but decimated, which surprised no one but the mature lady who produced the show, but we all commiserated with her. After all, she gave us six weeks of paid work and a better chance at the mandatory twenty weeks to collect unemployment. We opened on March 5th and closed on the 7th.

In 1974 my play *Occam's Razor* was presented at the Manhattan Theatre Club which was soon to become a prominent off-Broadway house for new works. Marlene, my girlfriend from graduate school, directed for we had run into each other in Manhattan not knowing we had both moved from California. My friend Martin Donegan played one role and Marlene cast an unknown Danny Hedaya in the other male role in the three, later four, character two-act drama.

I began working on Broadway by not being cast by the director/choreographer during the rehearsals of the musical *Mack & Mabel* in late 1974. I auditioned for Gower Champion and he asked me to join them in their last weeks of rehearsal before going on the road prior to opening on Broadway as "swing," the name for a dancer who covers all the other dancers' work, a sort of everyman's understudy. All musicals hire a male and a female in this capacity.

I had never been in this lowered status before and even though it was Gower Champion, Robert Preston, Bernadette Peters and producer David Merrick, I asked whether I could consider it over the weekend or whether it was mandatory to make an immediate decision. It was Friday and Gower said to give them a call on Monday.

I did and he had already cast someone else. I had made a very bad error in not jumping at this opportunity for this could be a good-paying, long-running job and I needed the money. It could also lead to doing better things as the show was constantly reworked before opening on Broadway. That was the case a few weeks later on the road. Hubris is not for the performer who manages to last in the business.

In 1975 after moving back to L.A. I read for a role, a number of scenes and lines, and had the unusual opportunity to read the entire screenplay while waiting to audition. Usually only principal players, leads and large supporting roles, get to see the whole script. It seemed very dumb to me and a rip off of *Champion* starring Kirk Douglas or perhaps the earlier *Body and Soul* with John Garfield in the lead. I did not get the role. But, like with Gower, you never know what is going to happen in showbiz. The film was *Rocky*.

Two weeks later I was called to work the final weeks of the *Mack and Mabel* rehearsal before going on the road; apparently the other guy did not work out—or the somewhat bizarre choreographer/director thought I should be taught a lesson. Once in rehearsal, while playing the Dorothy Chandler in L.A., the well known Broadway performer Lisa Kirk (who played the third lead in *Mack*) showed up late after lunch and, as I had been warned by my buddy Gerry, when she apologized and made an excuse Gower went nuts in the best manner of chewing up the rehearsal hall. She almost got fired.

Gower was known for casting "character male dancers," which meant they looked and danced like straight guys and had a character look, rather than being pretty and obviously gay. After changing this, that and the other at the David Belasco Theatre in NYC and never encountering the ghost of Belasco, we left for an opening week in underwhelming San Diego. Belasco was an actor, playwright, producer in the late 19th and early 20th century best known for his play *The Girl of the Golden West*.

One day before we left town I arrived for rehearsal and saw they were going to throw out the Belasco's very old sign that states in large letters on two lines: QUIET PLEASE /CURTAIN IS UP! which hung by the stage door to warn anyone who entered to not disturb the performance. This necessity has been handled in other ways for decades. I acquired the sign and currently have the weathered old words of theatre history hung above our bedroom door.

After a stop in San Diego we did eight weeks at the Dorothy Chandler Pavilion in Los Angeles. This is where Gerry and I solidified our friendship. There was a career chorus singer who was pedantic and intellectually snobby with everyone. I had heard enough of his boorish diatribes and when he began pontificating and giving Gerry a bad time about something I went after his particular niche, sociology, and with my one course on the subject years earlier I drove him speechless quoting experts in that field and refuting his premise conclusively. Being a member of Mensa, he later suggested I join, but his style dissuaded me from that course.

Gerry was a New Jersey street guy who also danced and sometimes said lines. He would come to the theatre offering inexpensive things which allegedly dropped off a truck somewhere. Chet, a tough, scroungy looking street guy type, with whom we shared a dressing room, was even more unlikely as a stage performer. It was an interesting number of months with these two guys. Chet was always late, arriving with a large black coffee and a racing form and only one part of the paper: sports. I am sure that there were many gay guys who were thrilled not to share a room with either of this duo. Do not misunderstand. There are some very scary, tough individuals who are gay but they are not the majority in showbiz.

We were on the road about ten weeks with *Mack* before moving into one of the Shubert Alley Broadway houses: the Majestic Theatre. I managed to find an occasion to be on the stage at the Majestic with no one else around or, at least, within sight or sound. The only light was the ghost light, a single standard with one bright bulb that is left on when the theatre is empty. Being alone out there is a unique feeling. Unlike an empty sound stage on a movie lot or a TV studio, there is a sense of being enfolded by aloneness that is not at all lonely. It is as if the spirit of the audience and the other humans who will soon make the large enclosure buzz and hum onstage, backstage and in the loud silence of the audience, except for laughs, is there with you. On the stage you are the sole focus of the spirit, just as you are when you are doing a solo or a line and for a second or two everyone is focused on you. It lasts longer than a second and is a wonderful, unique feeling.

It cannot be emulated in 99-seat houses or theatre in the round or in academic theatres. This feeling is found only in some very old, very used venue that has a kind of character that sets it apart. The huge and well-appointed O'Keefe in Toronto does not have it, nor does the Kennedy Center, nor the Chandler in L.A.

Our oddest pre-Broadway house for *Mack* was the second largest outside theatre venue in America before a spate of 20,000+ seat venues were built in the last two decades. The Muny in St. Louis, formerly the Muny Opera House, which seats a little over 11,000 people, was built in 1919—and can be extremely humid. I have played the former largest outside venue, the Hollywood Bowl, which seats over 17,000 and was built in 1922. The Bowl accommodates orchestras and acts ranging from musical performers to comedians to classical orchestras, but does not do musical theatre plays. I performed at the Bowl with other Mouseketeers in 1956, twice in the late 'eighties, and last in 1990 also for Disney as Mouseketeer Lonnie.

The sets for *Mack* at the Muny had to be built there since most of our traveling scenery units would not fit, nor work, so we rehearsed one day with the quickly built units at this venue and played only a week. It was very dangerous climbing up tiny wooden steps to a second-story spot behind a shaky flat, the units on which sets and background are painted, which I had to do for one scene. There are numerous problems in playing *al fresco* including insects that love to fly into actors' and singers' open mouths and a sound delay that, to a lesser degree, exists in the round, between you and the pit orchestra.

The conductor of *The Music Man* and I disagreed about the tempo of my Act II opening solo *"Shipoopi,"* which translates to *"the gal that got away"* in the much earlier era depicted. I wanted it upbeat at the tempo Iggie Wolfington did it on Broadway because I had a dance added since the choreo knew how good I was. My late friend Iggie, whom I understudied and went on for in the L.A. company of *42nd Street*, was not a dancer. The conductor kept bringing the tempo down as I tried to push it up to where it should have been.

On opening night I began the number and, since I play to the cast rather than the conductor, I was not watching his baton as an opera singer would. The cast stared back at me as if I was in the path of an oncoming locomotive. I was about two bars in when I realized the scoundrel was going at his tempo and due to the sound delay I had not realized it. I adjusted immediately and made it work, but my number was not nearly as effective as it could have been. I discussed the problem heatedly with the director who agreed with me. With the proper tempo it came close to being a show stopper, which I later had with my gang in *Sugar* and previously with the three other buyers and Ginger in *Coco*. The number has cute lyrics but is simply an innocuous wake-up call that the second act has begun.

I had another disastrous musical number in *Mack*. This romp was added on the road and I was partnered with an impossibly nasty, willful young woman named Nancy who had an unpronounceable last name and insisted on leading. The female dancing backward does not lead in social dancing. It does not work because she cannot see where she is going.

I asked Gower (known originally for dancing with his wife Marge as his partner on stage and in film) about this problem which was always a dangerous proposition for he was unpredictable and it was better to go through one of his assistants. Gower was wired much of the time. He listened to me and decided to show me how to go about it.

He gathered Nancy as his partner and did that section with the rehearsal pianist. He managed to get through it, but not to his satisfaction. Nancy was so impressed with being partnered with Gower that she did not notice his glowering eyes. Gower left Nancy, came over to me and quietly said, "You're on your own, Lonnie."

This number had us dancing around other people with lines and blocking, three other couples dancing while tables, chairs and other set pieces were flying in (being lowered from above) or brought on from the wings on a very crowded stage. It was quite dangerous. Nancy fought me for the lead, getting bumped repeatedly, stepping on the foot of an actor speaking his lines and almost got a table bashed into her head but I managed to overpower her at the last second.

Nancy and I never spoke before going on, nor at any other time. Dancers are almost as weird as musicians. However, Sandahl Bergman, a beautiful blond chorus girl in *Mack* whom Fosse used as the featured female dancer in the film *All That Jazz* became a star in some minor movies later. I did not know her well at all but I would have really enjoyed dancing with her as my partner in anything.

Another of Gower's whimsical oddities was saying "Woof" to himself when thinking, to emphasize things and also to get things accomplished. Most of the company noted this but not everyone did. One day the stagehands in L.A. were moving a set piece from stage left to stage right on rollers and Gower was to let them know where he wanted it. They moved it in a few paces and Gower made the woofing sound; they really did not comprehend the dog jargon but they stopped. Gower woofed again and so they moved it farther stage right. He kept saying "woof" with more emphasis and volume and they kept moving until they disappeared into the wings on the opposite side. Hilarious—but no one laughed openly.

A story told to me that I did not actually witness was regarding a rare show of Gower's that opened and closed with alacrity. At the opening night party it was alleged that he declared, "This is a FLOP". He then lay down on the floor, began flopping from side to side and repeated over and over, "I'm a flop, I'm a flop, I'm a flop."

Gower was known for using unusual phrases. Once a show was open he would say, "Now we've got the elephant on its feet, let's see if it can walk." Apparently our pachyderm would not budge. *Mack & Mabel* got tepid reviews after opening on Broadway on October 6, 1974, and we closed about seven weeks later on November 30th. We did not play to large houses often but the cast had strange things occur, e.g. one chorus kid called the box office for tickets and was told we were sold out, but we only played to half a house that night.

Composer Jerry Herman, an award-winning Broadway veteran, was displeased with Merrick's lack of promotion for the show. Author John Anthony Gilvey quotes Jerry as saying that Merrick never even came to the theatre and spent nothing on advertising. Despite only sixty-six performances, *Mack & Mabel* received eight Tony nominations for book, direction, lead actress, lead actor, choreography, set and costume design and Best Musical. It was Jerry's first big flop after a number of hits.

Merrick had recovered the approximately $1,000,000 investment cost of the show—much lower than today's musicals—on the road before we opened on Broadway, which is unusual. There was word that a new hot musical coming to town, *The Wiz,* had lost its theatre to another show that extended its run. There was speculation that the real reasons we closed were that Merrick had already made his investment back and could give himself a nice write off and, perhaps, that he had received an under-the-table perk for allowing *The Wiz* to easily breeze into town.

I think *Mack* is one of Mike Stewart's (*Bye, Bye Birdie, Hello, Dolly* etc.) best books (musical theatre dialogue/scenes) and one of Jerry Herman's best scores. Bernie and Pres were terrific. Even though the show was not a light musical with a happy ending, which except for *Sweeney Todd* and *West Side Story* comprised 95+% of musical comedy in this era, it seemed premature to close it but, of course, we will never know what actually transpired.

What I did get from doing this show was my first Broadway credit and high blood pressure. After the aforementioned ten weeks on the road with rehearsal every day, eight shows a week, constant changes and only one day off every two weeks added to my unwinding with a couple of drinks after a show to bring down my adrenalin, I was not in great shape.

I went to a very unusual physician, Dr. Isadore Freed, a family friend and doctor to the Dickey family, who managed to be on the staff of the three most prominent hospitals in NYC, one Catholic, one Jewish, one Protestant.

He diagnosed my high BP, prescribed the normal diuretics and told me to cut out salt, and I beat it back down to normal in about four weeks. He also insisted that I start taking vitamins daily. My cousin Billy lobbied for and took vitamins for years but I thought the pills were just a con to take yokels' greenbacks. Dr. Freed explained it very simply to me: if everyone ate three meals a day that were not filled with salt, fats, sugar, preservatives and other horrible substances, if they did not have hereditary problems, breathed only good, clean air, exercised regularly, never consumed things bad for their bodies and so on, there would be no reason to take vitamins. Since no one does this, we need to supplement our diets, even if they are fairly good comparatively. Of course, you do this with knowledge and are careful about what you take and how much you take and from whom you acquire it. I have done so ever since my thirty-second year and I have been quite healthy.

As a kid, teen and young adult I was prone to respiratory ailments but since beginning my vitamins, in addition to later getting yearly flu shots, I have a cold or the flu about once every five or six years. When they do occur they are very mild and rarely drive me to bed. I heartily advise taking supplements with the help of a physician or at least acquiring a thorough understanding of what each vitamin is, what it does and what the limits of usage are.

In January, 1975 I had a piece on the MMC in *The Village Voice*. It was an epistolary satire of being Mouseketeer Lonnie that was misunderstood by Disney, but they are not known for their acceptance of anything but their POV on any subject at any time. In addition, surely no one employed by Disney reads *The Voice* (or would let on if they did).

That same year the MMC began reruns in black and white when everything had been in color for quite some time and five of us appeared on Tom Snyder's talk show, *The Tomorrow Show*. It was late night Snyder's

In formal attire with Diane for the "Women in Show Business" tribute to Annette Funicello in the early 1990s.

highest rated show and the rerun was his second highest—at least for that year. This really was the first Mouseketeer reunion of any significance after the series stopped shooting in 1958 and took place five years before the 1980 TV special for our 25th Anniversary. Roy and Annie joined us by phone; Roy died the following year.

Diane and I were interviewed and photographed for *In The Know*, which I later wrote for doing a profile of Bernie Peters. I placed an article with *American Film Magazine* AGAINST letting children be professionally involved in show business.

Diane and I started a poetry quarterly titled *Quiddity*. We got some unpublished poems from my friend, novelist, poet, composer and translator Paul Bowles. I took a course from him while working on my Ph.D. in the later 'sixties when he made a rare trip home to the U.S. from Morocco. Paul was a long-time expatriate American who lived in Tangiers and we continued our epistolary communication until his death in 1999.

I added to his obituary in the *Washington Post* what he had written to me about how a world renowned one-act play by Sartre got its English translation. Paul was a friend of Sartre and did the definitive translation. The title in French, *Huis Clos,* may be translated various ways but it ostensibly means being confined in a tight space, which the audience learns is Hell. Paul struggled with its translation until one night when he was in the N.Y. subway and looked up at a sign: *No Exit*. That has been the play's title ever since and the first translation—Paul's—is the best.

Much of our correspondence is in the Huntington Library in San Marino, California, which is known for its extensive collection of American authors. Paul and I exchanged for over thirty years. I plan to also donate my ten years of correspondence with author, essayist and critic Leslie Fiedler. Diane and I abandoned our poetry project when we moved to Southern California mid-year.

Epistolary exchanges, that for too long have been labeled "snail mail", have almost disappeared. I fear the communication inherent is now a thing of the past that will be missed, at least by the literate. Everyone will go on texting, e-mailing and being joined at the ear by their cell phones without ever actually putting serious thought into what they are thinking, writing or saying.

Our move to California in May 1975 forced me to observe the constant instances of my making large moves mid-year and always around my birth date of May 31st. I moved in with my grandparents in June 1958, went to Europe twice in June, went to NYC in May, I moved to Maryland/D.C. in 1998 during May and came back to San Clemente, California, in July of 2005. I do not know what to make of it but it does seem a little too coincidental. Maybe I really want to make sure I graduated.

I continued to publish poetry in NYC from 1970-75 and gave poetry readings in the Chelsea district of NY and the famous East 92nd Street Y, which also accommodated T.S. Eliot, Ginsberg, Dylan Thomas and Auden among the many notables that read there. I gave a reading at the Chicago Art Institute while doing *Syracuse* and another some years later in Santa Monica, California, with Bukowski, a poet and writer whose work I have never liked. Well, we almost gave a reading together. I showed up but he did not, which surprised everyone but me. I did a reading in Washington, D.C. and in this century, I gave my last reading in Maryland. I did not read my own work for once, but interpreted my favorite poem, "The Love Song of Alfred J. Prufrock" by Thomas Stearns Eliot, one of my very favorite poets and an unmet mentor.

The bits I did in three films in my five years in NYC were not remarkable for me in any way: Neil Simon's *Prisoner of 2nd Avenue* with Jack Lemmon, *The Hospital* starring George C. Scott and *The Panic in Needle Park* starring a young Al Pacino.

Like a fool, I once went up to Jason Robards, drinking alone at Charley's, a theatre bar started by Charley the bartender and Charley the *maitre d'* from Joe Allen's. I succinctly told Mr. Robards how much I liked his work. He was obviously drunk, which I had not perceived, and he garbled, "Ge'way from me ya' fagot!" Jason was famous for doing O'Neill's plays but I only saw him do a revival of *Moon for the Misbegotten* and he was drunk onstage. The fabulous actress Colleen Dewhurst, married for some time to another difficult individual, George C. Scott, managed to bring Jason back to O'Neill's lengthy book and get him through it. I am sure that some of Jason's performances of O'Neill were great, but his alcoholism clouded his life.

I had met my buddy Martin doing *Broadway* in which he played a gangster. Martin was a hard drinking, Irish actor and raconteur and he and his later wife Margo and Diane and I would get together to play cards. Margo did not smoke but Martin, Diane and I did and we played cut throat poker for pennies sometimes until 4 or 5 a.m. in their teeny sixth-floor walkup on the East side filled with smoke and booze and laughter. We had some damn good times.

After *Broadway* closed, Martin and I had drinks, sometimes lunch, without the ladies now and again and he was my closest friend in the city other than Jack, with whom Diane and I still keep in touch. Martin was a small man but was convinced he had the famous John Barrymore's profile; this was not thoroughly accurate, but no one wanted to tell him that. Later he took a bad beating in an alley outside a bar and had to have extensive facial surgery. We had a falling out right before I left Manhattan, both of us too far into the bottle, at a tavern he liked near his apartment.

I have an insight into people that I have to avoid or only use very carefully with someone who I am sure is receptive. It is one of the reasons that my group therapy members all thought I should be a shrink. I understand things about people that they almost always do not want to hear or know, even though they say that they do. It is a little like my prescience which I now accept but denied for my first three, almost four decades.

I had difficulties later in this regard with *WKRP* star Frank Bonner, with whom I became friends before his TV fame, directing him in an Ionesco one act and later in the world premiere of my stage comedy, *Over the Hill*. He had a good eye for directing and later went into directing television shows. I also wrote a magazine article on him after our schism.

Again, I have found that absolutely everyone insists you tell them the truth but you find that hardly anyone actually wants to hear it unless it agrees with their idea of the truth. The ending with Frank, but more importantly the earlier break with my best buddy Martin was final in terms of friendship, although I did see them both subsequently. Visiting New York, Diane and I were coming out of the Russian Tea Room after some great vodka, appetizers and Beluga and accidentally ran into him on 57th street. Margo and Martin had married, moved to Brooklyn and had a daughter. We made plans to meet Martin and his daughter after a matinee once and she was a lovely young girl, but he and I were never close again.

Some of my relationships with women in my NY years were serious, like Suzi during *Boys from Syracuse* in Chicago. Only eighteen years old, she was eleven years younger than I. This was the first relationship with a much younger women until that last short affair in the late 'nineties; also eleven years difference, her 39 to my 55.

Christine, she of the beautiful, long hair and quirky, innovative sexual tricks is someone I remember fondly. She managed to have me remain coupled with her through three orgasms for both of us; that was a first and a last. For some reason that was not explained, this could not happen on a bed but only on a built in bench in her apartment in the Village. Denise, my French lover from *Coco,* was cast in the *Syracuse* company also and we had remained friends. My twenty-ninth birthday party was celebrated in my Chicago hotel room with Denise, Suzi, Diane and the gay conductor of *Syracuse*; he and I liked each other and he fit perfectly with the other three girls.

I had a short affair with Terry, whom I met at an AFTRA workshop. She was very intelligent and sexy. She lived with her cousin Geoffrey who did something for Cooks Travel agency. One night they came over and Diane and I, being children of the early 'seventies in our twenties, decided to spend the evening after *Calcutta* with our clothes off. When they arrived we were nude and invited them to join us or not. Terry had no problem with it and disrobed but Geoffrey took a while longer then joined us—except he refused to remove his socks. Terry left showbiz acting and became a psychiatrist, so maybe she finally got Geoffrey to take his socks off.

Diane and I had one other Calcutta-like episode during *The Music Man* when she came to visit me on the road. Actor Mort Marshall and I were close during and after the show. One night after the performance and a few cocktails, this sixty-something funnyman knocked at our hotel room door. There he stood—all five feet two inches of him—totally nude, with a rose in his teeth. We fell down laughing and he ran back to his room.

In retaliation, I managed to somehow get into one of Diane's low-cut dresses and she into one of my outfits and we went down and knocked on his door. Mort opened the door and laughed so hard he almost became even shorter. That was the first and the last of our cross-dressing.

Back in New York Mort asked us over for dinner one night. His wife was very rude and unpleasant but I did get to see his Renoir which he often referred to on our museum visits on the road. It was a lovely original sketch that he valued highly and his wife subtly denigrated. Our love of art and being vets of the business is what drew Mort and I together as friends on the road.

I was not happy with the work I got in New York, even after the lead in *Broadway* and *Mack* on the Great White Way, plus the pressure of the city and the idea of buying a weapon for protection, the miserable streets in winter, the humidity, the dirt and litter everywhere and the aggression and combativeness of too many people. Diane was disenchanted with the city

During the run of The Music Man, *Mort Marshall and I always found the time for some off-stage schtick, 1973.*

too, particularly after getting stuck in the subway at rush hour for about ninety minutes and having to walk many blocks through the underground tunnels in her office clothes and carrying her usually oversized purse.

I wanted California and an easier life style, a cool car, the fantastic weather, the laid back style of people and all that I grew up with and accepted as comfortable in my early years. I went on my first TV game show in either March or April of 1975, *The Big Deal*, and won over 5K—no big deal in today's game show money, but enough backup along with my *Mack & Mabel* earnings to make it feasible for me to move back to my home bringing Diane with me to Cali-For-Ni-A.

But was Southern California as I knew it still there?

Chapter 14
Some Tough Guys Dance a Little

John Leonard Burr was a rough, tough man, but the late Norman Mailer who wrote *Tough Guys Don't Dance* was only partially correct. My gramp had no knowledge of, nor ability in terpsichore but he would do a hippity hop *Deliverance* sort of jig to rile my grandmother and eventually get her to giggle. It was the only way he managed to annoy her in their 60+ year marriage except for persisting to smoke, drink on holidays and get out to the race track.

John's family was never discussed; he and Gram met as young adults. Unlike Gram, John spent his formative years as a modern outlaw known as the Deacon with the Wicked Wrist in sporting houses. My grandmother grew up on a farm. She was a stringently moral woman and accepted no one else's idea of morality. She believed in God and prayed but never belonged to any formalized religion.

As a small child she saw where eggs came from, thought it was disgusting and refused to eat them, and at about ten she saw a chicken's neck wrung off by hand and watched the blood spurting everywhere. At that point in life she stopped eating all animal products and became a vegetarian. She was later, I assume, shamed by the fact her first marriage did not work out and she met John when Mom was about seven in 1921. This is probably why I did not learn he was my step-grandfather until I was in my fifties and he had been dead well over twenty-five years.

How Gladys converted this n'er-do-well to be an ever faithful, hard working middle-class bloke is a mystery. He was a fairly decent pool shark, a very solid card player and bowler, as was my father, and they both liked playing the ponies. Both of them managed to get there as much as they could, but much less than they wanted, against Glade's and Dot's wishes. But John was an outlaw no more.

He was a gruff man who enjoyed toying with me in nonchalant, covert ways. When I was five or six he left me in a wading pool so long that I had a close to unbearable sunburn and almost my entire body peeled. When I was about six he put some boxing gloves on me and poked me in the nose with his bare hands. He laughed heartily when I began to tear, not knowing that at even this young age I had an unsettling tendency to get so angry my eyes would tear up.

Another time he took me along when he went to pick up rental payments and I was bitten by one of the tenants' dogs. He pooh-poohed my pain and tears and continued collecting all the rental fees before taking me to a doctor. All kids in the 'fifties were scared to death of not just polio but also rabies from dogs, not bats and wild animals. I had been told time and again how excruciating the many shots were that they gave you to avoid your contracting mad dog disease. Kids were almost as afraid of the shots as the disease.

At their home in Altadena they bought me a small merry-go-round with six painted horses. It turned when kids worked the pedals on the ponies and I invited neighbor kids over to ride on it. One day a bully, both of us having on our cap pistols and gun belts, quarreled with me and then hit me on the head with the butt of his gun. I ran after the bully, but my grandfather picked me up and would not let me pursue him. This enraged me and seemed totally contradictory to his John Wayne demeanor.

In one way he always acted as if I was short of being a real Mailer male, a tough guy like him to whom pain was no big deal and, if challenged, from no man would he walk away—unless that man wore the uniform of a cop. Here, however, he frustrated my natural retaliation response to being struck. He was right, of course, because I could have really hurt the bullying schmuck, or been hurt, but I saw it quite differently then.

Only once, before I moved out, did we almost get into it. He was in his sixties then but over six feet to my 5'7" and his limp from jumping freights and having two toes cut off as a youth had become more pronounced. I was arguing with my grandmother and he misunderstood what I said. He somehow thought I had called her a dog, fighting words for him. He rushed across the room toward me and I gave no ground waiting to take him on. Gram shouted and he stopped. She told me to go and I got in my car and left. I think it may have been the only time that he thought of me as a man rather than an intellectual, girlie boy TV star.

Yet, the Deacon was my grandfather and, thus, had meaning in my life however he treated me. So when he had a major stroke in 1973 and I was in *The Music Man* moving from Indianapolis to our next theatre in Atlanta, Georgia, I received a late night call from my grandmother. I got the first flight to McCarran in Vegas early in the morning after calling the stage manager who was not pleased about my trip. I was picked up at the airport and sped to Boulder City hospital. I insisted on a second opinion and that kept him alive, although greatly impaired, for the next two years.

John died in 1975 and Diane and I flew in for the funeral. At his request the Masons were there, for he was a 32nd degree Mason, just below the final step of 33rd degree, and it was one of things of which he was most proud. I know little of the Masons but these particular men were pushy and aggressive at the funeral ordering us around in an intrusive and obnoxious way. I did the best I could to not bust the old crocks up side the head and I succeeded in that and getting through the service and my eulogy.

My grandparents had sold their house to supplement their Social Security and bought a condo. After the services the family and guests gathered here and their friend Jim Valint had driven up from California. He was a tenant in their apartment building and had bought it from them; they took back a second to facilitate his buy years before at below market interest. Valint was a heavy drinker and a crude man that I felt was untrustworthy.

Valint had the audacity to bring up his money problems and need of time, after three non-payments of the second mortgage, and he chose this occasion to tell me he needed time for a fourth nonpayment. I had no involvement in their deal. Prior to Gramp's death, he and Gram were living on Social Security, the savings they had left from the house sale and the interest Valint paid them. I told Jim that what he was doing in this situation, with my grandmother distraught and my grandfather just buried was contemptible. I later resolved the matter without having any further contact with this man.

My grandfather's inability to breathe and my alacrity in getting him to emergency in the 'sixties was most likely a precursor and that may have given him another thirteen years before his stroke. In her nineties my grandmother told me that the two years she had been given to care for John in his extremely limited state allowed her to go on.

She said that she believed she would have killed herself, something no one in the family would have ever believed she would do, if I had not fought for her getting those twenty-four months to care for and slowly let go of John. I really only did what I thought was the right, logical and caring thing to do while still maintaining my commitments to my work—the bloody show went on.

My grandfather's death preceded our move from Manhattan to California. I had been very fortunate and no one in my family had died until John. This always overpowering sense of loss, even if the person gone has not been kind or caring to you, threatens your very existence and reminds you forcefully of your own fears of mortality. You are going to die whether in thirty years or tomorrow. This is something we all ignore or avoid but in a funereal situation there is no way to sidestep the truth. I was thirty-two.

I missed the old bastard despite his treatment of me and the fact that he had set only negative examples, as did my father, as a male role model. It made me furrow deeper into myself, to change, and helped me contend with my ever-present struggles with my depressive states, which is odd given the grief and depression that is natural to feel when someone who has been around your entire life disappears forever.

By now all television shows were in color except for a very few reruns or older movies. Our MMC black and white films reran from 1975-1977 and Disney was so surprised at the enormous interest in the original series that they came up with *The New Mickey Mouse Club* in 1977. This was jazzed up as a "go-go show" and was ethnically filled out much more than the original but it was thought out, written and directed poorly and only ran for two seasons.

Later in 1975, our transition from one coast to another was relatively easy. I preceded Diane and stayed with my aunt Pudd the non-driving lady, and her husband, Bob, in Van Nuys and looked for an apartment. Pudd, her mother Mame, her brother Billy and my grandmother were probably the only humans in California who never had a driver's license. I found a duplex 2-bedroom, 1.5-bath about a thousand square feet plus with a built-in bar and far enough away from the pool to not be bothered. It was only $250 a month, which was less than in NYC and seems ludicrously low in 2009. Diane flew out, approved, and we had our furniture and paraphernalia shipped out.

California was not there as I had known it. Everything had started sliding downhill toward what I had encountered in New York, Baltimore, Pittsburgh, D.C. and other eastern cities. It was not an earthquake-quick jolt but the place had changed. It was still better than other places I had lived or worked in but my home proved that Thomas Wolfe just might be right.

We became Southern California habitués of North Hollywood not far from where I had lived before moving to Manhattan. I had begun writing a satirical memoir entitled *Confessions of a Mad Mouseketeer* in the Apple and I continued while working on a new play and a TV pilot titled *HIKE*. I sought an acting agent but the woman I signed with was not big enough to have much access to the studios for more than day player work. I was not going to go up for a support in a film, nor a TV series, nor a pilot but I could make some money and become eligible to collect unemployment.

Collecting unemployment bothered me despite the fact that money from your paycheck and also from your employer is held by the state on your behalf, so you are receiving money set aside specifically for that purpose. It is not charity, nor is it welfare, nor food stamps. At that time you had to appear at the unemployment office in person and stand in line once a week to collect your money. Film star Laurence Harvey arrived in a chauffer-driven Rolls Royce at the Hollywood office, and stood in line like the rest of us.

No young artist in any field, particularly acting, could get by without unemployment. Unlike other fields of endeavor, your years of good work, talents, accomplishments, credits, many recorded on tape and film and the whole caboodle rarely means a thing in showbiz.

The very best you can hope for is that your chance will occur and it is useless to think that your resume will get you even an audition, let alone the job, except in rare instances. This is why residuals, as well as unemployment, are crucial to actors and, very obviously in 2007-2008, writers and, to a lesser degree, directors but primarily actors, who, except for stars and second leads, make less than writers and directors.

After our move Diane had some temp jobs, then worked at American City Bank on South Beverly Drive in Beverly Hills as an entertainment consultant, which means she was part of a two-person team that tried to put together money deals between filmmakers and the bank. So there was more than one visit to Le Bistro but nothing was ever produced. She also worked briefly for Tom McDermott, who was hired to run Four Star Productions after founder William Powell became ill, but that was a dead end, too.

She then became one of two people involved in creating the West Coast second office of the W. Colston Leigh lecture agency and we were doing all right. We both became involved in ANTA (The American National Theatre & Academy) productions and I played a role in an original play at the small Merle Oberon Playhouse in Hollywood. Diane produced plays there and one I had written was performed through ANTA. Janyce and I tapped on a pilot of *The Lorenzo Music Show for* Louis DaPron; Lorenzo was an actor/writer/producer who played the voice of Carleton the Doorman on *Rhoda*, a spinoff of the *Mary Tyler Moore Show*. Lorenzo also was the voice of Garfield the Cat. While auditioning people for the role, the creator of Garfield, Jim Davis, is reported to have said, "I looked at the room full of [voice] actors and then in the corner I saw Lorenzo quietly licking himself."

I began writing articles and reviews for the ANTA magazine and then other magazines and newspapers opened up to my work. My magazine profile of Bernie Peters for *In The Know* came out in November, 1975 and I started to work regularly for *Valley Magazine*. I played Plato opposite character actor John Dehner's Aristotle for ANTA's drama *The Mask of Silenus*. Doreen and I did nude tests as a duo for *Playgirl* magazine but they decided to not go forward, which in many ways I am grateful for now. These were not to be sleazy or graphic like the shots she had done for more gritty girlie mags.

Diane and I had also both become involved with Actors Alley, a theatre group in Van Nuys that put together a season of four to five plays a year. Among the members were David Soul who went on to star in the TV cop series *Starsky and Hutch* and Frank Bonner, who sold the radio station's air time in gaudy suits on *WKRP*.

Diane began producing with an original, *The Ice Cream Sunday* by a TV soap writer and then T.S. Eliot's *The Cocktail Party*. I directed Ionesco's *The Bald Soprano* in an original manner: with no cross-dressing, nor indications of anything sexual, the women's roles were played by men and vice versa. A few audience members were confused, but it got huge laughs and Ionesco would have loved it.

I had also fallen into a meaningful relationship with Penelope, whom I had dated briefly in college in the late 'fifties. I called her and we went out during the months Diane was still in NYC and I was in California. We instantly fell in love. As always, she knew going in that I loved and lived with Diane and she accepted the situation. Actually she has had a number of relationships with married men and has never married. There were complications, naturally, and far too soon she called Diane and suggested they have lunch.

They were both mature and accessible women and found they got along well. My relationship with Penelope lasted about three years and was only brought down by her neuroses, which are comparable to those of just about every single one of Tennessee Williams' leading ladies. She was a fair-haired brunette, sexy and tall and lithe, a good actress and a pretty good artist who really enjoyed sex.

In the 'nineties, long after Pen and I had ceased being intimate, Di and I bought the house next door to our own and searched for acceptable tenants. Penelope moved in with two friends, a woman and a man and, for a while, all was copacetic. She and I never fell back into our love trysts. Actually, it was a bit trying having her that close and, unfortunately, our last meeting was a shouting argument outside my home which she instigated and I finished.

The *ménage à trios* of me, Penelope and Diane, which was more figurative than literal, worked really quite well. Any sensual pleasures were not between the two women, neither of whom had any sexual interest in each other. Pen was open to other male relationships but she was not very often interested in other men as she had been prior to our finding each other years after college. The two of us in any combination and the three of us had some wonderful times together and when I think of her it is not how she acted after we stopped being lovers, which was grim and nasty and cold, nor our last outburst, nor her despicable lack of control over her neuroses but as it was and how I hoped it could have continued for much longer. We ran into each other on a commercial audition in 2006. It was reserved, not nasty, but quite enough.

I occasionally would do a talk show anent the MMC, like *America Alive*, and I had written a two-act comedy titled *Over the Hill* which had its world premiere at the MET theatre in 1984. It was my first produced play. It had generally good reviews and ran longer than most plays do in L.A. I had another play published before *Hill*, a satire entitled *Who's Afraid of David Mamet?*

I had miscast my lead in *Hill*, a man whom I would later replace when he left a lead role in the play *Tamara*. He was a soap actor and just did not comprehend comedy timing. I believed I could bring him through it and I usually get much more out of actors than they think they have, but this time I failed. The producer and stage manager, Diane, fired him after a few weeks; I took over his role and things went much better. It is the only time I have written an original, produced play, directed it and played the lead. After we closed, I hoped it would get picked up but nothing much happened except a copy of the play is in the Skirball Cultural Center in Los Angeles.

I worked with a brilliant set designer, Keith Hein, who had put together the set for my *La Cantatrice Chauve* (*The Bald Soprano*) as he had Diane's Eliot play and he also moved from the surreal set for Ionesco in end staging—two audience seating areas, the stage against the back of the small theatre—to my realistic comedy in a proscenium house. He was excellent at his craft/art but unfortunately we did not work together again. He had been nominated for an Emmy for set decoration later in the 'eighties and I know would have been a major designer for Broadway and film but he died young of AIDS in 1987, the same year that Diane's brother Douglas died of this horrendous virus.

Meanwhile, Diane was offered a position in administration at the Norton Simon Museum in Pasadena, to my mind and prior to Diane's work there, the best museum in the Los Angeles area due to the impeccable, eclectic taste of the art chosen. I must say it was wonderful to be able to view the works in silence without all the rude slobs tittering and saying obtuse things, which I managed via Diane one day when the museum was closed. The only thing vaguely similar was being alone on an empty stage in an ancient, empty theatre.

She eventually moved into the position of Associate Curator and at Mr. Simon's request researched the attempts of the world's major museums to protect their art works from vandals and sun damage. The Norton Simon ground floor is very open to the sun to show off exterior sculptures, ponds and landscaping. Diane's work was instrumental in their decision to use more UV filtering Plexiglas, which corrects light reflection better than plain glass and is less friable. This re-sparked the philosophical, aesthetic and pragmatic debates among museum curators that had been around for a while: is it right to create a barrier between art and the viewer even when doing so preserves the work in a far superior way for later generations?

My literary agent in NYC had not been able to gather interest in my *Confessions of a Mad Mouseketeer* satire which was about 100 pages along, but he did get me my first book contract through a very easy exercise on my part. The Simon and Schuster publishing company was looking for a writer for a book on comedy teams. My agent gave them my background in show business and comedy including my work as a child with Martin & Lewis and Abbott & Costello along with my credits as a writer.

My pro heavy shot in the late '70s. Being a character actor, I always maintain five or six looks, not just a commercial smile.

I only had to write a three-page treatment describing how I would proceed and give them a page of chapter headings for teams ranging from the Marx four to George Burns and Gracie Allen to modern teams like Bob and Ray, the Smothers Brothers and Rowan and Martin.

Most people assume you write a book THEN try to get it looked at on your own or acquire an agent who then attempts to get it read and, you hope, published. That is the most frequent approach but I was making money writing for magazines and newspapers more than anything else although I did catch an acting gig here and there and got an advance for a book. It was not huge, I was not a known writer, but it helped.

I wrote a number of cover stories on stars like Robert (RJ) Wagner, Ben Vereen, Loretta Swit of *M*A*S*H*, Erik Estrada and Susan Anton, the latest pretty, blond starlet star on a short-lived TV series *Cliffhangers* which did not run, after which Ms. Anton seemed to disappear. Ben was open and easy; Ms. Swit was difficult and insisted on taking me to the Polo Lounge in the Beverly Hills Hotel which did not impress me. She was very closed and was accompanied by her press agent, which no star before, nor after, did. All she seemed to want to talk about was her French Provincial house and furniture. This article was never used by the magazine; there just was nothing interesting to write about.

I interviewed Estrada on location for *CHiPs*. Mr. Estrada was busy at the time designated for our interview so I waited and watched his trailer rock back and forth quite a lot. Then a young woman came out and I was invited in. He smirked through telling me about his growing up on the streets and accidentally getting his break. I managed to put together something readable but it was not easy.

RJ Wagner is a charmer. He either is one of the most disarming and friendly guys in show business or one of the best con artists; I will never know which it is but I enjoyed interviewing him in his trailer outside the sound stage on which they shot *Hart to Hart* which he also produced. He also took me onto the set and I wrote a very complimentary article about him. He is one smart business man.

I also accidentally met his remarried wife Natalie Wood, another child star and an HPS alumna, before her untimely and questionable death at sea. I had never been a fan of Ms. Wood, thinking her mildly attractive and more the memorizer majority of actors. She knocked and entered the trailer dressing room and was strikingly beautiful in person; she had the loveliest skin on a woman I have ever seen. It was clear that her star quality had to do, like Annie, with her charisma.

RJ had never been considered a strong actor but he was a good looking fellow who got by in light roles, a lesser Cary Grant. He married Natalie twice and his current wife is Jill St. John who also attended HPS during my years; Natalie was at the school before me. I must confess to a crush on Jill, who, as I have mentioned, is intelligent and beautiful. At this point, I was a bit old to have an instant crush on Natalie, but I sure would have if I had been younger.

I met but had little time with RJ's costar Stephanie Powers. She was extremely attractive and pleasant. I always think of her long relationship with William Holden as very similar to Kate Hepburn and Spencer Tracy.

I was a film and theatre critic, wrote a column for *Entertainment Monthly* called "On the Wry Side" and sold comedy pieces and more. Reviewing plays and films too quickly became drudgery for me. I could write great things about the movie *Gandhi* but then I had to suffer through horrid films and plays that I would have walked out of if I had paid to see them.

In my first semester of college I read an essay by John Stuart Mill in which he argued that you could not judge a thing or reject it until you were fully aware of its totality. This misled me for years as did his quote, "I'd rather be a man dissatisfied than a pig satisfied." The problem is, of course, that J.S. Mill had never been a pig, thus, could not judge it. In philosophy this is called begging the question. For years I would start reading a book and continue even though it held no interest for me. I stopped that in my late twenties and I still walk out of, or stop reading, anything that I cannot get interested in, only I do it much more easily and frequently. A critic must see too many popular movies or unknown plays that are crass, uninteresting, amateurish and unfunny. I knew that unless I was dedicated and could abide the good, so-so and terrible as well as persist in making little money unless I got hot and rose to the top of the field, which is precarious and not guaranteed whatever your insights and abilities, it would not work for me.

From the '70s and into this century I worked for such papers as the *Los Angeles Times, The Cincinnati Enquirer, The Sacramento Bee,* the *Los Angeles Herald Examiner,* the *Las Vegas Sun,* the *Santa Barbara News-Press* and *The Washington Times [D.C.].* The mags included *L.A. Weekly, Big Valley, American Film, Amtrak Express, Scriptwriter, Louisville Today, Kentucky Life, Film Notes* (Australia), *Dramatics* magazine, *Arkansas Times, Disney Channel Magazine, Antiques and Collectibles* and eventually e-zines. I was variously listed as Arts Editor, Editor, Drama Critic, Film Critic, Contributing Arts Editor, columnist or just Lonnie Burr.

In the late 'seventies I became involved with American Radio Theatre for which I wrote four scripts with a 224-station syndicate and in the 'seventies and early 'eighties I was a staff writer and did twenty-one scripts with a 500-station syndicate across the U.S for the radio drama *Heartbeat Theatre*. In this century

I donated these scripts and copies of the shows as aired live, which were translated from vinyl to CDs, to the Thousand Oaks Library in Thousand Oaks, California. I added notes and script rewrites also and they are held as the Lonnie Burr Collection. This library is one of the most copiously stocked and best known repositories of radio drama and comedy in America.

The radio shows were WGAw sanctioned so I was paid and had very strict format requirements so I learned at the same time I was creating. Despite their emotional rather than emotional-plus-intellectual approach, I always managed to get in an allusion to a poem, philosopher, artist or historical tidbit, something so that the listener would also learn while being moved.

My book was published by the Messner division of Simon & Schuster in 1979 as *Two For The Show: Great Comedy Teams*. I was not happy with many of the changes made by my editor, which is the case with many authors, and I did not like their lack of promotion for the book. I have had problems with editors in a number of situations. The last was in this century at the *Washington Post*. I had written about the MMC and used a sentence in which I said that the show embarrassed me until the 1980 revelation and I had a long agon regarding the experience for years.

I assumed this foolish, youthful editor could not find agon, which means argument, in his spellcheck and decided it should be the word agony without calling or emailing me to find out if I intended to use that word. There is a substantive difference between having an argument about an experience and feeling agony.

When I read this stupidity in the paper I was livid and e-mailed him. I explained politely, without anger, what agon meant. I added that it is in, from whence I learned it, the first sentence, "The agon begins." of the first novel, *The Black Book*, by the famous English author Lawrence Durrell, he of *The Alexandria Quartet* and other volumes. All the little twit had to do was inquire. His em response was a Seinfeldism, "My bad." I am convinced that this instance and hordes of others in the present is the result of children who learn via calculators and computers rather than using their minds and reading books.

Two For The Show had three editions, one of which I updated regarding deaths and other matters, but never made big bucks. I went on a promo tour on my own dollar along the West Coast up through Oregon. I also saw my old pal Clayton Moore (the one and only Lone Ranger) on my book tour when he and I anchored a NYC autograph show. I have never seen his face. The Wrather Corporation owned the rights to the Ranger and Clayton was

Dad (in remission) and Diane at the book signing for Two For The Show *at Dave Dutton's great book store in North Hollywood, 1979.*

prohibited from wearing the Ranger mask so he wore huge sunglasses that hid his face. They were making a Lone Ranger movie and after it bombed Clayton, in 1985, got the right to wear his mask again.

Since his partner Tonto, Jay Silverheels, was deceased, Clayton brought along Iron Eyes Cody, whom I had not worked with nor met previously. It was later learned that Iron Eyes was not a Native American but of Italian descent. He portrayed Native Americans in numerous films, married an Indian woman and adopted two Indian children. He did not put on his wig and costume just for specific roles but played this role all of his life, dressing in full regalia and wig when he left his home. He was eventually accepted by Native Americans after his lie was discovered. They felt his Italian heritage did not demean the fact that he had done good things for them. Who does not recall the early ecological, anti-pollution TV commercial that showed Iron Eyes with one tear streaming down his face after seeing images of humans destroying the earth in their uncaring hubris? It may be more wide ranging than learning to spell EN-CYC-LO-PEDIA from Jiminy Cricket, even though it is an incorrect way to put the word into syllables. Of course, those of us in the business might wonder if they used glycerin or post production work to make the one perfect tear.

Clayton and Cody both died in 1999.

This NYC autograph show was my first meeting with Leonard Maltin as well; I saw Leonard again when he was the host of the interviews a few of us original Mouseketeers did for the 2004 first DVD of the MMC which shows the entire first week of the 'fifties series without commercials, over five hours of programming, as well as color versions of some things never shown on television, except in black and white. We discussed our remembrances of Jimmie, Walt and other Mice, including Annie, who was too ill to join us. In 2006 the ten mostly badly chosen VHS tapes of the original MMC which came out in 1992 were translated into "the best of" DVDs. *Spin and Marty* became DVDs one year later.

After the comedy team collection, my agent next wanted me to write a book on religion. I had absolutely no interest in doing that. The agent apparently took umbrage at this and I have never heard from him since except when he rejected a manuscript I sent to him in the 'nineties. Since he was a literary agent, supposedly more literate than an acting agent, I was surprised by his supercilious, bizarre behavior.

I waited until the copyright reverted to me and in 2000 updated the book, redesigned the hideous cover S &S had used and under the iUniverse Back In Print series the book came out for the first time as a paperback: *Two For The Show: Great 20th Century Comedy Teams* updated from 1979 to 2000, thus covering the entire century.

Teams started in the late 19th century in vaudeville and moved on to silent films and burlesque. I used Smith and Dale as my first team and representative for they met in a bicycle collision, exchanged retorts, and decided they could make money doing it on stage. They started making moola in 1896 and much, much later played the Ed Sullivan Show. It has been alleged that Doc Simon used them as a prototype for his comedy *The Sunshine Boys*. Joe Smith was still alive and when I interviewed him he was living in the Englewood, New Jersey Actors Fund Home.

My book was concise and more comprehensive than other comedy team books, like Leonard's earlier one limited to movie teams. He also included Hope & Crosby, who did a number of films together but did not meet my definition of a comedy team just as Belushi & Ackroyd as The Blues Brothers did not make a team, nor did the Pythons, nor the later *Saturday Night Live* cast.

Cover of the updated paperback of my book on comedy teams, 2000.

I was also eclectic in not including teams that really did not make it big for a long period of time, like the Wiere Brothers, Olsen & Johnson and the well-known 19th century team of Weber & Fields, letting Smith & Dale, who also did some film work, indicate all of these teams.

My book also took teams through 1979, so I covered Bob & Ray, Nichols & May, the Smothers Brothers, Rowan and Martin, Stiller & Meara, Burns and Schreiber and, the least effective but financially productive team of the 'seventies Cheech y Chong. I also put in Mel Brooks and Carl Reiner, which could be challenged but I found them hilarious together, for their series of albums and TV performances with Mel as the "2000 Year Old Man." These two were friends and also both worked on Sid Caesar's writing team in early television. Michael Stewart, my late friend who became a prominent Broadway musical book writer and sometime lyricist did most of the typing for the comedy writers on this show and along with Woody Allen started out on Sid's quorum of writers.

I used one lesser-known team to show the transition that teams were going through in the 'seventies from performing to writing: Clair & McMahon. This is one of the explanations for the demise of team comedy. Dick Clair and Jenna McMahon had some success but gave up performing to be writers for *The Mary Tyler Moore Show*, *The Bob Newhart Show*, *Maude*, Dick Van Dyke's second sitcom *The New Dick Van Dyke Show* and finally on staff for *The Carol Burnett Show*.

Patchett and Tarses were a performing team who took the same path beginning with the *Alf* series. Most folks are unaware that George Carlin started out in a team, Burns and Carlin. They started in radio and were both DJs at the same station in Boston, like Bob and Ray before them and the two white men who played Amos 'n Andy even earlier. They moved to live performance and even cut an album but they were both two fast talking white guys. Comedy teams are made up of disparate elements and their similarity doomed the team. Jack Burns later became known with Avery Schreiber as Burns and Schreiber, whom I included, but eventually he made the transition alone to writing comedy for television and other outlets.

Diane and I became friends with the late Dick Clair and she almost physically forced him to replace one of the roasters at my surprise 40th birthday party, without any material written and against his better judgment. He came with his then well-known female shrink, Susan Forward, and she encouraged him to "just get up and do it."

Dick was the funniest roaster of the night beginning with saying that he was replacing someone who did not show up to roast me and that was, perhaps, the greatest roast of all. He then glibly mentioned my relentless heterosexuality, referring to some comments from previous roasters. The roast took place by the pool at Mouseketeer Tommy's house and Annette and some other Mice were present as well as the lady we had worked with at Disneyland who played Mickey Mouse and got into the Mickey Mouse outfit to surprise me—with a rare special dispensation from Disneyland.

Pointing directly at me, Dick said, "I recall *The Mickey Mouse Club*... but I don't remember *him*."

The fact is that after the breakup of Cheech and Chong in 1985 there has been no viable comedy team. The Smothers Brothers eventually did make appearances from time to time but not often, although in 2009 they are touring their act again. Team comedy, a staple of vaudeville, burlesque, radio, films, TV, records, tapes, CDs and now DVDs, just disappeared. I believe this should be investigated in another book but no publishing house has been interested—*wink, wink*.

I taught again, this time at UCLA—with no permanent commitment beyond one semester. The course was boorishly titled "Creative Writing"; I did not choose the course name but what is the alternative, "*Un*creative Writing"? This did not go as well as my later work as an educator in advanced tap and jazz dance, acting and directing, but it opened up another way for me to make some money, between acting

With Disney Legend Bill Justice at WDW—very close to being a comedy team! 1995.

jobs and paying writing jobs, that I was good at and enjoyed as long as I was not tied down to teaching the same things for a long period of time.

I was disappointed about the book but was working on another play, writing regularly for mags and papers and radio, and looking for acting jobs, which I got but less often than I preferred. I had no idea that there was going to be an amazing resurgence of interest in *The Mickey Mouse Club* as all those Boomers got nostalgic and Disney finally came to the conclusion that there was still interest in the original Mouseketeers.

The 1980s turned out to be a very busy, rewarding and well-paying decade for me and for Diane. Seeing the Mouseketeers after twenty-five years made a lot of folks in our age range, their parents who had watched along and even younger generations, feel young again—at least until the next news broadcast or paper delivery. Actually, the Mouseketeers seeing each other after twenty-five years was a bit like relocating lost members of your family. It was also a devastating decade of death.

Chapter 15

Renaissance Mouseketeers (or the Middle Ages?)

My dad contracted pancreatic cancer in 1978 when he was sixty-five. He assiduously avoided doctors so the disease had taken hold and begun to metastasize before he was diagnosed. He went through chemo and, although not cured, he went into remission for over nine months before wasting away quickly and dying.

As I mentioned, my dad and I had virtually no relationship when I was growing up for he blocked me out after Dot made it clear that her life focused on me and my career and a few years later also on her talent agency. He never said it, but Dad was jealous of the attention I received and seemed to have no interest in my success in school, in movies, TV, theatre or even in playing football. That one hug he gave me when I flew off for the first MMC personal appearance tour in 1955 was changed when I sought reconnection as an adult for I would hug him when we met and he did not seem to have a problem with that.

When they divorced just after I finished high school and turned fifteen, he absconded and I did not hear from him for years. I contacted him in my early twenties and began to build a new relationship with my dad. It was more like older brother to younger brother but he insisted from time to time on giving me a ten or maybe a twenty when I had been making my living on my own for quite some time and his truck driving job made him very little comparatively. Initially I resisted, but I needed to let him do this so I did. I knew it was what he wanted, perhaps in a small way to make up for excluding me as a child and teenager.

He remarried a very unlikable, NY tough, know-it-all female named Paula who was similar to Mom in size and also bleached her hair blonde. They met—as was the case with most women Dad met—at a bar that had a dance band; women found his dancing irresistible and sexy. According to Paula, he followed through in the bedroom.

When Diane and I moved to L.A. in 1975 we began seeing Dad and Paula. Usually we visited their place, played the card game Hearts and had a few drinks and laughs. I managed to put up with Paula, as did Di, despite her overbearing personality, very like Mouseketeer Darlene and my brother-in-law David's relentlessly pushy wife Barbara who once, shortly after we met, attacked Diane at a family dinner out.

I defend people I care about and I stopped Barbara dead without raising my voice, nor resorting to profanity, nor even a sarcastic retort. I merely told her that what she said to Diane was offensive to me, which shut her up for once. She never forgot that or the fact that she was a successful government economist with monstrous holes in her liberal arts education and general knowledge which showed when we discussed many subjects. Her sense of humor was in need of repair, especially if inference or knowledge was part of the equation.

I am a very funny fellow existentially, but not a joke teller. I have never had the impetus to go on stage and do a routine, preferring to get laughs behind the persona of a character or casually in a social situation. I have made Diane laugh with new material for about thirty-eight years and that really helps a long-term relationship.

One time I attempted to explain to Barbara, when she asked, the humor of something I said that Diane, Dave and I cracked up at. As all comedians and comedy writers know, an explained joke is no longer funny and that was the fact in this instance. I felt restricted around her because of this and her overbearing demeanor.

The last time (other than Hilda's death) that the four of us were together was for dinner at their home in Virginia. Over dinner she brought up a tender conflict between Diane and me that Diane had mistakenly mentioned to her in confidence while living with them prior to our finding our home in Maryland. She began her all too frequent Barbara-knows-it-all by telling Diane what she should do differently. Diane was embarrassed and chagrined; I was angry. The evening ended soon after the onslaught. From that time forward I bowed out of meetings with them unless it was mandatory. Diane communicates with David fairly often and visited both her brothers in Arizona in 2007. Diane had lunch with Dave and Barbara in Laguna in mid-2008 when they paid a visit to California.

I had cared a lot about Douglas, more than anyone in the family except for Diane and Hilda, but he had turned inward and sour, for no reason I was aware of, in our later meetings before he contracted AIDS. In our first meeting at Diane's and my apartment in NYC, before she got home from work, the two of us talked for a couple hours laughing and really enjoying each other. This is unusual for two guys who have never met and sports never came up once. During my first visit to the Dickeys' Georgetown home, where Doug lived, he began speaking English in an Indian dialect and I responded immediately and we made the whole family and a few close friends all the merrier. We had a very definite affinity for each other.

A third brother, Chris Bliss, is an exceptional juggler (a skill he learned, incidentally, from Diane). He was the opening act for one of Michael Jackson's early tours and later a juggling YouTube star. In addition to receiving millions of hits, he is known as a comedian in the corporate world. After Willie Nelson saw Chris juggle, he alerted others to his throwing things around in synch with rock music and Chris got work. He started adding Seinfeldesque comedy which he wrote. In time he made the transition to stand-up comic who would, once in a while, juggle. Chris seemed compelled to compete with me. He was quite hurtful, snide, and aggressive on many occasions; the last I recall was outside the L.A. comedy club where he was appearing.

When I returned to California in the mid-'seventies, I went on a commercial interview for which Jay Leno, not a star yet, was also auditioning. He incessantly made jokes that some were amused by, but those of us who depended on making a living spent time working with the copy and thinking about how we were going to approach the few seconds of camera time we would get. Leno never stopped and had no interest in anything but being the center of attention.

Chris is a fairly good stand-up but he is too similar to Leno at that commercial audition, his brother Dave's wife and Mouseketeer Darlene. Chris needs to be the center of attention and that is something for which I really have no affinity.

David and Barbara came to our house in Maryland once and he and I went to a nearby street fair without our wives. I asked Dave out for a drink once but he was unavailable and we saw them rarely even though only separated by about a half hour ride. David did not attack me as Chris did but he never called to talk to me or ever sought me out in the seven years we lived fairly close together. With Barbara in tow, I was unavailable.

Chris drove me back to the airport after the trip to Pennsylvania to bury Douglas' ashes in the Finch family cemetery and he suggested we get together for a drink, for we both lived in L.A then. That, of course, never happened and we only saw each other on Thanksgiving at their second home in the Valley. I disliked his inviting a seemingly stoned buddy of his, also a stand-up, and his lady without alerting us. The guy was on the whole time, Chris, for once, letting someone else be the center of attention.

Thanksgiving is for family, not ego-obsessed acquaintances. I did not enjoy a performance by a guy who was sometimes funny, sometimes not funny at all being forced upon me. I was reminded of Tommy and Darlene at Doreen's party. I do not recall his name and have never seen him do anything. I have not seen Chris, affable Daisy, nor her pleasant sister Dorothy except for Hilda's burial and memorial in 1995. Both brothers moved to Phoenix and it is easy for me to have no contact with them.

I recall criticizing both of Diane's brothers because they could not be bothered to remember their sister's birthday, the slightly older sister Hilda had made do much of the raising of all three boys, by sending a simple card. They apologized but they continue forgetting her birthday sometimes or remembering via e-mail. In-laws are in-laws are in-laws, except for Hilda.

Diane and I used to go out frequently in NYC but after we moved to L.A. Diane quit smoking and since the hardest place to not smoke was a bar, when that was still allowed, we did not go out for a drink—ever. She did not stop until 1988 but in L.A. there just is not that much to do at night except meeting with friends or going out to dinner. Our only close friends, the Coles, were raising two kids they had adopted in the 'eighties and Sharon's husband was a very difficult man from both of our points of view.

Then Paula had some serious problems with her eyes, after she and Dad bought a house in the north Valley. She was convinced they were the result of a gypsy woman who had come to the door to seek money, was refused and literally put the evil eye upon Paula, who was a believer in such witchery. Later Howard and Paula separated well into their second decade together and eventually divorced.

McGowan and Company was the metallurgy firm Dad had worked for from 1947 to 1978 when he was diagnosed with cancer. They promptly let him go and gave him five thousand dollars as severance pay. He had only that, an older vehicle he owned outright and he was beginning Social Security. No testimonial, no kind words, no Rolex—just five grand and a wave

Diane and I are happy and relaxed at the Seacliff beach house in 1980 and we're equally content six years later at a friend's house in 1986.

after more than thirty years of being on time, causing no trouble and doing good work. Not a golden parachute but one made of tissue paper. American business and greed marches on, unconcerned and prosperous.

Dad took a room in an older woman's house and managed to get out dancing as often as he could. I saw him from time to time and Diane and I took him out to dinner. He managed about seven or eight months before his cancer began to take over. After a few months of debilitating chemo, he began to recover and went into remission.

I first got him into a good assisted-living home and added what I could to the fees. It was soon clear he hated it there and I was ashamed of having him live in that situation. I asked my aunt Pudd to take him into her house with Bob for a while and she always liked Ham.

Pudd's mother, my aunt Mamie, took Dad in after a few months with Pudd and let him use one of her three bedrooms. Mame and two of her sons, Vernie and Billy, in their late fifties, still lived together in my grandmother's former apartment building. The two guys barely got by working sporadically and for little recompense. They shared a bedroom to make room for Dad and Mamie had time to see to Dad's needs. At least he was with family members he had known most of his life and not stuck in a room with a stranger. Jack, the fourth phantom sibling of Mame's, whom I only saw when I was very young, was "the black sheep"; he was a heavy drinker and had been incarcerated many times.

In the anger and sorrow of all he had not done and done to me when I was a youngster and teenager, Dad's death disturbed me greatly, as did his last Thanksgiving with the family in 1979, after just being released from a long hospital stay due to his dreadful pain and huge loss in weight and strength. This whole period was a sad one for me and pushed my depressive buttons. I drank more, but only at home.

By then my mom had divorced her second husband. She had visited in 1979 for our family Thanksgiving but she had not made the trip to see Dad. Later she would allow Don, her ex, to live with her when he was dying of cirrhosis. I took it badly that she had not seen Dad except by accident before he died, although I avoided bringing it up for it would only cause more rancor between us.

Even with his painkillers, Dad was in constant agony, could keep no solid food down and slept only fitfully. He asked me to help him kill himself. I knew this was right but I feared the law so I explained which of his pills he should take and the amount needed, then, like a coward, I left. He did what I said but could not manage to keep enough of them down.

The call from Mame early in the morning on January 28, 1980 came after she was unable to wake him up and an ambulance had taken him to the hospital. Diane and I rushed over. He survived for another day but he had managed to set in motion the process of his escape. When he and I were alone he gave me a look that made me feel as if I had failed him as a human by not helping him fully accomplish his exit from inevitable death and pain into peace.

The next day he died and, after seeing to the necessities, I attended an audition for a stage role at the Mark Taper Theatre downtown. I thought it best to go to take my mind off what I was going through. It was a supra-real experience but I ran into a couple of actors I knew and it helped. It was far superior to immediately dealing with my loss.

Diane and I took care of the paperwork and went through the procedures for his requested cremation. Dad had not designated a place to have his ashes strewn, telling me he really did not care, so I did what I thought was right for him. When my mom died twenty-three years later in 2003, Diane and I unofficially interred her ashes by putting them into the Burr dual burial plots for Glade and John in Boulder City, Nevada. I told Diane that I hoped Dot and Dash were somewhere together dancing forever, thus, unable to argue. They both would be very happy and all would be swell.

I was grateful my dad was alive to see my first book published the year before, my first play produced, to know that I was able to take care of myself and that Diane and I would stay together. I later wrote a radio play based on a son's failing to help his father take his own life and eventually a quite different two act stage drama, *Exeunt All*, in which a son has a relationship with his dying father in scenes after his dad's death while the son is at an actual Thanksgiving with the rest of the family. The son confesses his lack of character and strength to help his father fulfill his wish to defeat his horrid pain by death. These two works (both of which were produced) seemed to expiate some of my guilt but never all of it.

Writing the play also gave me an opportunity to get some anger out at Scotty's brashly intruding priest and, worse, the doctors and specifically the oncologist who would have my pained, weak, frail father sitting in his wheel chair in the waiting room unable to even read the boring magazines, one time for over an hour, to be seen as the doc paid for his BMWs, Hawaii vacations, expensive home and golf bets by shuttling people from one cubicle to another. I have found that the Hippocratic Oath is only taken seriously by some physicians. I did the best I could for Dad and it was not good enough.

So much for being a perfect son.

Diane was much more effective with her brother Douglas, who died of natural causes while suffering through AIDS in 1987. Douglas specifically forbade Hilda's participation and help but without Diane I do not believe that her two living brothers would have been as efficient at helping Douglas find the peace he sought just as my father had. If his father Ray had lived to see Doug diagnosed with and die of AIDS the SOB would probably have disowned him.

Women are stronger than men in many ways; they just do not brag about it. They use their testosterone not as a weapon, but as a tool.

The 1980s were a decade of death for us as well as many others. Diane's father died in 1981 of a brain tumor. He had always feared he would die at sixty since all the males in his family had died at that age and he only made it to sixty-two before he succumbed. My aunt Mamie went from a heart attack in 1983; she had been obese for decades. Mame's son Vernie died in 1984 of lung cancer. I visited him in the L.A. Vets hospital

350   Confessions of An Accidental Mouseketeer

and it was a horrible place and experience. Vern had smoked since his World War II service in Germany and drank at least two six packs of beer daily.

Pudd now has her brother Billy living with her. Billy, who is eighty, drank two six-packs daily of Pepsi-Cola, but he also took vitamins and finally quit smoking so he is still with us after becoming debilitated by a stroke in 2002. He has more locomotive ability than my grandfather had after his stroke. Pudd, who had a minor stroke herself in 2007, helps him out although she is eighty-eight, with the predictable pains and problems of aging.

The first original Mouseketeer died in 1983. Mouseketeer Mike Smith was on the first season and was likable enough but was very prissy; his mother highlighted his auburn hair with blond streaks and forced him to wear a cap like the girls when he swam. He was not excessively talented and left after his first year. Our 25th Anniversary TV show only managed to have 31 of the 39 kids on the original series; some could not be found, others, like Jay-Jay refused to take part.

Diane took this shot of me, Mickey and Cheryl at a photo session for the press in front of the bridge to Fantasyland during the 1995 MMC 40th Anniversary celebration at WDW.

I was so consumed by doing *George M* in Vegas, two shows a night, six nights a week and being one of the hosts of the special that I am not sure of everyone who showed up for the taping of the live finale in which we hosts were joined by all the other Mice that could be gathered. I do know that Mike, Charley and Tim were there on that day and it was the last day any of us saw the three again.

Mike had not come out but we always assumed that (like Dennis on seasons one and two who came out of the closet in 1978) he was gay. Mike would have been thirty-seven the year he died.

Mouseketeer Charley died in the 1997 by his own hand and the third original Mouseketeer to die was Tim Rooney. Tim and his brother Mickey Jr., were the sons of Mickey Rooney. Tim died at sixty on September 23, 2006 after a long, tough battle against dermatomyositis, an inflammatory disease of connective tissues, manifested by skin inflammation and muscle weakness.

On January 6, 2009 our graceful "tenth" Mouseketeer, Cheryl Holdrige Reventlow Post, became the fourth original member of our show to die. She spent a brave and exhausting two years fighting lung cancer and decided, finally, to stop her medications and life support. Her warmth, smile and talent live on for all of us as well as for millions of fans. She devoted much of her life, after being successful in TV subsequent to the MMC, to charitable works.

The 'eighties was the decade of the AIDS crisis as well as other national and world wide disasters but with tragedy there is always rebirth, joy and positive activity and memories. A renascence is a renewal of life, vigor and interest and in 1980 the Mickey Mouse Club was revived in the minds of millions of fans from the 'fifties and many from the reruns in the 'sixties and 'seventies who wanted to remember their insouciant, happy days, singing along on the floor or the couch in front of the tube. They also wanted to see how their aging Mouseketeer buddies were and what we were doing as adults also nearing forty.

I started the year promoting my comedy teams book on the road after doing a signing at Dave Dutton's Books in North Hollywood but, alas, Dave later closed his store. His brother Doug's store Dutton's Books in Brentwood closed in 2008. They were like City Lights in San Francisco, great independent book stores. Dave's store was our second favorite after Bart's Books in Ojai, CA, south of Santa Barbara, which was sold by Gary Schlicter to Dave Ray and remains a rare and wonderful place for book lovers. They leave paperbacks on wooden shelves outside when they lock up at night and if you really need a read you take one or two and just toss the change over the gate into a courtyard.

My radio plays continued for Heartbeat Theatre and an original comedy radio play, *The Cat's out of the Closet*, aired for American Radio Theatre; it also won an award and was nominated for a more prestigious PBS award.

In 1978 the Mouseketeers were asked to participate in a reunion of sorts at Disneyland in which I refused to be involved. My problem was that they wanted the original Mice to appear for free at a media event to publicize something of Disney's at Disneyland, a long drive from my home. I asked for at least gas money and a small fee for the long drive and my time; they refused. I did not show up. None of the others would have even considered such a request for fair treatment. There is only one Mouseketeer Mensch [mensch n. a decent, mature and responsible person—Yiddish.] and that would be me.

We nine Mouseketeer hosts were in every scene of the NBC 25th Anniversary Special but we were paid union scale. Everyone else jumped at the opportunity. I thought we should be paid more for our larger roles, not an exorbitant fee but we were the only original stars, except for Sherry, who lasted the entire filming of the ground breaking, unique MMC and

Mouseketeer Mensch as a pegleg pirate in Hook *for Spielberg, 1991.*

the first humans to represent Disney and all of Walt's characters. I also knew that I would get no support from any of the other Mice, so I signed.

I did contact the producers and sent them my writing resume, suggesting that they could use a second writer who knew the show more intimately than they or their writer or director could. The only other Mouseketeers to become pro writers were Paul Petersen who wrote some paperbacks and Jay-Jay who wrote stories for biker magazines and has a book out compiling them.

Disney hired me to join the production staff and I was paid for my role as second writer and idea man. I was credited as Creative Consultant which was negotiated with WGAw, the Writers Guild of America west, of which I am now an emeritus member. Rod Warren, who was pleasant to work with, is listed as the sole writer.

Knowing Paul Williams, who tried out for the Mouseketeers and like Candice (Candy) Bergen, Edgar's daughter, did not get hired, was going to star, I came up with the idea he would look funny as a small, somewhat round adult male in glasses wearing the wrap-around horse used on Talent Roundup Day. This gag was successful but would return to haunt me later.

I joined the production too late to change some other things—for instance I did not have a featured number like some of the others—but left it alone. Nor could I do anything about Doreen being in the mouseka-doghouse because of her two nude, blatant photo layouts and being replaced by Sherry who was not remembered that well from just season two.

So eight of the nine who lasted the entire filming of the show were hosting and, in this instance, the ninth was Sherry. It is a mystery how she managed to become one of the principals in the show. I was told by one of the producers that Eileen had tried to do the same thing but failed.

Perhaps because they are both Italian and Catholic, Sherry instantly became close friends with Lorraine, the Disney liaison who took over after the Special, and later wrote the 1995 paperback that was published by Disney-owned Hyperion, which made sure the tome followed the company line: *The Official Mickey Mouse Club Book*.

Sherry has been featured ever since 1980 with the rest of us and even more in the last decade as she and Bobby became Disney spokespersons, I believe, due to her relationship with Lorraine who most likely passed them along to her replacement when she retired a few years ago. Ostensibly, Sherry has replaced Doreen for sure, Darlene, Sharon and Karen. Maybe Mouseketeer Mark could replace Mouseketeer Tommy if he gave it a shot.

Sherry's husband, Richard, has been our physician, except for our move back East from 1998-2005, since the beginning of the 'eighties. Even during our years back there we occasionally called him for medical advice. I hope that continues to be the case for he is a first-class, well-informed, caring doctor who adheres to the Hippocratic Oath.

I worked preproduction for the special earlier in the year and we began rehearsals for two weeks to shoot in July but the 1980 SAG strike shut down production. At the same time I was cast in *George M* at the downtown Union Plaza Hotel in Vegas which provided me with time to try to bridge a gap that existed between my mom and myself since I stayed at her house, the salary at the musical being less than overwhelming.

The 25th Anniversary Special started shooting after the SAG strike ended. After we broke from shooting, Diane picked me up and I tried to catch a commercial flight back to Vegas to do the show. This did not work out and for most of the daytime shooting at the studio and my panic race back to Vegas I had some financial help from Disney to hire a single prop plane to fly me from Burbank to McCarran Airport. Once there, I leaped into my car, drove lickety-split to the theatre, threw on makeup and raced onstage. I have ear problems in small aircraft and do not trust them but I needed the money and work. What I made as a writer over and above the other Mice was used for part of my daily transportation before the strike.

When they got behind in shooting, I had to miss the biggest tap number in the show. They knew that our choreographer Dee Dee Wood, who had done *The Sound of Music* and *Mary Poppins* was, like Gower and most choreos, not a tap expert. They decided to have Sharon do the tap choreography. I did not fight this, although I am and was an excellent tap choreo myself, because I was working behind the camera and making extra money. I did call Sharon and suggested she negotiate for money and screen credit, which she did.

The all-tap number in the special was to feature Sharon in the center in a threesome with Bob and me in front of one Mouse threesome on camera right and another threesome camera left behind us. The final special has Bob and Sharon in front of the two back groups. Such are the perils of being a working performer being overworked.

The show was a big hit. *Variety* said, among other things, it was "A marvelous evening of nostalgia…" and it gave Disney ideas for further revivals. Before I started the Vegas production of *George M*, Cubby, Sharon,

The first live show at Disneyland included kids from the New MMC in the '70s; here I am with Curtis Wong and Shawnte Northcutte, 1980.

Tommy and I did a live variety show on the Tomorrowland Stage with six of the kids from the 'seventies *New Mickey Mouse Club* and of course Mickey and other characters and the Disneyland band.

Many noted that the four of us, who had not worked together for over twenty years, seemed like a team while the six kids, who had worked together three years earlier, were like six separate performers. This show was put together by the usual Disneyland and WDW choreographers who are never going to work for Joe Layton, Fosse, Gower, Vincent Paterson, Twyla Tharp nor Kenny Ortega as I have. Kenny is the choreographer of the current *High School Musical* phenomena for Disney and the movie I did that he directed and choreographed, *Newsies*, was for Disney. He later used me as a dancing surgeon in a rare musical number on the last season of *Chicago Hope*.

The Disney choreographers with whom I have worked and others whose work I observed might do a halftime show at a football game, for it is much like the academic school style of dancing, too much cheerleading and no relationship at all to Alvin Ailey.

Bonnie Lynn Fields and I are trying to kick our boots off on a Talent Roundup number in the 1984 Disneyland show.

The producer of that first show with some kids from the "New MMC" in the 'seventies, Barbara Epstein, pushed through a second live performance at the Park in October through Thanksgiving with just the original Mouseketeers and Mickey and his gang of characters. She wanted me to write it, which I did, and she and I would co-choreograph some original numbers and do some on our own. I was very proud of the most complicated number that I created, with straw hats and canes à la Astaire. She also wanted me for the frequent Disney-no-credit-and-no-money to consult about the directing as well. After seeing the four of us dance as pros and as a unit, much better than we did as kids, Disney knew we could easily do it and with style.

But we had to find two more original girls so there would be three couples for dance numbers. We ran all the names but I really convinced Barbara that we needed Bonnie Lynn, the second Bonnie, with whom I had done Fosse's first film *Sweet Charity*—she was featured in "The Big Spender" number—for her dancing skills. I fought for Sherry because she was a good enough dancer and singer and she had a very solid stage presence which not all the other Mice had. This made me an accomplice to the caper she has pulled off since 1980 in her new position vis-à-vis the original nine of us and Cheryl.

This show was an even bigger hit than our first live venture earlier in the year and ran weekends in October and November through the Thanksgiving Day weekend. Many people saw the special and loved seeing us in person more, so we did three shows a day and a parade. One overheard comment as we waved to fans from the float we rode on: "God, they look great! I thought they were dead." I was once again into the flying back and forth to Vegas since the musical lasted into 1981. Disneyland had us back every year in a similar show around Thanksgiving through 1985, the MMC's 30th Anniversary.

Diane and I had rented a beach house in Seacliff, just south of Carpinteria and north of Ventura, before I moved for months to Vegas for the *George M* gig. After my double duties for the special and the live shows and the musical closed, I leased the beach house for a year. Diane came up on the weekends and I got a lot of writing and running done.

After deciding bike riding in L.A. was too dangerous on the streets and it was too far to go to find a safe place, say Griffith Park, where I

My first 10K, 1975.

could bike, I became a runner in 1975. I wanted to exercise, but my main purpose was to change my circadian rhythm. I had always been a night person, even when not in a play, and I learned that I preferred days but could not get to bed early, consumed as I was by Johnny Carson.

I ran a mile and soon managed two, then three. I began running three times a week at the Valley College track. Then I began training for my first 10K. I never found the commitment for a marathon and I, indeed, was still a smoker but I did well in the 10ks; I have a medal for winning one for my age group—mid-thirties.

I continued to run for almost two decades and added to my dancing now since the age of four my orthopedists have all considered me an athlete. I had always been careful as a dancer and never sustained an injury of any lasting import. I read about running properly, bought good equipment and ran on a track, saving my back and knees unlike the untutored who train and strain on cement or asphalt. I began to enjoy my free drugs: endorphins.

The orthopedist told me not to run after the first knee procedure but I went out and tried anyway. I found that I was feeling a sensation that was not promising, so after two attempts I gave it up. While living at the beach house in Seacliff in 1981 I did my longest run one day—ten miles along the coast—and that was as close to a marathon as I wanted to get. Much later I learned that Cubby had become a runner too, which helped when he was on the road for his continuing drumming gigs. He and Bob and I are the only Mouseketeers who are still doing what we did as kids.

I had a second right knee arthroscopy in 1999 and everything has been fine since then but age began creeping up on my stomach, so I became a hiker. Our former home in San Clemente was surrounded by nineteen miles of hiking trails. Two trails converge about a half a block from our house.

Twice a week I take a 3.5 mile hike, 1 mile of which is raked up to about a 19% grade on a dirt trail up to the top of the mountains in the area—okay, tall hills—to a water tower and back down in fifty-one to fifty-four minutes, depending on my pace that day. I also give myself an advanced jazz warm-up for fifty minutes once a week and do other exercise for short spurts. Thus, at sixty-five I have a thirty-three-inch waist and I do not look like a display for a tire store with one whitewall stuck under my shirt.

I have been very healthy all of my life which is to some degree genetic but also the way I live and exercise. My only other operations besides a tonsillectomy as a teen, a benign tumor on my vocal chord in my mid-twenties, a cyst on my wrist and the arthroscopies has been the rotator cuff surgery in 2005.

My heaviest weight was after the first knee op inaction when I was neither taking nor giving myself dance classes and before I started hiking. I bulged up to 197 pounds, far too much for a man my size. I went on the DeBakey Living Heart Diet and got down to 165. I stay now between 160-163. I have never looked buff like my dad and my buddy Bill Boss but I do look in shape.

Bill Boss was my closest friend in the 'seventies doing *Boys from Syracuse* in Chicago. He played one of the leads and was a handsome, muscled guy who worked out and did not seem gay onstage—except he often walked to the theatre in overalls with no shirt on. Of course, Bill was gay. He was not Nellie but offstage he did not care what anyone else thought. He was not effeminate, he was just Bill. He and Diane and I were close and one night smoked a doobie and went to The Magic Pan in Chi. We had the best crepes in the world although it was very difficult to eat and laugh simultaneously. I have often wondered where Bill is now; he was a good man.

A chorus guy in the show known by all to be gay was getting married. Bill and I were invited to the bachelor party where I'm fairly sure I was the only straight guy. Bill and I had smoked a roach before arriving and the conversation was more about men's fashion than sports and female attributes—it was unlike any guy's bachelor party ever before. It amused Bill and me immensely as they all tried to act butch.

Then Bill stood up, wearing his overalls and no shirt, rested his arm on the fireplace mantle and in a very loud voice began discussing how much he loved and was accomplished at eating pussy. The room became deadly silent and he went on and on. I was tearing from laughter and rolling from side to side on the couch. It was a priceless moment that should be put in a film.

In the Vegas musical I shared a dressing room with Phil Ford (of the vaudeville and stage Phil Ford and Mimi Hines duo) and R, who was in the closet. Phil and I knew R's preference and Phil instigated a discussion of the same subject. R went on and on about his love of this oral act and Phil and I both almost got hernias from NOT laughing. R left the room and the two of us looked at each other and laughed for at least five minutes.

At the Toys for Tots Harbor Parade before boarding our boat. It's a fake fur folks, 1981.

    Phil was also known by the bartenders as a no-tip rip-off and he once brought a suitcase to our dressing room and had the entire cast check out his "dropped off the truck," like Gerry in NYC, knock-off watches. Everybody has to make a buck.

    Some of the Mice got together for the Marina del Rey Toys For Tots boat parade in 1981 at the instigation of Bonnie Lynn who actually lived on a boat in the harbor at the time with her retired fireman husband. The group included me, Doreen, Sharon, Tommy and Larry Larsen, the eldest Mouse, who was one of the very best dancers and was on season two. He had become an engineer and made the finale for the 25th the year before.

    Nineteen-eighty-two was the year I shaved off my full beard which began in 1980 and performed in what had become the yearly live show at Disneyland and on the Merv Griffin and Mike Douglas shows to promote that gig.

    Disney had figured out that they could emulate what Barbara and I had done with in-house "choreographers" to adapt the script, choreograph mindless dances and sort of direct without using me or Barbara, thus, accomplishing the primary Disney directive: make money while not putting out money. This is when the horse-around-the-waist bit I used for Paul on the 25th bit my butt.

Marilyn the choreo—the same one from the debacle in 2005—wanted me and three other Mice to wear horses for a number. I was one year shy of forty and was not about to be cutesy and dancing with a horse around my waist even if we had been being paid appropriately, which, as always, we were not. The two girls and the other male Mouseketeer, Don Grady, said nothing. Marilyn tried everything but I quietly refused to look like a fool. Both the women and Don were grateful for another Mouseketeer Mensch stand but only Don thanked me later.

Mike Hoey and L.B. at the WGAw Awards Show in 1989. Mike is wearing the largest lifts in Hollywood, but don't tell anyone.

I continued to write radio plays and was working on a new stage play. I choreographed a play entitled *The Session* in which I was challenged to give each actor an animal and its movement style to motivate their character's movements. I have become known for taking people with little or no dance training and experience and making them look good in dance numbers.

In 1983 I played Billy Early, the slick dancer/lawyer played by Bobby Van in the 1971 Broadway revival of the old musical *No, No, Nanette* in L.A. for the Masquers, a long-lived actor's social club. I also met film star Ruby Keeler who was a smash in the revival with Van. Ruby came backstage to the bar downstairs and met with cast as well as doing a little mature hoofing on the dance floor. Mike Hoey, who had started as an editor on the MMC and moved on to screenwriting and directing, introduced himself and we soon became friends. He wrote a number of films for Elvis including *Live A Little, Love A Little* which I had appeared in before meeting him.

Mike also helped me get a story idea to the TV series *Fame* and cast me in *Falcon Crest* when he directed an episode, which led to a recurring role as a club owner, and later cast and directed me in Hal Linden's short-lived *Blacke's Magic* cop series.

Hoey is one of the very, very few people in sixty years in the business who has believed in my work and helped me. He later asked me to choreograph six non-dancing writers in a number for our 1989 WGAw Awards at the Beverly Hilton, which was a smash. Mike also asked me to choreograph the world premiere of an original musical based on Dorothy Parker's life which he directed. *The Lady In Question* had lyrics and score by the irascible Tony winner Albert Hague who played the irascible music teacher on the TV version of *Fame*.

The others who have helped me are my friend Jack Lee the Broadway conductor—I know him to be one of the very best and an even bigger help than Mike—and an NYU instructor of voice and musical theatre; my friend producer Marty Wiviott, for the Nederlanders at the Pantages in Hollywood; and my former agent and for many years a casting director, Jim Tarzia.

There were other people, of course, who cast me, including Broadway director Lucia Victor, choreographers like Kenny Ortega and Louis DaPron who used me more than once, writer Carl Gottlieb (*Jaws*) who got me a TV/film writing agent, agents who sent me out and many other people but only these four really gave a damn about my work. The rest of it was all up to me and I have gotten a lot of work on my own.

*Jack Lee visiting us in California in the late '80s.
Jack is not wearing lifts; neither am I.*

    The agents in L.A. get you auditions but you nail the job. In NYC you do both but there is much less work except for theatre; the same is true in Baltimore & D.C. My first literary agent got me looked at for my first book and had a chapter printed in a national paper, but everything else I submitted on my own, including this book.

    Thanks Jack, Mike, Marty and Jim!

    I had great reviews as suave dancing/singing lawyer Billy Early:

    "Burr's Eddie Cantor type of agility is another asset," said the now defunct *Los Angeles Herald Examiner*.

    "Lonnie Burr is brisk and deft as Billy Early," from the *Hollywood Reporter*.

    "Lonnie Burr's turn shows good comic timing and his excellent dancing gives dash [as in Dot & Dash?] to his performance," by the *Los Angeles Times*.

    "Lonnie Burr gives the best performance in the show," the local *Tolucan*, from Toluca Lake, which is near Burbank.

    I won a short story contest from the *Los Angeles Herald Examiner*, a former rival of the *Los Angeles Times*, and two of my short stories were published despite this not being my métier. My two-act play *Children Are Strangers* was done at the Playwright's Public Forum and my book went into its third, updated edition.

Diane and I got away for our first vacation to British Columbia; she took me there in 1983 for my fortieth birthday before the surprise roast which was successful because it was two weeks AFTER my birthday. We returned to B.C. for my fiftieth in 1993 due to the beauty and nature of the people. Canadian people always seem to be like Americans before Vietnam and the changes in our ethos and personalities. A bonus was that only one of us got a mosquito bite. We had no bear encounters in B.C. but when we went to Alaska for our 25th anniversary in 1995 we came within 20 feet of a full grown male. We had learned and remembered what to do and, fortunately, he was neither hungry nor in an ill temper.

We also went to the Hollywood Bowl every year, usually for a jazz night, and we were there for Joe Williams, Carmen McRae and the Velvet Fog, Mel Torme. Sadly, Mel had just suffered the stroke that led to his death and did not appear that night. On the positive side, I was asked a question by the most prominent and still ongoing jazz station in L.A. which I answered correctly and we got free tickets to see Miles at the recently refurbished, marvelously Deco (which we collect as Streisand does but on a much, much smaller scale) Wiltern Theatre in L.A. on Wilshire Boulevard, not too far from the excellent Perino's restaurant, which is now long gone.

I had seen Miles at UCLA as a teen and I disdained his unfriendly rebuffs, ignoring the audience by facing upstage most of the night and walking offstage in the middle of a musical phrase so I had refused to pay to see him perform again. I still bought and listened to his unique horn style, except for the fusion crap he got caught up in for a decade, so I would not have had the chance to see how he had changed. At the Wiltern he did no old schtick, like "Kind of Blue," nor "Sketches of Spain" with Gil Evans, but all new tunes with a great young sax player and two percussionists, one an excellent young Hispanic female. It was a marvelous experience and not that long before Miles died in 1991.

My TV and film work picked up with two episodes of a short lasting sitcom *It's Your Move*, a *Mike Hammer* and guesting and choreographing a dance for Hayley Mills and myself on *Saved By The Bell*. Originally titled, *Good Morning, Miss Bliss* this sitcom has provided the best residuals of any show I have done. I did the TV movie *Lots of Luck* starring Annie and Martin Mull, making me the only Mouseketeer to work with Annie as an adult in a non-Mouseketeer venture, although the independent film was made for the Disney Channel.

In 1984 Gower Champion's second in command, Lucia Victor took over after Gower's death and cast me in the Los Angeles company of the last musical he directed and choreographed on Broadway. *42nd Street* opened at the Shubert Theatre, in Century City near Beverly Hills. My understudy did my three roles when I could not get back from shooting with Annie and also when I did other film or TV work and the next to last live Mouse show at Disneyland, now at a different venue for they scrapped the Tomorrowland

My psycho shot. Would you want your sister to date this man?

Stage to build the Magic Eye Theatre where Michael Jackson's 3-D *Captain Eo* directed by Francis Ford Coppola and produced by George Lucas starred Jackson and Anjelica Huston. It ran there for eleven years.

My best review in a year run in "*42nd Street*" was from the *Daily News*, the reviewer writing "Lonnie Burr is a master of disguises."

I played three different principal roles and my look and work were disparate. Robert Osborne mentioned me favorably in his column in *The Hollywood Reporter* as well. Bob knows Diane better than me, having been one of her clients at The Leigh Bureau, but he has always been supportive and friendly.

Oklahoma sugar daddy Abner Dillon commands respect in 42nd Street, *1984-85.*

Still wearing my stage manager's costume, this is my second meeting with Cary Grant; the first was at Cheryl's wedding. He came backstage after 42nd Street *and has just turned to autograph a cast member's poster, 1984.*

Broadway and Off-Broadway shows have a softball league and they play each other every year. L.A. does not have this tradition but the *"42nd Street"* cast got involved in at least one game. I got a hit and a slight injury and we beat the San Diego Globe Playhouse team 37 to 34. Both of our defenses needed a humongous amount of work. As a result of 42nd, the best money I had ever made in theatre, and my outside work in film and TV, I bought myself a 1967 fully restored Mark II Jaguar which I loved and kept for five years. They are temperamental and expensive cars to repair so I then moved to a restored 1973 Benz 280 SE, which lasted much longer and needed less repair work.

During the *42nd Street* run I became a regular at Harry's Bar which was part of the Shubert mall in Century City. Harry's was opened by the Cipriani family in Venice, Italy in 1931 and Hemingway hung there and even referred to the bar in one of his novels. There was a second Harry's opened in Firenze in 1952, not owned by but sanctioned by the Ciprianis. The first Harry's in the U.S. was much later and I believe began in L.A. with a later one in San Francisco. I had meals there between the weekend matinee and evening performances, five shows in three days from Friday night to Sunday evening, which is much more difficult than the usual Wednesday and Saturday New York matinees.

Harry's put a name plate with my engraved signature by the deuce I sat at, isolated from the rest of the tables in the small room off the bar. Northern Italian cuisine replaced French, Thai, sushi and Mexican as my favorite forever. From shrimp *grigliati* to delicately seasoned pasta to their always delicious soups, I was devoted. Harry's has made a final exeunt just like the fantastic Scandia on the Sunset Strip.

I moved on to *Hill Street Blues*, commercials for Ford and McDonalds, *Hollywood Beat* and other TV series and the television film *Copacabana*, playing a sleazy club manager with my second Annette (O'Toole, also from HPS). Diane and I bought a house in North Hollywood and I was the M.C. at the allegedly final reunion of HPS in 1985, the year Mrs. Mann died and the school closed forever.

Diane had left the Norton Simon to spend over a decade at Financial Management Consultants, a small business management firm run by Nathan Cohen, an accountant and investor who handled mostly writers and actors, like David Jacobs, the creator, producer and scripter of the television series *Dallas* and then *Knot's Landing*. Nathan was both Jewish and Scottish and very good at money matters. Diane was second in command and fully enjoyed her relationship with Nathan, other staff members and her work.

Mouseketeer Karen was in a car accident in 1983 that left her paraplegic. She needed time to adjust to living in a wheelchair but by 1986 she got a number of us Mice involved in "National Barrier Awareness Day" in D.C. Each celebrity, about six or seven Mouseketeers along with others, took on the disability of someone and went through something similar to their problem for a day, so one might have to get around in a wheelchair, like Karen.

I had lunch in L.A. with a fresh standup comedian and later actress Geri Jewell who has cerebral palsy and whose disability I would emulate. Geri is best known for her role of Cousin Geri on *The Facts of Life* and more re-

Geri Jewell and I take a break on The Mall in D.C. during Barrier Awareness Day, 1983.

cently as one of the stars of the hit cable series *Deadwood*. We decided I should walk with a weight attached to my ankle for the entire day visiting Congress and other political notables. The visit to Congress made exactly the point of the movement to help people with disabilities. The only wheelchair access to the Capitol at the time was halfway around the building from the regular tourist access. I met affable Richard Dean Anderson, then starring in *McGyver* who was another of the celebrity participants.

I dined with Geri in the Congressional dining room and I was confronted once again with the way people with impairments get abused socially. The waitress looked at Geri, who was tired and as a result had some uncontrolled movement of her head and left arm (uncontrolled movement is part of cerebral palsy and something Geri has worked very hard and successfully to overcome). The waitress saw this, looked back at me and asked, "And what will SHE have?" I was angered but all I said was, "I suggest you ask HER."

This reminded me of an earlier problem with my mom's MS. She refused a wheel chair and I assumed, although it was not discussed, she considered walking to be her last bastion of freedom. She was forced to drag her right leg and could not use her right arm to help her up stairs. Since I lived with her in Vegas when I did *George M* she wanted to see me onstage and she had to climb ten wide stairs to the door where the *maitre d'* waited. I was helping her but I let her do it on her own, which she preferred, using her left arm on the banister and dragging her right leg up after attaining the next step.

The uncaring and aloof *maitre d'* showed great consternation that she was taking so long by his sighs and in other ways. I was livid with him and his typical Vegas behavior. I wanted badly to attack him, but that would not have helped Mom, so I stayed with her. When we got to the door he hurriedly went ahead and pointed to the table, accessible by more steps down. He had no pressing duties for there were no other patrons yet being seated. I brought her early knowing her problems were better kept in an environment that could allow her time and not embarrass her.

Many people have cruel reactions to the disadvantaged, which is why I participated in this event with Karen and Geri and everyone else. I believe that all of us there and the event itself had a little to do with changing things. Many people are much better now, but there is a lot more work to be done.

I began my recurring role as Arnie Sardie on *Falcon Crest*, made commercials, shot a *Hunter* and played a yacht club snob on *The New Gidget*.

Nineteen-eighty-seven brought two more deaths: Diane's middle brother Douglas, who was Director of Research and Development and the Vice President of Solid State Logic, died from AIDS. The talented Keith Hein died of AIDS in July, Doug in early August. Doug was one of the creative geniuses for the music world and film at Solid State for their beyond-state-of-the-art recording studio consoles. His memorial service a number of weeks later at the National Cathedral brought colleagues and friends literally from around the world. At the service Diane spoke with gentle humor about her brother and I read a poem I had composed in his memory.

Keith had been nominated for an Emmy as set decorator for a television remake of the Tennessee Williams play *The Long Hot Summer*. I was very troubled by both these deaths; it goes without saying that Diane took it even harder. Losing young, talented people in their prime is more devastating than the expected death of an aging parent. The only thing worse that I can imagine is losing a child. My friend Sharon lost her son in his early twenties. Personally, one of my most difficult cases of grief and loss was "my daughter" Syny, our kitten of eleven years who died in 2005.

In fake nose, makeup and costume as W. C. Fields, 1989.

    I played a caring son in novelist Henry Denker's play *Horowitz and Mrs. Washington*. I met this well-known author during rehearsals. I next shot some court TV shows, one with Raymond St. Jacques as the judge, and a forgettable flick titled first *Nameless* then *Time Bomb*, which it did, in 1988. In 1989 I impersonated W.C. Fields in full costume and makeup, fake red, bulbous nose and all, for the Television Academy Hall of Fame television special honoring Red Skelton, whom I had met and auditioned for as a kid. I was in the same number as Broadway choreographer and dancer Tommy Tune.

I was a principal and co-choreographer of the Carl's Jr. commercial right before I filmed *Lionheart* starring Jean Claude Van Damme; I played the main bookie in a number of scenes over three weeks. Jean Claude is arrogant and full of himself but maybe that is how he managed to become one of the few stars from Belgium. It is my opinion that the Belgians and the world prefer to think of the Flemish masters and modern painters, their beautiful architecture and the world master of the jazz harmonica Toots Thielemans, as more representative of this charming country.

I first saw the bizarre play *Tamara* while I was doing *42nd Street* and really wanted to do it. It began in Canada, later played two years in NYC but had its longest run in L.A., about seven years. This is highly unusual for nothing has ever run a long time in L.A. except for a mindless extended burlesque work called *The Drunkard* many years ago. After *42nd Street* I was cast as one of the leads, Capitano Aldo Finzi from 1989 through much of 1990.

This intense drama is staged not in a theatre but inside many rooms of a building which is supposed to be Il Vittoriale, the palace of the Italian poet Gabriel D'Annunzio. In L.A. they redecorated the large VFW hall on Highland immediately south of the Hollywood Bowl. The play takes place in different rooms in the palace and the audience is literally inches away at all times.

As Capitano Finzi I began the evening by explaining the rules to the audience in formidable fascist style after checking their passports—the tickets were in the form of a visa—as they entered. The two producers of the 25th Mouse show and Mike Eisner came through and tried to get me out of character, but I reprimanded them soundly. Eisner sent me a nice note after the performance. "Lonnie—We loved *Tamara*! You were great! Congratulations—sorry we didn't see you after the show—keep up the great work—Mike." It was mandatory that the audience follow rules and that they choose which characters to follow, for after my speech the characters moved off to different rooms to enact their scenes.

It is very tricky to work so close to people and move past them and around them as if they are not there. It was even more difficult because of the intricate timing. There was no way of knowing what had transpired in the other rooms and scenes and you needed to arrive on schedule for your next location and scene and the other actors had the same constraints. It was a little like early '50s live TV which I had done decades earlier.

I was very pleased to nail the role. However, due to the intimacy of the acting and some of the personalities of the actors involved, it became emotionally divisive. So, like *Oh, Calcutta!* they had a resident shrink with whom you could consult. Due to the physicality of the show, the Capitano being the most difficult, there was also a resident chiropractor whom I also saw from time to time. I was in the show for over a year but their shrink was not enough, thus, I began therapy again for the first time since the late 'sixties. Diane and I were having problems, too, so we went to a very good couples' therapist.

Finzi is a closet Jew, an Italian *fascisti* who is a murderer and womanizer. He has an inferiority complex despite his striding around, ostensibly in charge, in an all-black uniform, black boots and gloves and a holster containing a German Luger.

The show also brought about my only incident of being stalked. A man in his early twenties saw the show one night and came back a few nights later, appeared to be on drugs and had on a T-shirt with a picture of me as Mouseketeer Lonnie. I knew that he had done it himself or paid to have it printed because there were no such garments on sale at that time.

I talked to the stage manager, a very difficult individual, and he said he would keep track of him. The truth was, despite our constant proximity to the audience, there was no official security. Everyone had to get by me as the Capitano to see the play and when the stalker returned two more times and continued to wear the same T-shirt, I became more apprehensive. I complained to the SM more heatedly. All I had in Capt. Finzi's Luger were blanks that I used at the very end of the play.

After paying to see this play three times you paid less and after five performances you got in free. This scary, doped weirdo was getting in for free. I asked for and got random checks of patrons' bags, backpacks etcetera when they entered and before they got to me with their ticket/visas. The next time he showed up—Diane was there to observe him for me that night—they found a knife on him. I do not think they called the police but they confiscated the knife and ushered him out and told him never to return. I was still concerned, but he did not come back; I do understand why celebrities have to hire security. There has never been a problem in appearances with other Mouseketeers but the Disney approach to our security was not nearly effective enough for this kind of dangerous weirdo despite the overbearing nature of Disneyland's private security force.

At a Tamara *cast party, Shelly Hack and I celebrate New Year's Eve 1989.*

Il Capitano Finzi has numerous violent moments such as hitting a wall at one point and socking a woman in the stomach. Making the physical action seem real with people inches away and NOT hurting the woman, nor your hand on the wall, takes a lot of craft and effort. I learned that my predecessor as Finzi actually hit at least one other actor once, just as my understudy in *42nd Street* had almost knocked out another actor.

However, I did get to play the lover of two very pretty women: Shelly Hack one of *Charlie's Angels* and later the "Charlie Girl" in the perfume commercial, and Sherri Belafonte, who wanted her boyfriend from a soap to play my role and, I believe, got me canned.

I was replaced for indefensible reasons and Equity helped me fight for a cash settlement. Equity and I were successful but it was time for me to get out of this play anyway for it was doing very bad things to my mind and my depression battles.

On a friendlier note, Shelley Fabares, who had started on the MMC and remains one of Annette's closest friends, saw *Tamara* one night and came back to congratulate me on my work. That one stood out more than others who would come to my dressing room door.

Diane and I finished our couples' therapy and our relationship improved but the shrink work was helped by the calming influence of our cats. We have always been cat people; I only discovered I was one after I moved in with Diane and met Floomerfelt in New York, for if you recall it was my reaction to the surly Siamese at four that prompted my second attempt to run away from home.

Floomerfelt was the name of a school friend Diane had and she thought it was silly enough to fit the personality of this fixed, male pinto feline who just may have been the dumbest cat in NYC and then California, perhaps the entire U.S., but he was charming, warm and as lovable as can be. We had to put him to sleep on July 29, 1989. We had added Myrrhy (pronounced, Murray) in NYC but he died of an infection when he and Floomer were kept by a vet when Di came out to visit before moving to California.

We got Leibniz, named after the philosopher rather than the cookies, a long-haired grey cat in the late 'seventies so Floomer would have a buddy. These guys usually slept together rolled up unless they slept on our bed with us. Floomer made twenty years and Leibniz about seventeen but they were not outside cats save the occasional supervised foray in the backyard. Mnemosyne (Syny) came to us from the street after the Northridge earthquake and was our first female. After two years of grieving over Syny's death in 2005, we gave it up and adopted Asta Astaire, another young female who is a black and white tuxedo cat.

The long run of *Tamara* was only interrupted for me by a short cruise we took in early 1990. We enjoyed the four days and understood why Arte Johnson and his wife Gisela seemed to make a second career of cruises. Before e-mail Arte sent me and others weird, absurd, tacky postcards from wherever he and Gisela visited.

Now I am a bit leery of cruises due to pirates, infections and food twenty four hours a day.

I have to sidestep to a short study of my history with women and specifically my last serious love from 1983-85 with the second most difficult female name for me, disregarding the dreadful two Karens—the first is Darlene, as in my first wife and the much earlier Mouseketeer, the second is Susan and, worse, a Susan, never Suzi, with red hair everywhere.

Chapter 16
Such Women Do Not Exist

Women, even after I gave over trying to peer up their skirts as a small boy, have always compelled my interest. I unquestionably get along with them better than I do with men. Unfortunately, after six decades of politely and desperately, at times, inquiring just like Freud, I have not one iota of information as to what the hell they want. I have known almost from the start that you must always strive to contend with them for they are formidable partners and more formidable opponents who keep changing the rules on you.

How to interact with females as an adult, rather than as a somewhat sophisticated boy trying to emerge as a man, was within my purview, or so it appeared, as another of my precocious accomplishments. That is a chasm away from actuality. I was popular and dated at every opportunity but I was sometimes misused by young women; I am convinced that there are a few women who feel that I misused them but I would object and need to know the reasons that made them feel that way.

I never said I loved a woman unless I felt it. I never stood anyone up, nor did I intentionally hurt them, nor lie to achieve sexual advantage. I do not claim spotless perfection but I have always attempted to be honest, understanding, fair and caring. I am moody, caustic, and temperamental, but too many times my honesty, most pointedly, got me into contentious, sad situations and it was clear to me that we would have both been better off if I had lied. I loathe lying and being lied to—that is not who I am and I will not change into another person's idea of what I should be for any reason that is not some literally extreme threat, say an automatic weapon.

I believe I was so disturbed and conflicted by the devious and deceitful actions of many people, both as a child and as a young adult, that I had to follow a different path. I vowed to myself that I would not lie unless I truly had no other choice.

Some of my mother's homilies were accurate. Just because everyone else is jumping off a bridge does not mean you have to do the same thing is so like a Doddism that it surely fed my need to be independent in many ways, one of which was telling the truth as I perceived it. At some point or other, my almost compulsive truthfulness has never ceased to frighten everyone with whom I have come into contact.

Obviously, there are ways of presenting the truth so that you are not constantly harping and criticizing and hurting others. Disagreeing with a person's choices, actions or beliefs is one thing, but insisting on only your way or besieging them incessantly is quite another thing. The manner in which you present things is also an integral part of pursuing the truth without appearing to be misanthropic, which I am not.

I was dumped at a party by a college date, a pretty-faced Melissa. She gravitated toward a braggadocio lawyer who spoke casually of his pilot's license, charmed her with compliments and enticements and his tantalizing, most likely untrue, accomplishments. While it was a very atypical experience for me, once is quite enough to feel the blunt thud of this emotive cudgel and feel demeaned publicly.

In my early teens I took a date dancing at the Hollywood Palladium, being dropped by my mom and later picked up to take the young lady home. I was not pursuing her as a girlfriend but she was a very good dancer. She had not expressed anything explicit to me so I did not know her feelings or her expectations, except we were on a date. You bring her, stay with her, have a good time and you take her home.

Going for refreshments between swing dances in the huge ballroom, I accidentally met a very attractive girl. My pheromones flushed. Some guys might have dumped their date but I somehow managed to juggle the two girls for a whole feverish evening. I got the new girl's phone number and my date seemed either unaware or uncaring regarding my two or three slightly extended absences. I do not think this may be misconstrued as the cruelty of abandoning your date. I never tried such an absurd endeavor again but, as mentioned, I have been in romantic situations with two women on a number of occasions subsequent to this chrysalis adventure.

One substantive yet bewildering issue of my honesty was that I continually insisted that my girlfriends be honest, too—from the late 'fifties forward. I wanted full partners, which showed an unusual male prescience in an era in which superior male roles and diminished female roles were clear and accepted by almost everyone. However unfair or unequal, there was no question about who was opening a door, who was calling whom, who was asking for a date or picking up the young lady and paying the check for entertainment and/or dining out.

I reasoned with young women and drove them into making decisions that they had been told were not theirs to make. Guys act this way, girls act that way and never shall the twain be untwined. This bothered them all enormously, even those who verbalized their appreciation of my idea of a relationship. It seemed to stimulate their ire and they took it out on this pushy fellow who made them make these rude, distasteful, unheard of choices.

When gliding past the Statue of Liberty on a ship with Gloria Steinem, Yoko Ono, a few other men and many women to celebrate the first anniversary of *Ms.* magazine in the early 'seventies, I felt I belonged there because I had paid for it in increments long before the first sensitive man became fashionable sometime in the late 'sixties.

In my forties I decided to think of libido as a cheap, boring club on the outskirts of Vegas. I kept my pheromones inactive. I was convinced that much ado about something so fleeting and strewn with imminent emotional hazards and dreadful pain was not going to capture and hold me hostage as I had let it previously.

Sometime in my twenties I was watching a movie (it might have been *For Whom the Bell Tolls*) and I muttered, "Such women do not exist." I went on to recall many films, plays, teleplays and even radio scenarios when a female character acts so unlike most of the women I have known, that this sentence almost became a recurring mantra.

This should not be translated to mean I hate women—quite the contrary. I certainly do not deny that there are some unusually caring, brave, giving, steadfast women. It may not be misinterpreted to suggest that I have never met such a woman. There is also the consideration of my subjectivity as a possibility for my opinion but it does explain why I have from a young age been leery whenever a woman tells me she loves me. It does not change my hormonal response when I encounter a lovely woman of any age beyond early twenties but I merely appreciate her beauty, whether just physical or beyond; I do not pursue her. Since my relationship with Susan in 1985, I have made it clear that I have no interest in women other than Diane even if interest in me is indicated by a female.

At three years ahead socially and academically, I was interested in older young women until my mid-twenties; my first wife was five years older than I. Girls and very young women, however beautiful, *louche* and magnetically charming far too often are boring, obtuse, unread and solipsistic—like little girls—and that turns me off. I seek mature women who are intelligent, funny and receptive to humor, educated, perceptive and attractive—in that order. I deviated from this norm at times in my younger, more hormonally driven and imbibing days but that, if you will excuse the phrase, "petered out" in my early forties.

From my childish, furtive glimpses in ballet class in the late 'forties to early crushes and my first dating experience with Jerilyn in 1951 when I was nine, through the decades to the brief affair with the insatiable L'il K in the late 'nineties, I have questioned the promises of love that women repeat over and over in a loop of meaningless undying ardor. Love needs to be proven over time and trial for me to be convinced.

I have lived with Diane as a partner for thirty-eight years and she has been by far my best friend. She has meant more to me and done more for me than any parent, family member, friend or lover.

She did change enormously after our first sixteen or seventeen years together and I have found difficulties in the last two decades at times in believing her implicitly when she says, "I love you." My corny but very likable first year college speech professor, Bob Rivera, would in his inimitable style say, "The world is not interested in excuses, only results!" If you do not act like you love someone it really makes little difference what you say to them or how you believe you feel. It is not tangible, it is not fact, it is not the truth. I am sure Diane would not express it in the same way but has similar feelings toward me. We are both quite human.

I must acknowledge here that after a decade or so, Diane and I began referring to ourselves as married because many other humans have miniscule, closed minds. We are actually latter day bohemians who have absolutely no need of a legal, bureaucratic set of papers to clog our lives and force us to stay together. We stay together because we choose to stay together.

We have never wanted children and do not need to prove to anyone, nor to each other, why we have lived together—and in love—for almost four decades. We do not want money-grubbing lawyers making sure that fifty percent or more of our worth will be attained if we should decide to live separately.

Subsequent to Sharon at seventeen, I have said to every female lover when they have whispered or blurted out, "I love you," after a time and we really discussed the meaning of the phrase, that they would stay around long enough to say it in a year or, maybe two years—not forever, not a lifetime, not two or three or four decades. Of course, there were some one night stands where the phrase was not broached. I consider this three-word phrase a commitment to more than just hormonal satisfaction and that is certainly not what many other people, men and women, think "I love you" means.

Every single one for whom that was possible promised that she would do just that. The few that made a year or the rarer two years never made a full third year. And only one, who was not in the top five or so relationships for either of us, has made any contact since our love interests ended. It is quite like everyone saying they want the truth but never actually wanting it.

It is impossible *not* to be able to reach me. Even if I had not started my own website in 2000, I can always be found through SAG and my other unions before PCs and presently Google, in which I have far too many entries. Apparently, not one of the women who professed her love is interested enough to make the minimal effort to find out if I am still alive. Or if so, she certainly has never attempted to contact me just to say hello despite the depth and intimacy of our words and acts when we were in love.

I have always believed that after a serious relationship ends, if you truly loved the other person, whether the breakup is uncharacteristically easy or the more common, desperately spiteful, ugly situation and verbal attacks, that there must be thoughts and interest in the lost lover. If not, you did not actually feel the love you professed. Did you lie to your lover or to yourself? It may take healing time but wondering about a former, serious lover, this great, deep hunk of your life, will occur.

That is why I contacted and saw my first wife over a year after our divorce was final in 1970, despite my having asked for the separation and having been the one who filed for divorce, fully convinced as I was that she had the character and personality of a predatory viper. She had moved to Vegas while I was living in Manhattan and, on a visit to my mother, I called Dahr and asked her out to dinner. I was interested in how and what she was doing, in seeing how she had changed or grown or prospered and, if not, in finding out how I could be of assistance.

She began the evening grimly when I picked her up and she still showed a monstrous animus toward me. She was nastier and more verbally aggressive than before we split up in 1968. Actually, it was as if we had not parted. I am not a masochist and so I have never attempted to meet or to talk to her again, nor has she ever tried to contact me, just as she had not since the divorce. I confess I have tried a web discovery in the last decade and was unsuccessful until 2008 when I discovered that she was deceased.

Women have an escape mechanism that men do not: they marry, are hidden by an alias and disappear. Thus, women are difficult to trace and I have also tried alumni news and other avenues for the few lovers that were so important as a part of my life, but I have not found them.

I do not harbor any platonically ideal thoughts about how they look or how they think I look, nor how they act, nor feel toward me now. In truth I would prefer a pleasant exchange over tea rather than acrimony and recriminations, but most of all it would just be nice to make contact with a few (particularly Nora, Renata, and Janyce).

My later negative encounters with JoAnne, the two Karens, Barbara and a few others have made it obvious how soon love is forgotten, how easily it can turn to hate and, eventually, to boredom.

I have rare moments of fantasy in which I envision a significant lover, but these do not involve sexual intertwining; they are about the love and tenderness we felt for each other: a smile, a dance, a sunrise or sundown, a grasp of a hand, sharing a drink, a kiss. They are warm, good and meaningful memories that give me strength to move on, sometimes slouching, sometimes standing tall (at least for a man my size) through the no longer endless days towards a suburb of Bethlehem.

Marlene, my only unconsummated lover after I turned sixteen, did contact me online three years ago. We were both sure in 1962 that we could not coexist together forever, nor even for a long time, a bit like the more mature first Betty and my last lover L'il K. Naturally, I would have preferred that we had made love completely, as opposed to advanced canoodling, but I had alternatives in grad school from my lingering involvements as an undergraduate.

The behaviorist shrinks, zealously entrenched in dogmatic dogma, blames it on you, the *therapee*. You choose these neurotic individuals (name three individuals who are not neurotic) to whom you give love, trust and hope, thereby gifting them with power over you and over your friable heart and soul. You are told you intuitively search for these evil lovers and seek their battering ways just as you somehow sought out parents who misused you.

Amazing.

I attribute something to this shrink persiflage about our choices in love but find it impossible to come up with consistently common traits in each and every single one of my Keatsian *"Belle Dame[s] Sans Merci"* for whom love, defined as forever, lasted only as long as she felt it or until the next forever male came along. A number of them do fit the shrink paradigm but not ALL of them. The word "love" appears to have much more longevity for me than for the women I have loved, known and merely sexually encountered on a short-term basis.

My first recollection of sexual interaction dates back to my first play at age six at the Playbox, a small theatre that was part of the Pasadena Playhouse. The drama was titled *The Willow and I* and starred B-movie lead George Nader as my father and a supporting actress who was very kind to me, Ann Doran, who later became the Secretary of SAG and played James Dean's mom in *Rebel Without a Cause*.

An attractive, sexy young actress in her early twenties played the French maid and we had to go offstage and remain in a tiny, dark, space closed off from the audience's view downstage right for what seemed eternity—it was actually about fifteen minutes—before we entered again. We could not stand, but had to lie flat out, close together and had to remain silent due to the audience proximity on the other side of the wall, merely a thin flat that masked us. This would have been tedious for an *adult* pro—and I was only *six*.

We whispered in each other's ears succinctly on an infrequent basis and we began fiddling with each other, tickling and touching. I am not clear about who instigated what but some things sensual did occur. There was no blatantly consummated sex act but I was concerned that my stiffened member might betray a stain on my short pants when once again exposed to the folks in the front rows. Yeah, I could and did at six and after the first night I kept a handkerchief in my front left pocket, being a left dresser.

My early interest in onanism was practiced many places including the isolated, rarely lit or used, second story of my grandparents furniture store on Colorado Boulevard. All that was kept there were mattresses and extra furniture not used in the large downstairs display area. I came armed with hanky or tissues so I never crudely soiled anything.

Explaining dry, sticky spots on the upper inner thigh of your pants to anyone, particularly your mom, is very embarrassing and shaming so I learned the value of Kleenex (beyond proboscis necessities), dark pants and the assets provided by a wisely placed school books or homework, which backpacks do not allow. The alert eyes of my grandmother would have grown huge and fierce at a mattress stain and would have seemed like I imagined Armageddon since she would shudder and voice a retching noise if anyone mentioned the horror of *French kissing*. The concept of sticking her tongue in someone's mouth, or, worse, someone's tongue in her mouth, was anathema to Gram and would help explain my grandfather's nasty comments to everyone else in the family.

After our sexual involvement when I returned from Manhattan in the mid-seventies, Sharon and I have remained friends and I care a lot about her. She is the only former lover who has consistently instigated or returned contact. In essence, she is the only close friend I have left since Jack Lee and I have little contact.

Sharon and I had a misunderstanding which, I believe, is resolved. We were just leaving a jazz club in Toluca Lake in the 'nineties and this issue came up: she thought that I still loved her sexually, which has not been accurate for some time. Sharon is a handsome woman in her sixties, but we all have to admit that over time pheromones change and it is up to each individual to keep themselves true to what they believe.

The two of us do grouse about this or that anent our partners, but friends do that. I am afraid, unfortunately, of bringing up many things that are substantive. Sharon and her third husband joined our friends the Coles for services for Bob, my aunt Pudd's husband. If they had not been there, only a couple of relatives would have been there for Pudd. This was a magnanimous and tedious task for both my friends and their spouses and I appreciated it greatly.

Sharon and I look like we're dancing—maybe we are—at her going away party in 1990. She and her husband spent a year in Saudi Arabia for his work.

The threesome with Penelope in the late 'seventies was pleasant much of the time and we all got along well; we cared about each other. Eventually Penelope, after a few affairs with other men, decided she could no longer abide the bifurcation of time and emotion for I continued to live with Diane and she knew that was not going to change. She had cast herself in the Blanche DuBois role one time too many and we parted.

In 1982 while playing Billy Early in *Nanette* I met Susan, who was working crew on the musical. There was a pretty, zaftig, blond young woman, obviously from an affluent family, who was the focus of the few other straight guys, but I found her uninviting in all ways. Susan and I crossed pheromones quickly and, after I explained my living arrangement and commitment to Diane, we made love and fell in love.

She was very different than women that I had been attracted to previously, mainly due to her lack of education, life experience and her youth. Her beautiful red hair, freckles, flashing eyes and wide smile were mitigated by a street toughness, at times, crudeness that could become a challenge and should have been seen as a warning.

In this threesome there was an early engagement in which she showed interest in Diane sexually but Diane, without rancor, explained she was not of that mind at all and it never occurred again. We had marvelous times together and at one point, during an Easter meal at our apartment with the three of us, I felt that I may have achieved something I have always missed: a real family. I had hoped for the same thing with Penelope.

Susan, Diane and I spent a long holiday in a rented beach cottage and survived a harrowing experience when Di burned herself cooking and we rushed to emergency. Another apparent threat of a home invasion turned out to be some drunk, rowdy teens flowing over from a nearby public beach; otherwise we shared wonderful moments of peace with the calming, indomitable waves of the ocean a few steps away.

I have found more peace and provident solitude living at the edge of the ocean than at beautiful inland nature stays or the wonders of the city's museums or orchestras or theatres. The possibility of buying a small home on the ocean in California or anywhere is about as remote as winning the lottery, perhaps more so. Before I tap dance on the bucket, these houses may be swamped by melting glaciers anyway.

Diane and Susan had become friends and shopped or went places on their own. When I worked a Disneyland gig they went out into the Park rather than hanging around as I rehearsed, focused elsewhere, or during shows, for there was no need for either of them to see every single performance from any of our points of view. They even bought the same dresses once and wore them together on a couple of occasions.

When I landed *42nd Street* in 1984 I knew it was going to be difficult for Susan. She was not accustomed to the hours commuting to eight shows six days a week, my being nearly exhausted after five shows from Friday night through Sunday night, and our differing schedules. I lived with Diane and so I would come home from the show or to Susan's apartment but I would be less of myself. Susan would have to be up later, which made it difficult for her to get up early for her job. In essence, we spent much less time together and, although we had sex, it was rarer than previously.

She made a few complaints but they were about our lack of time together in general. It would have helped if she had been specific, extrapolated more; I might have found a way to change the situation. This tension was exacerbated when I shot a TV movie or a series or a commercial while doing the eight shows a week. Diane was used to the lack of my presence during such times just as she was used to my constant presence when not working and only auditioning and writing. Susan was not.

Susan began a new job and, apparently, after being pursued for a while, she began an affair. She was not mature, nor caring enough to discuss it and talk about a separation and keeping in touch, which, when you are family or at least have a basis for a meaningful friendship that alleges love, is the best approach for everyone concerned.

I went over one afternoon and she said something to the effect, "I am f—-ing someone else and I never want to see you again." I was unaware of any change in our sex other than there was less of it and would have done something about it if there had been some communication, but there was not.

I became very depressed but still had to work. I began drinking too much, never affecting my performances nor before driving to the theatre and home, but it was the worst depression since my father's death five years earlier. I called Susan, but she would not return my calls. Finally, after two weeks, I managed to reach her and asked to take her to a final dinner and talk caringly and civilly about the situation.

Susan agreed to the dinner meeting on the condition that she picked me up in her vehicle. I assumed this was because she wanted to be in control. I agreed. I drank at our dinner since I was nervous and would not be driving. She used this in every negative way possible. I was not slurring words, nor was I unable to walk, nor was I irascible. I was most assuredly in a state of sadness and desperation at my imminent loss and the cavalierly nasty way she was treating me. My fears of abandonment one more time were at the forefront of my thoughts.

We went to a nice restaurant we had visited before. I asked if we could continue our relationship in spite of her new lover. She laughed at me.

She dropped me back at our place and drove away, forever. I went through three months of extreme depression (in a time before there existed pills that could obviate some of the depressive symptoms). I considered suicide for the first time in many years. I wondered if she was a lesbian and her lover was a woman.

Explaining someone's cruelty is a purely intellectual endeavor that is never successful and does not in any way mitigate the emotive pain that is caused. I had never been quite so badly hurt before by anyone. The way she treated me reminded me very much of the bullies we have all encountered from school years forward. Bullies come in all shapes, sizes, colors, ages and sexual orientations and they are not always violently physical but they are always intent on demolishing your tangible self.

Except for a major mistake for a few weeks in 1998, 1985 was the last time I had any relationship or just sex with another woman. I was and am determined that no matter what my hormones dictate, whomever I find alluring, I will never again put myself in a position to be scalded to the soul as I was by Susan.

So, the saga of my skewed lovers and, apparently, a family, are over and I have the sometimes good, sometimes wonderful, sometimes spiteful and difficult times with Diane and our cat, but we have a bond that is solid and enough love to carry us through. People who believe in one god or another would say I am "blessed." I prefer to say that we have made our way through almost four decades without the need of religious beliefs, nor a marriage certificate, nor raising children together, but because of our choices and actions, the way we have lived our lives.

The too often meaningless words, "I love you," like showbiz hugs and kisses, are often merely metaphorical. Very few, if any, of my younger loves could have sustained a relationship like the one I have with Diane. We have fought and struggled to stay together, making the inevitable adjustments of years, my depression as well as Diane's, as we hike through the hormonal valleys and vistas that aging decrees.

True love has less to do with sex than we all believe and good sex has less to do with love than I have always insisted on from myself and those with whom I have had intimate relations. Most of my experiences with women have been wonderful; they just have not been able to go beyond to a superlative relationship. Without patience, compromise, hard work, fearless tenacity, luck and a partner who has the same substance and character that you have, the success of a long relationship is doomed to failure far beyond the divorce rate of fifty percent or more.

In my twenties I formed a theory that heterosexuals, or perhaps any two people in a significant, substantive relationship, have to get beyond having sex in order to be either in a lifetime partnership or to become long term best friends. Until that natural sexual tension is somehow dealt with, put in its proper place, the normal hormonal surges for something new and different and unexplored will wane and the relationship will dissipate. After sex, you must daily follow through in forming a relationship that works and you might have a lasting marriage or friendship or both.

There is still life, discovery, accomplishment, wonder, tragedy, hope, failure, excitement, shock, ill health and boredom afoot every day even though we have fled much further from large "R" romance, the faux pretense of *amour courtois* in the Middle Ages and from the Camelot view of a formal wedding. There is love, but you must maintain a quotidian struggle to keep it alive and vibrant even when you are as wearied as a constantly recovering patient.

The chapter heading and statement no such women exist is draconian and overblown. Diane is enough for me.

Chapter 17
The Desperate Silence of Testosterone

Men have trouble communicating their feelings to women, other men and themselves. Most poets and philosophers have been men but they are individuals and applying words to paper involves only communicating with yourself, despite the sharing of their ruminations, rather than with another human. Some of this may be attributed to the roles men play and have played, but it was as true before the Greeks and Romans as it has been for all of us who have come after them.

I have sought and nurtured friends, male and female, straight and gay, with no thought of race, country of origin, nor religious beliefs throughout my life but it has been problematic, arduous and, in too many cases, ultimately fruitless.

This does not mean that friendships that do not last are useless; they include fond memories, but the inability to sustain relationships makes life less tolerable and much less joyous. Of course, a smile unconsciously opens our faces when we see someone from the past. A meeting in person has much more effect than an e-mail or text message. If it is impossible to meet in person due to distance, a well-thought-out letter is far superior to machine to machine connections and the phone, a McLuhan "hot" medium, also beats our most common form of contact in 2009. Curt, inelegant text messaging and a plethora of boring old jokes are anathema to me, although I do like animal pictures.

Diane has one close friend from her childhood and she has many other people she considers friends but she is not that close to any of them. The majority of our friends have been mine since we first met.

Patty and Diane have known each other since the third grade and grew up as next-door neighbors in Washington, D.C. They attended grade school and high school together. Patty's parents were godparents to Diane and her three brothers.

I respect Diane's relationship with her. They are good friends to each other, but Patty and I do not mesh well at all. I am not comfortable with people who interrupt conversations without excusing themselves and otherwise assume they are the center of the universe. Even after Diane and I lived together for years, Patty did not include me in the address in seasonal cards. It is only in the last few years that Patty managed to include me in that way and I was surprised by a birthday card from her this year. I put no constraints on Diane's interaction with whomever she chooses just as she does not with me, but I prefer not being hypocritical in regards to Patty, although I was for many decades.

I have had some long-term friends, but two, one from my childhood, are lost forever to the male inability to open up, to understand, to show respect, and much harder, love to their own sex.

I was friends with Mouseketeer Tommy during the MMC but we lost touch until 1980 when we began working together for the various shows anent the renascence of the MMC. My friend Ed from Valley College in 1959 remained in my life off and on until the late 'nineties. We had an argument one time when I called with a few scotches in tow and he introduced an absurdly mundane topic.

He was a drummer and photographer who became a DP (Director of Photography), primarily for television (*The Virginian*, *The Incredible Hulk*) although he did work on some films including Hitchcock's last: *Family Plot*. Hitch and Ed did not see eye to eye, which is very bad for a Director of Photography who is using his eyes to accommodate the director's vision. Ed said that Hitchcock seemed more interested in breaking for his martini at four when his limo arrived than in making a film. Since Hitchcock then owned a fair amount of Universal Studios no one could do anything about it and that is why his last film is not up to his usual level.

Ed and his first wife Marilyn and their autistic son Tod and later his second wife Suzie and Tod lived in North Hollywood. They moved north to Montecito, California, and in the 'nineties they settled in Santa Fe, New Mexico, but by that time we were no longer speaking.

In the argument that stopped our friendship, Ed stated that he found stand-ins for stars during cinematic set-ups to be equals to actors. Being a stand-in requires no more, nor less than being an extra, people who fill out the background of scenes and only on rare occasion are given a line. Having been through all the actor's difficulties and rejection for decades,

I strongly disagreed with Ed. It is quite possible he met a stand-in who was making some needed money and was an actor, but that is not what he said.

I do not recall us calling each other names, nor swearing at each other but, even if something that termagant occurred, it is small-minded to end a friendship that has lasted more than four decades because of one argument. I tried to reach him by phone and failing that, I wrote him three letters, but there was never a response. Finally, many years later in 2004, I wrote one last letter to Santa Fe and he called me.

Ed would not go over what had made him so angry that night, nor would he explain his initial lack of response—but I had made contact. Ed does not, apparently, write letters and he does not have a computer, thus, no e-mail. I am not one much for chatting by phone, but after that first phone call he made one call eight months or so later and we talked for a half-hour. The next year he called again seeking my help in finding something from our college years for a private film project and I gave him what help and suggestions I could. There has been nothing since, and after the years of silence and my making a final overture to communication, the rarity and pedestrian nature of our phone calls, I do not see any reason to pursue this past friendship.

Ed and his familiar-looking buddy at the Seacliff beach house in 1980; he only lived about 15 miles north in Montecito, which is just south of Santa Barbara.

Men can complain about or lust after women easily, discuss sports, cars, weapons, music and food. If they are unusual they will talk about literature, art, philosophy and, very carefully, politics. They are good at non-revelatory problems or complaining about bozos with whom they work. That seems to be just about all that the men I have met can do unless they are very different and match my efforts to sustain a relationship. I had been through a lot with Ed and made sacrifices for him as he had for me but that was not enough to break through to each other as caring, committed humans.

I sometimes miss the good times that Ed, Susie, Diane and I had. I miss seeing Tod, too, who is doing well as an adult with his disability. Ed has always taken care of Tod and I respect that. One of Suzie's daughters has a drug problem and they are now raising a grandson. I miss much more when Ed and I would have tequila shooters and talk or listen to his extensive jazz collection on his excellent sound system. But when something is over, it is futile to feel bitter or to try to resurrect it.

Martin, whom I met in NYC during my lead in the drama *Broadway*, was last seen when he met Diane and me for a drink in the late 1990s. He seemed not to be actually present and was talking about upcoming things like too many actors who are out of work. He does do book readings for money at times and teaches acting, is still married to Margo and dotes on his daughter.

Gerry and I became friends when we shared a dressing room in *Mack & Mabel*. I did not like his officious, disagreeable wife, one of Gower's assistants, but the four of us did some things together. We did not correspond after I left New York but he was a bartender when not doing chorus dancing and I ran into him when Diane and I took a short trip to Manhattan. One time the three of us went out for drinks at our favorite, nearby Greek restaurant off West 112th Street and he seriously and crudely proposed that the three of us have sex. I found that offensive, as did Di, and I have never seen him since.

After Tommy and I became friends again in 1980, he and his wife Aileen and Diane and I did things together a lot. I did a funny bit at his fortieth birthday party as MC and roaster and my later roast was held in their back yard by the pool.

Tommy and I referred to each other as best friends, but he was hard to tack down individually. While he appears to be very accessible to everyone, I came to realize he is a closeted man—his inner self *not* his sexuality—whom I almost had to beg to have lunch with once or twice a year. That does not seem like a "best friend" to me.

Tom surrounded himself daily with his family, drop-by friends and acquaintances, biz associates and neighbors. His countless phone calls, both receiving and calling and which were exacerbated when he acquired a cell phone, became a recurring joke along with his numerous references to his hemorrhoids. Tommy and Aileen could not have kids so they adopted a girl, Lindsey, and about a year later adopted a boy, Casey.

They added an illegal live-in maid who brought along her grandson whose mother gave birth to him a week after being smuggled into the country. Tommy eventually became this Hispanic boy's godfather. Tommy then moved his mother into the house and finally his older brother joined the roost. Since I am the only son of an only daughter whose family gatherings were a very rare birthday or Thanksgiving and Christmas and since I live with one woman and a cat or two, I was frustrated that there was never a moment of privacy or intimacy in this conglomerate of different individuals, however literally or figuratively related they were.

Tom's house in the Valley began as a small three-bedroom with one bath and eventually grew three times its size—into a two-story, six-bedroom with four or five baths. He was constantly consumed by his make-up work and sweat labor on his house.

When we did talk away from everyone else he was focused only on his work or some familial problem or what the kids were doing and, oddly, he is the only straight guy I ever met who had no interest in ANY sport at all. Even many gay guys are into sports. Our rare lunches were as if we were not best friends but two people chatting on a talk show.

Diane and I had a falling out with Aileen and Tommy about their self-involvement when we brought up the fact that all the four or three or two of us ever discussed was Tommy's work as a make-up man, Aileen's as an airline attendant or their two growing children. One night they began exchanging and for a few minutes did not refer to us at all; it was as if we had disappeared. I rarely talk showbiz and Diane is not preoccupied by any of her careers. For a couple of years we did not interact because of this, but Diane and I did visit our godchild, their son Casey, and his sister Lindsey, although we were not her godparents. The Coles had always complained that the other godparents really did not keep in touch with the kids even when remaining their friends but we did even after the separation from the kids' parents.

Tommy was extremely remote and betrayed our friendship once too often. In the early 1990s when I was excluded for the first time from a Mouseketeer TV event when some of the originals including Annie visiting the third "Earless" version of the MMC on their TV series. Tommy did the show but did not tell me. My problem was that as my best friend he knew I was being screwed, but he said nothing. I was told by someone else. He was angry at me when I brought the subject up; if you do not discuss problems, they fester. I was not happy that he failed to tell me.

Friends give you bad news; they do not ignore you and hide in silence.

Contrarily, when we did the live show at Disneyland in 1980 and Tom wanted to do a rather boring song he had done on the original MMC, I had to almost tie down Barbara Epstein, the director/choreographer of record, to get her to let him do the number. I had him get some charts done to beef up the song and I choreographed Bonnie Lynn and Sherry in a soft shoe with twirling parasols around Tommy to make the weak number more palatable.

Tommy's thank you for my fighting for him to do his number was typical. Aileen, Diane, Tom and I had made reservations for an intimate, expensive dinner at a nearby dinner house as close friends to celebrate the opening of the show we starred in and I had help put together, as the writer and co-choreographer and "third eye" director. The ladies even surprised us by hiring a limo to take us down to Anaheim and bring us back. Their second secret was having unique satin jackets, the kind that most TV shows had by then, made for us which stated "Original Mouseketeer Lonnie" (Tommy on his) on the front, with the Disney liaison getting them dispensation to have the Mickey Mouse logo on the back.

Diane and I got a call in our hotel room after the last show and Tom said he had cancelled our plans and instead was going to treat all the Mouseketeers in the show and their others to dinner at something like Denny's without even asking if we minded. I was offended, as was Diane, but she talked me into going. I took a couple of trips from the table for some shots at the bar and was considered much more sullen than my usual amusing fellow. I was hurt and felt betrayed.

When Diane was planning my surprise fortieth birthday party/roast she reminded Tommy and Aileen that the only person I truly disliked was Tommy's buddy Dick, who had been consistently insulting to me over many years. Diane said she really did not want him to attend. She even offered to hold the party elsewhere if Tommy felt it would insult

Dick to exclude him from an event at their home. Tommy and Aileen said it was not a problem, but then Dick showed up and both Coles said they had no idea how he heard about it. They did not ask him to leave.

Diane and I were complimented when we were asked to be Casey's godparents but I made it patently clear that I would have to decline if I had to participate in any religious mumbo jumbo, which would be acting hypocritically for me. If this was required, I would understand and would just attend the service as a supportive friend and spectator. They told us we would have no involvement in the service and said that they wanted us to be Casey's godparents not for the religious aspect but so he would have two more caring adults in his life. I forget if they were Lutheran or Methodist, but except for Tom's recently deceased mother June, the Coles attended church like most people, sporadically, and none of it seemed to be part of their lives, no grace before meals except Thanksgiving, no prayers, and so on.

Diane and I arrived at the church and we were called to join other godparents and religious leaders in the center to go through a bunch of arcane, solemn hocus-pocus that I objected to enormously. If I had walked out, which was my first instinct, I would have hurt Casey and everyone would have thought I was a complete pr—k. The "pr—k" part did not bother me, but it was not Casey's fault that his parents lied to me. I did it for Casey.

When Tommy's friend Don was dying of pancreatic cancer as my dad had a year earlier, Tom asked me to go see him, knowing it would upset me; he even said he would understand if I could not do it. I was not a close friend of Don's but Tom asked, so I went.

We were alone and Don told me something I am not sure that anyone else knew. He told me he had been in love with Mouseketeer Bonnie Lynn Fields and she was the biggest love of his life. Then she dumped him. She made no effort to contact him as he lay dying. This hurt him deeply in his last few days. I tried to comfort Don but I thoroughly understood.

Tommy had recurring knee problems. I have had two arthroscopies on my right knee since 1993. Before I moved to Maryland in 1998, Tom's knee had not become severe enough to require surgery. As a make-up person, like actors who are not stars, Tom usually had to park a mile or so from the shoot site of a TV show or film and walk to and from the makeup room or trailer. His doctor gave him a handicapped sign so Tom could park closer in these circumstances.

I had no problem with his using it for this specific purpose but I frequently saw him take advantage of the placard when we were out and his knee was not bothering him just to get a closer parking space and once to save seventy-five cents on a meter. Considering that Annie and my mother had MS and his own mom had some mobility problems and actually needed the handicapped parking spots, it was clear to me that he misused a privilege.

The last time he tried this when I was present was one of our rare lunches away from the madding crowd. In a small, corner strip mall with every store within feet and many open parking spots, he pulled into the only handicapped place. He seemed to feel entitled to the space just because he had the card. I told him if he did not move the vehicle I would make my own way home and would never ride with him again. He got very angry, but he moved the car. I think it best to let his actions speak for themselves. He no longer discussed his sometimes gimpy knee.

Another moral decision that Tommy and Aileen made bothered us both. They allowed a known molester of pre-pubescent girls, including the man's daughter and granddaughter, who had never been identified to the law and prosecuted, nor even dealt with properly by his own family, into their house when their children were growing up. Lindsey was at just the right age for this predator. Their justification for allowing this man to spend time with their family was that they would not leave their daughter Lindsey alone with him. I am convinced that child molesters rarely, if ever, reform and are always a threat. Taking even the smallest chance that one more child will be scarred forever should not be allowed. Actually, having knowledge of a molester's history, I would be against him being in my house even with no children present.

Finally, or so I thought, my affair with L'il K, whom Tommy also knew well, was apparently one of her cruel jokes to break up the two of us as friends. She succeeded because of Tom's gullibility, his not really knowing his best friend and his refusing to come to me to seek the truth. When you are told about something that a person who is very significant to your life has done, you first go to them and see if it is accurate; you never assume it is true and act is if that individual is guilty. This harks back to my nightmare about my mother and grandmother leaving me in jail and assuming I was guilty when I had done nothing wrong.

Diane had seen Li'l K do something similar to others including Tom when he had been a victim of her deviousness and pathological lying. I was unaware of her problems with the truth, except for this one nefariously cruel act.

Li'l K was a very pretty, sexy woman just shy of forty but still noticed by males everywhere. She exuded sex. I have seen guys walk into stacks of cans in a market as they turned to follow her natural, sensual, sexual walk.

Diane and I had been bicoastal for nine months, with only two short visits. I ran into L'il K and we decided to go to a movie. She came back to my house; we talked and laughed for hours then had excellent sex. I saw her six more times and that was that. One night I was having dinner at her house and Aileen called to speak to Li'l K's teenage daughter. The teenager showed a wry smile and toyed with Aileen, putting her on outrageously as the teen and her mom cracked up mutedly. I did not know quite what to do but I felt that what they were doing would have alerted Delmore Schwartz—"Do the others talk of me mockingly, maliciously?" It should have alerted me, too.

I found out later that Tommy had been misinformed—as had I—by L'il K, but he assumed that I was going to do something totally uncharacteristic and sent me an insulting letter. He wrote that because he cared so much about me and Diane and our relationship that he was sending the ill-conceived letter to save me from making a horrible mistake

He began by condemning my drinking although he had never talked to me directly about it, like a friend, nor did he ever attempt to help me except by answering his phone for a late night call for help on rare occasions. I was never bombed at his house whether just visiting or at a party. Yet he maintained a bottle of Jack Daniels as an enabler for a mutual HPS friend who we both knew was an alcoholic.

He then outlined how wrong it would be for me to leave Diane for this new relationship, which should be inconceivable to anyone who knows me even slightly, more so if one knows me as a best friend. Everyone is very clear that I am not going to leave Diane for any reason other than an impasse between us and certainly not for another woman, however enticing. That has been my word, history and the actuality since 1970.

I did not respond immediately to his written railing because I was too damaged and enraged, but I told L'il K about it. She gave me a story about his sneaking by my house, seeing her vehicle outside and inferring that we were involved. Her story went on that Tom confronted her and she told him we were having an affair. She did not extrapolate further.

Thus, I thought he had jumped to a shabby inference without even showing me the courtesy of meeting me face to face. This hurt me the most because it meant that my best friend had not one clue about me and my character. It reminded me of my grandmother thinking I would do what she wanted because I liked her money so very much, prompting my exiting her home. They were both categorically wrong.

I discussed our romance with L'il K after our first night together, as I always had in the past, and it was very clear from the beginning that our interlude was limited. I was moving to Maryland/D.C. in a few months and she was omnivorous in her *louche*, obsessive need for sexual adventures, having coitus with almost anyone whenever she could—including, I found out over dinner at her house, my auto mechanic for twenty years. In addition, she had a teenager and was raising a three-year-old she had out of wedlock. The worst was that she clearly had problems of character and mind that were as far gone as V's in Manhattan.

In time I inferred she told Tommy that we were having an affair and that we were going to run off together. His letter and actions prompted my epistle in response that was unpleasant, but not nearly as nasty as I wanted it to be. He was very offended.

Subsequent to Tommy's letter, I knew that he could not be trusted. I was afraid he or Aileen would tell Diane of this short, meaningless sexual dalliance. I immediately called Diane, told her what had gone on and abjectly apologized. I hoped she would be able to forgive me, after so many years of my not being with any other woman. It was difficult, but she did. She never had to know of my error for it changed nothing between us. She would not have had to feel the pain I found necessary to inflict on her because of Tommy's actions and words. None of the Coles bothered to inquire about Diane's distress.

After that it was all over. This was not Tommy's first, second or third betrayal, but it was his *last*—if I had anything to do with it. Yet despite having no contact after early 1998, Tommy managed two more betrayals.

At the 2000 HPS second "final reunion"—the school closed in 1985—I made it clear to everyone involved in putting on the event and performances by alumni that I specifically did not want to be singled out, nor did I want to be on stage. I merely wanted to see people I grew up with and see how everyone was doing. There is no question that Tommy was made aware of my request. The real highlight of the night was the Steiner Brothers, in from Canada, who did their old act, good tap, singing and great vaudeville-style joking with each other. It was excellent seeing older pros strutting their stuff. Some, like Tony Butala, were good, others were not, but I really felt I was past another HPS Aud Call. Whitey on the sax, Alan on skins, Chuck on guitar and Pat on piano were great, and talking with friends, dining and dancing is more to my liking.

Tommy, who is a failed but still eager pop singer, had charts written and rehearsed and rehearsed to get up and perform two songs. After his numbers, knowing full well I did not want to be up there, he called out for me and Ronnie Steiner, a first-year Mouseketeer and the only other one present, to come up and sing the well-known Mouseketeer song. I could embarrass myself and everyone else, as I could have at the church with Casey, exit with Diane and be considered a rude pr—k, which is what I should have done but did not want to embarrass Diane, nor leave a bad after dinner taste in my colleagues' mouths. So I joined them onstage.

My former best friend's actual final betrayal was at WDW in late 2001 when Walt Disney's centennial prompted a year-long promotion called "100 Years of Magic." While Tommy is not a writer, he managed a copycat script for a short show that no one from WDW told us —or at least told *me*—that we were doing.

Since we were living on the East Coast we had little communication with the other Mice. After receiving the invitation stating that we were going to be Disney's guests for a vacation at the "100 Years of Magic" kickoff, I had asked the Disney liaison twice what was expected of us during the time we were there. Both times I was assured that at most we might be in a parade. We were their guests in thanks and appreciation for many decades of being part of the Disney family.

Instead, we had little time to see or do anything and were shuttled between meeting the press, filming things, going to formal meals, attending awards programs, for which we received nothing, and rehearsing and performing. Apparently, the guests had to pay for their visit in many ways.

If I had known all we were expected to perform for free, I would not have attended, but I decided that since Diane and I were there I would not say anything and try to make the best of the situation. I, of course, was angry about once again being misled by a Disney representative, but I was really frustrated with Tommy for trying to usurp my position as the only professional writer, the person involved with the scripting of the NBC Anniversary Special in 1980 and the writer of the live show later that year at Disneyland. At minimum, he could have let me know in advance, for he obviously had told the other Mouseketeers.

Tommy asked Aileen to hand out copies of his little ditty. The director of the entire show including our ten-minute bit asked what it was and when told it was Tommy's script he said he had the script they were using. Tommy and Aileen became apoplectic, which was fitting, and I must admit to feeling pleased. This final betrayal by Cole closed the book for me. I will never shake Tommy's hand again, which he had done much too eagerly at the HPS reunion and at the arrivals at the hotel at WDW for this event.

In all fairness, I did make a few midnight, drunken calls for help to Tommy since the mid-'eighties as I had to Ed but one night in the early 'nineties he told me he would not tolerate it any more. I apologized and never called him in that condition again. *Never.*

One night I called my mom in a depressed and drinking situation and she actually helped, that one time, even though she was the source of most of the problems. That was the last time I sought help outside myself for my struggles with depression and falling into, from time to time, my habit of seeking solace from liquor, which is like seeking comfort from a predator.

The fact that Tommy is incapable of sharing his closest views with anyone, including the one person he called his best friend, is something I accepted and dealt with for almost two decades. The fact that he has to provide for his family, extended family, friends and acquaintances by being Mr. Big Brother to everyone was not easy to contend with, but I managed it. The further truth that he refused to be honest with me and talk about his concern and problems with me face to face, I accepted until I no longer could. Tommy's treacherous behavior to me dictates, like Susan, V, L'il K and others in this category, that I will never again allow anyone who shows certain tendencies, like mendacity, to be in a position to hurt, diminish and betray me.

Apples, from whatever tree, do not fall far from where they are nurtured. I kept in touch with my godson Casey but unless I contacted him, there was no communication. This bothered me particularly during our seven years in Maryland/D.C., but Diane encouraged me to communicate and said all the things said about young men and their obvious lack of care for others being preoccupied by themselves, sex, thrills and as little time as possible spent on studies. After the fallout between Tom and me over the letters, Casey told me he had resolved the matter in his mind and we remained in contact. I told him I would be glad to discuss what had and had not happened, but he felt he was okay with everything as he understood it.

As godparents, Diane and I had always remembered his birthday; Casey seems unaware of mine and Diane's. We gave Casey many gifts including a poem I wrote about him when he was a child. He was quite young and the verse was about trains, written after I made the Mickey & Lonnie revamped Fantasyland/Amtrak tour through eleven states; Diane did some nice collage work for it too; when in the mood, she makes excellent collages, as did her late brother Douglas. I also gave Lindsey and Casey a song I had written for kids, although writing for children is not my forte, titled *The We of Me*. Of course, there were Halloween surprises at our house and Xmas and birthday visits and gifts. Casey and Lindsey always were directed by their parents to give thank you notes for things received; I still have them all. For Casey this later became maybe a phone call, then a terse e-mail.

Later I broke one of my own rules—never give anything to which you are emotionally attached to anyone else no matter how close you are to them. In his mid-teens I gave Casey an English penny well over a hundred years old that I found on the street during my first trip to London at eighteen and had added a chain after a jeweler mounted it. When his sister seemed to be getting financial help from Tom and Aileen and Casey was not as he continued to pay off his college loan, I sent him some money. Noticing the small library in the apartment he shared with his girlfriend, I gave them about fifty books. Later I gave him the black star sapphire ring which I had kept and worn from my teen years through my fifties. In his twenties, I gave him my black star sapphire cufflink set with three studs which I had purchased to match the ring. All these items had been mine for years and meant a lot to me. I did receive a thank you for them, but now they are gone forever and I imagine not used at all.

I had given his dad a Tiffany money clip like the one I still have from Joel Grey when he left *George M* in 1969 that read: jg/GM/lb. Tommy lost the one I gave him, which read TC/MMC/LB and did not tell me until I pressed him on it much later after not seeing an item used daily for some time. He apologized and said he lost it. How in the hell do you lose a money clip without losing your money? He responded by giving me a Tiffany key chain which represented a movie "clacker," the slate they hold up before a shot to identify it. I did not care much for it, but accepted it pleasantly.

However, I put up with Casey's insularity and non-communication for years even though it bothered me and I, of course, was always available if he needed something and responded quickly to any rare communication that I did not instigate.

When visiting L.A. prior to the July Disneyland appearance and moving back in 2005, Casey and I had a contretemps, nothing of any importance, on the phone. We did not use scatology, call names, shout, nor use negative adjectives, we just had our first argument after two decades as fairly close godson and godfather. I was taking him to dinner the next night but he wanted to talk before we went out, so we went into the backyard of Sharon's house where I was temporarily staying.

He began a mini-tirade about the way I had addressed him and our disagreement. I knew then that our relationship was over. I wanted to call off the dinner but I always give people at minimum a second chance. I apologized for whatever he thought was so important, which certainly was not. At least Ed managed over forty years before abandonment.

I only heard from him once more, after my shoulder surgery, Syny's death from cancer and my being abused by Disney for the last time. Casey had to have known at least about the Disney show and the shoulder, if not Syny's long bout with cancer, for I wrote an e-mail to all the Mouseketeers involved in the show so they would understand why I did not return after the first day of rehearsal.

Casey never contacted me to see how the surgery went, just as he had shown up late years before, after being out most of the night, for his mother's serious back surgery, which I reprimanded him for whether Tommy did or not. Casey's last, terse e-mail in 2005 explained his breaking up with his live-in girlfriend of about four years, whom he had planned to marry. He had moved into a house with some guys in an arrangement that sounded like an ersatz fraternity, which might not prove the best of choices at twenty-six.

I knew that we were not close enough for me to tell Casey much earlier that this girlfriend was going to screw him in one way or another and that he should get the hell out of the relationship and not marry her. I had never liked her. At least he came to his senses on this one and has saved himself from that disaster.

I did not respond to his e-mail in November, 2005 and have not heard from him since, so he must not really care very much, which I have thought for years. Casey seems to have absorbed many of his father's puerile, nugatory, whiney qualities. So, sadly, Diane and I no longer have a godson.

I apologize to the reader for seeming to carp about my problems, enigmas and failures with lovers and friends but it is part of a whole man and I am not writing just to please, inform, get a laugh, nor entertain. I am learning about myself as you are and I am certainly not pleased, nor happy about some of my actions, nor my experiences with other humans. Cats, however, have always shown me kindness, except for that first Siamese.

By asking questions as in Socratic methodology, why should we stop when the negatives are out of the way and our journey is so near its end, the now of 2009? Take heart, there is not much left to cover: the 1990s past 2005 when my Disney farewell could best be described by the Scottish poet Robert Burns: *"The best laid schemes o' mice and men/ Gang aft a-gley…"*

Chapter 18
Back Home, Candide Weeds His Garden

I learned recently that, unbeknownst to the folks who gave me the unused Leonard as my first name, it is derived from ancient German and means "prepared for battle." I did not come into the world ready for a fight and I have, since my volatile younger days, tried my best to avoid negative interactions. I did take on the role of nonconformist early when I decided that my individuality was more important than other people's opinions and the compulsive need of others for conformity to feel complete. Finding myself ultimately alone in the world, I have battled for my individualism and what I believe to be the right, moral, ethical way.

Nonconformists know they face overwhelming odds at all times. Ralph Waldo Emerson said "whoso would be a man, must be a nonconformist." I do not pledge that I am a big Emerson fan but Nietzsche had nothing quotable, even though he is a famous nonconformist. I still had to deal with a line from Le Carre's 1990 novel *The Secret Pilgrim* in which a character asks, "Who the hell is Leonard Burr?" I only know that I am Lonnie Burr, not Leonard Burr Babin, and that is all that really matters.

Babin is not the French equivalent of Smith in America. The only place I have ever found it, except for a few others with the cognomen, is in Rabelais' satire *Gargantua and Pantagruel*, which seems fitting to me.

I was a studio executive in the *Write Man* sketch (a take off on the film *Rain Man*), choreographed writer/non-dancers for the 1989 WGAw forty-first Awards show and continued in *Tamara* through much of 1990. I played a cop in a number of scenes in *Equal Justice* on TV, made the last Mouseketeer Hollywood Bowl appearance with Hayley Mills hosting, the Carl's Jr. commercial was recycled, I made the movie *Time Bomb* and I endured three knee-throbbing, painful peg leg weeks on *Hook*, which was released the following year, in 1991.

I have always been a Robin Williams fan but when in pain waiting to shoot a scene, Robin doing his club act is a monstrous pain in the knee, which on these days was much worse than my ass. I wanted to tell Robin: 1) take some downers or 2) you got the job so shut the hell up!

I was cast as one of four drunken, cockney, pirate buddies of Bob Hoskins as Smee, Dustin/Captain Hook's first mate. The three other gentlemen and I were concerned about both rehearsing and shooting on the peg legs which were difficult to walk on and much more so in dance steps. They were dangerously unwieldy making it easy to fall. Fortunately, since I was the only actor, the very affable John Williams gave me a couple of solo lines in cockney dialect for our section of the long musical sequence. Much of it was cut since Spielberg thought it told the audience that they were going to see a musical like *Peter Pan*. The good news is we still get residuals.

We all felt we should be making more money for our endangerment but the others had no idea what to do. I told them to be quiet and let me deal with it. The production people had been lackadaisical about having us sign our contracts. In the second week of rehearsal and the day we were to record our song, an assistant brought us the contracts. The three guys said, "Talk to Lonnie." I explained that the problem in signing had nothing to do with any of us personally but SAG would require us to be paid more because of the danger involved. Under a SAG contract "hazard pay" is given for anything that is more dangerous than normal. Having guys rehearse and dance around on slippery, painful wooden peg legs was just that, particularly given our ages. He balked at the suggestion and I thought the best way to resolve it is with the proper person at SAG.

They could not shut down recording, scheduling and production to hire four new guys to learn the dance and song. SAG, of course, supported our request for hazard pay. We received a nice raise for our three weeks on the film. Mouseketeer Mensch does not just work for the other Mice.

Diane had returned to school and became a paralegal, rising first to Secretary and then Vice President of the L.A. Paralegal Association. She quit smoking in 1988 and, predictably, began to gain weight, but managed to slim down by the time we took our first cruise in 1990. She looked more elegant than ever before and I convinced her to cut her hair very short and slick it back with gel. We were having a drink at the upstairs bar at the Dorothy Chandler Pavilion when a smartly dressed, good looking woman in our age group took the time to compliment

Dancing with Goofy (he's the one on the left)—one buddy who never let me down. We are on the now-defunct Tomorrowland Stage, 1982.

Diane on her hair style. We also danced together very well in the cruise ship music club, receiving compliments from various onlookers. Prior to this, Diane was always too nervous to dance with me, but she gained confidence knowing how stunning she now looked.

I started teaching commercial acting and auditioning for film, TV and stage at Learning Tree University. Again, I did not deal with Hamlet's favorite color being chartreuse, nor his zodiacal sign as subtext, but the pragmatics of auditioning for different media and the punch and pulse of auditioning—all the vagaries that are different in all the formats of acting.

In 1991 we remodeled our kitchen and bath, closed up a wall, extended a room and installed new carpeting except for the refinished floors in the living room. I have never remodeled again and hope to never undergo such a contentious and draining experience.

My Native American regalia for Mr. Saturday Night *as I played, sang and danced as one of the four guys from Billy Crystal's character's TV show.*

As far as professional work during that time, I played Uncle Stanley in *Pink Lightning*; I played a bad cop opposite the self-impressed, feckless and otiose Robert Davi, in an indie film, *Illicit Behavior*; I became a businessman in *Murder, She Wrote* with the aloof, or perhaps older and overworked, Angela Lansbury; I choreographed the Dorothy Parker musical *The Lady In Question* for its world premiere; I did *Mr. Saturday Night* with Billy Crystal and *Newsies* at Disney for choreographer/director Kenny Ortega; and I went to Maui to play a director for a live Coke Industrial show and played Sherlock Holmes for a tour group in Montecito, California.

My next appearance for Disney was solo as Mouseketeer Lonnie at the Chicago Museum of Broadcasting with Allison Fonte who was a star of *The New Mickey Mouse Club* in the 'seventies. Without asking us to sign a release, the Museum taped our hour-long dialogue and began selling a DVD, viewable and available for sale. I had no knowledge of it until later when a fan informed me. They even charged me when I called to acquire a copy. I guess some museum folks are just like some showbiz folks. I did manage to get a slight discount for the DVD of my own appearance.

Diane and I went to Mouseketeer Sharon's fiftieth birthday in Palm Springs with Annie and other Mice and I choreographed another play, *The Bonnie Earl Tapestry*. Marty Balsam was my sidekick in the very corny comedy, *Silence of the Hams* in 1993 and I played an IRS agent in the "Robo Sammy" sketch on Robert Townsend's *In Living Color*. In another odd twist, I found out that Townsend bought the HPS building and land on Hollywood Boulevard, but thus far nothing has been done with it.

The first psychotherapy Diane had was in the 'eighties for depression and some related problems. I was once asked by this therapist to sit in on one of Diane's sessions, which I found odd but agreed to do. This female was surly and very aggressive in attacking me. I got through it but Diane realized this lady could not help her when she violated her trust with Diane by assaulting me, no matter what Diane had said in private and confidence. In the 2000s in Maryland, Diane found a more effective therapist.

We were facing menopause and andropause, which has more to do with hormones and changes in the human body than mere mood swings and buying a new Ferrari, which I had no interest in doing.

I moved on to two different roles on *Lois & Clark* in '94, the second one being the sleazy, look-alike agent Sammy in the "That Old Gang of Mine" episode. I was a gay Muscovite in the film, *Police Academy VII—Mission to Moscow* and choreographed the play *The Session*.

I also played grizzled old Lobster, a character in an original play *Strays*, and made an appearance at Disneyland with a few other Mice and both Karen and now Annie in wheelchairs for a Disneyana Convention in the same year 1995.

My play *Exeunt All*, which I also directed, was at the Ruby Theatre in Los Angeles. I also co-choreographed and tapped with hoofer and tap teacher Stan Mazin, with whom I had worked on *Newsies*, as the Price/Waterhouse team (à la the Oscars) for the L.A. Dance and Choreography

Annette, Sharon and Karen in front and Lorraine Santoli, Tommy and Mouseketeer Mensch behind at a Disneyana convention at WDW.

awards for LADAS. My poem "Above the Bike Path" won the thirteenth annual poetry awards and publication for the Triton College of Arts and Sciences and I began getting in touch with my natural self and nature while acting as a docent at Descanso Gardens. This continued as a weekly chore until moving to Maryland/D.C. in mid-1998.

Lorraine's book *The Official Mickey Mouse Club Book* was published in 1995 for our Fortieth MMC Anniversary and we attended the Disneyana conventions at Disneyland and WDW, after first meeting at Annie's house. We did a dialogue/song/dance variety live show at WDW, too. Tommy Kirk made a rare appearance along with us as did David Stollery and Tim Considine, but they did not sing or dance. Bill Justice, one of Walt's famous "Old Men" who started with him and created, among many other contributions, Chip 'N Dale, had been asked to attend and decided to get married. It was Bill who had brought his friend and tennis partner Jimmie Dodd to Walt's attention in 1955. Diane and I were the only Mouseketeer witnesses to the small ceremony of Bill's marriage to his bride Kim in our WDW hotel. We also went to Cheryl's surprise birthday party for Annie in Santa Monica and later took Fess up on his overnight visit, hosted dinner, stay at his hotel in Santa Barbara and a tour of his winery in the Santa Ynez Valley, California.

My next difficult death occurred on May 19, 1995 when my mother-in-law Hilda died very suddenly. I felt very close to Hilda because she allowed me to be myself, not the person she wanted me to be, Beyond unusual and unique. Hilda was in the hospital and Diane was flying to D.C. when Hilda suddenly went into surgery but she did not survive. Diane never got to see her mother alive again. She was devastated.

Later that year Sharon's twin boy Jeremy, in his early twenties, died in a skiing accident. Diane and I helped coordinate the services and I spoke for us both. We both really liked Jeremy a lot and remembered he had thought it cool when Diane and I gave him and a buddy a ride, years before, and we were playing Blood, Sweat and Tears. There were good times and bad times in 1995.

Annie and me at Sharon's 50th birthday in Palm Springs, 1992. The vest with the Hook *logo is the one from Dustin.*

Hilda and her only son-in-law in her home in the late '80s.

In 1996 I received a residual intended for George Chakiris. I returned it to SAG and could only wonder how Burr and Chakiris got mixed up. I joined other Mice in the Burbank Day Parade and my first Betty, the older woman from the 'sixties, rushed out of the crowd to say hello. She looked trim and sharp and her smile had never changed. Very cool.

My grandmother turned 100 in 1997 and I managed to get her a birthday greeting from President Clinton and a mention by Willard Scott on *The Today Show*.

Diane and I stayed at her friend Patty's beach house in Bethany Beach (Delaware), in Patty's absence, and took a boat over to Chincoteague National Park, known for its wild horses, and were pleased at the beauty everywhere on our bird-watching excursions. The owner of Diane's business firm and her employer Nathan Cohen had moved to Santa Barbara, with Di running the business from the office; they communicated daily by PC and phone and he, of course, made all the final decisions on matters for his clients. Not too long after this, Nathan became ill and died.

With Gram in the '90s and in her late 90s.

Diane had been recruited for the position of Director of Alumnae at the National Cathedral School, a girl's independent school on the grounds of the National Cathedral in Washington, D.C.. Diane had attended the institution, which was soon to celebrate its centennial, before receiving her B.A. from Bucknell and her M.F.A. from Catholic University. One of her classmates at NCS was Lynda Bird Johnson. I met Lynda when we attended an NCS party at the home of the former President's daughter and her husband Senator Chuck Robb. Other children who became famous, like Gore Vidal and Vice President and Nobel Prize winner Al Gore attended St. Albans, for boys, on the same grounds. The Beauvoir School is part of the campus for younger children. Schoolmates for Diane from her M.F.A. at Catholic University included Susan and Chris Sarandon.

We had been looking for a way out of the San Fernando Valley and California for a few years and this seemed the perfect fit. I had played the National Theatre, the Kennedy Center and done stock outside of D.C. and also visited Diane's parents in Georgetown often and later just Hilda. So in 1997 we became bicoastal with Di moving in temporarily with her brother

David and his wife in Virginia, just across the bridge from D.C. I stayed in North Hollywood writing and auditioning and did the last season of *Chicago Hope*. I also was stuck with the tedious process of selling our two houses.

We finally moved to our great home in Sligo Park Hills, Maryland, just fifteen-plus minutes from downtown D.C. in my birth month of May, 1998. The house was all on one level (that would be called a rambler in the East and a ranch house in the West). Older eastern homes usually have at least two stories and a basement. We had a finished basement as a large family room with a third full bathroom and access to the washer/dryer and large sinks, storage and the single-car garage. Everything else was one level up.

I was amazed at how many houses in the eastern part of America have single garages or no garage at all. I assume they were built in earlier eras when people had only one vehicle and there is little land left but the weather dictates a two or three-car garage. The living room in our 1934 home was quite spacious with great light which was true of all the upstairs. There was outside light downstairs in the family room but it was limited. There was a separate dining room and just past it a large master suite with a full bath, walk-in closet, large clerestory windows plus a built-in chest of drawers and sliding-door closets added on in the 'sixties.

Our den served as our media room with another full bath and through an open window-paned door from the LR was another added-on room which was my study, used as a writing and reading and PC room. It also had a separate heating system so I could rise earlier than Diane (which I have since I changed my circadian rhythm in my thirties), and not overheat the house. I get up every day around 5 a.m. I really miss that room; it was definitely *mine* more than any room I have ever had.

There were wonderful large trees on the property and a lovely, spacious rear garden with a nice-sized patio. I had created a small Japanese garden in our Cartwright home before this and I added a large rock circle at 3 Belmont—Diane insisted on moving these large California rocks from L.A. with the furniture movers, who thought her a bit barmy—to enclose our sweet bay magnolia tree in the center of the backyard. We also had two hemlocks, a huge gum locust, an apple tree, a crepe myrtle, some rose of sharon, azaleas, forsythia and lilac.

We added flowers and vegetables in one section and, as previously at 5749 Cartwright in North Hollywood, it was a maintained habitat for birds and other animals. This time we included butterflies by adding buddleia and other flutterbys foliage. There were also the resilient, indomitable but laughter-producing squirrels and a rare groundhog or other small critter now and again since we were only about one hundred yards from a park that ran miles north and south. Together and separately, Diane and I identified 46 different species of birds in our years at this address including pileated woodpeckers, a Cooper's hawk, red-winged blackbirds, and flickers.

In our front yard, two feet from our property, was our neighbor's huge willow oak which was over 150 years old, two dogwood trees on each side of our yard, flowering crabapples at the curb which flourished in springtime up and down our cul-de-sac street making things bright pink and white, as well as hydrangeas, more azaleas, honeysuckle and mint.

Since my Descanso integration with nature I have become something of a gardener. I rely on Diane's knowledge of plants, but I do the designing and all the trimming and upkeep. I also got exercise shoveling snow every winter but at least we were not in Minnesota or upstate New York—still, I think I shall find a way to avoid this exercise in the future.

Securing an agent, I also started looking and, on my own, did VO (Voice Over work) for the most visited museum in the world, the Smithsonian's National Air and Space Museum. One of the things I recorded was for their IMAX films; the previous voice for the films was Sir

In Death of a Salesman *by Arthur Miller at the Olney Theatre, Maryland, 2001.*

Alec Guinness. I also became a member of the Edwin Forrest Society, a part of the Actors Fund of America which is a section of Actor's Equity that helps out-of-work actors subsist.

I had overestimated the amount of acting work I would find in the D.C./Baltimore area, although there is more paying theatre than in L.A., but I did shoot an episode of *Homicide—Life On The Street* in 1999 and played a run of *Death of A Salesman* at the Olney Theatre in Maryland. I continued writing, more on a new play than the memoir which became one with a drawer.

In 2000 my writer friend Jerry Bowles helped me set up my website, which is the only Mouseketeer website out there except for mousestars.com, which I helped webmaster Steve assemble in 1995, but which shut down in 2005. I still assist webmaster George Grant for the much more comprehensive originalmmc.com which started in May, 2006 and Don Grady finally set up a website for his new CD, music and conducting and Bob a site for his dancing school in 2008.

I took early retirement from SAG to have regular money coming in when I was fifty-five, much earlier than other pensions allow. I decided to take less payment and early retirement from Equity and Social Security at age sixty-two, the earliest allowable, in 2005. In all three instances you can earn more by working and paying into the pension fund and I have in no way retired.

For some time I have been concerned about the mounting problems and what I believe to be the inevitable misuse of the Social Security system. I had been contributing since a child and they already changed my full retirement from sixty-five to sixty-six and some months. If not Bush, which was my main concern, some politician(s) will be doing something to dissipate S.S. in the next ten years, at least in my opinion, altering it to the detriment of the Americans who have been paying into it for many decades. Despite my accountant's denial of this, I think being a part of the system already will be much better than waiting for the next negative change.

I did the play *Typhoid Mary* in the role of Francis Morgenborg at the well known Arena Stage in D.C., which I had not played before, and played two roles in an Industrial film—meaning a film made for just a specific business group. This short movie was made for the Teamsters. I portrayed an ecumenical, politically incorrect co-worker who first inappropriately comes on to a female and then heckles a gay male coworker. Before any wags begin wagging their tongues, this was NOT typecasting.

The paperback of *Two for the Show* came out with the revisions from 1983 to 2000 and Diane and I went on our first visit to Philly, which we enjoyed, and got to see the wonderful Barnes Foundation collections. which, like the Phillips in D.C., another favorite, is in the home of the late collector—against the man's will, the collection is fighting being moved to downtown Philadelphia. In early 2001 my second poetry collection was published, a compilation of thirty years of mostly published poems winning eleven awards and titled *The Gravity of Finity II*.

September 11th, 2001 changed the life of all Americans forever. Living as close as we did to D.C. and not that many miles from the Pentagon, we may have had more trepidations than those elsewhere, excluding of course people who lived in New York City. Diane was at work at the National Cathedral School where she had crisis responsibilities as an administrator. The entire administrative team had to remain calm and be reassuring to the students amid a terror alert right next to the largest Christian symbol on the highest point of land in Washington, D.C. where services for deceased Presidents and other major leaders are often held. It could easily have been another target.

I was appalled, oppressed and transfixed watching the attacks on TV at home and could not reach Diane by phone. She finally got to me over an hour later to say she was all right. I have been through the horrors of the assassination of JFK, then Martin Luther King, Jr. and Bobby Kennedy. I watched the ugliness of the 1968 Democratic Convention in Chicago. Nothing was like this attack, including Pearl Harbor which could not be SEEN but only heard about and was thousands of miles of sea away, not near our home in Maryland and in New York City where we had met.

It was eerily quiet with absolutely no air traffic; the sky was beautifully blue and the clouds stark white. For many weeks afterwards as soon as Diane got home we would have drinks outside on our back patio where the birds splashed and squirrels darted. We talked of this act that had terrorized all of us and many others around the world. As we recovered somewhat, there was a new alert; F-16s blasted over our home patrolling D.C. air space; the first night they stopped constant patrols months later, there were numerous calls to radio and TV stations about what was wrong, what was going on, were we under attack again? It was far worse and even more frightening than Orson Welles' radio broadcast of *The War of the Worlds* in 1938. This radio play was done in documentary style and hundreds of thousands did not believe it was fiction but the real thing.

I wrote an occasional poem and Jerry Bowles put it on his website and married it to some of his photos of the epochal destruction. It can still be found online. The poem is titled:

Le Chute [The Fall]

we crane our souls to
commiserate,
just as we congregate in
gothic edifices
which serve no purpose
but our propinquity

vonnegut's dresden
nagasaki
surreal yet real
like this abyss drawing us,
that we shun in full
mirror

assassinating an
important personage
good or bad, kennedy
or king, kills one's ideals

the holocaust
of new york
kills
idealism

2001 – lonnie burr

I wrote a longer poem on the first anniversary of 9/ll titled "The Day of Names" (see Appendix).

Diane and I continued bird watching although her executive hours were longer than they had been with Nathan and she had many functions to attend. Since I could no longer run, I did start doing some hiking, but only sporadically. I did, at least, give myself a fifty-minute, head to toe, jazz warm-up once a week but I started to put on a few pounds. Men's bodies change just like women's as they approach 60—unless you work at keeping fit.

I gave my last two poetry readings and my new play was *Phantom Pain*, in which dialogue explains that phantom pain is a medical phrase used when your brain feels a pain, for example, in the foot which a surgeon has removed; thus, it is a false pain existing only in the mind even though the pain is tangible. I used it as a metaphor for the lead character searching for his long-deceased father. The father's nickname was Bake (remind you of Ham?). The two-act was done at the National Conservatory of Dramatic Arts in Georgetown, D.C.

I had a nice conversation with Roy Disney, Jr. at the "100 Years of Magic" for he is a cordial man, or always has been to me, and I am sure he had no knowledge of our vacation being turned into unpaid work.

My grandmother turned 105, but was in a very bad state for which there was no cure but pills that put off some of the pain. Our last phone conversation before her death in 2001 tormented me greatly. She had not been able to hear for years and refused hearing aids. When she got on the phone she immediately began calling me hateful names and accused me of

Roy Disney, Jr. and a Mouseketeer named Lonnie at "100 Years of Magic" at WDW in 2003.

things that I never did. I inferred that she thought I was someone else, most likely the disreputable Jim Valint. I tried patiently to explain to her, but I failed to break through her senseless, repetitive anger. We never spoke again.

My mom had stopped calling Glade daily too for the same reason. I asked her to explain this unpleasant mix-up to Gram but she, too, was unable to discover who Glade thought she was talking to or what I was supposed to have done. Dot could no longer drive due to her MS; actually, she should have stopped her short trips to the market or anywhere long before she did but, like Gram, she would not listen to me. Fortunately, she and other drivers were spared an accident. She maintained contact by phone but Glade could not hear, nor could she communicate much at all.

I played Mr. Grogan in the musical of *The Human Comedy* by William Saroyan and one review stated, "Lonnie Burr is compelling as the hard-drinking but lovable old telegraph operator." This was an unusual experience that had no dialogue and was all song and was written by Galt McDermott who wrote the music for the very different musical, *Hair*. I made a solo Mouseketeer appearance in Nashville for a large corporation and went back to the Arena Stage for *The Marriage of Miss Hollywood and King Neptune*, an ineptly titled and written two-act in which I played one of my many hoods.

By this time I had had enough of the provincialism of both Maryland and D.C. Of course, if you run in the millionaire and political circles, there would seem to be a wealth of international diversity, intelligence and wit in the area but that is not what we found, except at NCS and I attended only a few functions for the school. I got over being a "party animal" by my thirties and since the onset of politically correct meaninglessness in conversation, even the weather can become a verbally contentious ordeal. Hence, I am not one for parties, nor have I been for well over thirty years. We rarely give them either; our last was for Diane's move to NCS in 1997.

One example of the provincial nature in Maryland: I attempted to find a comfort food from childhood that I get a hankering for every now and again, Swanson's Chicken à la king which my mom served on toast. The manager of our chain market had never heard of it and referred me to the foreign food section, I can only assume because he thought à la king was a French concoction or that it was some strange offshoot of Chung King Chow Mein. I checked another chain market and they did not carry it. This product has been sold for about seventy years. I finally had to have the manager of the closest supermarket order a case of it for me. It is in my favor that the canned goop keeps for a long time and still tastes the same as when I was a kid.

Granpa Joad in Act I of The Grapes of Wrath *and The Mayor of Hooverville in Act II, 2004.*

    I became the octogenarian Granpa Joad in the stage version of Steinbeck's *The Grapes of Wrath*. Granpa dies near the end of Act I, so in the second act I turned into a very different looking Mayor of Hooverville. "Hoovervilles" sprung up all over the U.S. during the Depression and Hoover's presidency. People were forced to live in open town squares or any area in which you could put up tents and not pay for anything. In 2009 there is concern about this becoming a reality again.

    People seem to think of the homeless people as being from the last two or three decades but there were tens of thousands more in the 1930s. My Mayor was a mite 'tetched and used a kid's wagon to contain all of his possessions and to scavenge for anything that he could use. We performed the play in the 19th century Ford's Theatre in downtown D.C. which I also had not played before.

    After President Lincoln's assassination at Ford's in 1865 the theatre was not used for plays or any public display. A century later it was refurbished and in 1968 it reopened and began producing only American playwrights' work as well as some appropriate touring companies. The theatre holds a fair amount of people but nothing like the huge, cold vacuums of some Broadway and other newer theatres. It is quite intimate for its size and the orchestra has rows of separate wooden armchairs as was done in the mid-19th century, rather than banks of theatre seats. The box Lincoln was in is never used and there is a full body likeness of him, facing the stage.

    The night we opened I walked out the stage door and there were MMC fans who were thrilled and surprised that Mouseketeer Lonnie was in the play. Granpa was about 25 years older than I and they were pleased I did not look like I did onstage. They wanted my autograph more as

Mouseketeer Lonnie than as Granpa Joad. I got some very nice notices and, due to my previous work, did most of the TV interviews which are generally done by the leads who have more focus, like the very good young actor, Craig Walker, who did Hank Fonda's role as my character's grandson in the film of the book. Jim Ortlieb, as Uncle John, was one of my makeup roommates and he made the experience much more pleasant.

In December of 2003 my mom died. I still keep in touch with my third cousins, Pudd and her brother Billy and Pudd's daughter, my fourth cousin Bev and her husband Jack, her son and grandkids. I was called from the hospital Mom was taken to in Vegas to make decisions about maintaining her life in a comatose state with no chance of improvement and I knew what her wishes were. Diane and I flew out from Maryland to do all that was necessary regarding her remains, will and the house she lived in, which I owned. She was just two months shy of ninety. She wanted to be cremated, as do I and Diane. As mentioned, her ashes are with her parents in nearby Boulder City, Nevada.

My ashes will be surreptitiously strewn in Disneyland whether by Diane, if I precede her, or my executor. If I explained where in the Park, Disney would definitely prevent it, so take a guess where I will be a permanent part of Walt's dream.

In 2004 we were visited by an ailing raccoon who took up sleeping in one of our basement window wells, the ones that, to my regret and sweat, filled with leaves and later snow every bloody year. On an earlier occasion, two baby raccoons who most likely were motherless, made attempts to get food from the birds (and the inevitable squirrels) that I fed daily. They appeared by the tool shed and I threw small, light, empty containers for the feed at them. They decided this was a swell game and I was like a referee at a basketball game, for they batted the containers around and returned a number of times.

In 2004 I made a Special Guest Appearance in "Musical Chairs" a recurring live show in Palm Springs, California. It is run by Derrick Lewis, with whom I went to college; I began calling him Derrick Merrick for he produced the shows as well as performing in them, casting and directing. Derrick puts together musical theme shows and had chosen Disney songwriters, like the Sherman Brothers, who wrote the songs for *Mary Poppins* and other films. I met and worked with the two Shermans, one now gone, in 1987 at the first of three Mouseketeer performances at the Hollywood Bowl after our very first in 1957. Derrick thought it would be

On the stage of the Hollywood Bowl rehearsing with Richard Sherman at the piano. Tommy and I are behind it with Snow White, and host, Disney executive Frank Wells is holding the mike, 1987.

great to have a real Mouseketeer to sing and dance and adlib and do scripted lines with onstage but it did not change my opinion of Palm Springs as one of the most boring cities in the world.

Both Diane and I were ready to return to the West Coast but I was much more eager than she was to get away from the humidity, winter snow, provincialism and the worst drivers I have ever encountered including Paris, Tijuana, NYC and, of course, Southern California. We found a home in San Clemente, which was only a couple of miles from the ocean. We put our Maryland house up for sale and it went quickly; being 2005 we made a bundle on it. We only had four days and three nights to fly out and find a home in San Clemente, a town neither of us had ever visited. Although D.C. had become excessively expensive for homes anywhere, California was worse. Our shipping date was imminent and unchangeable, thus, we had to have some place to put our furniture, art, collectibles, clothes, Syny the cat—and us.

We finally found something newly listed the last day we were there. What we had seen previously from $450,000 to $650,000 was not livable except by necessity for the three in our family. Ours was only slightly over a half a million, which is enormous when you grew up in the late 'forties and 'fifties.

We arrived early and stayed with Sharon in Studio City; she has always been a very gracious hostess. Syny began showing signs of illness soon after we arrived. She seemed to get better, we moved into our home and Diane started her duties in San Juan Capistrano but we were both preoccupied with Syny's illness, which took a desperately bad turn.

Our first vet was lousy but we found the very good and caring veterinarian by the name of Jack Mannix. Syny was diagnosed with lymphoma and Jack had us see feline cancer experts who started her on expensive, debilitating chemotherapy. Her personality began changing and worsened on this drug regimen.

I performed in the July 17th, 2005 live show at Disneyland's fiftieth anniversary before my shoulder problems began and then made the futile attempt to do the show for the MMC 50th at Disneyland in early October. My pain and absence did not appear to concern, nor interest anyone.

That Christmas Diane and I went on a holiday to not be around where Syny could no longer cavort, attack and slide through the wrapping papers, ribbons and her own gifts. We went to the Baja California area of Mexico and looked at some property as a possible future place to live. San Clemente was nice enough but was not the answer. We did not find much to our liking and I was concerned about the graft and danger of Mexican police, the banditos that are everywhere, the drug wars, escalating kidnappings and the language barriers.

Diane had begun gaining weight again after the 1990 transition, losing the weight she had gained from stopping cigarettes. There is one main reason; she does not exercise. I have done everything possible to entice and encourage her, but she refuses. She did start dieting seriously in 2006 because we had decided to spend Christmas, the second without Syny, in Europe, six days in Firenze, Italy then a week in Paris. There were fantastic museums, great comestibles, lots of walking, an excellent lunch at the haute cuisine Jules Verne restaurant high up in the Eiffel Tower as well as other very good wine and dining out.

Diane on the carousel we had started just for the two of us one evening after dinner in Firenze, Italy, 2006.

I searched for and found an agent on my return to California in 2005 but almost all of my auditions were for commercials, which are good moneymakers but are rarely fulfilling for an actor. I am older and there is age discrimination for men as well as women, although it occurs earlier for females; this is true for writers as well. There are not that many grandpa roles out there and a robust guy, in good shape in his sixties can be nothing else but a grandpa in our youth acculturation. Actually, the product people who represent the advertisers prefer silver-haired grandpas in their 70s.

My first love and largest roles have been in theatre but it is against my stage union's rules to work for free. There are numerous roles I would love to do, like Tobias in Albee's *A Delicate Balance*, but finding a paying company for this would be nearly impossible. It was bad enough to spend a three-hour plus round trip freeway drive from San Clemente to L.A. for an audition, but to do so daily for weeks of rehearsal and play dates in a 99-seat, no pay, union acceptable situation was impossible. The cost of gas from a round trip ranged from $23 to almost $40 each trip, depending on the current rip-off, for an audition, which precluded it.

Unless I have the opportunity to play a role I have wanted do for years like George in *Who's Afraid of Virginia Woolf?*, I do not have the same passion for acting and performing that I formerly did. Whether actor Barbara Gordon's memoir about her valium addiction and showbiz, *I'm Dancing as Fast as I Can,* or the aforementioned Broadway director Jose Quintero's memoir *If You Don't Dance They Beat You,* I no longer feel the need to knock myself out for an audience, nor for my own sense of accomplishment. If it is just for some commercial drivel, it is even harder to motivate myself, although the money would come in quite handy.

Diane performed very well in her slightly different capacity at St. Margaret's Episcopal School in San Juan Capistrano, CA amidst the returning of the swallows. She met the annual gifts' goal her first year and surpassed the increased figure by many thousands in her second year. She also created new programs and obtained a major foundation grant. Then her boss left and an evil vixen, whom I thin sliced on first glimpse before meeting her, fired her after two months for no defensible reason.

The full part of the snifter was this vile female due to her infamous, outrageous actions and behavior to my wife and others was fired herself two months later. We considered litigation but California is an "at will" employment state which greatly complicates things and, in addition to my feelings about the dangerous law system, we decided to decline the risk, stress and time that would be mandatory.

In September, 2008 Diane became the Director of the Annual Fund at the beautiful campus of venerable Lewis and Clark College in Portland, OR. We had considered moving to Oregon previously and we finally got into our new home in nearby Beaverton, OR in January, 2009. Oregon is not a "yankee" state but west of the Mississippi it is the state most oriented to an individual's rights. My kind of folks.

My memoir is being published and I am going on to something else, which may be more writing or not. I do not know. We are not affluent but we will not wind up on a street somewhere despite the ongoing massive real estate depreciation, the formidable price of oil and gas which has begun to affect everything from food to automobiles to tourism, in concert with the unnecessary, impossible to win, deadly war in Iraq and an economy circa 1929, all thanks to perhaps the worst American president we have ever had, including Harding, Nixon, et. al.—George Bush II. We were billions ahead economically when he came into office more than eight years ago and we are now trillions of dollars in debt—and it rises day by day. Even if President

Obama's efforts and plans solve some of our problems, we are a very long way from reclaiming America from the Bush destruction.

I contend with my depression much better now but it remains a part of life that must be dealt with far too often despite the pills and my former therapy. I do drink but in my home. If Diane and I have a martini and then wine with dinner she drives, but that combo is rare.

The Walt Disney Company began honoring people in 1987 with The Disney Legend Awards. Stars like Julie Andrews, Kurt Russell, Hayley Mills, Fess Parker and, from the MMC, Annette, Jimmie and Roy (J & R posthumously) became Disney Legends. Many artists behind the camera have also been honored. I recently found out that in 2006 Tim Considine and David Stollery, who respectively played Spin and Marty, Kevin Corcoran, who acted as Moochie, Tommy Kirk and, among others, Mouseketeer Ginny have also become a part of Walt's legacy by receiving this honor.

Mouseketeer Ginny?

For years I told the few fans who inquired that there was no Mouseketeer Ginny. I much later found out that Ginny Tyler, who looked very much like Annie including her coiffure, was the Disneyland hostess for the first reruns of the MMC (1962-1965) even though she had not been a part of our series.

Annie unquestionably deserves her Legend status and I have never held out hope for myself, nor the other seven original Mouseketeers who lasted the entire filming of the original MMC, to receive such an award. After this memoir, IF this oversight is rectified, I surely will not be included.

"Do you not see how necessarily a World of Pains and Troubles is to school an Intelligence and make it a Soul?," inquired John Keats of his brother Tom. Many contrary examples come to mind but Georgia O'Keeffe had a lifetime of problems with depression yet continued to do beautiful work and Handel struggled desperately most of his life but late in his years he wrote his best work, *Messiah*, after having many failures.

I do not, as I did as a young man, think you must suffer in order to be an artist. I do believe that all artists need to live life and experience pain and laughter, love and loss of love, the death of those to whom they are extremely close, pain and injury and sickness in order to convey emotions and thoughts to other humans who experience the same in their own way, in their own lives, in a fantastic richness of artistic modalities that no other species is capable of accomplishing. The elephant is more beautiful, the bee more productive and the ant stronger—but we do have this one rare gift.

My many decades in the entertainment industry have taught me one thing that is true of all of life: you must always respect what you do, whatever it may be, for if you do not respect it, no one else will. If you are forced to do things you do not respect, you must desist, leave at the first opportunity. Even if it involves how you make your living, you must find an alternative and escape the first day it is economically feasible. If you do not, you will really not be living at all.

In early 2009 I read in a newspaper that the Geological Society of London has declared that the negative impact of humans on the earth's atmosphere, air, land, seas and waters, animal species—just about everything—since the Industrial Revolution, has moved us out of the Holocene epoch and into the Anthropocene epoch - the time of humans - which is denoted by notorious hubris and destruction. I am forced to agree with this pejorative declaration and can only do what I can, as an individual, to not contribute in any way to the furthering of these deplorable acts in this sad, faltering world.

In spite of my candor and less than beautiful and inspiring view of our circumstances, I will continue reading daily and writing. I will also be acting/dancing/choreographing/directing, if these latter talents can find outlets here near Portland, Oregon. Diane and I plan to fulfill a long standing desire to start a theatre company: The Chez Nous Theatre. I also might return to educating or working in some volunteer capacity.

What I will not do is retire, nor give up, nor lose hope, nor sign on to do anything for Disney, nor anyone, without the elements of what I am to do and for how long specifically written out to my satisfaction. Since the early '80s our appearances for Disney have been primarily verbal, then changed radically and to our detriment. I also will require that I be treated with respect and receive decent, appropriate wages. Disney actually doing this would be as unlikely as their contacting me for future Mouseketeer appearances.

If Disney just needs a number of Mouseketeer bodies, as Sherry quite correctly put it, they will have to do without Mouseketeer Mensch's form, which is aging quite well, like a fine Brunello di Montalcino from Tuscany.

Back Home, Candide Weeds His Garden

Hiking into 2009.

Appendix

** page from original first year contract
between Lonnie Burr & Disney

9. The Artist grants to the Producer, without consideration other than the salary hereinabove agreed to be paid, the exclusive right and license to use and simulate the Artist's name, photograph, likeness, silhouette and voice in and in connection with its motion picture productions and in or in connection with advertising, exploiting and exhibiting the same, and in and in connection with merchandising and commercial advertising and publicity tie-ups in which its motion picture productions are advertised or exploited, and in and in connection with the services specified in Paragraph 1 of this agreement. The Producer shall have the exclusive right to issue publicity concerning the Artist, and the Artist agrees not to engage any publicity representative nor to issue or permit the issuance of any publicity whatsoever concerning the Artist except by the Producer as aforesaid.

10. (a) In addition to the rights granted to it in Paragraph 9 the Producer shall have and is hereby granted the further exclusive right and license to use, utilize and simulate, or to license others so to use, utilize and simulate, the Artist's endorsement, name, photograph, likeness, silhouette, caricature and voice in and in connection with any merchandising and/or publishing endeavors whatsoever (and whether such publishing endeavors be literary or musical) in which the Producer or its licensees and/or privies may be or become engaged.

(b) In consideration of the right and license granted to it in paragraph 10(a) the Producer agrees, subject to the provisions of subparagraph (c) next following, to pay to the Artist sums of money equal to two and one-half per cent (2 1/2%) of the gross amounts received by the Producer pursuant to or attributable to any such merchandising or publishing endeavors referred to in subparagraph 10(a) in or in connection with which the Artist's endorsement, name, photograph, likeness, silhouette, caricature or voice is or are used, utilized or simulated, provided, however, that the Producer's obligation to pay such sums to the Artist shall not accrue unless or until the moneys out of which the same are to be paid shall have been received by the Producer within the United States of America and are placed at the Producer's unrestricted disposal.

(c) The Producer represents to the Artist, and the Artist is aware, that during the term of this contract the Producer will be a party to contracts with other persons pursuant to which other contracts the Producer has been or will be granted rights, and has undertaken and/or will undertake obligations, substantially the same as, or similar to, those contained in this paragraph 10. It is agreed, therefore, that if, and whenever, with respect to any such merchandising and/or publishing endeavor, the Producer is obligated to pay compensation to the Artist under subparagraph 10(b) hereof, and also to one or more of such other persons pursuant to the corresponding or similar provisions of the Producer's contract or contracts with such other persons, then the percentage payable to the Artist pursuant to subparagraph 10(b) hereof shall be divided by the number of such persons (including the Artist) to whom the Producer is so obligated to make such payments.

-4-

WALT DISNEY PRODUCTIONS
CHARACTER MERCHANDISING DIVISION
COMMISSIONS PAYABLE (MOUSEKETEERS)
MONTH ENDED MARCH 30, 1957

LONNIE BURR

CHARACTER MERCHANDISING

Sawyers, Inc. - December, January and February Royalty Report

	December	January	February
(1) Tru Vue Card DA-7 D-22 Each participates at .25%	$ 44.67	$ 59.04	$ 40.53
(3) #865ABC	718.50		345.60

Participation	January	February	March	Total
1 and 3	$ 3.70	$ .15	$ 1.83	$ 5.68

WALT DISNEY PRODUCTIONS
CHARACTER MERCHANDISING DIVISION
COMMISSIONS PAYABLE (MOUSEKETEERS)
Month Ended September 28, 1957

MOUSEKETEERS

CHARACTER MERCHANDISING

Sawyers, Inc. -   June, July and August Royalty Reports

LONNIE BURR

	June	July	August
(1) Tru Vue DA-7 D-22 Each participates at .25% of	$22.60	$17.11	$29.20
(3) #865 A Each participates at .50% of	$82.68	$66.15	$73.50

Participation (1) and (3)

	July	August	September	Total
	$ .46	$ .37	$ .43	$1.26

Rcd 4/27/99

DEAREST LON: sent Homel owner's Day

AS YOU CAN SEE, I STILL HAVE THE EXPENSIVE STATIONERY!
(asset - takeover grands?)
BILL AND PUDD WERE UP TO SEE ME. THEY STAYED FOR TWO WEKS,
AND DID IT COST ME !!!!!

ARE YOU EVER GOING TO GET THESE THINGS OF MOTHER'S THAT
YOU WANTED? (it)   ("chanto")
not until house

I WIL ANSWER ALITTLE OF WHAT YOU ASKED ME SEVERAL MONTHS AGO.
FIRST, IT WAS BIG, OLD, FAT TRAVER THAT TOLD ME YOU WUOLD
BE BLACKBALLED IF YOU TOOK FLIKA BUT I SHOULD HAVE TAKEN IT
ANYWAY!

~~GARRAD AVE.~~   ~~KY~~   ~~6 MONTHS~~

PLACE	STATE	AGE
GARRARD AVE.	KY.	6 MONTHS
2700 ASHLAND AVE.	KY.	1 YEAR
316 E. THIRD ST.	KY.	2 YEARS

AT 2½ WENT TO CAIF. STAYED IN HOTELS FOR A WHILE
NO APARTMENTS WOULD TAKE CHILDREN! ✓

? STRICKLAND	CALIF.	3 YEARS	Highland Park
1353 KENT PL.	"	"	4 TO 6 years	Glendale
5039 BLUEBELL AVE.	"	6 YEARS	NoHo

I DO NOT KNOW THE PLACES AFTER THAT BECAUSE YOU WENT TO LIVE
WITH YOUR GRANDPARENTS.

Some of the People of Note With Whom I Have Worked

Stars and Celebrities

Jimmy Stewart
Elvis Presley
Rosemary Clooney
Roy Rogers and
  Dale Evans
Eddie Cantor
Julia Roberts
Jean Claude Van Damme
Bob Hope
Sammy Davis
Robin Williams
Dinah Shore
Clayton Moore
  (The Lone Ranger)
Ed Wynn
Keenan Wynn

Martin Balsam
Carol Channing
Robert Preston
Jack Benny
Scatman Crothers
Shirley MacLaine
Bob Hoskins
Abbott & Costello
Eddie Bracken
Ginger Rogers
Paul Winfield
Charlie Ruggles
Bernadette Peters
Jock Mahoney
Donald O'Connor
Dustin Hoffman

Ann-Margret
Cesar Romero
Ben Vereen
Dean Martin
Buddy Ebsen
Hayley Mills
Darren McGavin
Pat Boone
Jimmy Durante
Charles Coburn
Christian Slater
Billy Crystal
Jerry Lewis
Raymond St. Jacques
Gene Nelson
Jason Bateman

Directors and Producers

Steven Spielberg
Gower Champion
Bob Fosse

Norman Taurog
David Merrick
Walt Disney
Cecil B. deMille

Joseph Losey
Charles Vidor
Arthur Hiller

Composers, Choreographers & Conductors

John Williams
Mark Shaiman
Buddy Baker
Jerry Herman
Richard & Robert Sherman
Alan Menken

Jack Lee
Albert Hague
Peter Matz
Don Pippin
Twyla Tharp
Vincent Paterson
Dee Dee Wood

Larry Fuller
Kenny Ortega
Lester Wilson
Joe Layton
Louis DaPron
Bob Herget

AUTOGRAPHS

Between 1949 and 1955 I collected autographs of the stars I worked with. Some are included here. Those not shown are: Cesar Romero, Eddie Fisher, Rosemary Clooney, Edmund Gwynne, Keenan Wynn. Charles Coburn, Danny Kaye, Dean Martin, Jerry Lewis, Edward Arnold, Jeff Chandler, Kate Drain Lawson, Bob Crosby, Eddie Bracken, Marilyn Maxwell, Gene Nelson, Louis DaPron and Gower Champion.

> *Robert Preston*
>
> Dear Lonnie —
> Saw your opening and
> loved you — Didn't come
> back because I thought I'd see
> you later at the party —
> Love to the gang and special
> love to you
>
> Pres

This Note from Pres was for the opening of the Los Angeles production of *42nd Street* at the Shubert Theatre, 1984.

> Dear Mr. Saks —
> Have fun tonight!
> Love,
> Ginger
>
> Aug 10 1971

Opening night note from Ginger Rogers for *Coco* – she has a very dramatic signature!

> Dear Ronnie —
> I've really enjoyed working with you. You bring a respect and professionalism to your work that is a pleasure to watch and even more of a pleasure to play with. Night after night I always knew I could depend on you, whether I was in a faint and you were holding me up, or I was just trying to figure out when during that damned piano music, I was supposed to sit up! Thanks for everything — Shelly

Shelly Hack was a pleasure to work with in *Tamara*, 1990.

> Dear Mr Burr,
> Your performance in "No No Nanette" was superb. I was hesitant to see the show as I had seen the revival with Bobby Van in NYC years ago. I had wanted to keep the memory of Bobby's performance held pure. You matched him. Bravo!
> Sincerely
> Mary Belle Forrest

I really appreciated this note about my *"Nanette"* performance, 1982.

Published by The International Thespian Society

DRAMATICS

March 1995 *Volume 66, Number 7*

The Boy in the Bell Jar

BY LONNIE BURR

CHILDREN have been working in show business since at least the sixteenth century, when the Boys of St. Paul's used to entertain Henry VIII. But the child star is a twentieth century phenomenon, and it is only in the last twenty years that child actors seem to have proliferated like furniture in an absurdist play. After Jackie Coogan, Shirley Temple, and the *Our Gang* gang, kid actors moved into radio, film, television, commercials, videos, and now interactive CD-ROM. Today there are child actors and child stars everywhere.

In the nineties, kids are big business. There is a good reason for this: money. Macaulay Culkin commands millions for films, and even lesser lights of the child-star firmament like the Olsen twins of *Full House* aren't doing too bad in the emolument department.

Money attracts just about everyone, and the bigger the money the greater the attraction. So if it seems that there are a lot more child stars than ever before, there are.

Some people grow up and have marvelous lives after early stardom. Shirley Temple Black became an ambassador. Ron Howard is a successful and respected film director. They are in the minority. The majority have problems later in life. Lots of problems. We have read about too many young adults or, worse, middle-aged adults who, after great careers as kids, are arrested for shoplifting, drugs, alcohol abuse, and sundry other felonies and misdemeanors. This should not come as a surprise. It does not take a psychologist to see that the child star experiences a grotesque distortion of the normal process of growing up.

I was a child actor and then a child star in the fifties. I worked in Cecil B. DeMille movies, had recurring roles on television and leads in radio soap operas and stage plays, and ultimately became one of the nine stars to last the entire filming of *The Mickey Mouse Club*. Ask your parents; they probably remember me.

Occasionally other parents remember me, and ask my advice on their children's show business careers. It is always the same (and almost never what they want or expect to hear): do not induce, nor allow, your child to become a professional actor. Better he or she should be a cowperson. Let them, urge them, to take music lessons, dance lessons at the proper time, even acting lessons (once they're old enough, which in my view is about thirteen or fourteen). Support them when they perform in school shows. But insist that they retain their amateur status until they have finished high school. There is enough competition and stress in growing up without the complications and pressures of show business.

Even under the most benign circumstances, being a child actor is a lot like being in prison. You have very few choices. You can't

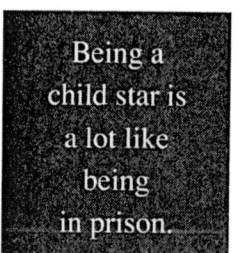

Being a child star is a lot like being in prison.

pick up your toys and go home or play with someone else because there's money involved. Your parents, regardless of how good their intentions, become wardens, and they're assisted by scores of guards: agents, producers, managers, casting directors, acting coaches, directors, and many others.

Along with the regimentation of the child actor's life comes an almost total loss of privacy. The child star is a kid in a bell jar, and these days, with the emergence of tabloid media and the triumph of sleaze over substance, it's many times worse than it was when I was young.

What's more, the kid who is being subjected to this confining regimentation and intense scrutiny is in a no-win situation. Even if he succeeds, the child actor fails. If you become a film or television star and get famous and make a great deal of money, you have nowhere to go as an adult. You cannot continue to be the child you no longer are, even though everyone would prefer you that way. The only place to go is ignominiously over the hill.

If, on the other hand, you don't get cast in that many roles, don't become rich, don't become a star, you're a failure—at the age of ten—in the more conventional sense. It matters little that not getting the role probably has nothing to do with your character, heart, attitude, creativity, charm, looks, or talent. Talent has less to do with show business than most people think. Knowing the right people, being in the right place, luck—these are the main ingredients in successful acting careers, especially in film and most especially when the actors are children.

IT IS AT ABOUT this point that the parent usually interrupts. Wait a minute, she says. Kids love to perform. They love to show off. I've been told my kid is a natural. What's the problem with letting him use his talent, and get paid for it?

One problem—and we are all of us usually too polite to talk about this—is the money. The money is enormous, and it is impossible to prevent the money from influencing the judgment of the parent. Not that I think stage parents are willfully condemning their children to difficult lives in exchange for financial gain. Quite the opposite: it seems to the parents. I feel certain, that they're doing something wonderful for the child, giving her a head start on her professional life, helping her become a success. The money is just a bonus.

But let us examine what actually happens, in the long run, to the young actor.

It's true that most kids love to perform, because they seek attention. Our cats and dogs and birds do it too. They—we— equate attention with love. It is not love, although it can be a form of love, but children cannot make that distinction, or if they do it is intellectually, not emotionally. Most *adults* do not make that distinction emotionally. After spending a few years at the focus of the intense attention that comes with early success in show business, how will the child react when that attention is taken away? Probably not very well. What did I do wrong? she will wonder. I'm still me. Why don't they love me any longer?

And for the vast majority of child actors, the attention will go away. How many television stars have viable careers after their series go off the air? Very few. How many adult actors who are members of the Screen Actors Guild make more than five or six thousand dollars a year as actors? Fewer than 10 percent of the approximately 80,000 union members. How many make more than $100,000 a year? About 1.5 to 2.5 percent. Around 2,000 people. Bad odds.

When I was a child actor, there were a number of kids in the business. We did not make nearly as much money as people thought and certainly nothing like the sums today's child stars are being paid. The smart thing would be to put the money—or anyway, what's left after the government, agents, managers, acting coaches, and others took their share—into some safe long-term investment.

But the lifestyle of the child star is a costly, high-maintenance proposition. There are classes, photos, image (clothes, cars, houses, parties), publicists, accountants, attorneys, chaperones, various hangers-on, and other accoutrements and trappings of public life. All of this stuff has to be paid for.

Kids don't make investments; their parents or guardians do. I believe that in most cases the parents and financial advisors of child stars try to handle the money responsibly, and there are laws that are designed to protect the interests of the child. But good intentions and legal constraints don't seem to prevent frequent ugly disagreements about what happened to the money once the child becomes an adult.

Let us not be totally negative. There are good things about being a child star. You do get attention. You meet many nice and attractive girls and boys. You sign a lot of autographs, get a lot of waves and smiles, and you are looked up to by many people. You have power very early in life. It is a limited power, since you are a child, but you have it, or are made to feel you have it. You travel a lot. You get pursued by the media. You have a humongous amount of things.

You do not get to shop alone, or go to sporting events, or play, or eat in a restaurant, because when you go out you attract unwanted attention. You do not get to have normal relationships with other boys and girls. You will always be that kid on that show. It is an abstraction, not you, that people admire, and their admiration is tinged with envy. You will not be you. You will be that kid on that show.

There is very little time to just hang, play ball, or goof off. You have lines to learn, school lessons to work on as best you can (four hours a day and good luck with the homework), and you must always be ready for the taping of the next scene.

When you are on hiatus or between films, you go back to your neighborhood, your school, your friends. You discover you no longer fit into your friendships in the same way you did before. If you work at it, over time you may be able to have a genuine relationship with a few people, but most are going to be responding—negatively or positively—to that kid on that show.

I had some good times and some bad times as a child actor and child star. I have managed to deal with it better as I have matured than I did in my twenties and thirties. When you walk off stage after performing Laertes and you're asked what it was like to be a Mouseketeer, it's confusing if you don't know how to handle it.

Today, being associated with *The Mickey Mouse Club* is something I feel good about, and I thoroughly enjoy the feelings I get from people who enjoyed that show that kid was on. But was it worth what it cost?

Noël Coward's lyric goes: "Don't put your daughter on the stage, Mrs. Worthington." I hasten to add: nor your son.

Lonnie Burr is an actor, author, director, dancer, and choreographer.

THE DAY OF NAMES

by Lonnie Burr Babin

We all take for granted, then we are stunned —
trapped in horrendous minutes that last for
years, just as years become minutes, second
when they have gone beyond touch, redemption.

Polish, Russian, Indonesian,
the day of names rolls on and on.

Crying has a purpose but not in print,
the high church of the eye, television
complex images of only now that
seem like some fictive trompe l'oeil screen play,

British, Arabic, German, Greek,
The day of names rolls on and on.

but these pixels were breathing, exploding
imploding to an ashen heap, thousands
now rubble. Howling evil drowns out our
song, our love, our hope, our humanity.

Indian, African, Chinese,
the day of names rolls on and on.

Lamentations from yoyo's soft cello,
one lilting flute, the solo violin,
a flurry of strings accented harshly
by the swirling, swirling wind and dust.

Balkan, Swedish, Mexican,
the day of names rolls on and on.

Fleeing the room at times, alone, deeply
exhaling to combat inner agon,
my duty: listen closely to each lone
consonant, each vowel of each victim's name.

Japanese, Irish, Australian,
the day of names rolls on and on.

Before all else I am American
now that I have lost my cynicism
now that the ideals of my youth lie slain,
slaughtered and wingless unlike the Phoenix.

French, Pakistani, Danish, Scots
the day of names rolls on and on.

Christian, Muslim, Buddhist, Jew and Hindu
an eye for an eye for an I must die.
Red, Brown, Yellow, Black, White, now grey like dung
in one nation where no one looks alike.

Korean, Canadian, Dutch,
the day of names rolls on and on.

Whether zealots' crusades or power gone
mad: manmade unnatural disaster
massacre sans remorse, confounds the soul.
We refugees need recall this monster.

As the day of names rolls on and on.

9.11.2002

Index

100 Years of Magic, 399, 419
2,000 Year Old Man, 59
20th Century Fox, 123, 256
42nd Street, 136 -137, 149, 316, 365-372, 386, 435
9/11, 417

Aadland, Beverly, 45
Above the Bike Path, 411
Actor's Chapel, 148
Actor's Equity Association (AEA), 149, 416
Actors Fund of America, 416
Adelquist, Hal, 122, 148-150
Aguilera, Christina, 119
Albee, Edward, 69, 97, 174-175, 188, 425
Alberoni, Sherry, 88, 230, 231, 234, 352-356, 394, 427
Alexander, Jane, 276
All My Sons, 246
All That Jazz, 317
Allen, Woody, 279, 340
American Radio Theatre, 335, 352
Amos 'n Andy, 22, 340
Amsberry, Bob, 139, 147, 150
Amtrak tour, 158, 306, 401
Andersen, Hans Christian. *See Hans Christian Andersen*
Andersen, Karl Eimer, 11
Anderssen, Miss, 45, 56, 205
Andrews, Julie, 103
Anthropocene epoch, 427
arbitration – SAG vs. Disney, 84-88, 116, 126-128
Arcaro, Eddie, 6
Arena Stage, 416, 420
Arroyo Seco Freeway, 19, 20, 21
Assault on Reason, The, 239
Associate of Arts degree (A.A.), 57, 102, 180
Asta Astaire, 108, 375

Astaire, Fred, 18, 24, 154, 267, 356
Astaire, Fred and Adele, 6

Babin, Howard A. (*also* Dad, Dash, Ham) 6,7,12,17,18, 21,66, 218, 359, 405, 439
Baird, Sharon, 119, 124, 129, 131, 147, 151, 157, 161, 163, 230, 353, 354, 360, 409, 410, 411
Baker, Buddy, 85, 147, 433
Bakery, The, 310
Bald Soprano, The, 132, 330, 332
Balsam, Martin, 409, 432
Bancroft, Anne, 298
Barnes Foundation, 417
Bass Lake, 95, 178, 179
Bates, Alan, 191
Beach Boys, The, 41
Beanblossom, Billie Jean, 82
Beast with Five Fingers, The, 23
Beaudine, Jr., Bill, 130
Beaudine, Sr., William, 130
Beckett, Samuel, 188, 298
Being There, 237
Belasco Theatre, 314
Benet, Brenda, 154
Bennett, Tony, 302
Berman, Shelly, 257, 279
Bertinelli, Valerie, 41
Beverly Hillbillies, 211, 265, 270, 271
Bible, The, 66-70
Bible home study, 67, 68, 70
Bible, New World Translation, The, 66
Big Spender, The, 302
Billy Early, 235, 362, 363, 385
Blake, William, 66, 268
Blink (by Malcolm Gladwell), 14
Bloom, Claire, 303-305
Book of Daniel, 66

443

Bon Voyage, 144
Bonner, Frank, 322, 330
Bonnie Earl Tapestry, The, 409
Boss, Bill, 359
Bowles, Paul, 320
Bowles, Jerry, 416, 418
Boy on a Dolphin, A, 106
Boys from Syracuse, The, 284, 309, 311, 321-323, 359
Brady Bunch, The, 41
Brando, Marlon, 174
Broadway, 1, 17, 103, 148, 181, 235, 284, 299
Broadway à la Carte, 260
Broadway (by George Abbott and Philip Dunning), 311-312, 321-322, 392
Bronson, Charles, 5
Brooks, Mel, 15, 59, 309, 340
Brown Derby, 106
Brown v. The Board of Education of Topeka, Kansas, 122
Brown, Gilmore, 176
Browne, Roscoe Lee, 104
Bruce, Lenny, 279
Burgess, Bobby, 88-90, 119, 124, 133, 142, 154-163, 229-230, 353, 416
Burns and Allen, 22
Burr, Dorothy Doloris (*also* Mom, Dot, Doe) 1-15, 17-27, 41-58, 64-68, 167-168, 205-206, 422
Burr, Gladys Olga Nethersole Andersen (*also* Gram, Glade) 9, 11-12, 91-98, 101-108, 205-206, 326-328, 348
Burr, John Leonard, 9, 12, 92, 96, 99-101, 263, 325-328, 348
Burton, Richard, 103, 181
Bush, George W., 225, 239, 416, 426-427
Butala, Tony, 41
Bye, Bye Birdie, 318

Cabaret, 104, 274
Cagney, James, 29, 36, 273, 311
Cahill, Don, 131, 140, 143, 163, 167-168, 179-180, 199, 229, 267, 348, 416, 433
Camelot, 103, 388
Camus, Albert, 59, 202, 250
Cannon, Dyan, 154
Cantor, Eddie, 2, 39, 40, 219, 432
Capitano Aldo Finzi, 75, 372-374

Capitol Records, 122
Captain Kangaroo, 2, 118
Carl's Jr., 266, 372, 405
Carol Burnett Show, The 85, 266, 340
Catch 22, 237
Champion, Gower, 1, 148-149, 208, 210, 262, 311-317, 354, 355, 365, 392, 434
Channing, Carol, 1, 307, 432
Chapin, Lauren, 41
Charisse, Cyd, 91
Chasez, J.C., 119
Chateau Marmont, 207
Chayefsky, Paddy, 63
Cheerios, 2
Chef Boy-ar-dee, 2
Chicago Art Institute, 277, 309-310, 321
Chicago Hope, 191, 355, 414
Chicago Museum of Broadcasting, 409
Chris Martin, 2, 106, 289
Ciro's, 165
Clair, Dick, 119, 340
Close, Glenn, 191
Coca Cola industrial, 169, 409
Coco, 288, 289, 306, 309, 316, 323, 435
Cohen, Nathan, 368, 412, 418
Cole, Nat King, 120
Cole, Tommy, 41, 76, 88, 90, 119, 128, 133, 139-143, 155-157, 163, 194, 290, 340ff., 390-402, 410, 423
Colgate Comedy Hour, The, 2, 39, 106, 130, 131, 150, 219, 220
Considine, Tim, 141, 411
Corcoran, Kevin (Moochie), 117
Cosmo Sardo. 207
Cowsills, The, 41
Cronyn, Hume, 191
Crook, Tommy, 76
Cruise, Tom, 106
Crystal, Billy, 408, 409, 433
Cummings, Robert, 119

Dahrlene, 167, 256, 261-269, 272, 301
Dali Museum, Montmartre, 277
Darley, Dik, 129-131
David Copperfield, 1
Davis, Miles, 302, 364
Davis, Muriel, 41
Davis, Sammy, 1, 103, 104, 152, 432
Day, Dennis, 119, 128, 141, 146, 152, 158, 351

Day, Dennis (singer), 119
Day, Doris, 6
Day of Names, The, 418
Death of A Salesman, 416
Debussy, Claude, 216
Delicate Balance, A, 425
DeMille, Cecil B., 4, 116, 138, 210
Descanso Gardens, 211-214, 411,415
Dickens, Charles, 2,20,29,30,74
Dickey, Diane, 54, 261, 294, 348, 398, 411
Dickey, Douglas Finch, 169, 332, 345-349, 370, 401
Dickey, Hilda Finch, 208-211, 345-349, 411-413
Dickey, Raymond, 208-209
Disney Channel, 119, 335, 364
Disney, Roy Jr., 419
Disney, Walt, 131, 135, 163
Disneyana, 410-411
Disneyland, 61, 82, 88, 117ff., 131ff., 156-163, 201, 211, 214, 228-232, 264, 290, 340, 352, 355ff. 410-411. 422ff.
Disneyland 50th Anniversary, 119, 424
Disneyland Circus, 118, 135-143, 215, 260
Dodd, Dickie, 120
Dodd, Jimmie, 120, 122, 139, 147, 150-165, 338, 411
Dodd, Ruth, 151
Dodge, Jerry, 148
Doll's House, A, 303
Donegan, Martin, 313
Donna Reed Show, The, 152
Dopey Drive, 43, 122
Doran, Ann, 383
Dorothy Chandler Pavilion, 148, 149, 195, 264, 274, 314, 406
Doss, Mrs., 44
Dostoyevsky, Fyodor, 171, 252
Dot and Dash, 6-8, 10, 20, 29, 77, 349
Dr. Paul 2,106,289
Driscoll, Bobby, 41
Dylan, 105

Ebsen, Buddy, 84, 147, 432
Edwards, Cliff, 147
Eisner, Michael, 234, 372
El Capitan Theatre, 2, 39, 220
Eliot, T.S., 62, 183, 321, 330
Elizondo, Hector, 191, 297
Elkins, Hilly, 303

Emerson, Ralph Waldo, 405
Enchanted Lady, The, 2,179
English Patient, The, 237
Epstein, Barbara, 356
Equal Justice, 132, 405
Equus, 181
Espinosa, Mary, 120, 154, 229
Estrada, Eric, 334
Evans, Bill, 257, 302
Evita, 309
Exeunt All, 349, 410

Fabares, Shelley, 374
Facts of Life, The, 119, 368
Falcon Crest, 178, 362, 370
Fantasies, 195
Fantasyland, 82, 119, 139, 142, 158, 159, 163, 350, 401
Fantasyland Theatre, 119
Father Knows Best, 115
Fiddler on the Roof, 267
Field, Sally, 4
Fields, Bonnie Lynn, 163, 356, 360, 394, 395
Firenze, Italy, 192, 368, 424, 425
Fleming, Peggy, 41
Floomerfelt, 374, 375
Flynn, Errol, 46
Fonda, Henry, 17, 191, 422
Fonte, Allison, 409
Ford's Theatre, 17, 421
Fosse, Bob, 1, 104, 147, 311, 317, 355, 356, 433
Foster, Jodie, 112, 203, 205
Frankel, Gene, 181, 298, 299, 433, 434
Frascati's, 207
Fraschilla, Jerry, 84, 87
Freed, Isadore, Dr. 318
Freeman, Morgan, 298
French Lieutenant's Woman, The, 237
Full Metal Jacket, 124
Fuller, Larry, 307, 309, 433
Funicello, Annette, 2, 41, 84, 85, 116, 119-124, 127, 133-139, 142, 144, 152, 156-166, 172, 179, 231, 319-320, 334, 338, 340, 364-365, 374, 394, 396, 409-411
Funny Thing Happened on the Way to the Forum, A, 194

Gangbusters, 22
Garden of Allah, 207

Garland, Judy, 41, 205, 288
George M, 23, 104, 107, 185, 227-228, 240, 265, 270-274, 281-282, 288, 311, 351, 354, 357, 370, 401
Gielgud, Sir John, 191
Gillespie, Darlene, 84-87, 119, 124, 138, 140, 144, 157, 161, 163, 230, 344-346, 353, 375
Giorgio's, 106, 107
Gladwell, Malcom, 14
Goetz, Bernard, 296, 297
Good Humor Man, 19
Goodman Theatre, 309
Gordon, Barry, *41*
Gore, Vice President Al, 239, 246, 413
Gosling, Ryan, 119
Gossett, Lou, Jr., 298
Goulet, Robert, 103
Grable, Betty, 41
Grady, Don, 143, 163, 216, 229, 361, 416
Granpa Joad, 17, 421, 422
Grant, Cary, 24, 154, 334, 367
Grapes of Wrath, The, 17, 421
Grauman's (now Mann's) Chinese Theatre, 106, 170, 220
Gravity of Finity II. The, 417
Grease, 275, 298
Great White Hope, The, 104, 276
Greatest Show on Earth, The, 4, *138*
Greenwald, Alvin & Audrée, 81
Grey, Joel, 107, 274, 275, 282, 283, 401
Grey, Terence, 104
Griffith, Melanie, 41
Grubb, Ronnie, 51
Guinness, Sir Alec, 105, 191, 416

Hackman, Gene, 5
Hair, 297, 420
Haley, Alex, 305, 306
Hall, Peter, 105
Hamlet, 191, 202, 226, 407
Hans Christian Andersen, 4, 11, 115
Hanson, Bill (*also* Billy, Doc) 347, 350
Hanson, Mamie, 68, 94, 95, 347, 349
Hanson, Vernie, 68, 94, 95, 347, 349, 350
Hart to Hart, 334
Hawkins,Mr., 45
Hayworth, Rita, 121
Heartbeat Theatre, 335, 352
Hedda Gabler, 303
Hein, Keith, 332, 370

Hello, Dolly, 148, 318
Helm's Bakery, 19
Hemingway, Ernest, 113, 171, 273, 368
Henri Cinq, Paris, 145
Herget, Bob, 284, 307, 309, 311, 433
Herman, Jerry, 216, 317, 318, 433
Heston, Charlton, *4*, 191
Hewitt, Christopher, 309
Hickman, Darryl, 282, 283
Hill Street Blues, 368
Hoey, Mike, 235, 361, 362
Hoffman, Dustin, 1, 5, 106, 282, 406, 411, 432
Holdridge, Cheryl, 88, 119, 126, 154, 156, 157, 163, 191, 230, 231, 350, 351, 357, 367, 411
Hollywood Beat, 170, 368
Hollywood Bowl, 105, 236, 315, 364, 372, 405, 422, 423
Hollywood Masonic Temple, 106
Hollywood Professional School (HPS), 41-57, 72, 78, 91, 105, 121, 147, 152, 166, 169, 180, 194-198, 205, 244, 290, 334, 368, 397-400, 409
Hollywood Reporter, 202, 287, 366
Holtzman, Burch, 131
Homicide: Life On The Street, 274, 416
Hook, 187, 282, 352, 405, 406, 411
Hope, Bob, 2, 133, 218, 432
Hopkins, Sir Anthony, 181, 191, 303
Hoppe, Hans, 115, 257, 258, 260-264, 267
Horn, Paul, 302
Horn, Shirley, 302
Hoskins, Bob, 406, 432
Howdy Doody, 2, 117, 118
Hughes, Linda, 161, 163
Human Comedy, The, 420
Hutton, Barbara, 154
Hutton, Betty, *4*

I'm a Fan, 307
Icons Are Not in Vogue, 49
If You Don't Dance They Beat You, 223, 426
Illicit Behavior, 409
I'm Dancing as Fast as I Can, 426
In Living Color, 409
In The Know, 79, 80, 320, 330
Inner Sanctum, 22
Ionesco, Eugene, 15, 188, 322, 330, 332
Irma la Douce, 100, 288-294

Iron Eyes Cody, 337
It's a Wonderful Life, 248

Jack Benny Show, The, 119
Jefferson, President Thomas, 74
Jehovah's Witnesses, 66-73, 101, 170, 243-244, 300
Jewell, Geri, 368-370
Jiminy Cricket, 147, 337
Joe Allen's, 286-287, 294, 310, 321
Johann, Dallas, 152
Johann, John Lee,134, 152
Johnson, Arte, 255, 262, 263, 375
Jones, James Earl, 104, 191, 276, 298
Jones, Spike, *41*
Joyce, James, 171, 285
Jumpers, 59
Justice, Bill, 341, 411
Justice, Kim, 411

Kafka, Franz, 76
Kant, Immanuel, 14
Kaye, Danny, *4*, 11, *434*
Keats, John, 427
Keeler, Ruby, 235, 236, 362, 410
Keeshan, Bob, 118
Kennedy Center, The, 17, 148, 149, 208, 210, 315,
Kennedy, President John Fitzgerald, 121, 167, 246, 417
Kennedy, Robert, 167, 246, 417
Keystone Kops, 149, 208
Kierkegaard, Soren, 70
Kilmer, Val, 41
King, Martin Luther, Jr., 167, 246, 417
Kirk, Tommy, 115, 141, 144-146, 192-193, 411
Krall, Diana, 302
Kubrick, Stanley, 124

L.A. Law, 297
Ladd, Alan, *41*, *106*
Lady In Question, The, 362, 409
Laine, Cleo, 302
Laney, Charley (Chuck), 156, 157,
Langella, Frank, 191, 298
Lansbury, Angela, 210, 409
Larsen, Larry, 133, 164, 360, 433
Larson, Gary, 124
Lavin, Jack, 123, 162
le Carré, John, 405
Le Chute [The Fall], 418
Le Jules Verne, 424

Leach, Britt, 132
Learning Tree University, 212, 407
Lee, Brenda, 41
Lee, Jack, 185, 216, 274, 302, 362, 363, 384, 433
Lee, Peggy, 41, 91, 302
Leibniz, 375
Lemmon, Jack, 288, 321
Lennon, John, 298
Lettermen, The, 41
Leveen, Lou, 202, 250, 251, 260
Leviticus, 70
Levy, Jacques, 297
Lewis and Clark College, 426
Lewis, Derrick, 422
Lewis, Jerry, 2, 106, 150, 433, 434
Lewis, Ted, 39
Lincoln, President Abraham, 7, 105, 421
Lindfors, Viveca, 298
Linkletter, Art, 119
Lionheart, 176, 177, 372
Lipton, Peggy, 41
Live A Little, Love A Little, 128
Living Stage, The , 49, 187
Lois & Clark, 410
London, Julie, 41
Lone Ranger, The, 336
Look Where I'm At, 311
Loren, Sophia, 106
Lorre, Peter, *4*
Los Angeles Times, 112, 202, 203, 335
Los Angeles Youth Theatre, 187
Losey, Joseph, 4, 303
Lots of Luck, 137, 364
Louvre, Paris, 192, 277
Love Song of Alfred J. Prufrock, The , 321
Lynley, Carol, 107
Lyon, Sue, 41

Mack & Mabel, 104, 148-149, 181-187, 208, 262, 313-318, 323-324, 392
MacLaine, Shirley, 103, 288, 432
MacMurray, Fred, 144
Macy, Bill, 297
Mad Max, 237
Mahoney, Jock, 4, 432
Mahoney, Tom, 133
Majestic Theatre, 148, 181, 315
Maltin, Leonard, 153, 338
Man in the Gray Flannel Suit, 121
Manhattan Theatre Club, 313

Mann, Mrs., 44, 51, 54, 73, 166, 368
Mann, Mr., 44
Mannix, Dr. Jack, 232, 424
Markham, Monte, 262, 283
Marshall, Mort, 281, 323, 324
Marshall, Peter, 309
Martin and Lewis, 2, 150
Martin, Dean, 2,
Martin, Tony, 91
Marvin,Lee, 298
Marx, Groucho, 15, 279
Masonic Order, 66, 327
Masonic Temple, 199, 219, 228
Masur, Richard, 87
Mathis, Johnny, 195
Matthau, Walter, 298
Maude, 297, 340
Max Factor, 106
May Company, 99, 211, 251
Mayor of Hooverville, 421
McAllister, Lon, 4
McCormack, Patty, 41
McDermott, Galt, 420
McDowell, Roddy, 103
McGavin, Darren, 259, 260, 432
McKellan, Ian, 104
McMahon, Jenna, 119, 340
McVeety, Vince, 130
Melnitz, Dean, 49, 187, 188
Merrick, David, 148, 149, 305, 313, 317, 318, 433
Merrily We Roll Along, 309
Metropolitan Museum of Art, New York, 192
MGM, 123, 128
Mickey Mouse Club (original, 1955-59), 1, 2, 4, 40ff., 76ff., 115ff., 144, 151ff., 187, 201, 205, 214ff, 259, 263, 265, 319, 328ff., 374, 390, 394, 411, 421
Micky Mouse Club 25th Annversary TV Special, 320, 350-354
Mickey Mouse Club 30th Anniversary, 357
Mickey Mouse Club 50th Anniversary, 228-232, 424
Mickey Mouse Club serials
Annette, 2, 124
Spin and Marty, 2, 84, 86, 115, 116, 118, 124, 130, 139, 338
The Hardy Boys, 2, 84, 118
Mickey Mouse Club (3rd version "no ears"), 119

Mickey's 40th Birthday TV special, 130
Miles, Harry, 154
Mill, John Stuart, 335
Miller, Arthur, 246, 415
Miller, Sidney, 130, 131
Mills, Hayley, 105, 364, 405, 432
Mimieux, Yvette, 41
Minister's Son, The 3
Mitchum, Robert, 41
Moore, Clayton (The Lone Ranger), 2, 336, 337, 338, 432
Morgan, Beverly Watson, 68, 422
Moulin Rouge, 103, 106, 163
Mouseketeer Lonnie, 1, 56, 79, 97, 123, 158, 187, 289, 315, 319, 373, 394, 409, 421, 422
Mouseketeer Mensch, 162, 352, 361, 406, 410, 428
Mouseketeers, 1, 41, 43, 83-90, 105, 116ff., 172, 187, 199, 201, 231, 232, 273, 283, 290, 338, 340, 342ff., 385, 399, 402ff., 412
Mr. Bumble, 74
Mr. Saturday Night, 408, 409
Ms. magazine, 379
MS (multiple sclerosis), 123, 124, 197, 369, 396, 420
Muny Opera House, 315
Murder, She Wrote, 210, 409
Museum of Modern Art, New York, 192, 277
Music Man, The, 103, 230, 266, 288, 308, 309, 316, 323, 324, 327
Musical Chairs, Palm Springs, 422
My Friend Flicka, 123, 124, 128
My Three Sons, 143, 216

Nader, George, 383
National Cathedral School, 413, 417
National Conservatory of Dramatic Arts, 419
National Theatre (DC), 282, 413
Network, 63
New Mickey Mouse Club, 119, 122, 328, 355, 409
New Testament, 66
Newley, Anthony, 265
Newsies, 355, 409, 410
Nietzsche, Friedrich, 57, 65, 225, 244, 405
Nimoy, Leonard, *5, 261, 305*
Nimrod, 70
No, No Nanette, 235, 236, 362, 385, 436

North Hollywood High, 56
Northcutte, Shawnte, 355

Obama, President Barack, 245, 246, 427
O'Brien, Cubby, 82, 83, 119, 131-143, 156, 163, 165, 229, 233, 354, 358
Occam's Razor, 148, 285, 313
O'Connor, Donald, 2, 41, 131, 284, 309, 432
Ogg, Sammy, 41, 152
Oh! Calcutta!, 297, 303
Oliver Quimby, 116
Olney Theatre, Maryland, 415, 416
On the Twentieth Century, 309
One Day At a Time, 41
O'Neal, Ryan, 41
O'Neal, Tatum, 41
Ono, Yoko, 379
originalmmc.com, 416
Ortega, Kenny, 355, 362, 409, 433
Ortlieb, Jim, 422
Osborne, Robert, 366
Othello, 73, 97
O'Toole, Annette, 41
Over the Hill, 310, 322, 331

Paget, Debra, 41
Palladium, The 106, 378
Pandit, Korla, 120
Pandora's Box, 207
Pantages Theatre, 106, 261, 362
Parade of Roses, Portland, OR, 161
Parker, Fess, 127, 147, 411
Parkins, Barbara, 1
Pasadena Playhouse, 5, 176, 191
Pasadena Rose Bowl, 19
Pasadena Rose Parade, 19, 94, 161
Pat Boone, 264, 432
Peabody Hotel, 305, 306
Pendleton, Karen, 102, 114, 119, 138, 139, 153, 154, 163, 196, 230, 353, 368, 370, 410
Pepsi Cola industrial, 309
Peters, Bernadette, 1, 79, 313, 320, 330, 432
Petersen, Paul, 152, 353
Phantom Pain, 419t
Phillips Collection, 417
Phillips, MacKenzie, *41*
Pickford, Mary, 107
Pied Piper, The, 176
Pink Lightning, 409

Pinter, Harold, 297
Plantico, Earl, *52*
Plato, 211, 330
Playbox, 383
Police Academy VII—Mission to Moscow, 410
Pool, Wakefield, 311
Porgy and Bess, 103
Presley, Elvis, 1, 124, 128, 129, 160, 267, 362, 432
Preston, Robert, 1, 103, 104, 149, 174, 313, 432
Price, Vincent, 305
Prisoner of 2nd Avenue, The, 288, 321

Queen for a Day, 5, 262
Quinn, Anthony, 121
Quintero, Jose, 426

Rachins, Alan, 297
Raft, George, 18, 262
Rall, Tommy, 41
Randi, Don, 207
Range Rider, The, 4
Ravel, Maurice, 216
Ready, Lynn, 143, 146, 163
Reagan, Ronald, 119
Redgrave, Sir Michael, 191
Reinhardt, Max, 105
Renaissance Club, 165, 178, 302
Revelation, 66
Reventlow, Lance, 154, 191
Reynolds, Debbie, 185, 212
Rhadamanthys, 76
Richard III, 14, 104, 182, 298
Rickles, Don, 140
Rijksmuseum, Amsterdam, 192
Rivers, Gerry, 158
Roar of the Greasepaint, the Smell of the Crowd, The, 97, 181, 265
Rocky, 78, 313
Roddenberry, Gene, 305
Rodeo Drive, 106
Rogers, Ginger, 1, 288, 306, 432, 435
Roget, Peter Mark, 112
Rooney, Jr., Mickey, 152
Rooney, Mickey, 41, 152, 288, 290, 351
Rooney, Tim, 152, 351
Roy Lane, 311
Roy Rogers Show, The, 2
Ruggles, Charlie, 4
Ruggles, The, 4
Russell, Keri, 119

Sahl, Mort, 15, 267, 279
Saint, Eva Marie, 298
Sam Goldwyn Studio, 123
Santoli, Lorraine, 117, 201, 353, 410-411
Sardi's, 312
Saroyan, William, 420
Sartre, Jean Paul, 65, 250, 320
Scherick, Mr. 45
Schopenhauer, Arthur, 248
Schwab's drugstore, 207
Schwartz, Delmore, 15, 397
Scientology, 69, 309
Scofield, Paul, 181
Scooter, or All For Love, 56, 192, 258
Scott, Bronson, 164
Scott, George C., 191, 321
Screen Actors Guild (SAG), 84-88, 116, 126, 227, 354, 381, 383, 406, 412, 416
Secret Pilgrim, The, 405
Selden, Samuel, 48-49, 188
Sellers, Peter, 15
Sesame Street, 117
Session, The, 410
Shakespeare, 114, 309
Sherman Brothers, Richard and Robert, 77, 422, 433
Sherry's, 207
Silence of the Hams, 409
Silliphant, Sterling, 130
Simon, Neil, 298, 338
Simpson, Orenthal James, 83
Sinatra, Frank, 106, 107, 160, 195
Skelton, Red, 140, 371
Smith, Maggie, 191
Smithsonian National Air and Space Museum, 415
Smithsonian Museums, 1, 415
Snell, Mrs. 45
Solari, Jay-Jay, 350, 353
Sommer, Elke, 289, 291, 292
Southern, Terry, *56, 192*
Space Patrol, 4, 129
Spats Palazzo, 262-263
Spears, Britney, 119
Spielberg, Stephen, 1, 187, 352, 406, 433
St. John, Jill, *41, 334*
St. Margaret's Episcopal School, 426
St. Moritz, 105, 179, 188, 194, 195
Stars Over Hollywood, 2
Steambath, 297
Steiger, Rod, 298

Steinbeck, John, 17, 421
Steinem, Gloria, 379
Steiner Brothers, 398
Steiner, Ronnie, 41, 399
Stevens, Connie, 41
Stevens, Wallace, 99
Stewart, Jimmy, 4, 93, 432
Stewart, Michael, 318
Stollery, David, 115-116, 141, 411
Stoppard, Tom, 59
Strawberry Circle, The, 5
Streep, Meryl, 191
Sugar, 262, 288, 316
Sunday in the Park with George, 310
Sunday Afternoon on the Island of La Grande Jatte, 310
Sweet Charity, 103, 274, 302, 356
Sy Devore's, 106
Syny (Mnemosyne), 232, 233, 370, 375, 402, 424

Take the Money and Run, 279
Talbot, Lyle, 4
Tamara, 75, 177, 310, 331, 372, 374, 375, 405, 436
Tandy, Jessica, 191
Tharp, Twyla, 262, 311, 355, 433
Trial, The, 74
Theatricalism, 49, 104, 105
Thielemans, Toots, 302, 372
Thomas, Danny, 120
Thomas, Dylan, 105, 321
Three Little Words, 24
Timberlake, Justin, 119
Time Bomb, 371, 405
Tomorrowland, 142, 355, 365, 407
Torme, Mel, 302, 364
Townsend, Robert, 409
Tracey, Bess, 157, 161
Tracey, Doreen, 119-120, 138, 142, 153, 156-163, 170, 185, 186, 230-231, 292, 330, 346, 353, 360
Traver, Lee, 123, 124, 126, 128, 152
Triton College of Arts and Sciences, 411
Troup, Bobby, *41*
Troup, Cynnie, 41
Tune, Tommy, 371
Twelfth Night, 174, 178
Two for the Show: Great 20th Century Comedy Teams, 336, 338, 417
Tynan, Kenneth, 297
Typhoid Mary, 416

Unbearable Lightness of Being, The, 237
Universal Studios, 85, 96, 104, 123, 390
Updike, John, 8, 124

Valint, Jim, 93, 327, 420
Van Damme, Jean-Claude, 1, 176, 177, 372, 432
Van Dyke, Dick, 307, 340
Variety, 202, 287, 311, 354
Vaughn, Robert, 191
Vault Disney, 119
Vereen, Ben, 334, 432
Vietnam, 172, 243, 245, 250, 256, 268, 364
Votrian, Peter, 115

Wagner, Richard, 65
Wagner, Robert (RJ), 334
Waiting for Godot, 188
Walker, Craig, 422
Walsh, Bill, 123
Walt Disney Studios, 1, 76, 84 271
Warhol, Andy, 1, 277
Warner Bros., 123
Washbrook, Johnny, 123, 128
Washington Post, The, 320, 336
Watson, Bob, 68, 384
Watson, Dorothy, 68, 94, 95, 328, 347, 350, 384, 422
WDW (Walt Disney World), 120, 136, 155, 163, 215-216, 229, 233, 309, 341, 350, 355, 399-400, 410-411, 419

Weld, Tuesday, 41
Wells, Frank, 423
West Side Story, 187, 259, 263, 288, 318
Westward Ho the Wagons!, 117, 124
Whelchel, Lisa, 119
Whiskey a Go-Go, 178
Who's Afraid of Virginia Woolf?, 426
Who's Afraid of David Mamet, 331
Wilde, Oscar, 49
Williams, Guy, 135
Williams, John, 216, 406, 433
Williams, Paul, 353
Williams, Robin, 406, 432
Williams, Roy, 117, 127, 139, 147, 150, 218, 320, 432
Willow and I, The, 383
Wilson, Brian and Carl, 41
Wings of the Dove, The, 237
Wiviott, Marty, 260, 362
Wolfington, Iggie, 316
Wong, Curtis, 355
Wood, Natalie, 41, 334-335
World War II, 19, 249, 350
Writer's Guild of America (WGA), 86, 336, 353, 361, 362, 405
Wynn, Ed, 2, 432

Yank in Korea, A, 4

Zeidler and Zeidler, 207
Zoo Story, The, 174-175
Zorro, 135

Printed in the United States
217839BV00004B/38/P